T0165956

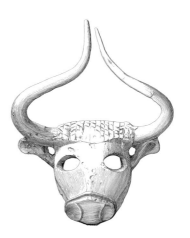

The Barbar Temples

P.V. Glob in memoriam

The Carlsberg Foundation's Gulf Project

The Barbar Temples

Volume 1

by H. Hellmuth Andersen and Flemming Højlund

With contributions by
Søren F. Andersen, Michèle Casanova,
Derek Kennet and Poul Kjærum

Jutland Archaeological Society

Moesgaard Museum
Ministry of Information, Bahrain

The Barbar Temples

H.Hellmuth Andersen & Flemming Højlund © 2003

ISBN 87-88415-27-9
ISSN 0107-2854

Jutland Archaeological Society Publications vol. 48

Editor: Flemming Højlund
English translation and revision: Geoffrey Bibby and Peter Crabb
Layout & cover: Orla Svendsen
Drawings: Orla Svendsen, Jens Kirkeby, Louise Hilmar, Flemming Bau,
Elsebet Morville
Photographs: P.V. Glob, H. Hellmuth Andersen, Lennart Larsen,
Peder Mortensen, P. Dehlholm, Rogvi Johansen, G. Franceschi
Printed by Narayana Press
Type: Palatino
Paper: Arctic Silk 130 g

Published by:
Jutland Archaeological Society
Moesgaard
DK-8270 Højbjerg

in association with
the Moesgaard Museum and
the Ministry of Information, Bahrain

Distributed by
Aarhus University Press
Langelandsgade 177
DK-8200 Aarhus N
www.unipress.dk

Published with the financial support of the Carlsberg Foundation

Contents

Volume 1

1. Introduction, by H.H.A. 7
2. Stratigraphy, by H.H.A. 23
3. Temple I, by H.H.A. 33
4. Temple II. The Central Platform, by H.H.A. 81
5. Temple II. The Oval Platform, by H.H.A. 111
6. Temple II. The Pool, by H.H.A. 147
7. Temple II. The Eastern Court, by H.H.A. 175
8. Temple III, by H.H.A. 187
9. Islamic Masonry, by H.H.A. 197
10. The Northeast Temple, by H.H.A. 199
11. Pottery and the Dating of the Temple Phases, by F.H. 209
12. Copper and Copper Working, by F.H. 255
13. Alabaster and Calcite Vessels, by M. Casanova 283
14. Stamp Seals and Seal Impressions, by P. Kjærum 289
15. Sasanian and Islamic Pottery, by S. F. Andersen and D. Kennet 307
16. Parthian-Sasanian Sculpture 311
17. Other Finds, by F.H. 315
18. Conclusion, by F.H. 323

Volume 2

Appendix 1. Animal Bones, by P. Bangsgaard 7
Appendix 2. Analysis of Wood, by M. Tengberg 17
Appendix 3. Metal Analyses, by E. Sangmeister 19
Appendix 4. Metal Analyses, by D.L. Heskel 21
Appendix 5. The Well at Umm as-Sujur, by H.H.A. and F.H. 35
Appendix 6. Phallic Cult-Stones from the Barbar-Temple Period, by H.H.A. ... 47
Appendix 7. Bibliography and Abbreviations 51
Appendix 8. Sections and Plans 57

Fig. 1. Barbar. The tell before excavation. From W (1954).

1. Introduction

The Barbar temple was discovered by P.V. Glob in 1954 in the course of the first Danish Bahrain Expedition (Glob 1954a p. 142). Immediately south of the village of Barbar in the north-west of Bahrain Glob noticed a gravel mound of unusual shape and considerable size (figs. 1-2). It lay about 800 metres from the north coast and according to Glob's description was squarish with rounded contours and about 60 metres in each direction. It showed three terraces and was about 6 metres high. During the years 1954-1961 this gravel mound was investigated.

E.L. Durand had already taken note of the mound in 1878 (Durand 1880), and both he and Glob based their estimation of the noteworthy nature of the mound on the presence of a large block of stone with rectangular holes cut into the top which protruded from the northern side of the mound. A decisive factor for Glob's decision to start an excavation was moreover the fact that scraps of copper and red ridged potsherds were found on the surface in large numbers, while there were not the same quantities of Islamic potsherds as on most of the mounds in the vicinity.

A trial trench through the mound in 1954 also swiftly revealed that it covered impressive structures of an early date. Various objects were discovered suggesting a third millennium dating, while altar-like constructions allowed a general interpretation to be immediately made: The mound was a temple-tell, containing several severely demolished temples, the one built upon and around the other. In the case of the older temples this took the form of a double platform, the lower rounded and the upper rectangular. The terrace walls around these platforms had, however, in many places been subjected to stone-robbery, and it was precisely these broad and deep stone-quarrying trenches which had left the broken lines in the mound surface which gave it its peculiar terraced appearance (fig. 1).

After further work in 1955 Glob was able to formulate a first working hypothesis of three main stages of constructional history (Glob 1955), and P. Mortensen and H.H. Andersen, who from 1956/1957 had assumed the responsibility for the continuing excavation, followed Glob's working

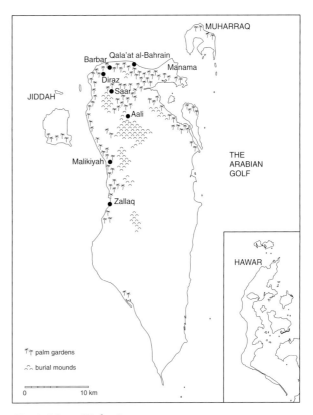

Fig. 2. Map of Bahrain.

hypothesis during the field-work, which ended in 1961. However, a complete investigation in the excavation's documentation between 1980 and 1983 by H.H. Andersen led to a critical revision of the working hypotheses and a re-interpretation of the constructional history of the temples. The main results of this work were presented in 1983 at the *Bahrain Through The Ages*-Conference in Manama (Andersen 1986). All previous publications on the Barbar Temple should be consulted with reservation as they are based on the provisional working hypothesis.

The Barbar tell covered three successive temple structures (figs. 3-5). Moreover, the first two structures are associated with such considerable rebuildings that it is possible to claim that the temple shows at least five building-stages: Ia, Ib, IIa, IIb and III.

The three temples had, as their dominating architectural centre, a rectangular platform. In each of the three structures this platform was built higher and larger, so that each successor encapsulated its predecessor. It is here that we find the constituent element for a tripartite division, by defining the floor-levels of the platforms.

These levels allow for an understanding of the structural history, and thereby also of the architecture of the temples in its entirety in each of the three main stages. This is the reason why a considerable rebuilding of the earliest temple (Ia) has been characterized as a direct derivation (Ib): The two buildings have a common platform-level. Temple II is defined as essentially a new building with a new platform-level, and extensive building changes in the outer works of this temple justify a subdivision (IIa and b). With Temple III a latest level is defined, and though the actual floor was not preserved, it can be shown to have been even higher.

As has been said, the three levels were easily recognizable in the central platform. The platforms consisted of outer walls surrounding a four-sided infilled terrace. On this stood the temple buildings and altars.

The central platform was itself standing upon a larger oval platform, though this has only been traced as a half-oval, and in the case of Temple III has not been found at all. In the time of Temple II this oval platform exists in two phases, as evidence of the building changes mentioned above.

At either end of this oval platform was found an impressive flanking structure, directly connected with the central platform. To the east there was a walled court, to the west a chamber built around a fresh-water spring. Both of these two structures must be assumed to have served important cult functions. The stratigraphy of the eastern area is dominated by thick layers of ashes. The pool on the west is even more remarkable. Architecturally it represents the diametrically opposite to the central platform – a deeply placed room with the ground-water surface exposed. It is presumably a structure of equal importance to the sacred structures on the central platform, for a stairway of an originally highly impressive nature, a processional stairway, connects the two areas.

Upon or beside the oval platform altars were also found, while in the south-west lay a well, which was in use throughout the whole history of the temple, and was consequently adapted to all five building stages.

Both the pool and the well required access to water. The structures associated with them had thus to lie at a low level. This required that the oval terrace wall in the southwestern area had to adapt itself to considerable differences in height between the oval platform's surface and ground surface close to the subsoil water level.

Viewed from the south-west the temple has therefore presented the appearance of an accentuated double platform. And in the time of Temple II a large building on the central platform has moreover added the impression of a third step. This layout of the structure could best be recognized in the case of Temple II. It was the best preserved, and the most accessible for investigation. Everything, however, suggests that already Temple I was laid out in the same pattern. In contrast, everything suggests that Temple III departed considerably from the pattern. In principle it consisted of an unusually large and high central platform of a strictly square shape, but without any oval platform, and without the pool and the Eastern Court. At least no such features could be recognized, but on the other hand this temple had been very severely demolished.

However, a related structure was identified and partly investigated immediately to the north-east of the Barbar temple. It had the form of a double platform and will be here treated under the designation of the Northeast Temple, to distinguish it from the main temple.

The excavations of the Barbar temple were commenced 18th February 1954 and terminated 14th December 1961. They were carried out in eight yearly campaigns, each of about 2½ months' duration. C. 35 local workmen participated in each campaign.

Excavations in 1954 (fig. 6) by P.V. Glob, T.G. Bibby and K. Jeppesen. A 55m-long trial trench, area I, was dug through the tell, and masonry belonging to Temples II and III discovered. Of particular interest were the circular stone constructions exposed in the centre, which led to local extensions. These revealed a relatively intact portion of a well-defined level, the flooring in the eastern side of Temple II's central platform. At the southern end of the long trial trench excavation was taken down to the bottom of the tell. Here masonry was located belonging to Temple I. Other trial trenches exposed more masonry of Temple II, while to the west the remains of the Temple-III wall was found. Excavation was thus in the main confined to the upper part of the tell, which was conspicuously lacking in finds. These sterile layers of fill were seen as evidence for a deliberate covering of the temples (Glob 1954a), but should be understood as the fill belonging to the platform of Temple III.

The same year the well-chamber at Umm as-Sujur near the village of Diraz was excavated by T.G. Bibby (Bibby 1954a). It is re-published here in Appendix 5.

Excavations in 1955 (fig. 7) by P.V. Glob, K. Jeppesen and R. Dyson. The supposed covering layer above

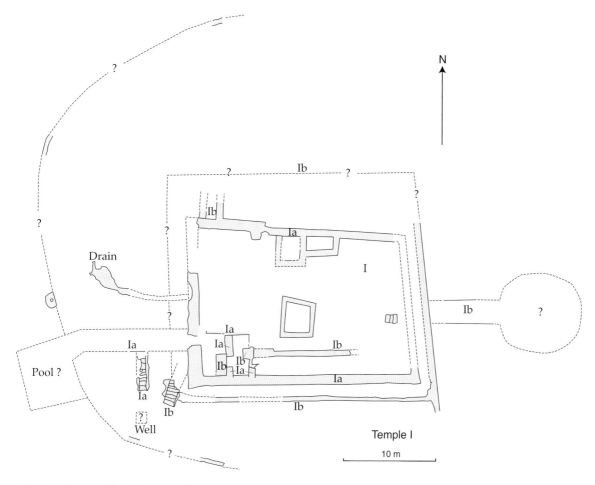

Fig. 3. Temple Ia and b. Schematic plan.

the centre of the temple, i.e. the sterile fill of the platform of Temple III, was machine-removed down to the Temple-II level. As an approximate outer limit to this exposure can be designated the terrace wall of Temple III. Within this area numerous excavations were now made to find masonry from Temples II and III. At two points, areas I and II, excavations were carried down to virgin subsoil, thus cutting through the accumulations of fill in the central platforms of Temple II and Temple I. The base of the structure was thereby shown to consist of a so-called "clay-core", which contained quantities of foundation-offerings. East of the platform a trial trench, area III, was dug to virgin soil, while in area IV the oval court and its ramp were exposed. West of the platform an excavation area, area V, was established, but was only superficially excavated (Glob 1955).

The observations made up to that date led Glob to propose a working hypothesis of three temples, a small earliest temple at the bottom of the tell, overlain by two larger ones. This hypothesis had thus seized upon the correct situation, but it contained unclear distinctions in the attribution of the masonry discovered; for example, portions of Temple II were interpreted as belonging to Temple III.

There lay implicit in this hypothesis that the levels of Temple II and Temple III were more or less congruent. The badly plundered "square outer wall" could not be recognized in its true interpretation as the terrace wall of Temple III.

It was the stone-robbery which obscured the picture. Temple III, which had lain more or less freely accessible, had been the first to be plundered, and thereafter the terrace walls of Temple II lying within it. As the floor level of Temple III had also disappeared, the layers of fill highest in the tell were interpreted as a deliberately applied covering. Thereby all conditions were present for "the square outer wall" not to be given the significance which it deserved, even though it was correctly attributed to Temple III.

Excavations in 1956 (fig. 8) by P. Mortensen, K. Jeppesen and Harald Andersen. Excavations were carried out to the east and south of the central platform. In area I the Eastern Court was investigated in detail and was shown to comprise several building-phases (Mortensen 1956). Here, however, virgin soil was only reached in a separate trial trench, laid out as a longitudinal section through the centre of

9

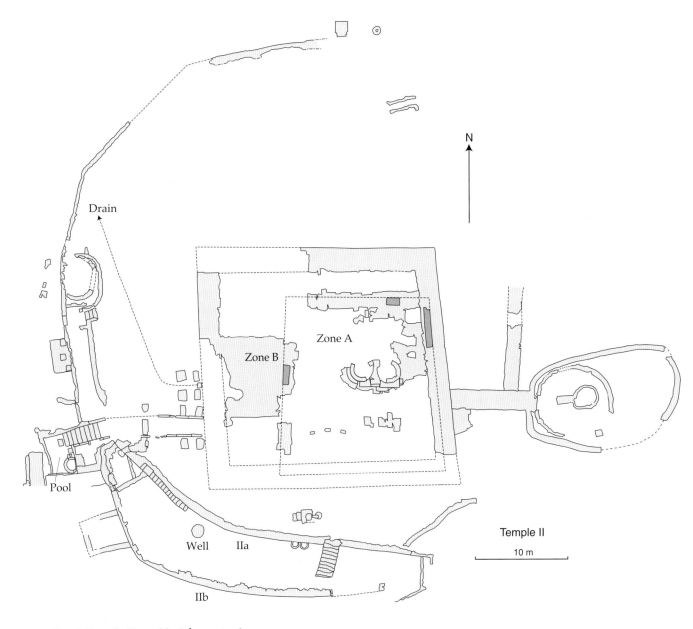

Fig. 4. Temple IIa and b. Schematic plan.

the structure. The north face of area III from 1955 was documented in detail stratigraphically. In the south the long trial trench from 1954 was extended in a southerly direction, area II. At the same time the excavation was begun to expose, in area III, the wall thereby discovered, a wall that in the course of time would prove to be a terrace wall of the oval platform. In addition a neighbouring tell, north-east of the temple, was excavated by Harald Andersen, and proved to contain the severely plundered remains of another temple, the Northeast Temple. This excavation is described in chapter 10 (Harald Andersen 1956).

Excavations in 1957 (fig. 9) by P. Mortensen and H.Hellmuth Andersen. With the object of making as total an investigation as possible, a series of cam-

paigns started in this year with the aim of systematically uncovering the temple, section by section, although the Eastern Court was considered to have been already completely investigated. As a starting point for this project a new transverse trial trench was made, comprising areas VIII, III-V, XI, XII, XIV and XV. For the original trial trench from 1954 gave scarcely any insight into the lower part of the stratification. It was naturally impossible for the new trial trench to include the upper stratification of the tell, as this had been removed in 1955. It therefore commenced at the Temple-II level and was taken down to virgin soil. The measurements here, combined with those from 1954, give a general impression of the total stratification of the tell, the so-called Main Section, which is the basis of the second chapter's description of the temple stratification.

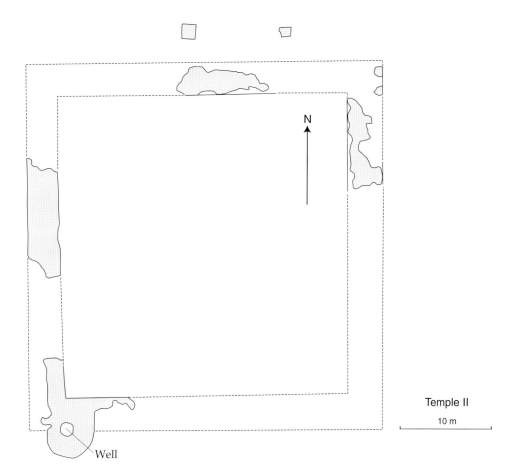

Fig. 5. Temple III. Schematic plan.

The trial trench was also a decisive contribution to the determination of the Temple-I level, which here appeared clearly as a plaster floor with remains of buildings, on a central platform bordered by terrace walls.

The trial trench brought to light in addition two deeply-founded terrace walls south of the central platform, walls which formed part of the oval platform. The earliest of these two walls – with a built-on stairway – must be attributed to Temple IIa, the later one to Temple IIb.

It was now evident that there existed, in the south, west and east, structural parts associated with the temple. Most of the excavation areas were sited in connection with this peripheral masonry, particularly in order to draw sections at clearly important points, especially in the west and southwest. In areas I, II, VI and XVII there were investigated the earlier of the two high oval walls, a built-on side-stairway and the well at that point, as well as earlier stairways behind the wall. So far as possible excavation was carried down to subsoil, and from these excavations there exists important documentary material for an understanding of the constructional history. In the west, in area XVIII, the walling of the oval platform at that point was excavated, but only to subsoil along a section-wall at the

north side of the area. Most of the other areas represent local investigations of masonry which was most often of a surface nature (Glob 1958).

Excavations in 1958 (fig. 10) by P. Mortensen and H.H. Andersen. In areas III-V and VII the floor of Temple I was exposed after a temporary removal of such parts of Temple-II's floor as were involved. Under the floor the earliest temple-core was searched through, and the outer face of the northern terrace wall of Temple I was exposed. To the south, in areas VIII and IX, the two high oval walls were dug free down to their footings. In the west excavation stopped in area VI at a subsoil-like surface, without contact being made with the underlying pool. In the east a section, area I, revealed the existence of several building phases in the ramp from the Eastern Court up to the central terrace (Glob 1959a).

Excavations in 1959 (fig. 11) by P. Mortensen and H.H. Andersen. The investigation of the central platform continued with the uncovering of the Temple-I floor in areas III, IV and IX. In quite a large section of the western half it can be seen that an area has been left undisturbed with the Temple-II level intact. In area VII the southern terrace wall of Tem-

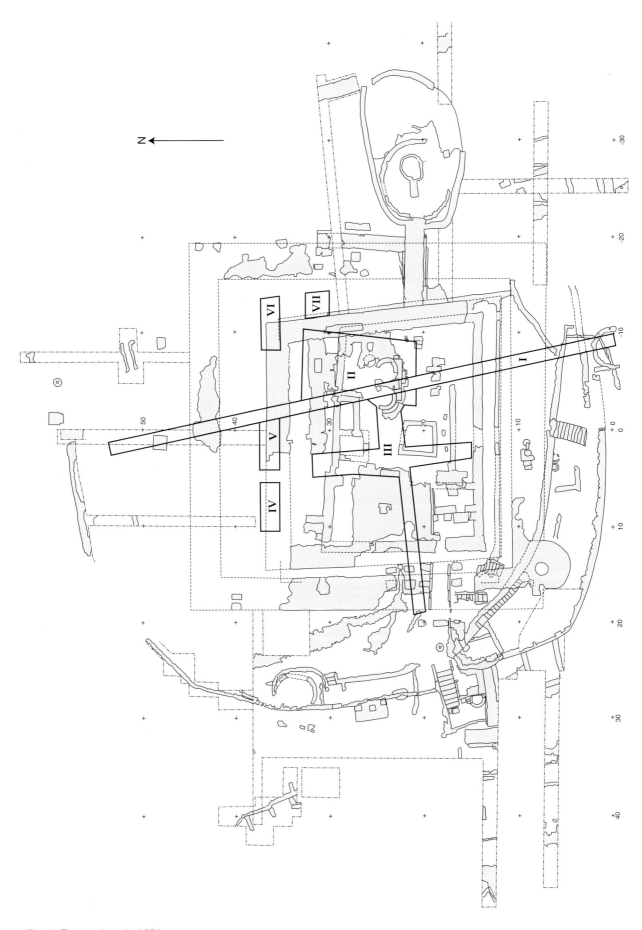

Fig. 6. Excavations in 1954.

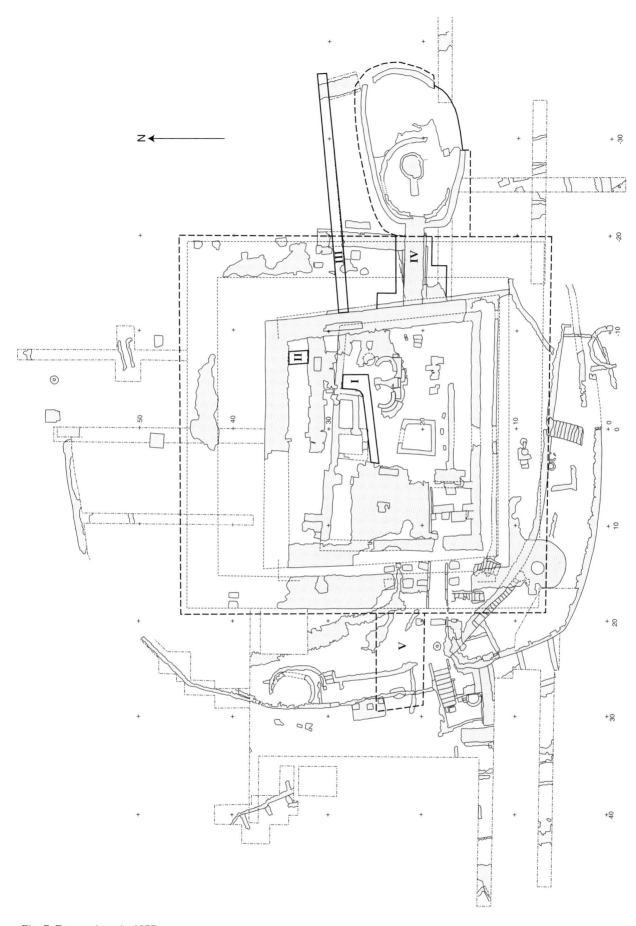

Fig. 7. Excavations in 1955.

13

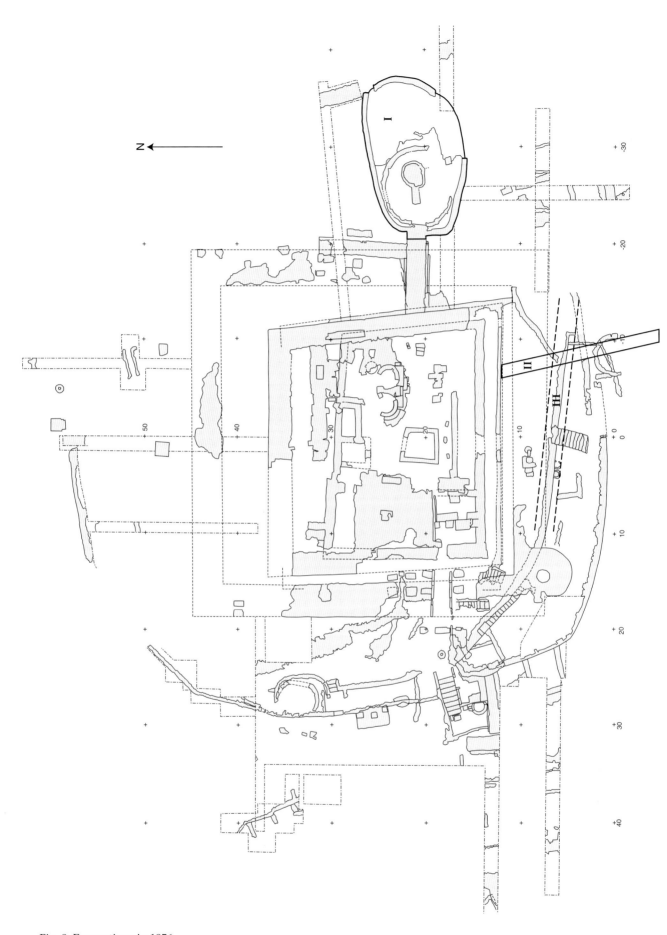

Fig. 8. Excavations in 1956.

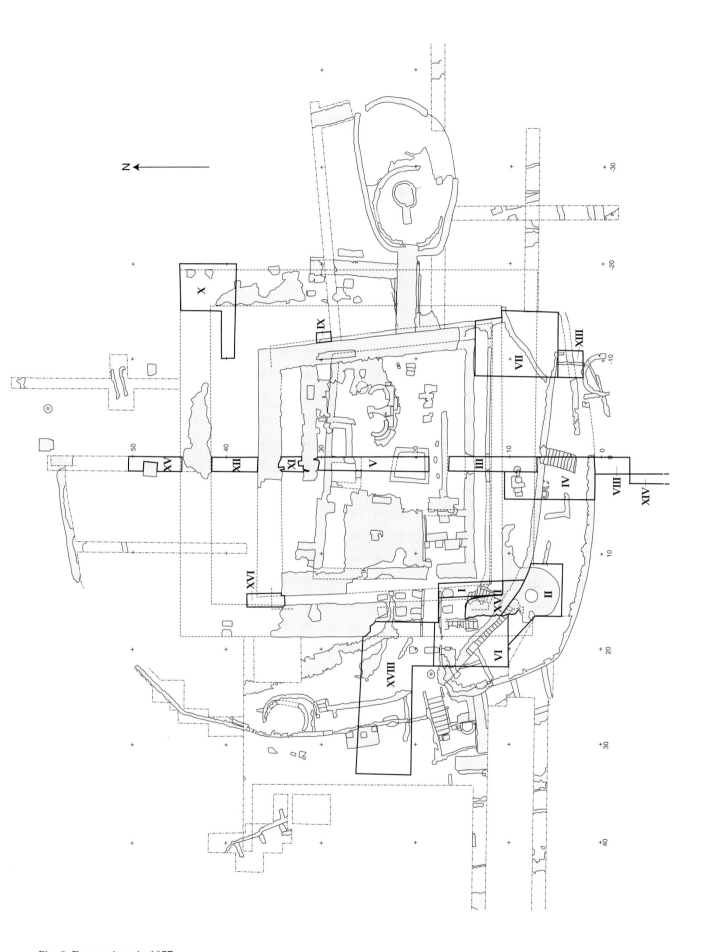

Fig. 9. Excavations in 1957.

15

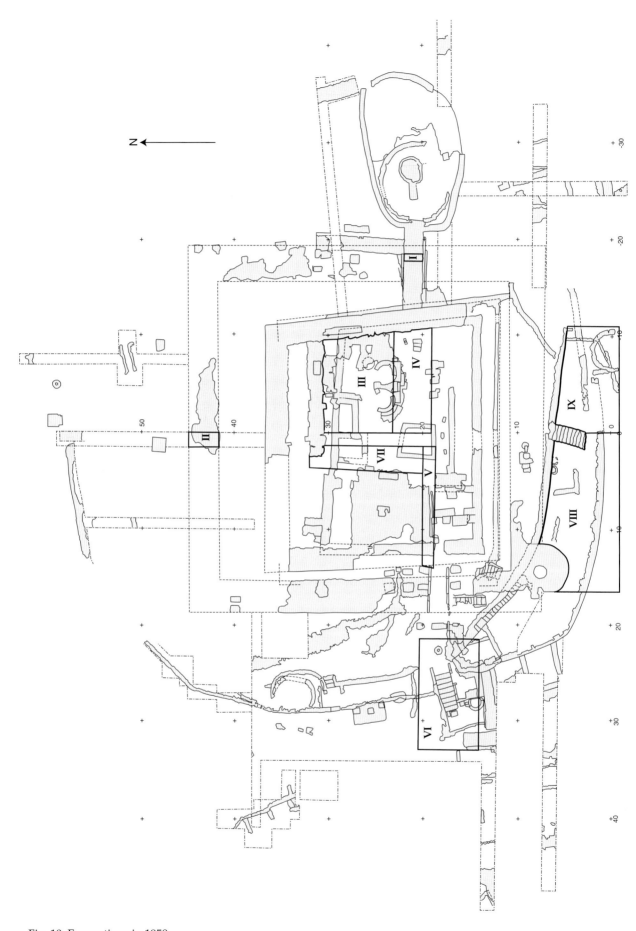

Fig. 10. Excavations in 1958.

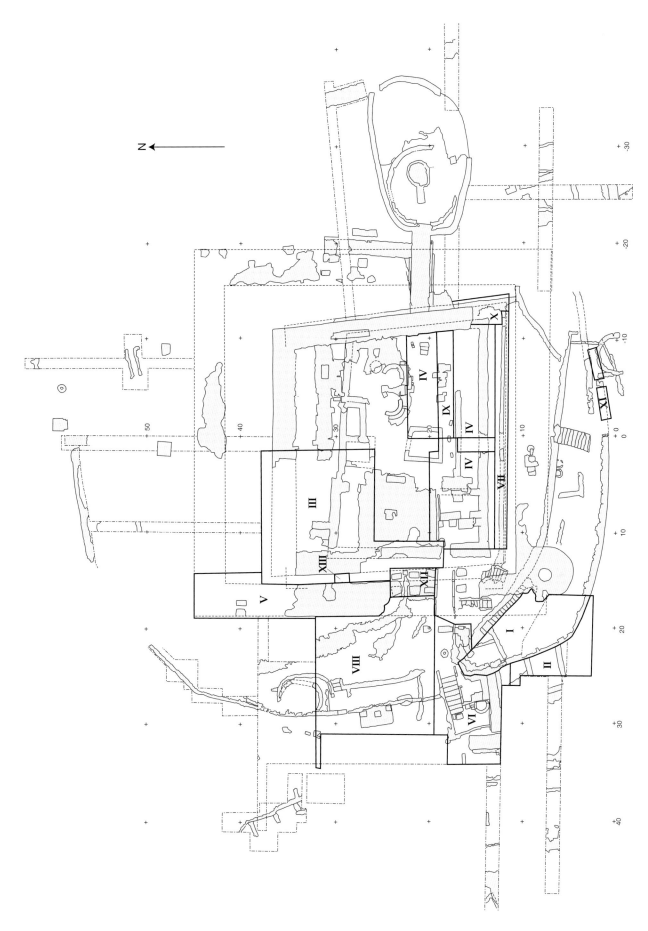

Fig. 11. Excavations in 1959.

17

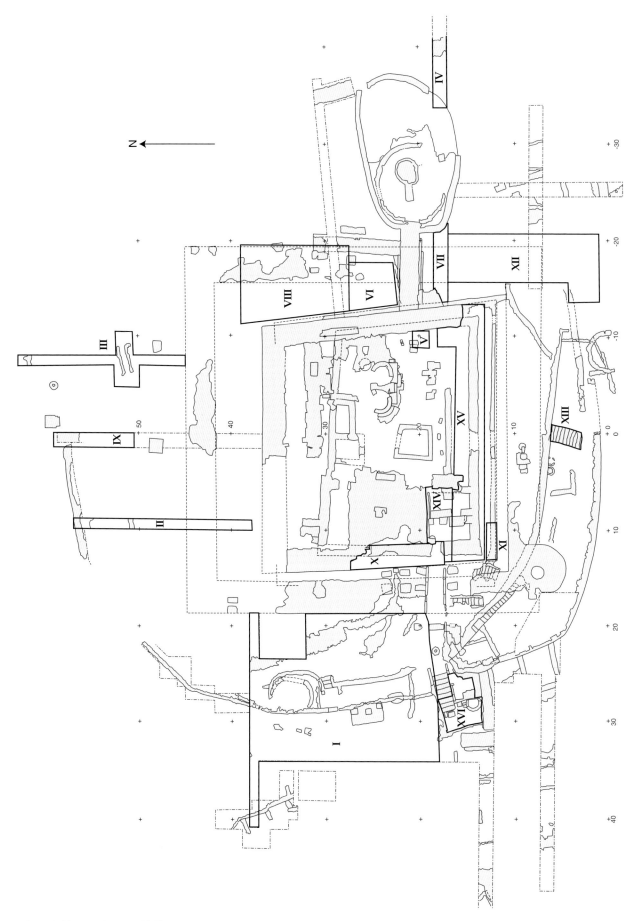

Fig. 12. Excavations in 1960.

18

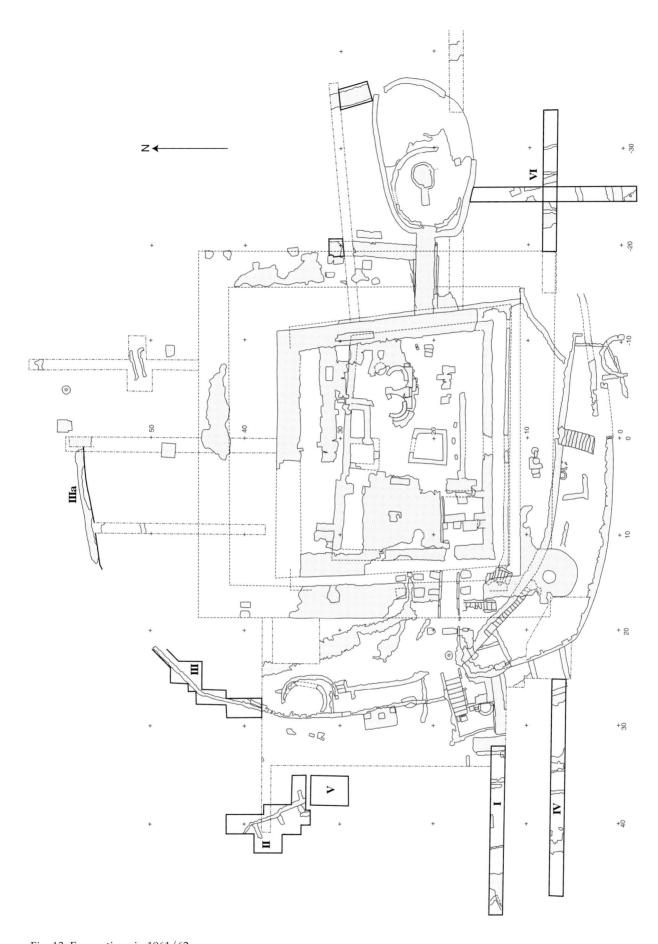

Fig. 13. Excavations in 1961/62.

19

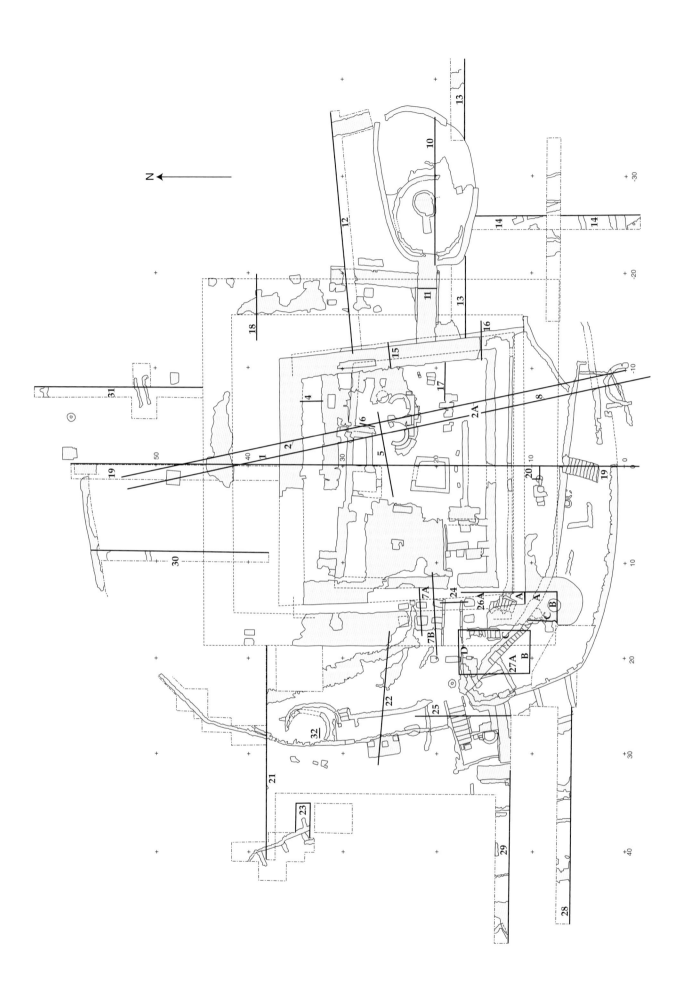

ple Ib was exposed. In area VI in the west a flight of stairs in continuation of a ramp-like stone structure, which had previously been uncovered, proved to lead down to a stone-lined chamber in the subsoil, filled by the natural subsoil water. The ramp-like masonry was thus the ruins of a stairway which had united the pool and the central platform (Glob 1959b).

Excavations in 1960 (fig. 12) by P. Mortensen and H.H. Andersen. The excavations in the central platform were brought to an end with investigations in depth in areas V, X, XIV and XV. The investigation was to some degree incomplete, due to leaving in position intact portions of the later temples, but it did show that the southwest corner of the central platform in Temple-I's period was not solid, but on the contrary formed a room, which was later filled up. In the west, in area I, excavation of the walling of the oval platform was continued, but only carried down to virgin soil along the north side of the area. The pool was emptied. In the south, in area XIII, the inside of the stairway was searched, and the stairway thereafter reconstructed. In the east the remains of the Temple-III wall were exposed in areas VI and VIII, but the deeper layers remained undisturbed. The sondage in the south-east, area XII, was superficial, but the trial trenches in areas VII and IV were in contrast carried down to subsoil. The northern foreland was also investigated with trial trenches, but a garden north of the temple prevented any continuation to the north (Glob 1960).

Excavations in 1961/62 (fig. 13) by P. Mortensen and H.H. Andersen. Concluding investigations were made at selected points, partly in order to follow the courses of walls in the west, north and east, and partly in the form of new trial trenches in the southeast and south-west. The Northeast Temple was re-investigated (Bibby 1965).

At the end of the excavation, in January 1962, the ruins were covered up for their own protection. They were, however, exposed again by re-excavation in 1970, directed by H.H. Andersen, in relation to the *Third International Conference on Asian Archae-* *ology*, which took place in Bahrain (Porada et al. 1971). Again in 1983, in relation to the *Bahrain Through The Ages*-conference (Al-Khalifa & Rice 1986), the monument was re-excavated, again directed by H.H. Andersen, and restored by the Ministry of Information (Rice 1983).

With regard to the technique of excavation it should be stated that the horizontal measurements are based on a west-oriented coordinate system. The measured sections are given in a special key plan (fig. 14). All heights are given in relation to a datum-point (0.00), and measurements are expressed positively below and negatively above the datum. The height of the datum-point above sea-level was measured on December 12th 1961 at 8.36 metres. The datum-point was situated in the easternmost hole cut into the top of the large stone block on the temple's central axis towards the north (cf. plan 8:3).

The excavation of the main temple mound is registered at the Prehistoric Museum, Moesgård, as no. 517; the Northeast Temple as no. 681; and the well-chamber at Umm as-Sujur as no. 516. Objects are designated by letters, 517.A-ASF, 681.A-EY, 516A-M.

As stated above, the final study of the architecture and stratigraphy of the monument was carried out by Hellmuth Andersen, who submitted his manuscript in 1981. The analysis of the finds was begun by Peder Mortensen, who published some preliminary studies (1971a; 1971b; 1986), but other obligations prevented him from continuing the work. In 2000 the treatment of the finds and the editing of the publication were entrusted to Flemming Højlund. They were carried out in 2001-3.

The excavation of the Barbar Temple was supported financially by the Bahrain government, the Bahrain Petroleum Company and the Carlsberg Foundation. The preparation and the printing of the present volume was made possible by the Carlsberg Foundation as part of the *Carlsberg Foundation's Gulf Project*. The assistance of the Directorate of Culture and National Heritage in the Bahrain Ministry of Information is gratefully acknowledged. For help and inspiration thanks are due to Khaled Al-Sindi and Poul Kjærum.

Fig. 14. General plan with all the sections, 1-33, indicated. The so-called Main Section is compounded of three sections, 1, 2 and 19. Two of the sections, 3 and 9, were impossible to place, and two others, 6 and 8, were uncertain. These four sections have not been published. Four other sections, 7A, 23, 26A1 and 27B, were considered redundant for the purpose of publication. Section 32 is merely a local description of strata without a drawing, and is therefore only mentioned. Section 33 is a reconstruction-section. Sections 1-9 were produced by the first excavators, sections 10-32 by P. Mortensen and H. H. Andersen.

2. Stratigraphy

The general stratigraphy of the temple can most clearly be seen in a main north-south section through the tell. No corresponding eastwest main section exists, but a series of sections nevertheless provides information concerning the deposits to the east and west of the central structure, a four-sided platform. It is the constructional history of this platform which gives the sequence of Temples I-III, since the platform contained in fact three markedly different stages of development. Each platform had its own surface height, here called the floor level, and this was constantly raised, at the same time as the platform was built larger and larger.

A number of sections were also drawn which concern mainly details. They can best be treated in connection with these details, and will not therefore be discussed in this chapter. All sections are localized in a general plan (fig. 14).

The Main Section

This section is a combination of three separate sections, 1, 2 and 19. Sections 1 and 2, comprising the soil-walls of the first trial trench from 1954, were drawn from the surface of the tell to the level of Temple II's platform floor, only occasionally going deeper so as to reach virgin sand. Section 19 represents a continuation from the level of Temple II down to virgin sand, but slightly displaced in relation to sections 1 and 2. A combination of these sections gives a complete picture of the stratigraphy through the centre of the mound, from end to end and from surface to virgin soil. This picture presents the outline of a tell with a transverse measurement of 63 metres and a height of 5.60 metres above virgin soil, measured at the 20 m point.

The result is a Main Section which by its placing gives a basic insight into the stratigraphy of the tell, first and foremost into the three floor-levels of the temple's central platform and their terrace walls, but also into the underlying oval platform with its massive terrace walls to the south. The stratigraphy also includes building levels and architectural remains, and in addition deposits from the period when the buildings were in use, laid down in front of the respective terrace walls.

In addition the traces can be seen of large excavations: the disturbances caused by secondary stone-quarrying.

An examination of this stratigraphy forms the starting point for the presentation, in this chapter and those following, of the architecture of the separate temples. It should be noted that the border between the two portions of the composite Main Section is shown by a continuous broken line. Andersen and Mortensen have only been able to make personal observations of the levels under this line (2-142).

Almost without exception these latter levels concern the stratigraphy of Temples I and II. The few exceptions are the result either of earlier archaeological trial-trenches (142) or of blocks of earth which were not removed, being left *in situ* out of consideration for building works above them (A, D, E, G, H and J).

The original surface of the site can be seen in the subsoil sand (10), the surface of which shows the outline of a low natural rising which to the south has clearly been dug away to accommodate the wall of the oval terrace (N). The northern foot of the rising lay at level 4.00, its central portion at level 3.20-3.30, and from there it fell to level 3.50 immediately before this excavation.

On this low rising the oldest temple (Ia) was laid out in the form of a central platform surrounded by a terrace wall. The distance across the platform from side to side measures in the section 16 metres. The terrace walls with their foundations stand directly upon the underlying sand at level 3.30-3.40, and the northern wall (F) is preserved in its full height. The southern wall (K) has been partly demolished, the demolition taking place in connection with the building of Temple II.

These two walls formed the outer edges of an almost 2 metre high platform, the inner core of which had been filled up. At the level of the top of the wall a plaster floor (71) had been laid, approximately at level 1.50. In the actual section this floor is only partly preserved, the remainder being broken up. It gives, however, the Temple I floor-level, which was retained in both phases of this temple (Ia and Ib). On this floor remains can also be seen of temple buildings (G and H), wall-footings which remained after a demolition prior to the building of Temple II.

The "fill" below the floor-level of the earliest temple consisted of sand (65, 66, 68 and 69) with stripes of clay (67 and 70). But the lowest level (64) consists, oddly enough, of pure clay. In this so-called "clay-core" objects were frequently found, deposited as foundation offerings.

This clay core was, however, not confined to the platform. Outside the terrace walls (F and K) a bottom horizon appears, composed predominantly of clay and also containing offerings. It should probably be interpreted as a continuation of the clay core in the surrounding oval platform, less pronounced to the south (93 and 95-96), more extensive to the north (41, 43, 56, 63) and here containing unconnected wallings (B). Above this bottom clay level, which must have reduced the visible height of the central platform, came deposits from the time when the earliest temple was in use, but they cannot be delimited with certainty, either vertically or horizontally. Among other factors, levelling can have taken place in connection with the subsequent reconstruction. The only immediate observation that can be made is that the footing of the terrace wall (L) in the next building-phase (Ib) has been raised about 0.75 m.

This terrace wall is our main evidence in the section for Temple Ib. This temple is thus here represented by its southern terrace wall, the footing of which stands at level 2.75. The corresponding north wall cannot be identified in the section, and was in fact never determined. It should probably be sought under the northern terrace wall (D) of Temple II, but investigations directed to determining this were not made.

With a footing level of 2.75 and a floor level at the same height as Temple Ia (1.50) this platform has only had a height of 1.25 m, in other words apparently lower than the platform of its predecessor, though the visible height of the earlier structure may have been reduced correspondingly by the surrounding layer of clay already described. The terrace wall which we are here concerned with (L) has also been partly demolished, a demolition which took place with the establishment of Temple II's southern terrace wall, which originally enveloped it but was itself completely demolished by stone-quarrying (1c).

In any event, we can describe the central platform of Temple Ib as an enlargement of the original platform, while retaining the same floor level. The dimension across the platform in the section can be estimated to have been 24-25 metres. It is worth mentioning that the reconstruction of the terrace wall in the south manifested itself in a special construction layer (92) which was packed so closely with stones that the two walls (K and L) appear in the section as a single composite mass. This feature has also been observed in other sections through the terrace walls of Ia and Ib.

Surrounding deposits from the period of use of Temple Ib cannot be separated out with requisite certainty.

Nor is it possible to read directly from the section whether Temple I was already laid out in the south as a double terrace with a central four-sided platform standing above an oval platform of greater dimensions, as was the case with Temple II. As the terrace walls of such an original oval platform could easily have been removed during the building of Temple II, and thus have been eliminated from the picture given by the section, we will here only call attention to one particular layer (108), a heap of stones deeply embedded behind Temple II's first oval terrace wall (N) in the south. It could be interpreted as a sign of a demolition of such a wall in an earlier version.

There are other indications that Temple I was demolished with a view to building Temple II. On the central platform the walls of buildings (G and H) have been demolished down to the footings, and the layers of the fill for the platform of the new Temple II (57, 58 and 76) are significantly full of fragments of stone and plaster, forming a regular demolition layer. This layer was thereafter covered by further layers of fill, predominantly of sand (77-79 and 89).

The foundation was thereby laid for a completely new central platform, belonging to Temple II. This temple was an architectural masterpiece, decisively characterized by a new building technique with massive use of finely shaped blocks of limestone. This is unmistakably present in the section.

The remains of the northern terrace wall (D) of the central platform can be seen directly, with its base at level 2.20, i.e. about ½ m higher than its predecessor of Temple Ib. Indirectly, the original location of the southern terrace wall can be determined by the presence of a layer of fill (1c and 90) marking the remains of a secondary quarrying excavation which stops at level 2.20-2.30. It contains, moreover, a block of stone (M) left behind in the fill.

The building of this wall led at the time to the demolition of the underlying walls of Temple I down to the level just named. The transverse width of the platform can thus now be determined, and measured from wall-face to wall-face 25 m. Its original height can also be given, since at an optimally preserved point in its eastern course an intact upper edge of the terrace wall was found at level 0.20. The wall has thus been 2 m high.

This determination of height shows that the northern terrace wall (D) in the section is only present as the remains of a footing, as a ruin of an original wall construction. It has not, however, been secondarily robbed like the wall to the south, for the stratigraphy shows undisturbed layers covering it (1), and belonging to Temple III. The state of the wall is thus ancient and cannot be attributed to a later secondary quarrying, which is in fact attested by the presence of a large local excavation down from the surface of the tell (1b). On the contrary, this robber pit here "missed its target." The Temple II wall (D) must consequently here have been demolished before the building of Temple III, and its stones probably re-used in the building of that temple.

The floor level of the central platform in Temple II can also be accurately determined. Admittedly in the section the floor has been broken up, but elsewhere quite considerable connected portions still remained, consisting of large limestone flags at level 0.50-0.60. Only the plaster layer (81 and 82) from the broken-up floor can still be seen in the section. At level 0.60, i.e. at the same level as the platform, there appears moreover the upper edge of a foundation wall (E) for a large temple building on the platform. To the same level can be attributed a pierced cult-stone (J), still standing in place.

The disturbances to the platform of Temple II here mentioned, in particular the broken-up floor and the demolished buildings, point to the same destruction process as named above, to demolition with a view to secondary use in Temple III. Undisturbed Temple III layers (1) cover large sections of the remains of Temple II.

Temple II's central platform has thus represented a totally new construction. The floor level has been raised about 1 m compared to Temple I, and the surrounding terrace walls have given the platform a new type of frame through the change in material. They were moreover raised about 25 cm above the floor level.

South of the central platform, at the southern end of the section, the oval platform of Temple II enters the picture, in the shape of deep-going wall constructions (N-P). They take the form of high terrace walls and a stairway. As two high terrace walls appear, both with frontage towards the south, and as the outer one enfolds the inner, a later reconstruction must be assumed.

The construction of the first of these walls (N) has necessitated digging away the original ground in a sheer excavation (106), which goes deep into the subsoil (10). The base level of the wall was here established as about 5.70, and its foot stood therefore below the groundwater level. The wall is completely preserved in the section.

From the surviving wall-top projects the upper step of a built-on stairway, and it can thereby be seen that the crown of the wall lies at level 2.20, a level identical with that of the foot of the central platform's terrace wall. This agreement, together with a plaster floor (115) at the same level on the interval between the two platforms, is the main evidence that the oval terrace wall (N) should be attributed stratigraphically to Temple II. This statement is made because the stratigraphy is not completely unambiguous, and because the wall is built of a material differing from that of Temple II.

The face of the wall showed at level 3.00 a ledge, a horizontal bevel edge which is concealed in the section by the built-on stairway, but which explains the upper pulling back of the wall which can be seen on its reverse face.

This wall is replaced in a subsequent period by a new oval-terrace wall (P) of finely cut ashlars of the same type as the rest of Temple II. This wall is even more deeply sunk than its predecessor, its foot lying at level 6.50, while above it another wall had been secondarily built of smaller stones. The wall here reaches its highest point at level 3.20, but it was not intact. That this was so is shown dramatically by the fact that, a few centimetres behind the section, the wall (P) has been robbed to the last stone. The excavation associated with the robbery is presumably to be seen in the section, in the fill of all the layers drawn in above the wall.

The wall (P) is thus, as it appears in the section, not in its original condition. Its crown has initially lain at a level corresponding to that of its predecessor (N), a circumstance still demonstrated at a fortunately preserved point west of the section. The shelf between the oval and the central platform is thus recognizable, though disturbed in the actual section. We can in this circumstance, as before, see evidence that the wall (P) is associated with Temple II, even though an unambiguous stratigraphy is absent.

The two stretches of wall (N and P) are evidence of a comprehensive, even though local, reconstruction of Temple II, which makes it reasonable to talk of two phases (IIa and IIb).

The Main Section was unfortunately not continued further in a southerly direction, and it is therefore uncertain how the area in front of this oval platform has been structured. But the extensive building activity in the period of Temple II has resulted in the destruction of any predecessors of the oval platform that may have existed in the period of Temple I.

Fig. 15. Surviving portion of Temple-III's platform with horizontal stratification of sterile fill (1955).

Furthest to the north the section ends arbitrarily at a wall (A) which stratigraphically can also be associated with Temple II. Further investigation here was prevented by the presence of cultivated land right up to the foot of the tell. The stretch of wall can best be interpreted as the remains of a corresponding northern portion of the oval terrace, though here quite low.

Of the layers (1) above the level of Temple II no specific information exists. They are summarily described as "sterile" sand or gravel. The layers present themselves, however, as far from undisturbed, insofar as massive traces (1a-c) of excavation can be seen. The object of these excavations is obvious; they originate at the surface of the tell and are the result of secondary robber activities.

These robberies have had a markedly destructive effect upon Temple III, the latest structure on the site, which may be assumed to have been directly accessible for stone-robbery. Our knowledge of Temple III is correspondingly reduced, but it is nevertheless possible to identify its main architectural feature, a new central platform, larger than its predecessor and of a considerable height.

The walling of this platform is only present in the section as a fragment of the foundation of the northern terrace wall (C). The foot of the wall has been laid at level 1.50, almost 0.75 metres higher than the corresponding wall (D) of Temple II. A robber-excavation (1a) gives the reason for the poor state of preservation of the wall. A similar robber-excavation (1c) at the southern edge of the tell reveals that the plundering of the southern terrace wall of Temple III has been total. The more centrally situated excavations (1b) can only be interpreted as traces of larger robber diggings. One may imagine that such holes have been scattered over the surface of the tell, and have in some cases given richer results for the stone-robbers than here, where the walls of Temple II (D and E) have not been reached. In this particular case (1b) it can only be mentioned that parts of a double-circular cult-structure on the floor of Temple II seem to have been encountered on its northern side and disturbed by stone-robbery, though this circumstance does not appear in the Main Section because of the displacement of the section.

It has been already mentioned that Temple II had not only been subject to secondary stone-robbery, but had also been already dismantled to a considerable degree as a preliminary to the building of Temple III. In support of this supposition can be adduced a remarkable feature in the layers (1) in the upper part of the tell, where they are undisturbed.

This situation is only found within the bounds of the Temple III platform between the terrace walls (C and the lost wall in 1c). This stratum shows a degree of layering caused by horizontal strips of some material containing plaster (fig. 15). These strips "seal", at least partially, the underlying features, including the above-mentioned walls (D and E) from Temple II. When these strips were laid down Temple II must already have been demolished to the degree that the section discloses.

The layers described here (1) were interpreted by the first excavators as a deliberate covering up of the temple ruin (cf. Bibby 1996 p. 50). In reality they represent the fill forming the platform of Temple III, the terrace walls of which are only represented in the section by the remains of the northern footing (C). The internal layering of this fill, the horizontal strips (1) must be explained as temporary levellings during the construction of the platform.

Concerning Temple III the stratigraphy in the Main Section can in reality only tell us that the terrace walls of the platform were founded at level 1.50, and that its fill was laid over the remains of Temple II. A surrounding raising of the ground level covered the oval platform of Temple II.

On the floor of the new platform the buildings of Temple III could then be raised, but this level has not survived. The height can only be defined as approximately identical with the surface of the tell or at a hypothetical level above this.

The foot of the terrace wall at level 1.50 must be assumed to lie at approximately the level of the surrounding terrain at the time when building commenced. In support of this is the fact that a massive shaped block of stone was embedded in the tell about 2½ metres north of the wall with its base at about the same level.

The highest surviving height of the tell seems to suggest a platform raised about 4 m above the ground level of the time. With a cross-section of 38 m and a height double that of its predecessor Temple III has thus stood as a comparatively colossal platform. It is square in plan, and these changes appear to be accompanied by an abandonment of vi-tal features of Temple II. The oval platform and the large flanking structures - the Eastern Court and the pool - can no longer be found. On the basis of our present knowledge Temple III has consisted in the main of the central platform.

The main result of the section here described is thus the demonstration of the way in which the tell contains three central temple platforms, the one above the other, contained by terrace walls. These walls continually change their footing-level as a result of the level of the earth surrounding them at the time, while their siting outside their respective predecessors continually increases the cross-section width of the platform. The floor level of the platform is established three times, each time at a higher level.

We have Temple Ia with a cross-section of 16 m and with a wall-footing at subsoil level (3.40), and Ib as a reconstruction with a cross-section of 24 m (?) and now with a wall-footing at a higher level (2.75). Both platforms have their floors at the same level (1.50). Temple I is superceded by a regular rebuilding, Temple II, with a cross-section of 25 m and a wall-footing at an even higher level (2.20) than Ib. The platform-floor is laid at a level (0.50) about 1 m higher than Ib. Associated with Temple II there is moreover a larger oval platform, which appears in two different forms as a result of reconstruction, Temple IIa and IIb. Temple II is superceded by Temple III with a cross-section of 38 m and a wall-footing at a higher level (1.50) than that of II. The floor-level is missing (about -2.50?).

The interpretation of the three temples here sketched can be stratigraphically defended, but it is impossible to deal exhaustively with the stratigraphy of a so complicated structure as the Barbar temple on the basis of a single main section. We shall therefore now present a series of sections which supplement our knowledge of the stratigraphy in all four cardinal directions. The north and south-going sections will of necessity be related parallels to the Main Section, while the east and west-going will to some degree be of a different character.

Section 2A

In the southern part of the initial trial trench of 1954 Glob carried out a local sondage down to subsoil, and made a special measured drawing of this portion. As this section partially contains the whole history of the building of the central platform, as well as the history of its robbery, it is a valuable supplement to the Main Section.

The section was placed to cut through the southeast corner of the central platform. Undisturbed subsoil (12) was found at level 3.50, and on this was built a wall (E), which can be identified as the rear side of Temple Ia's terrace wall. Later, at a higher level (2.85), another wall (F) was built, being the outer face of Temple Ib's terrace wall.

Both walls (E and F) were demolished down to a common level (2.20) and covered with plaster, so that they have the appearance of a unity. The demolition and the plastering are attributed to the construction of the wall of the superimposed Temple II, a wall which has here been removed. The removal has left extremely distinct traces of the robbery (3 and 13-15). The level of demolition (2.20) consequent on the building of the Temple-II wall, as well as the bottom level of the robber excavation, are precisely the base level of Temple II's terrace wall. About 1 m south of the robbed Temple-II wall the similarly robbed wall of Temple III should be sought, in the robber-layer (3).

The three central temple-platforms are also identifiable. Temple I's platform consists of the fill-strata (7-11) and the "clay core" (10). Upon these are the remains of local walling (C). The floor level of this platform is admittedly broken up, but a demolition layer (6) and a shaped block of stone (B), left standing *in situ* at floor level, formed visual markers of this level for Temple I (1.60). Above this follows a stone-filled demolition layer (5) from the levelling of Temple I and a building layer (4) for the platform of Temple II, overlaid with plaster for its flooring of large stone flags. These flags had been broken up, but a single one of them (A) had been left *in situ* and thus plainly marked the floor level of Temple II (0.50).

The fill of the Temple-III platform manifests itself in the uppermost layers of sand (1 and 2), divided by a strip of a different nature. The floor-level of this platform cannot be determined, on account of stone-robbery. All of these features are in excellent agreement with the evidence of the Main Section.

Layers (3 and 13-16) in the section show how the terrace wall of Temple III was first totally removed. After that the similar wall of Temple II was systematically plundered, only leaving a single loose block of stone (D). The layers of broken stone (13 and 15) bear witness to the destruction. This specific robber-trench is an optimally exact reflection of the southern terrace wall of Temple II's central platform, originally present but now totally disappeared. The stone chippings (18) come from the shaping of the ashlars of the wall, while the sand (19) may be the fill of the oval platform in front of the wall.

The remaining layers south of the terrace walls, or at least the lower ones (20-23), should probably be understood as successive original accumulations from the time when the temples were in use.

Section 30

In 1960 a trial trench was dug through the northern border areas of the temple, from the surface then existing down to virgin soil. By then the upper part of the tell had long been removed by excavation, so that only the lower part appears in its original state of preservation.

With a subsoil (6) sloping down from south (3.30) to north (4.00) this section is in good agreement with the Main Section. The secondary robber-activity can be seen in particular in a large change of fill (2) going down to level 1.50 and thereby revealing how the northern terrace wall of Temple III, which ran here with its base at this level, has been completely removed. Another change of fill (1) probably marks the robbery of some architectural feature, unknown to us, on the Temple-III level. The other undiversified deposits do not suggest any considerable building activity in the northern reaches in the period of the older temples. Large parts of the upper layer (3) can be interpreted as fill to raise the ground-level for Temple III.

Only two masonry walls survive, both in ruined condition. The one (A) can from its stratigraphical position best be attributed to Temple II, and it does in fact also appear in the Main Section. The other (B) ties up with Temple I. In both cases the remains of the walls can be interpreted as vestiges of the low northern terrace walls of the oval platform. The latter wall (B), however, is only known from this section 30, but to judge by this it has the appearance of a little terrace wall placed against a cut-away edge of the subsoil, so as to make a terrace of the clay strata lying behind it (8 and 9).

It should be recorded that any further excavation in a northerly direction was blocked by the presence of a garden.

Sections 21 and 22

The western border areas of the temple showed traces of a more intense utilization than in the north, moreover a utilization of an unmistakably cult character, culminating in the highly remarkable pool in the southwestern sector. When this was found the layers above it had, however, been long ago dug away, and it therefore does not figure in any westward-running section.

Here therefore only sections 21 and 22 are of interest. They cut through the oval platform with its terrace walls, while the central platform is only contacted by the sections in its third and latest phase. The sections were drawn in 1960 and 1957, with the consequence that only the foot of the tell can be shown in its original condition, whereas the upper layers of the tell had been dug away at the time when the sections were drawn.

Section 21 shows the subsoil (12) at levels dropping from 3.40 in the east to 4.60 in the west. This fall in ground level, together with that from south to north, suggest the original presence here of an elevation in the territory. The section covers the distance from the lowest course of Temple III's western terrace wall (J) in the east to some deep-going walling (A-D) in the west. The ashlar (J) is a facing-stone in the wall of Temple III. Its base lies at the normal level for this wall (1.50).

An immense uniform layer of sand (1) is the most dominating feature in the succession of levels, and by its sheer monotony seems to smother the stratigraphical information of the section. The upper parts of it represent the covering of the older temples and thereby the raising of the level of Temple III's forward area.

The more differentiated layers of the lower part of the section consist of a bottom level of clay or of sand and clay (10, 11 and 13-23), and this can reasonably be ascribed to Temple I. The same applies to the masonry (A-D) in the extreme west, where an edge dug out of the subsoil is held by a terrace wall (C) with a flagged floor (B) in front at level 5.55. This masonry is only known at this point and is therefore difficult to bring into a more general association. The wall (D) behind it was completely without association and only appears in this section.

The oval platform of Temple II can also be identified in the west, though in a lower form. In a layer full of stones and plaster (3) we can see its floor at a level (2.30) corresponding to the foot of the terrace wall around the central platform of Temple II. We can see the terrace wall of the oval platform in the walling (F and G), which in the situation here drawn forms a unity, though only because two walls are here built together, an earlier one (G) with its base at level 3.45, and a later (F) with base at level 3.25. The former has probably its root in Temple I. In section 22 appear two separate terrace walls belonging to Temple II, so that we can recognize two phases in the constructional history of Temple II's oval platform in the west just as in the south. The walling (F) is badly broken down in section 21, but it has to all appearance terraced the oval platform with a floor at level 2.30, and has therefore been about a metre high. This oval platform has had an area in front which has also been utilized. A stone pillar (E), which stands in the section, had several parallels in this excavation area.

In the platform there was a large excavation (6), at the bottom of which was embedded a stone-set drain (H). The course of this drain indicates a connection with Temple II, as its stratigraphy also strongly suggests.

The area in front of Temple III does not appear to have been terraced in the form of an oval platform. A surface layer (2), which resembles closely the floor-level (3) of Temple II's oval platform, can be seen on a level with the footage of the Temple-III wall (J), sloping slightly down.

Section 22 is shorter than section 21, but richer in architectural features. It shows subsoil (15) at a level (3.40-3.55) falling towards the west. The section extends from the partly surviving Temple-III wall (G and H) to a little walled structure (A and B). The ashlar (G) is a facing stone in the westwall of Temple III and forms the lowest course of that wall, while the stones (H) are roughly cut blocks within the substance of the wall, which rests upon a plaster layer (7) at level 1.50. A firm layer of plaster fragments (3) probably represents the surface around and in front of the foot of the wall.

A thick uniform layer of sand (5) covers all the older deposits, of which the lowest (14, 17, 22, 25 and 31) form a clay-like bottom level which should most reasonably be ascribed to Temple I.

The masonry appearing in the section consists of broken-down terrace walls (C and D), stone-set drains (E and F) and a particular walled structure (A and B). There is a strong stratigraphical probability that all this masonry is associated with Temple II, with the exception of one of the drains.

In that case, the terrace walls have delimited two successive phases of Temple II's oval platform, an earlier (D) with its foot at level 3.35 and a later (C) with its foot at level 3.25. The floor-level of the platform is absent.

In front of the later terrace wall (C) there was built at its foot a special structure, here seen in section. It consisted of a little square platform with three stone pillars. The platform had a floor (B) and surrounding masonry (A).

In the fill of the oval platform two drains occur. The earlier drain (E) is laid on the subsoil, the later (F) somewhat higher at level 3.00, to which it has been dug down, as is shown by a consequent change in fill (27). The earlier drain had been taken out of use, being broken up immediately behind the section. The later drain is identical with that shown in section 21. They belong respectively to Temple I and Temple II.

The interpretation given here of section 22, ascribing the structures to Temple II, must nevertheless seek support in other evidence based upon a more general interpretation. An isolated analysis of the layers – such as is here attempted – can in fact only show that this general interpretation is not directly contradicted by the stratigraphical situation.

Sections 13 and 12

The temple's eastern extension was, like the western, highly utilized for cult purposes, but the deposits here were of a completely different nature. First and foremost, the layers here were dark, powdery and wasted by fire. The architecture was badly preserved, apart from a large oval area surrounded by a wall and from underground drains and channels.

This eastern extension has, to judge by the stratification, been a centre for special cult ceremonies, which have included the cooking over a fire of the sacrificed animals. The remains of ashes from these fireplaces have been allowed to remain on the site with constant addition of new material, which at regular intervals has been coated with plaster. These plaster layers divide up the strata, apparently as floor levels.

Both sections have been drawn after the original ground surface had been mechanically removed, so that it only appears sporadically. It must unfortunately also be added that archaeological trial trenches following the walls have partly removed interesting stratigraphical associations at the point where these sections approach the central masonry of the temple. The excavation of the oval structure has, moreover, left a considerable gap in the stratigraphy between -20 and -35 m. Here the subsoil, the original ground level, has been projected in from the neighbouring section 10, which will be considered later.

In the almost 70 m long *section 13* the subsoil (13) appears at levels between 3.00 and 3.60. The original ground-level thus lay in places a little higher than elsewhere on the temple site.

The layers fall otherwise into three main types – sandy, plastered and powdery. They can best be seen on an interpretive section which has been included. The powder-like layers from the cult activities stretch to a point about -62 m, though this far to the east only in deep deposits. The plastered layers appear widely distributed and certainly for the greater part represent surface levels. The sandy layers are predominant both in the upper part and in the eastern part of the section, though they also appear as local separating layers.

Seen in relation to the constructional history of the temple, it is most likely that the deposits in this section were laid down in the time of Temples I and II. The condensed interpretation given here of the stratigraphy in the east should adequately document the singularity of the deposits in this sector of the temple; for details the reader is referred to the section descriptions (1-57).

The architectural remains, on the other hand, require further consideration. The footings of the terrace walls of the central platform figure directly; they comprise the 2.25 m broad wall (A) of Temple II with its base level at 2.25, which only survives in its lowest course, and the outer face (B) of the wall of Temple Ib, which has been demolished down to the base level of the superimposed wall. The wall of Temple Ia cannot be seen; it lies beneath the Temple-II wall. The Temple-III wall has been completely removed by stone-robbery, but originally ran, with its base at level 1.50, in the uppermost stone-filled layer of sand (1).

The surface of a stone-set drain (C) has been superficially uncovered, but, together with a change of fill marking an excavation (3), can best be interpreted as belonging to a level contemporary with Temple II.

The oval wall (D and E) surrounding the Eastern Court has been drawn in to give an impression of its placing in the total stratigraphy. As we know already that it belongs to Temple II, with which it is directly connected by a ramp, it is sufficient to note here that the section supports this conclusion.

Finally there is found here an underground, stone-built channel (F), almost the height of a man. It has clearly been dug down from above, and the excavation's change of fill suggests a stratigraphical association with Temple II. The groundwater level (G) was established at level 5.55 at -70 m.

Section 12 extends from the central platform to the channel just described. The subsoil (16) ranges from level 2.75 to 3.60, and the stratigraphy is marked by the same main types as in section 13, as shown in the appended interpretive section. The sandy layers can here be roughly subdivided into very stony (9, 12, 14, 23 and the upper portions of 6) and less stony. The former appear particularly prominently in the lower half of the section under an almost continuous level of grey-black plaster (8). The powdery layers are less prevalent than in section 13, while plaster levels occur in large numbers.

There seem to be deposits from all periods of the temple, even though the surface of the tell had been removed by machinery. At the foot of the central platform layers (13 and 15) can be seen which underlie the wall (E) of Temple Ib, while stretching out from this wall is a concentrated stone layer (11) which may be a demolition level for the wall. As a level belonging to Temple II we may point to the grey-black plaster (8), which extends through large parts of the section. Similarly there appears in the upper portion of the section a level of white plaster (5), which belongs to Temple III. Both these levels have a strong tendency to orient themselves with the footings of the temple walls.

Here too, all three temples are represented architecturally in the section, in the form of their terrace walls. Thus Temple Ib is represented by its outer face (E), the base of the wall lying at level 2.90. It has been demolished down to level 2.30 to allow for the building of the Temple-II wall above it, and the part remaining is surrounded by stones (11), presumably from the demolition.

Temple II is represented by an unusually well-preserved portion of wall (A-D), with its base at level 2.35 and a partially intact top at level 0.35. The terrace wall is seen here to have been 2.30 m broad and 2 m high. Above it stands a piece of vertical masonry (B and C), which is part of the wall of a building. The face of the terrace wall (D) has been damaged, but has films of plaster in place at the edges of the breaks. The lowest course of the face is also preserved *in situ*, and here a roughly cut footing appears below.

It should be noted here that the partial demolition of the Temple II wall must be regarded as primary, and not as a result of secondary robber activity. The demolition has taken place before the construction of Temple III, as will be shown immediately below. Similar observations are known from the Main Section.

The terrace wall of Temple III is present in the form partly of stones *in situ* (F) and stones *ex situ* (G) and partly of an underlying local strip of plaster, west of F (5), where the stone-robbed wall

originally ran. The wall was preserved in almost its full foundation breadth 2 m north of the section. The bottom level of the wall lies at about 1.50, and the level here established includes the plaster layers (3 and 5) in the terrace-fill behind the wall. These building deposits overlie the break in Temple II's wall, and therefore seal the condition in which it was found when excavated. The one of the plaster layers (3), which extended over a considerable area north of the section, has been dug away along its eastern edge, probably in connection with the robbery of the Temple III wall. Other signs of this robber activity can be seen in a disorderly layer of stone fragments (4) and a disturbed layer of fill (17).

Two drains (H and I), of stones set in plaster and still empty, are parts of a drainage system which seems to have been dug down from a higher level. At least one of them connects up with Temple II, from the platform of which a run-off is found in the east wall in the immediate neighbourhood. Also Temple I had a run-off at this point.

Rising up from the plaster layer (8) of Temple II in the area in front of the wall there can be seen in quite low relief a stone-set road (J). It runs from the north to the ramp of the Eastern Court some 8 m to the south, a circumstance which adds strength to the view that the plaster layer (8) forms a Temple-II floor-level in the eastern environs of the temple.

Mention should finally be made of the underground stone-built channel, which could also be seen in section 13. The changes of fill from an excavation again suggest a stratigraphical association with Temple II. The bottom of the channel was paved with long stones, about 35 cm broad, in which a conduit had been cut. In the exposed part of the channel just in front of the section there was, in the roofing stones, a four-sided cleaning hole, measuring about 40 × 40 cm, and it is possible that the internal changes of fill (26 and 33) in the excavation layers are the traces of a shaft down to the channel.

3. Temple I

The recognized parts of Temple I consist first and foremost of a central platform. An extensive reconstruction of the original platform, involving enlargement on all four sides with a new terrace wall, gives basis for a division into two building-phases, Temples Ia and Ib (fig. 3). These two phases are associated by the fact that they have to all appearances had a common floor-level, consisting of large stretches of surviving plaster floors.

Temple I was demolished to allow for the building of Temple II above and around it, and is therefore damaged accordingly, but the solid platform and its terrace walls could still be identified. There therefore appears a complete plan of Temple Ia and a partial plan of Temple Ib, so far as the central portion is concerned. There can, however, be scarcely any real doubt that this picture should be supplemented with a lower terrace step, an oval platform with the same main structure as in Temple II.

The central platform's terrace walls

The platform of *Temple Ia* has an askew four-sided ground-plan, oriented after the cardinal points of the compass. The terrace walls which encompass it have been raised on a natural rise in the original terrain. The two southern corners were fully excavated, while the two northern corners were overlaid by the masonry of Temple II, which was not removed (plan 1).

Section 16 shows the two terrace walls of Ia and Ib near the southeast corner (fig. 16). On the subsoil at level 3.50-3.60 stands the wall-footing (5) of the eastern wall of Ia. East of this is the later terrace wall of Temple Ib (2) at level 2.90, and between the two walls there is a filling of stones (3). Both walls have been demolished down to level 2.20, and are overlaid by the terrace wall (1) of Temple II.

The south wall of Temple Ia was about 25 m long and was exposed in its full length as fairly continuous, only interrupted in the middle by the Main Section (figs. 17-18). The wall consists of two parts, a foundation footing (plan1:1) on the subsoil and a vertical wall (2), which further up has been systematically demolished down to the base-level of the overlying Temple-II wall. A characteristic breakage-line intervenes between the foundation and the wall proper. The foundation consists of larger stones, the upper part of large and smaller stones, the binding material used being clay (figs. 19-20).

The southeast corner of the wall was severely damaged, so that only the lowest courses were preserved. It could thereby be seen that the outer corner of the foundation projected slightly (fig. 21).

This feature was repeated in the southwest corner. At the western end of the wall was found an original opening (3) in the wall, though the foundation was continuous all the way (fig. 22). Precisely here there was an inner "room" in the platform, in sharp contrast to the solid fill which otherwise comprised the inner composition of the platform.

The west wall consisted of two stretches (4 and 5/6), separated by an opening (7) which led into the same inner "room" as has just been mentioned (figs. 23-24).

The complete course of the west wall measured about 17½ m. The northern stretch (4) was badly damaged, and showed in addition a large break in the outer face, old damage caused by a drain which here issued from the central platform and continued in a drainage channel (35). The southern stretch consisted of both foundation (5) and superimposed wall (6). Here there was in addition an extra projection on the inner side of the foundation (fig. 22). The upper part of the wall has been demolished down to level 2.36 to give room to the overlying Temple-II wall. The building technique was the same as that of the south wall. The north end of the wall could not be exposed on account of the Temple-II walling.

The north wall was remarkably intact, 23½ m long, but less homogeneous than the stretches of wall already described. It will be considered in its two halves. Only the outer face was systematically exposed.

In the western half of the north wall two facts point to local rebuilding having taken place: an applied section of walling (8) was not founded upon

33

Fig. 16. Temple I, central platform, southeast corner, terrace walls, from S. Dug to virgin soil. Left wall Ia, right wall Ib, both demolished and overlain by lowest course of Temple II's eastern terrace wall (1960).

Fig. 17. Temple I, central platform, southern terrace walls, from E. Dug to virgin soil. Right wall Ia, left wall Ib, both demolished and overlain by Temple II's southern terrace-wall, here robbed to the last stone. In foreground the eastern terrace walls of Temples Ib and II. On the plateau to right remains of Temple I's plaster floor and archaeologists' stone-heap (1960).

Fig. 18. Temple I, central platform, southern terrace wall Ia, from W. Dug to virgin soil, SW corner exposed. The wall was demolished down to bottom level of Temple II's southern terrace wall, here robbed to the last stone. The plateau to left shows remains of masonry on the Temple-I floor, and completely exposed remains of a foundation-wall – of cut blocks – buried in the Temple-II platform (1960).

Fig. 19. Temple I, central platform, southern terrace wall Ia, outer face, from SE. Dug to virgin soil, foundation visible. In foreground corresponding wall Ib. On platform archaeologists' stone-heap (1960).

Fig. 20. Temple I, central platform, southern terrace wall Ia, rear side, from W. Dug to virgin soil. In background the wall's inner SE-corner with deeply-founded stones. At the demolition-level of the wall is a projecting portion of the lowest course of Temple II's eastern terrace wall (1960).

Fig. 21. Temple I, central platform, SE-corner of wall Ia, from above, south at top (1960).

Fig. 22. Temple I, central platform, SW-corner of wall Ia, from N. Dug to virgin soil, demolished down to bottom level of Temple II's terrace wall, here robbed to the last stone. In background opening in south wall, in foreground opening in west wall (1960).

Fig. 23. Temple I, central platform, western terrace wall, Ia, from S. In extreme north the wall is overlain by a surviving remnant of Temple II's west-wall. To right parts of the floor of the Temple-II platform can be seen, overlying a wall of roughly cut stone blocks, which is interpreted as the northern wall in an inner room in Temple I's platform at the SW-corner. In the west wall of the room, which is formed by the terrace wall, there is an opening, and in front of this can be seen flanking foundation-stones for walling which has presumably edged an approach to the opening. To left project large slab-like cut edge-stones out above the general level. They belong to the side-structure of Temple II's pool stairway, which was flanked by cut stone blocks with rectangular holes (1960).

Fig. 24. Temple I, central platform, western terrace wall Ia, from N. To left at top masonry on Temple II's platform, to right flanking foundation-stones in front of opening in wall, cf. fig. 23 (1960).

Fig. 25. Temple I, central platform, western half of northern terrace wall Ia, outer face, from N. A secondary wall has been built on at a higher level. In front of the wall excavated to virgin soil, behind the wall Temple I's plaster floor can be seen, overlain by remains of masonry on Temple II's platform. In foreground to right extension to platform, belonging to Temple Ib (1959).

Fig. 26. Temple I, central platform, western half of northern terrace wall Ia, outer face, from N. As fig. 25, but secondary walling removed (1959).

Fig. 27. Temple I, central platform, western half of northern terrace wall Ia, outer face, from E. Behind the wall remains of Temple I's plaster floor. In middle distance surviving remnant of Temple II's western terrace wall. In background remains of Temple III's western terrace wall (1959).

Fig. 28. Temple I, central platform, eastern half of northern terrace wall Ia, outer face, from E. Excavated to virgin soil. At upper right exposed south side of foundation-wall buried in Temple II's platform (1958).

Fig. 29. Temple I, central platform, eastern half of northern terrace wall Ia, top of wall at platform's floor level, from E. Behind the wall remains of chambers on the platform. They lay in a row along the wall, in background covered by fill in Temple II's platform. To right exposed parts of foundation-wall buried in Temple II's platform (1958).

Fig. 30. Temple I, central platform, detail of northern terrace wall Ia, outer face at east end, from NW. At top of wall can be seen the plaster floor from the Temple-I platform, Ib; to right a drain emerges on the wall-face, indicated by an arrow, a little below the top of the wall. The wall runs in under the rear side of Temple II's eastern terrace wall, consisting of massive ashlars (1958).

the subsoil, but on a layer of clay, while an extension of the platform's floor level could be seen north of the north wall (fig. 25). On removal of these secondary extensions the facade of the primary north wall (9) appeared in all clarity. The wall consisted of a lower and an upper construction, the lower being set slightly back (fig. 26).

This stretch of wall followed a straight course and again consisted of stones set in clay (fig. 27). It was fully preserved, and still possessed a wall-top at levels between 1.42 and 1.33, so that the top of the wall was higher than the floor-level of the platform. This wall-top is, however, certainly secondary, and belongs to the platform of Temple Ib.

The eastern half of the north wall continues the course in the form of the original wall (10) and carries a wall-top (11) with in places very high top levels (figs. 28-29). Parts of this wall-top can here be seen to be walls of small buildings which have stood on the platform. Also in this case it must be a matter of secondary masonry relating to Temple Ib.

At the east end of the north wall an upper portion of somewhat smaller stones has been inserted, a repairing of damage caused by a drain-outlet which issues on the outer face (fig. 30). The wall has naturally been demolished at the eastern end to make room for the Temple-II wall, but its lower portions continue in under the Temple-II wall, where its

northeastern corner, which was never excavated, must lie.

The east wall was covered by the east wall of Temple II and was never dug free, apart from a minimal portion at the southeast corner. Its length must be estimated at about 15½ m.

On this basis the masonry around the platform of Temple Ia can be summed up as a terrace wall about 0.8 m wide with an original height of about 2 m, built of local stone mortared with clay. Its footing was based on the subsoil sand, and its bottom level was quite uniform, averaging about level 3.60.

In many places the wall can be seen to have had a separate foundation-footing, which has been encased on both sides with a packing of clay. The foundation has probably therefore not been visible after the completion of the platform.

The problem of access to this platform will be dealt with below in the section on the outer wallings. No stairways directly built onto the platform were found, but they can easily have been removed during later reconstruction, or may be hidden under portions of the platform walling which have not been investigated, being covered by later constructions which were left *in situ.*

Temple Ib comprises a renewal of the terrace walls (12), but they were only observed along the southern and eastern sides, where they stood very close

Fig. 31. Temple I, central platform, southern part of eastern terrace wall Ib, from SE. Demolished down to bottom level of Temple II's eastern wall, which can be seen overlying the older wall, where it still survives – in background all the way up to the crown of the wall, where double blocks form a wall on top of the terrace wall. Projecting walling for the ramp to the Eastern Court blocks the view of the continuing course of the Temple-I wall (1959).

to the preceding walls. Their stratigraphical placing has been already described. Every survey shows the same picture: of a wall which is secondary in its relation to the wall of Temple Ia, but primary in relation to the overlying terrace masonry from Temple II. For the building of Temple II's walls it was demolished to a uniform level, and thereafter functioned as a foundation. It is this fact which provides the main argument for the view that Temple Ib represents an independent reconstruction. There are unsolved problems concerning the north and west walls, the solution of which was not attempted through the easily available opportunity of investigating the structural situation under the overlying Temple-II walls in the north and west.

The actual wall-construction is easy to describe. It consists of large and smaller stones, with a greyish white plaster used both as mortar and as a rough layer on the outer face (section 16:2). It lies here in a layer 1-1½ cm thick, though badly preserved on the south wall. The eastern wall was demolished down to the base level of the subsequent Temple-II wall, which all the way followed precisely the course of the Temple-Ib wall, but was set slightly back. The wall of Temple II thus, as it were, used its predecessor as a foundation-footing, and the same was also the case along the southern course, though here the Temple-II wall had been later completely removed.

Technically it can be said that the face of Temple Ib's wall has been moved out about 1.75 m in front of the face of Temple Ia's wall, and the space between the two walls filled with stones. Thus in principle the reconstruction resulted in a cavity-wall with the old wall as the backing. The later wall was therefore carried out in a much slighter construction than the earlier, though on the other hand with the use of plaster instead of clay. This method of construction resulted in the combined masonry of Ia plus Ib achieving in the south and east a considerable breadth, of about 2.75 m.

The eastern course of the wall could only be partially exposed, by reason of the wall of Temple II (fig. 31). At the northern end it can be seen to have been more thoroughly demolished than in the rest of its course, and it ends in a completely demolished condition. It has presumably been longer, but that circumstance was not systematically investigated. At the southern end it could be completely excavated, and the southeast corner exposed (fig. 32). Here, however, a complication in interpretation arose. The course of the east wall continued in an inexplicable way onward to a portion of walling for which it is difficult to find a place in the history of the building. It stands across the course of the east wall and will be dealt with as a part of Temple II's architecture.

Fig. 32. Temple I, central platform, southern part of eastern terrace wall Ib, including SE-corner, from N. The wall apparently continues in a southerly direction as far as a curved wall-course at the top of the picture, probably belonging to Temple II (1959).

Fig. 33. Temple I, central platform, southern terrace wall Ib, from E. To left of centre of wall can be seen masonry on Temple II's oval platform, to right remains of temple I's plaster floor and a fragment of masonry upon it. Behind this appear larger blocks from a foundation-wall buried in Temple II's platform (1959).

The course of the south wall, on the other hand, came clearly to view and was totally exposed, in so far as it was preserved (fig. 33). Archaeological trenching explain the breaks at the east end and in the middle. The western half of the south wall showed gaps in the state of preservation, and a portion which survived was, by a mistake, never drawn, but can be seen on an excavation photograph of the exposed course of the wall (fig. 33). Finally at the west end there was found a fragment of the wall's lower courses, and this was built in one piece with a very badly destroyed stairway (26).

At this stairway the terrace wall (12) ends, and the stairway (26) itself bears further witness to support the assumption that Temple Ib is a separate phase in the constructional history of the first temple. For the stairway is secondary in relation to another stairway (25), close by and to the west.

Concerning the terrace walls of Temple Ib in the west and in the north we can only at the moment put forward hypothetical considerations. Negative evidence in areas actually investigated north and west of the walls of Temple Ia suggests that the missing walls of Ib should be sought at a greater distance from the Ia walls than was the case in the south and east. If remains exist, they can therefore be hidden under later masonry which was left *in situ*, in the west, for example, under the wall of Temple III.

As for the north wall of Temple Ib, its eastern portion may be covered by the wall of Temple II. In the matter of the western portion specific investigations were not made. There are, however, two indications which argue for a more extensive advance of the wall in this area. It can be seen that the east wall (12) continues its course northward, before it breaks off; it apparently is aiming towards a northeast corner at an unknown position. And moreover, there appears a badly destroyed but sporadically visible extension of the platform's floor-level north of the wall of Temple Ia at the west end of the platform (figs. 25, 49-50). This stratigraphically late extension would be inexplicable, unless it was aiming towards a termination at a terrace wall to the north, belonging to Temple Ib.

Assuming the correctness of this hypothesis – and it could easily be confirmed or refuted by excavation – we can describe the platform of Temple Ib as an askew quadrilateral surrounded by terrace walls. Measured along the central axes the platform has had a north-south extension of about 25 m and an eastwest extension of about 30 m. For comparison the corresponding measurements for Temple Ia were 16 and 24 m.

Like its predecessor this platform was built at a uniform base level, as regards its terrace walls. It lay at about level 2.80, or about three-quarters of a metre higher than in the time of Temple Ia. As the platform retained the former floor-level, there was in fact a reduction in height, but it is doubtful whether this was apparent. We have recorded above that the foundation of Temple Ia was covered in clay, whereas the plaster coating on the outer face of the later platform went all the way down to the lowest edge of the wall, cf. section 16:2. The platform's terrace walls, built of local stone, would as a consequence of this coating have stood out in a white or grey colour.

The problem of access to this platform – and here we really have a directly built-on stairway (26) partly preserved – will be dealt with separately in the section on the outer wallings.

The central platform's floor-level

On the top surface of the platform, at an average level of 1.50, a plaster layer had been applied to form a floor, on which remains were found of temple buildings (plan 2). As we are unable at that level to distinguish between the two phases of Temple I, the description must combine the two. The picture is certainly influenced both by continuity and by local shiftings of parts of the structure.

A closer examination of the plaster floor already shows that it is not formed as one homogeneous surface, but has been repeatedly renewed, cf. section 17, which will be described later (figs. 34-35). It consisted in fact in many places of several layers of plaster, separated by thin layers of sand. Dependent upon the circumstances of preservation it appeared as a stretch of larger or smaller portions, some belonging to the uppermost, some to the underlying layers.

The actual plaster material is described as white or grey-white granular plaster, perhaps containing clay. The layer was on average about 10 cm thick. It was, moreover, far from well-preserved; on the contrary, it showed many original breaks (2), often with layers of stone fragments. It was also naturally broken up along all the border areas, where the walls of Temple II had been sunk through it. There are, however, also break-throughs (3) which must be attributed to initial excavation activities in 1954-56.

The following description deals first with special phenomena found in or under the floor, next with the architecture of rooms and buildings, and finally with special features placed on the floor.

On the eastern side could be seen a little semicircular raised platform of plaster (4), directly built into the floor (fig. 36), while in the southwestern portion there occurred a number of small pits, sunk into the floor (fig. 37). The pits were filled with clay mixed with sand, and in several cases had bottom and sides lined with a layer of yellow clay. They were 10-15 cm deep and in section resembled a round-bottomed pot. Their purpose could not be further determined by reason of objects found or other circumstances.

Under the floor ran a number of drains. Thus in the northeast corner there was such a drain (5), which stood open for a short stretch. It was here 10 cm deep, with walls of plaster and a clay-lined bottom. It issued on the face of the Temple-I wall in the north (fig. 30). South of this drain another channel (6) issued in the eastern wall, coming from a round structure (24) close by (fig. 38). It formed a 20 cm deep channel with walls and bottom of plaster. Just here Temple II also had a drain. A third drainage channel (7) debouched similarly in the east. It came from another round structure (25) and resembled the one just described in appearance (fig. 35). A fourth drain (8) in the form of a hollow-cast plaster pipe was found in the middle of the platform (fig. 39). It probably issued in the middle of the temple's west wall (plan 1:35).

On the floor of the temple there were numerous remains of demolished buildings. A centrally placed chamber (9) commands most attention. It stood isolated in contrast to other rooms which were built onto each other. A special interior and the choice of prominent location suggest that it should be interpreted as a cella.

Despite damage caused by the cutting of the Main Section this chamber can be described as a room measuring $3 \times 2\frac{1}{2}$ m, askew four-sided like the platform, and oriented north-south (figs. 40-42). The walls were built of stone and lumps of plaster, mortared in plaster and with a 1-2 cm thick layer of plaster applied to both sides. The floor, too, was of plaster and was divided into sections by plaster baulks. A transverse baulk, 6-8 cm high, divided the chamber into two halves, the northern of which was again divided into three sections by slighter plaster baulks, one on each side and 2-3 cm high (fig. 43). The southern half was reserved for a square podium measuring 80×80 cm and built directly against the south wall. During the cutting of the Main Section this podium was broken up before it could be photographed, and thus is only registered in the form of survey drawings. It was partly demolished, but nevertheless rose to a height of 30 cm above the floor. It was built of the same materials as the chamber-walls, and its three outer faces were coated with plaster. It presumably served as a standing place for cult objects.

Access to this room must have been from the northern end, but the threshold was not identified in the excavation of the investigatory trench. The assumption of a door here is supported by the fact that there was found, under the floor by the eastern part of the north wall, a plaster block with a vertical depression cut in one end (fig. 43), and in the bottom of the depression could be seen remains of copper. It had probably functioned as a hinge-stone of the door.

The other buildings with rooms were concentrated along the north and south edges of the platform in the form of connected suites of rooms. Along the eastern edge no corresponding traces of buildings were found, while the western area was never exposed.

Along the south side ran from east to west a quite long wall (10) of large and smaller stones mortared together with plaster containing clay. In the centre it could, however, only be seen as an impression in the plaster floor of the wall's northern edge. A termination was missing in the east, but was present in the west, partly overlain by remains of Temple II (fig. 44). The wall was here quite broad and coated on the outer sides with a 1-1½ cm thick layer of fine grey-white plaster. At the same time it turned south, forming an east wall, the south end of which, however, is broken off. Unless other partition walls have been overlooked by the excavators there has thus stood here a room of more than 10 m in length, the south wall of which must have rested upon the demolished terrace wall.

West of this narrow room the remains of a wall (11) in the same building technique further divides up the southwest corner of the platform floor, resulting in two small rooms (fig. 45). Here the small pits, already described, were concentrated, while in a wall-corner there was found a tiny quarter-circular enclosure (12) with a plaster bottom, bounded by a low ridge, formed of small limestone flakes and pieces of plaster set in grey-white plaster (fig. 46).

Along the north side of the platform there was a suite of smaller rooms, the best preserved being a little chamber (13) built in the same technique as the cella (figs. 47-48). Its interior measurements were $3 \times 1\frac{1}{2}$ m, longest from east to west. It was built together with the wall (14) of an adjoining room, but a skin of white plaster allowed the two walls to be distinguished. The north wall, of large stones set in clay-mixed plaster, was placed directly upon the terrace wall of Temple Ia. The west wall was broken down, and it was here that the entrance to the chamber must have been found. The plaster floor in the chamber lay higher than that of the rest of the platform. The adjoining wall (14) is evidence for the presence of a further chamber here, but it was extensively demolished, so that only portions of the west and north walls could be recognized. The ma-

Fig. 34. Temple I, central platform, northeastern portion of floor level, from NW. Partly preserved plaster floor with remains of structures, bordered by: on left northern terrace wall Ia, above eastern terrace wall of Temple II, to right an unexcavated portion of Temple II's platform with floor-slabs *in situ*, and below Temple-II fill. In background can be seen blocks from Temple II's platform temporarily removed from their place (1958).

Fig. 35. Temple I, central platform, detail of plaster floor in several layers, near east wall, with drainage channel, from E. On the floor can be seen the east side of a stair-like pedestal (1958).

Fig. 36. Temple I, central platform, detail of plaster floor with formed circular platform, near east wall, from N (1958).

Fig. 37. Temple I, central platform, detail of plaster floor near SW-corner, with unexcavated pits, from N. In background remains of Temple III's southern terrace wall (1959).

Fig. 38. Temple I, central platform, detail of plaster floor on east side, with cast-in drainage channel, from E. At bottom Temple II's east wall with cutting for a similarly placed drain outlet (1958).

Fig. 39. Temple I, central platform, detail of plaster floor in middle of temple, with cross-section of underlying drain, cast in plaster, from E. To left can be seen remains of a chamber-wall on the floor, in background exposed parts of a foundation-wall buried in Temple II's platform (1958).

Fig. 40. Temple I, central platform, plaster floor in centre of temple with chamber, so-called cella, from N. Partly damaged by trial trench for Main Section. In foreground remains of buildings along northern terrace wall, in background temple II's platform with pierced cult-stones *in situ* (1958).

Fig. 41. Temple I, central platform, plaster floor in centre of temple with chamber, so-called cella, from E. In background remains of Temple-II masonry – a wall-fragment, standing upon an exposed foundation-wall buried in the platform (1958).

Fig. 42. Temple I, central platform, plaster floor in centre of temple with chamber, so-called cella, from NW. The area is edged by parts of Temple II's platform, including part with floor-slabs in situ (1958).

Fig. 43. Temple I, central platform, detail of NE-corner of cella, from W. Division of room with plaster baulks. Under the plaster floor and against the north wall can be seen a plaster block with a cut depression – perhaps a hinge-stone? (1958)

Fig. 44. Temple I, central platform, plaster floor along southern side with course of wall belonging to buildings, from W. It is overlain by fragment of exposed foundation-wall buried in Temple II's platform. In background can be glimpsed the upper edge of the broken-down east wall in Temple II, and to its right, in the trench, the upper edge of the southern terrace wall Ib (1959).

Fig. 45. Temple I, central platform, plaster floor in SW-corner with remains of wall, from NE (1959).

Fig. 46. Temple I, central platform, detail of plaster floor in SW-corner, from SW. An inner corner of a chamber can be seen, with a little quarter-circular wall, overlain by the exposed foundation-wall from Temple II, buried in the platform. In background appears the rear side of Temple II's eastern terrace wall (1959).

Fig. 47. Temple I, central platform, eastern half of northern edge-portion with remains of chambers, from SW. The chambers are built onto the terrace wall Ia. To the left, the foundation-wall dug down from the Temple-II platform, and behind that in a parallel course the upper edge of Temple II's northern terrace wall. In background Temple II's east wall, rear side, preserved to the uppermost edge of the wall (1958).

Fig. 48. Temple I, central platform, detail of north-western inner corner of chamber on north side, from E (1958).

sonry was in the same technique as that of the previous chamber.

To the west the succession of rooms continues with a little chamber (15) (fig. 34). It was almost square, with inner measurements of 2 × 2½ m. The building technique was the same, but only remnants of the vertical portions survived. The east wall was common with the above-mentioned chamber (13), the north wall was demolished, but existed as an impression, the west wall showed the remains of a footing, and the south wall similarly. Here too the floor lay higher than the platform outside.

Thereafter followed as the neighbouring rooms to the west, first a little chamber (16) and then a long but poorly preserved room (17). The limits of the rooms were also obscured by the overlying masonry of Temple II. Large and smaller stones in clay-mixed plaster formed a stump of a partition wall between the two chambers. The north wall lay on the terrace wall of Temple Ia. A 10 cm thick layer of white granular plaster formed the floor in the little room, but flaked off in several layers from repeated renewals. A 5 cm thick layer of grey-white plaster formed the floor in the long room.

As Temple Ib is assumed to have been characterized by an extension towards the north, it would be natural to expect remains of floors and building-complexes north of the terrace wall of Temple Ia. Un-

fortunately this area had been badly damaged by the establishment of deep-going masonry belonging to Temple II, and therefore only sporadic remains can be adduced. A weak reflection of the assumed extension should perhaps be seen in the north-east, where the plaster floor clearly has a tendency to overlie the old terrace wall (fig. 30). We have in addition, in the Main Section, demolition layers from walling lying at the appropriate level about 1.50 m north of the old terrace wall, cf. layers 57 and 58.

The most conspicuous evidence of this situation must, however, be sought at the western end of the old terrace wall, where the disturbances from Temple II no longer intruded. Just here, north of the wall at the platform's floor-level, were found the remains of a chamber (18) (figs. 49-50). This placing would make it a late construction in the history of Temple I. The northern portion was missing. It has only been a little over 1 m in width, and possessed a 5 cm thick floor of grey-white plaster. Its walls were built like those of the previous chambers (16 and 17).

Another wall-fragment (19) of stone in plaster, lies 4 m north of the earliest terrace wall, out from its centre (fig. 51). Its position allows it to be interpreted as a modest foundation-fragment in the complex here described.

On the eastern part of the platform, which so far as we can see was devoid of buildings, there were

Fig. 49. Temple I, central platform Ib, detail from NW-corner with masonry – plaster floor and wall – built out from wall Ia, from NW (1959).

Fig. 50. Temple I, central platform Ib, detail from NW-corner with masonry built out from wall Ia, from NE, cf. fig. 49. Here can be seen the stratigraphical situation out from the crown of the oldest terrace wall. In background Temples II and III's western terrace-walls (1959).

Fig. 51. Temple I, central platform Ib, detail of semicircular wall-foundation north of terrace-wall Ia, from N (1957).

found a number of features which, on account of their distinctive character, must be ascribed functions in connection with the cult here represented. They comprise the following:

In the south-east there stood *in situ* on the floor two shaped limestone blocks. The first (20) was well-preserved, about 20 cm high, about 35 cm broad and about 1.35 m long. A break at its west end could be seen to have been carefully repaired with a little, finely fitted limestone slab, applied with grey-white plaster (fig. 52). Its positioning is shown in section 2A (B) described in chapter 2. The other block (21) was more damaged (fig. 53). Its curved upper surface showed a remarkable form of shaping, with a groove along its greater length and parallel bevelling along the edges.

Northeast of these two stones there was a staircase-like structure (22), built of stone slabs held together by clay-mixed plaster and with a core of clay (figs. 54, 34-35). The height of the treads was about 20 cm. As it is difficult to imagine any actual stairway function in connection with the structure it should perhaps be understood as a podium divided into three steps at the east wall of the platform.

A special structure (23), badly preserved, is interesting in that it is a forerunner for a similar structure in Temple II. It has moreover been placed at the same point and is thus overlain by its successor (fig.

55). What is preserved can be described as the foundation of a circular construction, consisting of large, roughly shaped stones, the upper surfaces and edges of which were covered with patches of white plaster (figs. 56-58). To fit the round construction the stones are all cut with curved edges, apart from one rectangular block of stone which protrudes somewhat from the northern curve of the structure. As the surrounding area had been broken up, it is impossible to know whether this structure has had a double form like that of the later structure in Temple II. It must be the foundation for an altar.

The foundations of two other round structures (24 and 25) were found north-east of the construction just described (figs. 59-60). They were very much alike, and formed as rings of stones mortared with plaster. One of them (24) was coated on the outside with clay-mixed plaster, while the other lacked this plastering. The latter (25) has been more thoroughly demolished than the former, which was perhaps its successor. The position of this feature (24) in the stratigraphy will be made clear in the description below of section 5. The base of the features was not marked.

Between the two features – under the floor-level and partly covered by the plaster of the floor – protruded a white block of stone or plaster. There were drains from both stone circles, and the drain associ-

Fig. 52. Temple I, central platform, plaster floor in southeast portion with shaped limestone blocks *in situ*, from SW. In background can be seen the stair-shaped pedestal and the rear side of Temple II's east wall, here preserved to the original wall-top (1959).

Fig. 53. Temple I, central platform, detail of plaster floor in southeast portion with shaped block, from S (1959).

Fig. 54. Temple I, central platform, detail of plaster floor in southeastern portion with stair-shaped pedestal, from S, cf. figs. 35 and 52. In background Temple II's east wall (1958).

Fig. 55. Temple I, central platform, detail of circular altar-foundation on plaster floor in eastern half of temple, overlain by corresponding Temple-II construction, left standing on pillars of earth, from NW, cf. figs. 56-58 (1958).

Fig. 56. Temple I, central platform, plaster floor with circular altar-foundation exposed, from S. In background remains of chambers along northern edge, and behind them a foundation-wall and a terrace wall from Temple II (1958).

Fig. 57. Temple I, central platform, circular altar-foundation on plaster floor, from SW. Behind it a round stone-setting of smaller stones (1958).

Fig. 58. Temple I, central platform, circular altar-foundation, from NE (1958).

Fig. 59. Temple I, central platform, plaster floor and fragment-layer in northeast section with round stone-settings and channels formed in plaster, from E (1958).

59

Fig. 60. Temple I, central platform, plaster floor and fragment-layer in northeast section with round stone-setting and channels formed in plaster, from NE (1958).

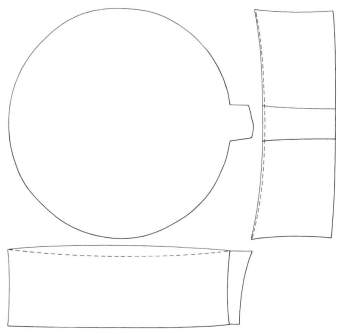

Fig. 61. Temple I or II. Circular altar-block. 1:20.

ated with one of them (24) was particularly elaborately fashioned. It consisted of channels shaped in white plaster in three separate sections, which together enclosed the stone ring in a V-shaped pattern. The western end, however, of the course of the drain was broken up (fig. 60).

If these stone rings have served as the foundations for circular altar-stones, it should be mentioned that one of these stones has in fact been found, though not in its original position. This altar-block (26) was of a particularly magnificent form (figs. 61-64). Its position in the excavation unfortu-

Fig. 62. Temple I or II. Circular altar-block *in situ* between the two platforms, from N. Behind are floor-slabs on the Temple-II platform (1958).

Fig. 63. Temple I or II. Circular altar-block, from S. Behind can be seen the foundation-wall from Temple II, with remains of wall built upon it (1958).

Fig. 64. Temple I or II. Circular altar-block, from E, from above (1958).

nately does not preclude the possibility that precisely this altar-block could have been dug down from Temple II as a deposited cult-object. Its exceptionally fine shaping, in fact, lends support to this view. For its position in the excavation we refer to section 5, which is treated below. Despite this doubt we choose to describe this object here.

The stone was cut to a particularly elegant shape, circular with smoothly polished sides, a finely grooved, slightly concave upper surface and a slightly convex lower surface. A projecting vertical tenon curved inward on its downward path. The stone's diameter was 122 cm, and its height was 43 cm.

On the basis of the evidence here presented we can give a general description of the upper surface of Temple I's platform as a raised four-sided court with a plaster floor at a relatively uniform level. Under the floor were traces of a branching drainage system. In the centre of the court were the outlines of a little building which is interpreted as a cella, while along the north and south sides were suites of rooms of varying sizes. On the probably open courtyard area to the east were found remains of small features, altar-sites and other structures of cult character.

This architectural assemblage, together with the terraced form, shows that we are dealing with a temple. Its chronological and cultural historical aspects will, however, be first considered subsequently.

The central platform's inner structure

The Main Section has already shown how the interior of the platform was filled up with a clay core as a bottom layer, and above that with layers of sand. The top was covered with a plaster floor.

This typical picture of a solid platform is shown also by *section 5*, which was drawn in 1955 in a trial trench about in the middle of the platform. This section, running from east to west, showed the subsoil (21) at about level 3.30, the clay core (17) and, above it, several layers of fill. Remains of the floor of Temple I (7) were preserved, and two of the features discovered and described above appear as partly excavated, namely a stone circle (8 = plan 2:24) and a circular altar-stone (4 = plan 2:26). The layers above the plaster floor comprised fill for the platform of Temple II, two flooring flags (1 and 2) showing the level of this floor. The overlying part of the tell, up to its original surface, had been dug away, before the section was drawn.

There was an anomalous feature in this stratigraphy, a layer of sand (20) interposed between the subsoil and the clay core. It can be added here that, when the inner northeast corner of the platform was excavated, a layer was found similarly interposed between subsoil and clay core. It was up to 15 cm thick and extended over several metres. In colour it was brownish black, in consistency powdery, without charcoal but containing particles of lime.

In the southeastern and southwestern corners of the interior of the platform masonry also occurred (plan 1). In the case of the southeast corner attention should be called to deeply lying stones, cf. section 2A (C) described above and an excavation photograph (fig. 20). The details of this discovery remained undescribed and undrawn, but another arrangement of stones (plan 1:13) was described, though without its significance being determined (fig. 65). *Section 17*(13) shows that it was deeply embedded in the clay core (8-10). The subsoil appears at level 3.55 (12), and the section continues upward to terminate with Temple I's plaster floor (3-6). To the left can be seen Temple II's east wall (1). In this section, too, brown sand (11) appears at the bottom as a layer separating the subsoil from the clay core.

A much more substantial impression, however, is given by the masonry in the platform's southwest corner (fig. 66), where we must assume the presence of an inner room (plan 1). Unfortunately this room could only be partially excavated, as later walling was allowed to remain undisturbed. At some point the room has been filled in, as there existed, as has already been described, on top of the platform in the south-west, both masonry and floor belonging to Temple I.

The room is delimited to the south and west by the earliest terrace wall, and it is divided into two by the foundation for a partition wall (14) with an opening (15), forming thereby a western foreroom and an eastern back-room (16) (fig. 67). The partition wall is contemporary with the terrace wall, based on the subsoil in the same building-technique. It must have been secondarily demolished.

West of the partition wall there had been placed three foundations (17-19), of stone set in clay, each with its own base-level (fig. 68). They are presumably later foundations, dug down into the room. The centre one overlies the partition wall, while the southern one may have been partly removed in the course of building the Temple-II wall.

The north wall (20) of the foreroom was remarkable in being built of roughly squared limestone blocks. Uppermost in the wall's western end there had moreover been inserted a portion of walling composed of smaller stones, which to the west broke

off in a vertical line. This break must be seen in connection with the construction of Temple II's west wall, though this had here been removed by stone-robbers. It was impossible to determine whether the north wall of the room was original.

The back-room also had a north wall (21), in continuation of the wall just described. Only the inner wall-surface was exposed, and this, like the earliest terrace wall, consisted of a foundation of large stones and an upper structure of large and smaller stones, all mortared with clay. This wall (21) is in the east bonded with a corresponding portion of walling (22), which forms an east wall of the back-room. It was mistakenly not surveyed in, and its approximate position is given by a broken line. It is considered that a final, badly broken down piece of walling (23) forms a continuation of the east wall of the back-room.

The terrace wall of Temple Ia had openings at two points, formed in such a way that one may assume entrances to the room at these points (3 and 7) (fig. 66). At the western entrance could moreover be seen flanking foundation stones from a westerly directed approach, which will be described in more detail in the following section. Functionally this room could then provide an entrance route from the southwestern foreland of the temple to the platform. No traces of a staircase was, however, visible in the room, nor could any well-defined floor-level be recognized.

In the course of final investigations (1961) in the west side of the platform some observations were made, north of the abovementioned foreroom in a re-examination of an earlier trial trench, of some special features. Their investigation, however, was quite limited.

Here there was found a stone receptacle (24) *in situ* in the clay core, standing in a little room cut out of the clay and filled with loose clay (figs. 69-71). The receptacle, which had a stone slab as lid, was empty.

In addition, a four-sided stone-setting was uncovered in the clay core. It lay about 1 m east of the terrace wall (4) and in connection with the north wall (20) of the foreroom. The stone-setting measured about 80 × 110 cm and consisted of two courses.

In the eastern side of this excavation there appeared the cross-section of a truncated conical-shaped clay projection, which rose from the surface of the clay core and reached up to the plaster floor of Temple I's platform (fig. 72). It consisted of solid clay and was at the bottom a half metre in diameter. The presence of another similar projection was noted. They were perhaps floor-height indicators connected with the building of the earliest temple.

We can thus describe the platform summarily as a large soil-filled terrace, though with a built-in

Fig. 65. Temple I, central platform's clay core, dug to virgin soil, stone-setting in southeast portion, from NE. The stones at upper right are an archaeological clearance-heap (1960).

Fig. 66. Temple I, central platform, SW-corner, dug to virgin soil, with walling at several levels, from W. Foreground: western terrace wall Ia with opening to inner room in platform. The north wall of the room is built up of ashlars for the first portion, the rest – here hidden – and the east wall are built of smaller stones. The east wall is only partly exposed. Across the room can be seen a demolished partition-wall with an opening, and, in front of the partition-wall two foundations at a higher level. Above the east wall there is masonry from Temple Ib, overlain by a foundation-wall from Temple II. Top left are parts of Temple-II buildings (1960).

Fig. 67. Temple I, central platform, SW-corner, dug to virgin soil, from N. Inner room in the platform, bordered top and to right by terrace wall Ia, with opening in southern wall. A partition-wall with an opening divides the room into two, in one of which are placed two foundations at a higher level (1960).

Fig. 68. Temple I, central platform, SW-corner, from S. Inner room in the platform, overlain by Temple-II buildings. The north wall in the room consists of one section of ashlars and one of smaller stones. The northeastern inner corner can be seen. In the centre are foundations at a higher level and a demolished partition-wall below (1960).

Fig. 69. Temple I, central platform, detail of clay-core in western portion with stone container, from N (1961).

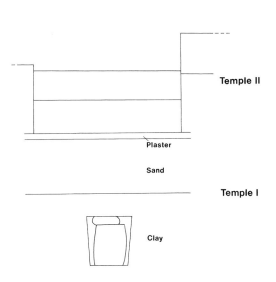

Fig. 70. Sketch of stone container's stratigraphic placing, cf. fig. 69.

Fig. 71. Stone container (517.ARJ) 1:5.

room in the southwest which may have provided access to the platform of Temple Ia. A special feature with the building of the platform is a bottom layer of clay, which, however, also extended outside the platform – a distinct preliminary building activity. As this base layer of clay does not appear to

have served any practical purpose, it is assumed to have been part of some project of ritual character, a ceremonial feature in the foundation of the temple. This view is supported by the fact that it contained large numbers of votive offerings.

Fig. 72. Temple I, central platform in western portion, from W. Clay projection in the form of a truncated cone, issuing from the clay core. Overlain by plaster floor in Temple I. Above that is fill in Temple II's platform, and then masonry upon that. On right can be seen the rear side of the ashlar-built wall of the inner room in the platform's SW-corner, cf. fig. 68 (1961).

Outer masonry around the central platform

Masonry belonging to Temple I in the area around the central platform was relatively poorly preserved (plan 1). This situation is explained by the fact that Temple II is in a high degree a direct continuation of Temple I, though in a completely new form. The new building-works consequent on this are of such a format that they either destroy Temple I or – insofar as the architecture of Temple II was left untouched – involve an overlay which covers the remains of Temple I. To a certain degree, also, the description of the outer masonry must be coordinated for both phases of Temple I, as we cannot differentiate with sufficient certainty between Temples Ia and Ib.

For an understanding of the observed remains of Temple I in the surrounding terrain we are moreover forced in a high degree to draw analogous conclusions from related phenomena in Temple II. The main features in Temple II comprise, as already described, a central four-sided platform standing on a lower oval platform. To the west comes a deeply sunk pool connected to the central platform by a stairway. To the south-west lies a temple-well, and to the east an oval walled court, connected to the central platform by a ramp.

There seems to be evidence that all these main features are also true of Temple I, though the evidence is often more indirect than direct. The south-west sector appears here to be of conclusive importance; it showed very intricate structural complications, the solution of which is more a matter of logical argumentation than of comprehension at the time of excavation.

The northern environs of the temple were comparatively little investigated and only by means of trial trenches. The stratigraphical information given by the Main Section and by section 30 has been presented already. They give the impression that construction in the north has been of limited intensity.

It appears from *section 30* (B) that there was at the 51 m point on the subsoil an east-west-running terrace wall of smallish stones set in clay and edging a step cut in the subsoil. The terracing held back layers of clay lying behind it, but it is only known from this one observation. The overall plans show its placing in relation to the central portions of the temple (figs. 3 & 14). In analogy with the corresponding later masonry in the northern environs belonging to Temple II, it is reasonable to interpret this wall section as the remains of an earliest oval terrace in the north. Its distance from the central platform of Temple Ia is about 20 m. The height of the wall has been 1 m, and the oval platform's surface has lain between levels 2.50 and 3.00. This situation has parallels in the south, as will later be shown.

In the Main Section (B) can be seen at the 55 m point a similar deeply lying piece of walling consisting of one course of stones set in clay, cf. the plan attached. So far as it was exposed it formed a crescent-shaped demarcation, accompanied on both sides by burnt layers. It lay about 25 m north of Temple Ia's central platform. Precisely at the point where we should expect a continuation of the northern wall of the oval terrace of Temple I the Main Section has by chance not been carried down to the subsoil.

A third trial trench in the north, east of the Main Section, was only in places dug to full depth, and therefore helps little. Here *section 31* was measured in, and it shows, on the subsoil at the 61.5 m point, a portion of walling (A) of clay-set stone running from east to west. In the opposite side of the trench a burnt layer, 5 cm thick, ran out from the upper edge of the wall. With this little irregular wall-fragment ends our knowledge of the temple's northern foreland. It was not possible to dig further in a northerly direction.

Finally it should be mentioned that there was no trace, along the exposed facing of Temple Ia's northern terrace wall, of any stairway architecture, though on the other hand an intensive layering rich in finds.

The temple's eastern foreland was likewise not intensively examined, apart from the large area-investigation of the court which belongs to Temple II. Trial trenches in the east produced the walls of earth where sections 12 and 13 were drawn in, and they comprise our main evidence for the use of this terrain. The basic interpretation has been given in chapter 2 – an area dedicated to the large scale cooking over fire of the sacrificed animals resulting in distinctive powdery, often dark layers of earth.

Evidence of building to the east is particularly involved with underground channelling, insofar as a drain in section 12 (I) suggests through its location on the subsoil a possible connection with Temple I. It was a hollow pipe constructed of stones in yellow-grey plaster, and it may have functioned in connection with gutter-like drains in the plaster floor on the east side of Temple I's platform. Another early drain ran in under the ramp in this area.

It was this ramp which connected the platform with the Eastern Court and it had clearly several building-phases, the lowest of which could with reasonable certainty be attributed to Temple I. The more detailed documentation will in this case be given separately, cf. chapter 7. For the remains from the period of Temple I form only a minimal part of the documented evidence concerning the eastern installation, though sufficient to support the assumption of the existence of predecessors to the ramp and court of Temple II.

The southern foreland was first and foremost dominated by the mighty terrace walls of Temple II, which here in two phases delimit the oval platform of the temple, cf. the Main Section (N and P). As these deeply sunk walls, with footing levels at under 5.00 and 6.00 respectively, have necessitated large-scale preparation of the site before they were built, they can have had a destructive effect on the earlier strata. There have in fact only been traced very few remains of earlier masonry, and these are concentrated in the southwest sector, where old and new are mixed with each other. Two excavation photographs give some idea of the consequent complications during excavation (figs. 73-74).

In order to keep one's bearings on the plan this sector has been drawn together with parts of Temple II (plan 1). In the north the sector is thus delimited by a row of three large stone slabs, which form the wall-face of the stairway down to the pool. The sector is cut across diagonally by the oval terrace wall, and this has on its outer face a sideways-built stairway.

This stairway leads down to the temple-well. As has been said, we are here describing a Temple-II situation. In a later period the well-construction was changed, when a later advanced oval wall extended the oval platform, and the well was encapsulated within this platform. A shaft was led down through the enlarged platform, to ensure continued use of the well. The two stages are marked by a four-sided well-head at the foot of the stairway on the older oval wall, and by a circular well-shaft as a later addition. An even later reconstruction allowed the well to be also incorporated into Temple III.

These later building-works, here described out of their proper order, demonstrate the extraordinary continuity which characterizes the well. To this can now be added that special features in the excavation allow us to carry the tradition back to the time of Temple I. The well thereby stands out as the only feature in the temple, apart from the central platform, which can be documented for all three temples. The constructional history of the well thereby supports in an important special field the general interpretation. This support extends all the way to the subdivision of the temple-phases into a and b. In the case of Temple I it consists of the following circumstances as excavated:

Two stairways (25 and 26) lead straight down to the area of the well, and alone the fact of their placing behind the oval terrace wall of Temple II is enough to show their connection with Temple I.

Fig. 73. Temple I, outer southwest sector, partly dug to virgin soil, from SE. Stairway to right of Temple II's terrace wall for the oval platform, phase IIa. The earth-face in background is section 22, and in front of it can be seen remains of Temple II's pool stairway with the remains of the portal – the upright stone pillar (1957).

Fig. 74. Temple I, outer southwest sector, from NW. Stairway-structures to left of Temple IIa's oval wall on the outer side of which a side-stairway has been built. This stairway leads to the temple-well, here seen in late phases belonging to Temples IIb and III. The earth-face in the middle distance is section 26A, with stratified layers from the plundering of Temple II's terrace wall in the SW-corner of the central platform. On the surface can be seen remains of Temple III's southern terrace wall, built together with the contemporary well-phase above earlier phases (1957).

The construction of this wall, in fact, amputates the lower portion of the stairways. The situation can be checked stratigraphically by means of sections 26A, 27C and 29, and it is with their help that the stratigraphy of the southwest sector will be described, before we proceed to look at the stairways as parts of Temple I's architecture.

Access to the underground water-table, which was a precondition for the well, could either be achieved by digging down to it or by it appearing naturally as a spring in a dip in the ground. We have taken the latter as being the situation, though the large excavations in connection with the building of Temple II's oval platform have obstructed any direct observation of the original ground surface in the relevant section.

Section 26A cuts through the layers from the southwest corner of Temple I's platform as far as the Temple-II/III well (fig. 74). The course of the main layers in an undrawn portion around the 10-m point is indicated for the sake of clarity. It is done on the basis of excavation photographs and of section 26A1, which stood at a right-angle to the section (26A) at point 10.85. In addition the stairway (B = plan 1:26) is projected in. It gives an indication of the stratigraphic position of the eight surviving steps.

In section 26A the subsoil (7) is visible at its normal depth of about level 3.50. It has been dug away for the building of Temple II's oval wall (D), and this digging (12) has removed any indication of the natural location of the original ground surface.

Above the subsoil the clay bottom layer (5-6), here very thick, can be seen. Here stands the foundation (A) to Temple Ib's terrace wall around the central platform. The corresponding Ia-wall does not appear on account of the placing of the section, which lies outside its southwest corner. The clay (5) is overlain by stratified layers of clay (3 and 11), which are the upper fill in the two platforms, the central platform north of the wall (A), and the oval platform south of it. In the one of these layers (3) there is admittedly missing the one side of the excavation which has demolished the wall (A) down to the foundation. All the layers so far mentioned are broken off by the large excavation (12) in which the later oval-wall (D) of Temple II has been placed.

As we see in the section layers of fill for an oval platform from the period of Temple I, the question of its terrace wall obtrudes. It cannot, however, appear, either because it had been situated in the large excavation (12) or because its remains lie hidden under the layers south of the later oval wall (D), cf. remains of walls on plan 1 (31 and 32), which have a connection with this problem.

For the remaining layers in section 26A the situation is as follows: A large secondary robber-layer (1) represents the breaking-up of temple II's terrace

wall in the southwest corner of the central platform. Of the wall itself only the plaster (2) at its bottom remains. The plaster floor (9) on the contemporary oval platform ended, as it should, with the terrace wall (D). Above the floor come deposits (8) which can best be understood as fill for the Temple-III platform; the bottom of its terrace wall (C) can be observed directly in the south, and it widens out into a large pendent mass – part of the well-construction of this phase.

The stairway (B) was secondarily demolished both at top and bottom. From the third step from the top inclusive, remains of masonry survived on the sides of the steps, but the two outer sides of the stair were not built up as walls. Even though it is only projected in on the section, the situation must be read as representing that the stairway led up to Temple I's central platform and down through the oval platform to the subsoil. It has never been a free-standing stairway, but rather a staircase in a shaft, which as in a cellar led down through the oval platform, and even down into the subsoil. This explains the masonry on the sides of the steps as a lining of the shaft. The stairway belongs to Temple Ib and is bonded into its terrace wall.

Section 27C repeats many of the conditions here described, but demonstrates an earlier situation, where another stairway (D = plan 1:25) is found, here directly in the section. It is situated between the south side of the stairway to the pool, of the walls of which the two surviving slabs (B and F) suggest several phases, and the oval wall (C) of Temple IIa.

The subsoil contour is disturbed, since the stairway (D) has been dug down into it, but undisturbed subsoil forms the main part of the block of earth (8) on which the stairway rests. From section 27D, at a right-angle at point 17.5 m, we know that it lay at about level 3.50. Here the clay base level (4) is also visible. These strata can also be seen in section 24 cutting across the stairway to the pool, cf. below.

As section 27C cuts across the stairway, it demonstrates the abandonment of the stair-construction by a filling-up, since here also it was clearly the case of a shaft-staircase. The stairway is preserved from its uppermost step at level 2.90 until it breaks off at the foot. The rear edge of the uppermost step connects with a row of slabs standing on edge (F) and resting on the foundation-stone (E). In other words, the stairway leads down from an old passage of a type which was succeeded in the time of Temple II by a new one (B), about 1 m higher, now in the form of an imposing stairway.

The shaft for the stairway (D) is filled up with sand (7). The stratification is otherwise strongly influenced by the massive reconstructions occasioned by Temple II. This temple is also present with its oval platform, of which there can be seen remains of a plaster surface (10), the terrace wall (C) and the already mentioned surviving slab (B) of the stairway leading down to the pool. The excavation for the terrace wall has been filled up by various layers (11-17). The upper edge of the section has been formed by the preliminary archaeological excavation.

On the terrace wall (C) can be seen the two uppermost steps of the stairway down to the well, built sideways onto the wall. But everything is out of proportion because of the angle at which the section is cut, both the excavation, the wall and the wall-stairway. In against the outer face of the wall, with its characteristic bevel at level 3.00, are deposited the layers (18-21) which filled up the interspace between the wall and its later successor further to the south. Above these, as in section 26A, follow the deposits (9) which form the platform of Temple III, the bottom of whose western terrace wall (A) is visible.

The western foreland is documented in *section 29*. We are here at the other side of the pool, and the upper part of the section is only of interest in relation to the later phases of the temple. But the deeper strata bear witness to the original situation, and therefore assist in an understanding of Temple I. We find here an "original surface" at a level under 5.00, and, above that, a probably equally naturally originating layer of plastic clay (24) containing very small crustacea. Above that again come the earliest deposited layers (22 and 23) of clay, together with the remains of an earliest wall (19) and occupation layers (20 and 21). In the neighbourhood of the pool – to the east – can be seen an excavation (25).

This stratification, with its deep subsoil-level, provides the main evidence for a natural depression in the original terrain, and the lowest layers (24 and 26) appear to have been laid down in water. Here appears, then, the presumed spring in the south-west, and it is associated with an excavation which demonstrates that already in the time of Temple I the inhabitants have regulated, or at least have shown a reaction to, the source of the spring.

In all probability the excavation (25) means that we have here an indication of a pool which is older than the clearly recognized pool of Temple II, which naturally stands in the way of further investigation. In the excavation was found a fragment of one of the pottery beakers so characteristic of the "clay core" (see below, p. 212).

While the sections hitherto described have shown virgin soil in the form of a natural rise of ground, section 29 is the first to show virgin soil in a depression with water-laid strata. On the rise of ground the central platform was constructed at a level of about 3.50. The depression, with a level under 5.00, was used for the construction of a pool and a well. These features were either constructed directly in the water, or else the water-table was easily reached. In our day the water-table manifests itself at level 5.50, or about 2.85 m above sea-level.

With this knowledge of the stratigraphy of the southwestern sector we can now turn to the survey plan (plan 1), and first to the two stairways (25 and 26), which lie at different levels (fig. 71). The one is built at a right-angle to the remains of a feature (27), a row of slabs which should presumably be ascribed to Temple Ia, while the other is built into the southwest corner of the platform of Temple Ib, with the south wall (12) of which it is directly bonded.

The deeper lying stair (25) is about three-quarters of a metre broad (figs. 75-76). The northwest side has suffered damage on account of later constructions in this area. Otherwise the stair is preserved up to its uppermost step, but not down to its lowest. Here, though, our excavation ended at a chance level, so that we lack direct observation of its continuation. Attention can, however, be drawn to the presence of some irregular stonework (28) at the foot of the later terrace wall on the outer side. Assuming a regular succession of steps the stairway would at this point have reached the water-level. The stairway is built of stone set in plaster and clay.

The sides of the stairway are flanked by masonry rising from the steps, but these are not supported by lower walls. The flanking walls must therefore be regarded as the remains of the walls of a stair-shaft. Section 27C shows the local surface (4) of the clay core, which almost coincides with the uppermost step of the stair. The stair-shaft thus cuts down through the clay core and the subsoil, and therefore through the assumed oval platform.

The function of the stairway is obvious; it leads down to water-level, and thus presumably to a primary well-head, cf. the situation in the time of Temple II with terrace wall, adjoining stairway and well.

The hypothetical Temple-I well was perhaps situated in the neighbourhood of the above-mentioned stonework (28), but the problem was not posed and a solution sought during the excavation. It can have been constructed either within or outside the oval-terrace wall of the period of Temple I. In the first case the stairway has ended in a terminal well-chamber, and has thereby been a parallel to the well-chamber at Umm as-Sujur (cf. Appendix 5); in the other case we must assume an alcove in the oval platform.

As has been said, the uppermost step of the stairway connects with an earlier feature, which is a predecessor to the stairway leading to the pool of Temple II (fig. 77). Little is known of this feature (27), which reveals itself mainly through three slabs of cut stone in a row, together with a fourth which had fallen. They have edged a passage-way almost without slope. The row of slabs is clearly a forerunner to a corresponding feature of Temple II, which, though, is built of much more massive slabs. This later feature can be reconstructed as a stairway, the

Fig. 75. Temple I, outer southwest sector, stairway from Temple Ia, from SE (1957).

Fig. 76. Temple I, outer southwest sector, stairway from Temple Ia, from S (1957).

Fig. 77. Temple I, outer southwest sector. In lower right corner, stairway from Temple Ia, from W. Seen in relation to Temple II's pool stairway with a single step *in situ* (1957).

Fig. 78. Temple I. Stratification in section 24 at east end of Temple II's pool stairway, from E. The upper layer is edged by side-stones of that stairway (1960).

Fig. 79. Temple I, outer southwest sector, stairway from Temple Ib, from SE. Broken off at the top by later building. In bottom right corner appears a remnant of terrace wall Ib, built together with the stairway (1957).

sides of which were flanked with the massive slabs. And this stairway connected the pool with the central platform. The earlier feature gives the impression rather of a passage-way, perhaps in the form of a gradual ramp, than of a stairway. Its function must have been to connect the central Temple-I platform with an unknown feature to the west. This unknown feature was presumably a pool, a forerunner for the known pool of Temple II, cf. also the comments on the excavation (25) in section 29.

Section 24 now cuts this passage-way 1½ m in front of the western terrace wall of Temple Ia (fig. 78), and contains the following stratigraphical information: The subsoil (6) appears at a normal level of 3.50. Above this come layers of clay (4 and 5) and an earliest building level, a plaster layer (3) flanked by stones (E and F), which must be interpreted as foundation stones for a bordering of slabs as on plan 1 (27). The stratigraphy ends with later layers of fill (1 and 2), which form the inner structure for Temple II's pool stairway, which has here been demolished. The borders of this stairway are revealed in the lowest course of sheathing-stone (C and D), thick oblong slabs at the sides of the stair. These are in turn flanked by large cut blocks of stone (A and B).

We conclude from this section that the stones (29) on plan 1 close to the west wall (4 and 5) of Temple Ia are connected with the remains of the passage-way (27), to which the stairway (25) has been attached. These stones have been placed so as to flank an opening (7) in the west wall. The passage-way would thus lead from this opening inward to the inner room in the southwest corner of the platform, and westward out to a pool of which we know nothing. On the way there has been attached a stairway which leads by way of a shaft down to a well.

These features can best be understood as belonging to Temple Ia. How the combined relationship functioned in Temple Ib is completely obscure. We cannot even establish with certainty the western terrace wall of Temple Ib's central platform.

Only at one point can an adaption to a new situation be clearly recognized, namely in a new version of the shaft-stairway. And this new stairway (26) is demonstrably associated with Temple Ib (fig. 79). It runs in a different direction from that of its predecessor (25) and is also placed at a completely different level. It is only preserved as a ruin of its middle portion. Its northern end was demolished in the building of Temple II's terrace wall around the central platform, and the southern end in the building of the same temple's wall around the oval platform. The archaeological excavation stopped at a chance level at the lower end of the stair. The stair-

Fig. 80. Temple I, outer
southwest sector, remains
of wall, possibly remains
of terrace wall for temple
I's oval platform, from
above, N upwards.
Deeply founded at foot
of oval-terrace wall IIa, at
top of picture. Foot of
temple-well, to left. Of
the latter the upper edge
of the Temple-III well is
seen, cf. fig. 130 (1958).

Fig. 81. Temple I, outer
northwest sector, deeply-
founded walling with
floor at ground-water
level, from S (1961).

Fig. 82. Temples I and II, outer western sector, north of pool, from N. Older walling at top of picture and base-stone, overlain by Temple II's terrace walls for the oval platform, IIa on left, and IIb on right (1957).

Fig. 83. Temple I, outer western sector, base-stone exposed, from N, cf. fig. 82 (1960).

way has been about 1.25 m broad and was built of stone and plaster.

From section 26A we can obtain an idea of the relationship of the stairway to the surrounding architecture. We reconstruct the Temple-Ib wall to a given height of 1.50 m, calculated on the basis of the plaster floor on the central platform at level 1.50. The stairway must be assumed to have led up to this floor, incorporated into the southwest corner of the platform. The surviving portion of the stair leads down through a contemporary oval platform and ends "blind", but must have continued down approximately to water-level. It has been a shaft-staircase, and some irregular stonework (30) at the foot of the later Temple-II well-stairway may mark surviving remains of the lowest structure of the shaft-stair. This stairway must also be regarded as a stairway to a well. Furthermore it must be assumed to have ended in very close proximity to the well of Temple II.

All in all, the southwest sector's complicated structures stand as eminent testimony to the architecture of Temple I. While revealing otherwise unknown aspects of this architecture, they at the same time confirm its subdivision into two phases, Ia and Ib. In addition the interpretation of the entire complex as a construction with three stages of history stands out clearly. This local sector in the southwest, with its special stratigraphy and architecture, provides an important confirmation of the general stratigraphy dealt with in chapter 2, but it also extends it. We can here deduce the existence of an oval platform surrounding the central one. On, in or beside this oval platform from the time of Temple I we can infer such distinct features as a temple-well, a pool and an established connection between pool and central platform. All these features appear clearly in the architecture of Temple II, but the arguments here put forward indicate that they have had antecedents in Temple I.

It is obvious that Temple I's oval platform presupposes terracing walls, to counter the difference in level between the upper surface of the oval platform and the ground surface in the depression to the south-west. These two levels can best be expressed as the approximate levels of the foot of the central platform and of the water-table.

The main element in the fill of the oval platform appears to have been clay, just as in the case of the so-called clay core in the bottom of the central platform. We can only give a vague estimate of the surface level of the platform as between 2.50 and 3.00. The foot of its terrace wall to the south should from the observations available be sought at levels in the neighbourhood of our datum-point 5.00. But it is masonry at precisely this level which has been in the danger-zone during the construction of Temple II, and as possible remains we can only point to two

small stretches (31 and 32) (plan 1). The one of them (31) is 2½ m long, especially deeply placed and consisting of somewhat small stones mortared with clay. The other (32) was not plotted in, but is located on a basis of excavation photographs (fig. 80). It disappears into an unexcavated block of earth. These surviving remains presumably represent foundations of walls which were demolished when Temple II was built.

In the context presented here these remains of walls are evidence of a terrace wall around Temple I's oval platform (fig. 3), and in that case the span from this wall to its parallel in the northern foreland, if an identity exists, is 46 m, a measurement which could approximately represent the greatest width of the oval in the time of Temple I.

At this point we leave the southwestern sector. In the rest of the southern foreland neither sections nor area excavation produced any evidence bearing on Temple I. The picture is completely dominated by the architecture of Temple II, whose two deeply founded oval-terrace walls, with their associated landscaping of the area, have removed all trace of earlier works.

Only in the south-east do we, by way of *section 14*, which is treated more closely in chapter 7, have knowledge of wall remains from the time of Temple I, but they were not further investigated. The subsoil-contours in section 14 give the following levels: the terrain falls from north to south from 3.60 to 4.00, which are well-known average measurements for the rise of ground on which the temple was built, the top and slope of the plateau. Clearly in the south-east we are beyond the depression which we have met in the south-west.

In the western foreland, sections 21 and 22, cf. chapter 2, have given insight into the stratigraphy north of the southwest sector. This stratigraphy could not be viewed in isolation, so far as the layers from the periods of Temples I and II are concerned. Interpretation must here be based on a combined evaluation, excluding stratigraphical contradictions, and it is the situation in the period of Temple II which is basic for an understanding. This area of the temple was at that time characterized by two low oval-terrace walls just as in the south – to all appearances continuations of these southern walls, and therefore successive structures, the one replacing the other.

The level of the original subsoil sank as usual from about 3.50 to 4.00 in a westerly direction, only going lower in the extreme west of *section 21*. Here, characteristically enough, terracing masonry (C) was met with, and will be described below. The clay bottom-level also appeared plainly, and we have good reason to consider this level as especially associated with Temple I, here as fill-material in an oval platform with no closely defined limits. For it

Fig. 84. Temple I, outer western sector, base-stone on underlying stone, from W. In middle distance oval wall IIa, and beyond it a drain. In background to left, lying high, the west wall of Temple III. On right remains of western portion of Temple II, here unfocussed (1960).

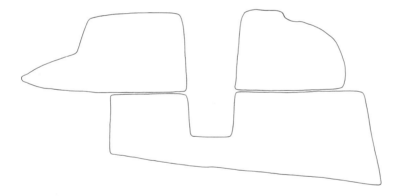

Fig. 85. Temple I, sketch of base-stone, cf. fig. 84, 1:20.

must be admitted that no terrace wall was detected, though this may be because the area was not systematically excavated in full depth. The only possible evidence of an oval wall in the west, of earlier date than the oval walls of Temple II in the area, is a piece of wall (plan 1:39) that was followed for a distance of 2 m. It was badly broken down, and consisted of stone mortared with clay. At its south end it converged with a later oval-wall (plan 5:1), which resulted in its demolition, but further north it diverged in a northeasterly direction. Section 21 cuts just through the point where the two walls (F and G) meet, each with its individual bottom level. The older wall (G) stands approximately on the subsoil and terraces clay-mixed sand lying behind it; east of

the wall could be seen a little plaster surface, apparently at level 3.00. On the overall plan we have joined this stretch of wall to the stretches to the north and south (fig. 3).

From the time of Temple II there are found in addition here in the west drains leading out from the central platform and various cult-structures. Both these features have had, or seem to have had, forerunners in Temple I.

Architectural remains from Temple I in the west sector are first and foremost represented by local masonry at the western end of section 21, cf. the overall plan (fig. 14). Its appearance here occasioned a provisional area excavation in two squares, of which the one to the south proved to be

Fig. 86. Temple I, central platform, clay core with pottery beakers as foundation offerings *in situ*, from S (1957).

empty. The masonry formed a sunk room, divided into two chambers (fig. 81). The building technique was stones laid in clay. The long stretch of walling had an irregular rear face and an even front. A wall built onto this face at right-angles formed the northern side of the room, while there was a partition wall in the middle and an enclosed staircase in the south. The floors showed the remains of stone flagging. In the northern chamber the water-table appeared. Outside the room there were other walls both to the north and the south.

Its position indicates a connection with Temple I, but otherwise the function of this cellar-like building is unclear. It lies very peripheral to the temple, and has its own individual orientation. In any case, it shows that the people of the time were capable of building, with a simple technique, rooms with floors at ground-water level.

Close to the terrace wall just north of the passageway described above there appeared a stone-setting (33) beneath three pairs of fashioned stones belonging to Temple II (plan 1). It consisted of scattered stones in a single layer, though the western edge was more wall-like, the stones here lying in 2-3 courses. It is probably a case of tumbled masonry from Temple I.

West of the stone-setting a pit resembling a post-hole (34) was emptied, and along its northern edge

a channel (35) came to view, formed of small stones mortared with grey-white clay-mixed plaster. It was disturbed by a channel from Temple II running above it, but a continuation could be seen in the form of a stone-set drain (36). The positioning of this drain, which was built of stones laid in clay, is shown in section 22 (E).

Due west, at the edge of the presumed oval platform, there was an unimpressive fragment of walling (37), preserved in its lowest course of stone set in clay (fig. 82). Its position is given in section 25, which will later be described, and it should perhaps be viewed in association with a remarkable stone construction (38) close by (figs. 83-84). It consisted of two massive rough-hewn limestone blocks placed the one above the other. A schematic section along the longer axis gives the sizes and relation of the blocks (fig. 85). A perforation of the upper block continued some way down into the lower. The hole was in all 67 cm deep, with an upper diameter of 29 cm and a lower diameter of 22 cm.

With a base level of 4.00 for the lower block it was presumably placed at the local original ground-level. 1 m further west the ground level could be established at level 3.80, cf. section 25. This deep positioning suggests a connection with Temple I. The blocks can have been used as a base for an upright structure, presumably a cult-figure.

Section 29 cut through the more distant western foreland, and in the trench was found deeply lying walling which must be attributed to the time of Temple I. A wall across the trench (19) was of stone mortared with sandy clay, while a wall in the direction of the trench (27) was completely without mortar. In the limited space investigated we can only make note of their presence.

Summarizing the above, we consider that we can uphold a view that Temple I – like its successor – in addition to its central platform consisted of a larger, lower lying platform which outlines a half-oval shape. This platform, in addition to its architectural function as a step to higher things, has perhaps also served to delimit the clay base-level which is so characteristic of the construction. The terrace wall of the oval platform is, however, only known through small fragments of a long orbit. The wall was not of uniform height, as in the south-west it runs into a natural depression in the original terrain. Here the terrace wall must have been correspondingly high, but otherwise it was of moderate height. Over long stretches the oval platform has only taken the form of a huge dais to the four-sided central platform. Whether this dais has formed a full oval is not known.

Offerings at the lowest level of Temple I

Deposited on or within the clay level of the earliest temple construction, foundation offerings were found. The clay of the bottom level occurred in both the central and oval platforms, and the votive offerings here described were also found throughout.

Considerable efforts were made to locate these objects. Large areas of the clay core remained nevertheless uninvestigated, both in the central and in the oval platforms. Here it must suffice to delineate their extent, and to describe the type of objects found. Many of the finds were surveyed in three-dimensionally, while others were assembled individually or collectively from each specified investigated area, see plan 2. These last are shown on the plan with a registration number in brackets.

By far the most numerous single group comprises pottery beakers, of which over 50 can be localized (fig. 86). But this number is only a minimum figure. The quantity of fragments in the collective assemblies shows that the deposition of beakers has been of much greater extent. They appear also outside the area shown on the plan, for example in section 13, layer 10, where numerous beakers occurred, all, however, badly shattered. Other types of pottery containers were rare (see below, p. 212).

Of stone containers only one was found, cf. the description above (plan 1:24), besides two steatite rim fragments (see below, p. 318).

Votive finds of a special nature comprised a gold band, in addition to a fragment of lapis-lazuli and a carnelian bead (see below, p. 315-316).

The remainder of the finds were of copper. They comprise ingots and fragments of ingots, a copper vessel, a rattle, flat or cylindrical sheet mounted with nails on wood, and small implements such as knives and rods. Larger tools were represented by an adze, and weapons by crescent-shaped axes, a dagger and three spearheads (see below, p. 255).

Summary

With reference to the summaries given above we can briefly describe the first temple as a central platform with temple buildings, placed upon a surrounding oval platform (fig. 3). This temple should for various compelling reasons be separated into two phases, of which the later represents a constructional change which shows itself first and foremost in an expansion of the central platform. The architectural layout described was continued in the subsequent Temple II.

The two stages of the first temple have been built upon a low natural elevation. This elevation lies on the edge of a depression containing a spring, and here were constructed both a well and a pool. Later construction precludes detailed investigation. At an early stage in the building activity a bottom layer of clay was laid down with a number of offerings. Figuratively speaking, this level appears as a deliberately established boundary between the parts of the temple associated with regions over ground-level and those associated with underground regions, in our case strata carrying fresh water.

As a final primary factor in the temple complex is a specially formed structure to the east, which has served activities of a repetitive character involving fire. It appears in Temple II as a court with several building phases, surrounded by a wall. Both the features to the east and those to the west were connected with the centre of the temple.

4. Temple II. The Central Platform

With Temple II is inaugurated the first total reconstruction in the building history of the Barbar temple (plan 3). Despite continuing traditions, every part of the complex receives new forms, and the rebuilding finds its most pregnant expression in a complete change in the building material. The local, uncut stone is abandoned in favour of shaped limestone ashlars, which, with their smooth straight outlines, provided an excellent medium for construction.

These white ashlars could not be obtained in the immediate locality. Suitable quarries had to be found, and the ashlars transported to the temple site. Early in the expedition Glob identified the quarries used, and localized them to the island of Jiddah off the northwest coast of Bahrain (fig. 87). It must at least be considered as an obvious probability that the limestone deposits there were the main source of the thousands of large stone blocks that were employed in Temple II. Here the expensive material was utilized with lavish magnificence, completely without regard to technical considerations.

It has already been made clear that Temple II is well preserved in its ground-plan, despite demolitions for the construction of the succeeding temple, and despite large-scale stone-robbery in later periods. Both the central and the oval platform stand out clearly, while the same is true of the peripheral constructions to the east and the west, the court and the pool. Moreover, the original subsequent demolition respected numerous individual elements of the cult. They were allowed to remain standing or lying in their places.

The description of this temple-complex will take the form of a division of the total material between this chapter and the three following, which will cover respectively the oval platform, the pool and the Eastern Court. Here discussion will be limited to the central portions of the temple.

The central platform's terrace walls

The central platform of Temple II was, like its predecessor, trapezoid in its plan, which can be followed with very great certainty despite the severe robbery of the surrounding terrace walls. Thus only the lowest courses of one single corner, the northeastern, survive, while of the total wall-length of about 102 m only about 42 m remain.

The wall appears as fragments of its course in the west, the north and the east, while the whole of the southern course is missing. In the quite long eastern course a portion occurs – as a key, as it were, to an understanding of the wall – where it is preserved in its original height, and even carries on its summit a part of a vertical wall more than 4 m long.

We can take this stretch of wall as the starting point for an analysis of the terrace wall, while pointing out that it has already appeared in chapter 2 on section 12. About 4 m south of this section a further *section, 15*, was drawn as a typical cross-section of the wall, which here stands with its front edge on the remains of the demolished terrace wall of Temple Ib (1). Apart from the partly demolished face (3), the wall (2) here stands intact. It can be seen how its outer face has been clothed with slab-like blocks carefully fitted together, while the reverse of the wall shows a much rougher adjustment. Section 12 showed in addition that the outer face possessed, right at the bottom, a little footing with a somewhat coarser finish. Section 12 could also show that the lower part of the demolition of the outer face was original, in the sense that the remains of Temple III's construction "sealed" the edges of the break in the Temple-II wall. The reverse of the wall possessed at the top (7) a cut-away bevel, coinciding with the floor-level of the platform.

At this point the wall of Temple II had a height of about 2 m and a width of about 2.25 m. Its construction was characterized by total solidity, ashlar

Fig. 87. Jiddah. Old stone quarry (1954).

being added to ashlar without regard to the expensive material. The bottom of the wall lay at level 2.25, the top at level 0.20.

The stratigraphical relationships of the wall have been already discussed, and it has been shown that it was built – after a demolition of the original walls to about level 2.20 – at the edge of the earlier platform. Its base lies about ½ m higher than the base of terrace wall Ib. It follows the course of this wall in the south and east, while in the west it is built above the wall of Temple Ia, and in the north runs parallel with the Ia-wall.

Its base-level, which is very uniform, is at the same time flush with the surface of the terrace formed by the oval platform, at least where this relationship could be checked. The top of the wall rose about 0.25 m above the floor which covered Temple II's platform. This is deduced from the well-preserved portion of walling in the east, which at the same time gives the norm for the width of the wall all the way round.

Fig. 88. Temple II, central platform, general view of well-preserved walling in the eastern part of the temple, from NE. On left eastern terrace wall, on right northern terrace wall. In front of the human figure can be seen the exposed foundation-wall surmounted by remains of walling. Other corresponding remains of walling stand on the eastern terrace wall. In background a floor of large flags with altars and pierced cult-stones (1955).

Fig. 89. Temple II, central platform, eastern terrace wall, from SE. Outer face, partly broken down, overlying terrace wall of Temple Ib. At top remains of walling, standing on crown of wall (1955).

We will now examine briefly each stretch of wall separately. *The eastern side* (1) is preserved from the badly demolished northeast corner for a length of about 21 m, as far as a point only a few metres from the now non-existent southeast corner (figs. 88-89). It has in total been about 24½ m long, and its front edge follows a straight course, the only deviation from the smooth surface being a semicylindrical channel cut downward on the outer face (2), leading down into a subterranean drain (fig. 90). Access to it was from another channel (3) crossing the surface of the wall, but this was only preserved in the uppermost ashlar of the reverse of the wall, again as a semicylindrical cutting, here about 30 cm deep (fig. 91). On the floor of the platform a drain (15) led to this channel.

On top of the wall stood, as has been said, a portion of walling, which will be described in the following section. The same is true of a projection built onto the wall, which is part of the ramp down to the Eastern Court, cf. chapter 7.

The greater part of the wall (1) stood as a ruin in varying degrees of demolition. The binding agent was gypsum cement, which often had run out over the exposed stones and partly concealed their sharply angled outlines. (On plan 3 these gipsum patches have been outlined with a thin line). It is therefore difficult to determine their direction of laying; but there is a clear tendency for the stones of the back of the wall to have been laid as "headers" (fig. 91), and, if one disregards the outer facing stones, the use of "stretchers" was less prevalent. A

Fig. 90. Temple II, central platform, eastern wall, from E. Semicircular channel cut on the outer face leading down into a subterranean drain (1955).

Fig. 91. Temple II, central platform, eastern terrace wall, from W. Rear side with cut-out channel in crown of wall. Bottom left, inner side of northern terrace wall of Temple Ia (1958).

Fig. 92. Temple II, central platform, western terrace wall, from N. Surviving fragment. To left, outer face of northern terrace wall of Temple Ia; to right, Temple III's western terrace wall. At end of the Temple-III wall the east end of Temple II's pool stairway projects, with edge-slabs and plinth-stones with cut-out holes (1959).

Fig. 93. Temple II, central platform, SW-corner, from W. In the vertical earth-face, which is section 26A, can be seen the layers filled with stone fragments left by the robbery of the western terrace wall, and on left the pool stairway. In foreground the remains of the portal and the terrace wall of Temple II's oval platform. Behind this and in front of the earth-face are the earlier stairway-structures from Temples Ia and Ib. Upon the unexcavated block of earth can be seen on right remains of Temple III's southern terrace wall and on left remains of foundation-wall buried in the Temple-II platform (1957).

Fig. 94. Temple II, central platform, western terrace wall, from NW. Surviving fragment with front face of lowest course. On left Temple Ia's northern terrace wall and buildings on western portion of Temple II's platform (1959).

Fig. 95. Temple II, central platform, western terrace wall, from S. Surviving fragment (1959).

Fig. 96. Temple II, central platform, northern terrace wall, from NW. Behind comes the exposed foundation-wall buried in the platform, with the remains of a wall standing upon it. Behind the foundation-wall is the flagged flooring of the platform with altars and cult-stones. In background left can be glimpsed the upper edge of the eastern terrace-wall, with wall-remains standing upon it (1955).

whole row of the uppermost stones of the back of the wall, north and south of the channel (3) had been given a rough shaping, so that they met the floor surface at a right angle (fig. 91).

Of *the southern side* (4) stone robbery had left nothing, apart from individual ashlars left *ex situ*. They are of course important evidence for the wall's original presence, as are the distinct robber-trenches and the uniformity of the demolition of the underlying walls of Temple I. The robber-excavations can also be localized at the western end, cf. section 26A (1-2). The stratigraphical evidence permits an exact identification of the eliminated wall-corners in the south-east and south-west, so that the original length of the south wall can be given as about 27 m. The work of shaping the ashlars to fit, as the wall was built, manifests itself in a layer of clean stone chippings, cf. section 2A (18).

A part of *the western wall* (5) is preserved in its full width, but badly demolished (fig. 92). North of it there remains a further abandoned ashlar. The total

length of this wall has measured about 25 m. Evidence of its original course is given at the southern end by a 5-m long robber-trench with its bottom at level 2.30-2.50, cf. section 26A (1). It fits precisely the dimensions of the wall and is filled with broken bits of gypsum-cement (fig. 93).

Section 7B has a secondarily excavated surface-level, but shows clearly that a robber-trench (3) has removed the western wall. At upper left lie the remains (4) of Temple II's platform, a large slab of plaster. West of the trench appear two (7 and 8) of a total of eight shaped stone plinths with holes cut in the upper surface to support whatever they originally bore. These plinth-stones flanked the pool stairway at the point where it met the lost wall. The section also shows the remains of Temple III's western wall (2) with its own robber-trench (1).

The surviving portion of the wall (5) on plan 3 shows almost 7 m of intact wall-face, but only of the lowest course of stones (figs. 94-95). In this walling we find a mixture of "stretchers" and "headers", and once again the outer face is carefully aligned, while the inner side is more casually put together. In the block of walling as a whole there are between 1 and 3 courses preserved, held together by grey-white plaster. At its maximum the wall stands to a height of 1.30 m, and gives here the deepest base levels – between 2.30 and 2.45.

The northern wall (6) has been almost 26 m long, and a little over half survives, though in a demolished or robbed condition (fig. 96). The situation in the Main Section suggests a demolition prior to the building of Temple III, though the total removal of the wall's western end should be attributed to late, secondary stone-robbery.

Section 4 has a bearing on the stratigraphy of the northern wall, cf. the relevant part of the Main Section. Its top is an excavated surface and it goes down to the subsoil between two Temple-II walls, respectively the terrace wall and a foundation wall within the platform. The subsoil appears at a typical level of about 3.30, covered by an indeterminate layer (18) which probably represents the bottom layer of clay, though the drawer of the section interpreted it as subsoil. Above this comes a very layered stratigraphy, which even includes a layer of drift-sand (13). If this layer marks a transition between deposits from Temple Ia, the terrace wall of which lies somewhat to the south, and those from Temple Ib, then layers such as the stony bottom level in the layer above (10 and 11) and an occurrence of plaster (12) are possibly building layers that can point to Temple Ib. The northern terrace wall of this temple is, after all, hypothetically assumed to be overlain by the wall of Temple II (4). The layers of fill behind this earlier unidentified terrace wall Ib are admittedly in

that case missing, apart from possible remains (6-8). These layers of fill can, however, have been removed when the wall of Temple II (4) was built, involving a large excavation (5 and 9). The latter of these two layers consists of limestone chippings, which point to local trimming of wall-ashlars, while the former fills up the excavation necessitated by the building-work, and moreover contains discarded material from the construction of wall II. Finally, a layer of sand (1) fills up the space between the foundation-wall (3) and the terrace wall (4).

There can also be seen that a stone-robbing layer (2) secondarily disturbs the upper levels, with a limestone ashlar left loose in the soil. Thus in section 4 the terrace wall has been the target of later disturbance, in contrast to the situation in the Main Section, where a planned demolition was carried through. In other respects the northern wall resembles the eastern, with many "headers" but with predominantly "stretchers" along the outer face.

With the documentation here given the terrace wall of Temple II's central platform is considered to have been fully presented in its remarkable trapezoid plan – presumably an architectural legacy from its predecessor. In the succeeding Temple III it is given up in favour of a right-angled construction.

The platform has the following dimensions: its sides have been 24½, 27, 25 and 26 m long, and its height was almost 2 m. It has stood upon an oval platform, and there has been access to it from both east and west. Other stairways can have disappeared as a result of demolition or robbery. Upon the platform there were numerous remains of temple buildings – the theme of the next section.

The central platform's floor-level

Large flat-cut limestone slabs formed the floor of the Temple-II platform, now raised one metre to level c. 0.50 (plan 3). In the western part, however, it lay somewhat lower.

By far the greater part of the flooring had been broken up. We cannot follow in detail to what degree this was attributable to later robbery. To determine this would have necessitated an intense study of the upper stratigraphy of the tell, for which there was no opportunity. The Main Section (1b) must here stand as representative for the situation.

The actual floor (plan 3:12) consisted typically of a single layer of flag-like blocks. On this stood in the east a series of assemblages of a cult nature, often more or less *in situ*, implying that they were respected by the builders of Temple III. But there were

also stretches of masonry with foundations under the floor, while special conditions seem to apply for a large patch of building remains in the west, though we do not know what the archaeological situation was below these remains.

In the case of the masonry stretches below floor-level, they must be interpreted as foundations for walls of buildings upon the platform, and indeed remains of such walls appeared in places. Although incompletely preserved, these stretches of foundations give important hints of the structures whose walls they supported.

The most intact foundation-wall (7) lay in the northeastern portion of the platform. It was partly broken up, but all the upper stones which survived lay significantly at the same level as the floor lying

Fig. 97. Temple II, central platform, foundation-wall near northern edge, from W. Overlain by intact fill-layers from Temple III's platform. In centre of picture remains of wall standing upon foundation-wall, and on its right the adjoining floor of Temple II (1954).

south of them; nor has the wall ever been higher, for on the surface thus provided stood *in situ* four ashlars marking a vertical wall (8). Equally significant for this foundation-wall is the complete absence of "finish" to the sides, such as is found on the outer face of the terrace walls. Any suggestion that this wall has had any terracing function can therefore be dismissed.

With its surviving length it should have supported a stretch of walling of more than 12 m in length, and it goes without saying that such a construction in the material employed has needed other foundation than the comparatively flimsy floor (fig. 47). The foundation was massively built with extensive use of large blocks of hewn limestone, set in plaster as "headers" in two courses. It is almost 1 m thick and over 1½ m wide.

This wall can be seen being dug free in an early excavation photograph, and the superimposed layers which were still there at the time show no trace of robber activity (fig. 97). The condition of the wall must therefore be considered as reflecting a situation from the demolition of Temple II.

The placing of the wall in the stratigraphy can be seen on the Main Section (E) and on section 4 (3). As has been said, its upper surface was approximately at floor level, perhaps covered with paving stones.

On the foundation stood, in close order, four limestone ashlars (8), forming the north wall of a building. In continuation of them could be seen on the foundation impressions, metre-long stripes, which marked the further course of the south side of the wall – here shown as a broken line. The stones of the wall were all set as "headers", and they were exceedingly precisely shaped so that both faces of the wall stood completely smooth. These straight faces were evidently meant to be fully visible.

A portion of walling of the same nature (9) was to be found in close proximity, but using the eastern terrace wall as a foundation (fig. 98). It has formed the east wall in the same building. Here a mixture of "stretchers" and "headers" is used. Both walls (8 and 9) are of the same width, about 0.75 m, and the one is preserved in a length of 1½ m, the other of more than 4 m. Where their prolonged courses met there would be an obtuse-angled corner, and, as we shall later see, the floor-surface here bears evidence of a specially fashioned corner-interior. This naturally supports the assumption of an original connection between the two walls.

Their function has been to delimit part of the platform, either as a high boundary-wall around a courtyard or as a large temple building. In both cases this construction can be seen to have de-

Fig. 98. Temple II, central platform, NE-corner, from W. Surviving portion of floor, bordered in rear by upper edge of eastern terrace wall with remains of walling rising from crown of wall. On left corresponding remains of walling standing on not yet visible foundation-wall (1958).

manded solid foundation. It must consequently have been of a considerable order of size.

For the extent of the building, evidence is provided by a third stretch of wall (10) of the type already described. It forms part of the west wall, and is similarly founded. 2 m of wall of the usual width survive, consisting of five "headers", finely shaped ashlars held together by light grey-brown plaster. Patches of covering plaster and shallow dressing of the surface of the ashlars (marked by pricking on the plan) bear traces of subsequent courses of stone, now removed, while foundation stones north and south of the wall show that its course continued. In places where even the foundation has been removed there can be seen, as negative impressions, the broken edges in the plaster floor of the underlying Temple I running in a straight line to north and south, cf. plan 4. Nor is this all. Precisely in line with this wall we also find the only serious damage to the otherwise well-preserved northern terrace wall of Temple Ia, in the form of a large demolition. It can be assumed to have been carried out to make room for the foundation-wall from Temple II, which was later removed. We have thereby almost made contact with the northern foundation-wall (7).

In the southerly direction there comes a further piece of foundation-wall (11), of "headers" bound

with light grey-brown plaster. It reaches almost all the way to the vanished southern terrace wall of Temple II, in the same way as the northern foundation-wall (7) was built joining the eastern terrace wall (1).

The west wall of the construction here described thus seems to have joined a south wall which, like the east wall, stood on the terrace wall, and the whole combines to give a picture of a trapezoid frame for a building which has formed a connected whole. Above the floor its walls are represented by stretches of walling (8-10). In the north and west these walls stood upon foundation-walls, in the south and east upon the terrace walls.

This edifice has had a northern side measuring about 15 m, while the other three sides were each about 18 m (fig. 4). With such an extent it has taken up an appreciable part of the platform, and its size may well have given it the appearance of a third step to the temple. In the following description we shall regard this interpretation as a "fact", and call the area thus delimited zone A.

A concentration of assemblages of a cult nature in zone A suggests that the area – whether a temple-court or a temple-building – has comprised a special sacral area. No trace could be found of interior divisions or of the means of access.

In the northeastern portion of zone A there was a large area (12) paved with limestone slabs, about 20

Fig. 99. Temple II, central platform, east side, from N. Detail of surviving portion of floor. To left upper edge of eastern terrace wall, rear side (1958).

cm thick and of varying sizes and irregular shapes (figs. 99-100). They were laid in a haphazard mosaic pattern at around level 0.50. Intervals between slabs were filled out with plaster or smaller stones. This connected portion of flooring rose at its southern edge to a low platform (13), on which were preserved cult-stones (19, 20, 22) and impressions left by standing stones (21). In the floor there was also embedded a crescent-shaped block, clearly secondarily employed, perhaps a former edging-stone to some aperture (fig. 101). Immediately north of this stone the platform consisted only of plaster and smaller stones.

Another plaster construction (14) rose a short way up in the immediate neighbourhood (fig. 102). Its surviving northern end was finely smoothed on the surface, and its northern and eastern sides were straight-cut and met at an obtuse angle. Otherwise this plaster block was damaged, so that its interior, consisting of stones in fist to head size, was visible. "Irregularities" recorded in the floor at this point are possibly connected with repairs or minor local rebuildings.

Another fixed construction on the floor surface consisted of a double trace of a channel carved out of the floor to a depth of up to 8 cm, surmounted, when found, by edge-stones (15) (fig. 103). These edge-stones were particularly delicately cut, almost

as planks about a metre in length but only 5 cm thick. They stood in pairs, on edge, originally set into a plaster floor above the flagstone floor, the interval between them forming a channel with a combined length of about 3 m. Traces of bitumen were observed in the channel, probably to waterproof it. This channel led to the channel described in the previous section as running across the top of the terrace wall.

A special framing (16) was found in the northeast corner of the floor, though here the actual floor-slabs were missing within the framing (fig. 104). Here too the edge-stones were *in situ* when found, and beneath them were shallow grooves in the flooring, into which they had been fitted. These edge-stones had been cut like beams, about 0.75 m long and with a cross-section of 15 × 15 cm. They framed an area of somewhat over 2 × 2 m.

The excavators, in the first year of the expedition, interpreted this feature as a pit, but there is no documentation for this view. The framing does, however show that the place was special, cutting off as it does the interior northeast corner of zone A, cf. the wall-remains here (8 and 9).

Quite special, too, were the objects discovered here. Vaguely described as coming from layers in or around the "pit of offering" a concentration of unusual objects was found, including alabaster vases

91

Fig. 100. Temple II, central platform, NE-corner, from S. Detail of surviving portion of floor (1958).

Fig. 101. Temple II, central platform, east side, from W, from above. Detail of surviving portion of floor with secondarily employed, crescent-shaped floor-slab (1958).

Fig. 102. Temple II, central platform, east side, from NE. Detail of surviving portion of floor with plaster block inset in floor. Behind can be seen the circular altars (1958).

Fig. 103. Temple II, central platform, east side, from W. Detail of surviving portion of floor with double runnels as foundation-grooves for edge-stones, cf. fig. 104. Run-out into drain cut through the crown of the eastern terrace wall (1958).

Fig. 104. Temple II, central platform, northeast portion, from NE. Surrounded by the massive fill of Temple III. Framed four-sided hole in the surviving portion of floor in corner of zone A. In background altars with channel edged with double row of stone planks (1955).

and copper statuettes (see below, fig. 695 and p. 262, 283, 316-317). Such accumulations of objects are, however, also known from other parts of this temple area beneath the floor, and they appear to have been deposited here as special votive gifts, either placed there at the laying of the Temple-II platform or dug down later from the temple-floor. Our northeast corner only therefore tells us that it too has been used as a deposition-area. It must suffice to record the framing. Against the theory of a specially marked-off pit of offering must be counted the discovery of alabaster sherds elsewhere in the platform which belong to the above-mentioned alabaster vases from the "pit".

On the east-west-running axis of zone A there were excavated large portions of a cult interior, dominated by a double-circular structure (18). This structure takes prominence, by reason of its unusual nature, its size and its placing, as a particularly important feature in the sacral organization (figs. 105-107). It is unfortunately not intact, insofar as the whole of its northern side has been torn up, probably through stone-robbery. Naturally the two circles must be assumed to have been complete,

while the building technique moreover makes it difficult to determine to what degree upper portions have been demolished.

As it had survived, it had mainly the appearance of a low oblong platform, rising to about 40-50 cm above the floor, with a straight south side still intact. Into the platform were inset the two stone-set circles, one of which projected slightly higher than the other. The structure was about 6 m long, and the masonry-work is pre-eminent. The straight southern edge, the vertical side of which must have been visible, lies in the east-west-going centre axis of zone A, the large trapezoid building on the platform. From a temple-historical viewpoint it should be remembered that under it – on the plaster floor of Temple I – there lay a related structure, though of less finished workmanship.

The structure (18) was excavated in 1954 and reinvestigated in 1958, but a number of stones had been removed from it in the interim. The following detailed description can be given: The western circle had a diameter of about 2½ m; seven of the stone blocks had survived, of which five (A-D and G) were found *in situ*, while two (E and F) were re-

Fig. 105. Temple II, central platform, double-circular altar, from above, from SE (1955).

placed. They were all finely finished on all six sides, with level upper and lower faces and level joining surfaces, but with curved outer and inner faces. The upper surface had at its outer edge traces of a 2-3 cm deep dressing, and in places there was also profiling a little way down the vertical curved outer face.

Separated by floor-slabs cut to shape lay an eastern circle of just the same size, with nine stones (H-P) preserved, all *in situ*. Of these one block (J) showed traces of a centimetre-deep hack in the upper surface, while another (K), of irregular shape, had an incision along the outer edge which went quite deep.

All these blocks were 50-70 cm high and stood on the top of the layer of fill between the floors of Temples I and II (fig. 55). Fitted floor-slabs (12) were laid around them.

The frame was only identifiable in the south, surviving for a length of 4.25 m and consisting in all of 11 blocks (Q-X and AE-AH). There are presumably some missing in the west, but in the east an intact termination may be in place, if we interpret a block (Y) placed here as a step. It rises more than half-way up the framing.

This framing consists of three sections, a western (AE-AG), an eastern (R-X) and a central (AH and Q). The stones are set as "headers", apart from the two central stones. One of the blocks (AF) has an irregular scar on the upper surface, another (AH) a slight lowering of the surface across the western end, a third (Q) bears also signs of transverse cutting and a fourth (R) has a 6 cm deep cutting-away of the upper surface on one side. These dressings of the block surfaces must be interpreted as preparations for receiving another course.

All these stones have received an unusual finish with a polishing of the vertical south sides, which suggests strongly that they have formed a visible front face. Their upper surface varies from level 0.00 in the west to 0.07 in the east.

Support for the interpretation of the southern side as an intact facade is also given by the provision of a step, formed of two blocks (AB and AC). They stand on the platform floor and show signs of shallow transverse cutting, with, in between these, a particularly smoothly polished portion, about 40 cm wide. The polished portion may have been flanked by vanished blocks like a "casing" on either side of a "door", and indeed the trace of a door con-

Fig. 106. Temple II, central platform, double-circular altar, from above, from E. In background remains of wall rising from not yet visible foundation-wall (1955).

tinues in over the neighbouring stones (Q and R). Carried to its logical conclusion, this would imply that the south face had continued upwards as a vertical wall. It should be added that the central stones (AH and Z) form steps down to the narrow floor between the circles, but this may be due to the removal of stones here.

The whole structure has been interpreted as offering-tables or as a double-altar. In favour of the latter interpretation is the fact that the stone-set channel (15) runs in the direction of the structure's north side. The role of round altars in the cult is also evidenced by a particularly elegant altar-block (AD) buried under the floor (figs. 61-64). It has already been described under Temple I, with reservations concerning its association with the earlier temple. If it was placed where it was found as a "de-

posited" cult-object from Temple II, then it would have involved a relaying of the floor, including an overlaying with plaster (14).

Two fragments of a similar round altar cut in oolitic limestone, with a diameter of 87 cm (figs. 108-109) were found in the rubble layer below the flagged floor in area III, 1958.

If the eastern step (Y) really is a step, then a connection is here provided between the double-structure and the platform-like raised portion of the floor (13) to the east. On this there was found *in situ* a stone slab with a depression in the upper edge (19), standing in a foundation-groove in the floor. The groove was 4 cm deep and contained remains of white plaster. A precisely similar slab (20) was found fallen, and its foundation groove (21) could be seen in the floor, 3 cm deep and similarly with

Fig. 107. Temple II, central platform, double-circular altar, from above, from S. Eastern portion with cult-stones *in situ* on right. Above them the edge-stones of the channel (1955).

traces of plaster. This permits a precise re-erection of the two slabs, and their interpretation as side-pieces of a bench or a table (cf. fig. 251). The distance between the two foundation traces was 1.11 m. The side-slabs are registered with the following dimensions: 52 cm wide, 80 cm high, and about 20 cm thick. The depression in the upper edge was 4.5 cm deep and 31 cm wide, while the projecting ends, cut sloping, were 10 and 11 cm wide.

In association with the bench there was found a rectangular stone block (22) with a rectangular depression. Its dimensions are recorded as 45×36 cm, with height 33 cm; the depression was 27×19 cm, and its depth was not measured.

South of the bench lay a beam-shaped block (23), which was not measured in, with a continuous groove running its full length (fig. 107). It was about 0.75 m long. South again of this lay a block of stone (24) with a specific shape carved into it. The stone measured $64 \times 26 \times 20$ cm (figs. 110-111). In one of the narrower sides a round hole had been carved, 12 cm in diameter and 6½ cm deep, and from it ran, to one of the sides, a 2-cm broad and 8-cm deep groove. It was interpreted as a *yoni*.

Finally, there was found beside the double-structure one of the "pierced stones" (25) characteristic for the temple, an oblong slab with a curved upper edge and with a hole penetrating all the way through near the top. It was 85 cm tall, had originally stood vertically and shows a change in shaping between the buried third of the stone and the free-standing upper portion.

South of the circular double-altar there came further remains of the flooring (12), and on this could be seen a shallow depression, almost 2½ m long and ½ m wide, marked by pricking on the plan, presumably from a little masonry construction. At both ends of the impression small round holes could be seen, set in pairs.

The rest of the floor had been removed. Only a few slabs lying at floor-level, which projected along the south edge of the special central double-structure (18), can be ascribed to the floor-surface of zone A.

All this section of zone A end with the delimiting wall (9) standing on the terrace wall (1). As we have said, the rest of the flooring is missing, and by the western wall of zone A there survive only a "step" (26) and three "pierced-stones" (27-29) of the type just described, still standing *in situ* (figs. 112-113). They were set up in a slight curve with its apex towards the north. If a stairway has led up to the platform in the south, in continuation of the stairway that in fact exists, leading up in the south to the oval

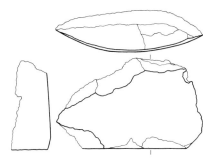

Fig. 108. Temple II, central platform, fragment of round altar in oolitic limestone (517.AJS) 1:10.

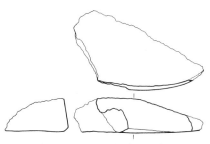

Fig. 109. Temple II, central platform, fragment of round altar in oolitic limestone (517.AJS) 1:10.

Fig. 110. Temple II, central platform, east side central, from above, from N, cult-stone, *yoni* (1955).

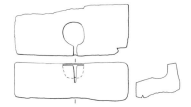

Fig. 111. Cult-stone, *yoni*, cf. fig. 110. 1:20.

platform, then these stones have stood centrally in the field of vision of those ascending to the central platform.

The reverence which has been shown these stones in an area otherwise demolished shows their especial importance. The centre stone is moreover notable in being furnished with a westward-looking animal head, carved in one with the stone (figs. 114-115). This protom was, however, later broken off and disappeared.

These stones can be shown in elevation drawings (fig. 116). They were 80-90 cm high and of varying thickness. All three cult-stones show traces marking the line to which they were embedded in the earth.

A further stone (30) of this type was found (fig. 117). It occurred *ex situ* in a stone-robber layer near the southwest corner of the platform, thus outside zone A, but it had been dragged away from its place. On both sides there were signs of a ring-shaped carving (fig. 118). As it was heavily chipped on the one edge it would be tempting to assume that it too had originally possessed a protom.

The platform outside zone A we choose to designate zone B. It comprises all the northern portion of the platform, which is demolished down to floor level, and all the southwest portion, which has suffered the same fate. Only in the centre of the western portion were there found connected remains of building (plan 4).

Concerning the demolished northern portion it can therefore only be said that the area north of zone A's northern wall (8) and onward to the terrace wall's face in the north comprised a good 5 m broad platform area. There was thus room for a suite of rooms such as those on the platform-floor of Temple I. The northwest corner of the platform can only be described as an expanse of about 9 × 9 m in a condition of *tabula rasa*. The same is true of the southwest corner, here in an expanse of about 7×8 m. This area even showed open breaks in the underlying plaster floor of Temple Ib.

On the other hand, the part of zone B which was only partially demolished attracts interest, since here are found remains of floors and standing masonry which were immediately construed as remains of temple chambers.

This portion of the temple was only exposed, never excavated *in toto*, so the parts that lie below it are unknown, apart from what could be seen in the exposed vertical edges of the area. Its north and east sides were excavated down to Temple-I level, while its west and south sides were dug deeper. There are unfortunately no section drawings of these faces, nor of the layers which overlay the whole area before excavation.

The investigation is thus concentrated on a square measuring about 8 × 8 m, with a robber-in-

Fig. 112. Temple II, central platform, southern central portion, from N. Three pierced cult-stones in a row *in situ* (1955).

trusion in the southeast corner and with an irregular western edge. A particularly deep intrusion (V) marks the inner side of a round change of fill at the building level, which has been hit by an initial archaeological trial trench.

The lack of detailed knowledge of the phases of destruction, the lack of understanding of the underlying layers, and the possibility of secondary rebuilding during the period of temple II, combine to make the situation somewhat obscure. To this must be added the fact that the recognizable remains are only a part of a larger whole. The area was excavated in 1955 and re-investigated in 1959, though it was little changed apart from weathering (figs. 119-120).

An important tendency of general application was a lowering of level in relation to zone A. The building level lies therefore in many places close to the floor of the underlying Temple I which extends under the level on the eastern and northern sides. The earlier plaster-floor can also be seen on the west side in vertical exposed surfaces, cf. for example figs. 70, 72 and 95. On the south side this floor had been broken up.

While we have no idea what there can have been in the missing adjoining area to the north, we can at least assume that the similarly missing surrounding area to the south has been involved in architecture which has been concerned with the transition between the upper step of the pool stairway and the entrance to zone A.

The preserved masonry in the west must furthermore be interpreted in the light of its proximity to zone A to the east and the terrace wall to the west, as well as to the underlying Temple I. On plan 4 these surrounding factors figure with the following main elements: Temple I's plaster floor (A), the western terrace wall (B), the pool stairway's junction (C) with the terrace wall, a large robber-breach (D) in the terrace wall, and broken-up portions of Temple I's plaster floor (E-H).

The eastern edge of the surviving masonry in zone B forms the boundary between zones A and B, and structurally belong rather to zone A than B (plan 4). It has therefore already been described as consisting of a partly demolished foundation-wall with the remains of a wall resting upon it. The foundation-wall appears in the form of two surviving portions (J and K), and two robber-holes (F and G). The surmounting wall (L) shows itself with five ashlars *in situ*. Both walls are mortared with light grey-brown plaster. On the west side of the wall-ashlars can be seen a shallow dressing of the surface.

Fig. 113. Temple II, central platform, southern central portion, from S. As fig. 112 (1955).

Fig. 114. Temple II, central platform, southern central portion, from S. Detail of pierced cult-stone with animal-head protom (1955).

It is the northern part of the surviving masonry in zone B that stands most prominently and most intact (fig. 119). For here was found a connected surface of large, almost square flooring-slabs (M). Their upper sides were finely smoothed, and they were laid in a regular right-angled pattern in long stretches. The slabs were in places spotted with daubs of grey-brown plaster, but this feature may be secondary. With a level of about 0.90 this floor lies almost ½ m lower than the floor-level which we know from zone A. It continues in a northerly and westerly extension as a surface (N) consisting of grey-brown plaster with impressions of the same floor-slabs.

Eleven of the surviving floor-slabs together form a connected whole, which is quite strictly delimited on three sides and thereby gives the impression of a room. Its floor-surface abuts in the east on the west wall of zone A, the abutment taking the particular form of a step or ledge (O). The ledge consists of smaller oblong ashlars, finely cut, laid in grey-brown plaster and partly covered on the upper side with a thin layer of the same plaster. The straight vertical faces of the ledge-stones are unplastered.

The southern end of the room has had precisely the same form, and here the ledge (P) abuts on a massive stretch of walling (Q).

To the west the area ends in a large vertical wall-fragment (R), but without a ledge (figs. 119-122). The actual wall (R) is a somewhat irregular piece of building, of limestone blocks in grey-brown plaster or just of grey-brown blocks of plaster with stones and fragments of ashlars embedded. It is also apparently placed "randomly" on the floor-slabs, which run in under it, and it has its own individual measurements with a wall-width of over 1 m. Its surviving length amounts to 4.75 m, its greatest height to 1 m. Its jointing, too, gives a different impression, and the plaster used resembles that which is found in daubs on the floor and the surrounding surfaces. Presumably all these are secondary features, showing that we are dealing with a later addition.

If we imagine these additions removed, then the flagged floor appears rather as a lower-level courtyard west of zone A. This court has in that case been edged to the west by the terrace wall (B). It can be seen, too, that the northwest corner of the floor's underlying plaster (N) ends inward towards the terrace wall in a straight edge over a metre long, a line

Fig. 115. Temple II, central platform, southern central portion, from NW. As fig. 114 (1955).

Fig. 116. Temple II. Elevations of pierced cult-stones from central platform. Left (plan 3:27): thickness above, 28 cm, below, 36 cm. Middle (plan 3:28): thickness 24 cm. Right (plan 3:29): thickness 25 cm. All three stones are differently weathered above and below, probably reflecting a level of insetting. 1:20.

Fig. 117. Temple II. Pierced cult-stone *ex situ*, here re-erected (1955).

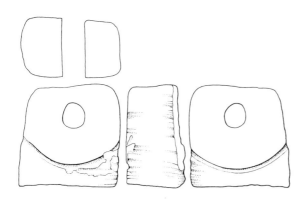

Fig. 118. Temple II, central platform. Pierced cult-stone, cf. fig. 117. 1:20.

of breakage which must be assumed to have followed an original vertical portion of the terrace wall.

The piece of secondary walling (R) seems to be broken off at both ends. The western face is built straight, whereas the eastern face bends slightly, and at this point a piece af walling (Q) starts, which runs to join the west wall (L) of zone A (fig. 123). This piece of wall is built of ashlars set in grey-brown plaster, and both sides are straight. On the upper side can be seen stretches of plaster. Its level, at about 0.50, agrees with the bottom of zone A's west wall (L), and it is perhaps the remains of a partition wall. In its southeast corner there was perhaps a hinge-hole for a door; at least there could be seen, in a projecting portion of the stone block there,

Fig. 119. Temple II, central platform, west portion, from N. Remains of floors and walls (1955).

Fig. 120. Temple II, central platform, west portion, from SE. Remains of floors and walls (1955).

Fig. 121. Temple II, central platform, west portion, from NE. Remains of floors and walls, cf. plan 4:M, P, Q and R (1959).

Fig. 122. Temple II, central platform, west portion, from NE. Remains of floors and walls, cf. plan 4:K-N and P-R (1959).

Fig. 123. Temple II, central platform, west portion, from S. Remains of floors and walls, cf. plan 4:K-L and R-T (1959).

Fig. 124. Temple II, central platform, west portion, from W. Detail from wall Q, plan 4, hinge-hole for door? (1959).

Fig. 125. Temple II, central platform, west portion, from N. Detail of opening, cf. plan 4:X. In background plaster floor and masonry belonging to Temple Ib (1959).

a four-sided hole, carved out to a depth of 5 cm, and very worn (fig. 124).

The southern part of the preserved masonry in zone B is even more difficult to understand. South of the wall (Q) described above there appeared at level 0.85 a smooth surface of grey-brown plaster (S), a layer of about 5 cm's thickness, and underlain by older layers of plaster (fig. 120). It looks like a smoothed floor and in its context again evokes the impression of a room. It changes to a somewhat deeper, uneven plaster covering (T), which is irregular and stony, and in which larger underlying blocks stick up. A new smooth floor-like plaster layer (U) surrounds the secondary wall (R) at level 0.90-1.00; it ends in the north in a broken edge which is straight-edged but bending at an angle. This layer, when first cleaned in 1955, stretched all the way out to the terrace wall's original course in its demolished portion (D). Its broken edge forms a transition to the broken-up flagged floor (N) lying to its north, and at the same time continues the line of the putative partition-wall (Q). In the floor-surface (U) a semicircular change in the material character (V) of unknown significance was observed, and south of this stood the ruins of a little step-shaped structure (X), or, more circumspectly, an opening in which the "step" formed the threshold (fig. 125).

The structure (X) consisted of four blocks, to the north a roughly shaped foundation block, thereafter a "double-step" of finely cut oblong blocks, partly covered in plaster, and to the south of this a similar block lying 25 cm lower. The accurate alignment of the blocks argues against them being a chance result of stone robbery, and the impression of a planned opening is strengthened by the constructions on either side, which seem to take the structure into account. A 15-cm thick plaster block (Y) flanks it on one side, and the plaster layer (U) on the other, with a straight-cut edge in towards the structure. The reader is referred to a schematic section, fig. 70, which shows these architectural remains.

The last element worthy of mention takes the form of a deeply embedded stretch of wall (Z) along the southern edge, built of ashlars carefully fitted together with a smooth south side. It was partly covered with plaster, and can be seen on an early excavation photograph, fig. 120. At its eastern end it deteriorates into a more haphazard building technique, at its western end it is overlain transversely by a row of three ashlars, presumably secondary, south of the large plaster block (Y). Along its southern edge the plaster floor (E) of Temple I has been broken up, presumably when the wall (Z) was built. It is evident that this wall is positioned to accord with the pool stairway (C), and it has probably once been higher. Its deep placing raises the question of whether the south-west corner of Temple II in continuation of the pool stairway may have been at a lower level, compared with the floor-levels north of the wall. In the opening (X) we would then have an ascent from the one to the other.

In summary it can be said of Temple II's floor-level that it has formed a trapezoid-shaped surface at several levels, but severely damaged in the north and in the south. Zone A seems to provide a well-defined formation, as a major structure with a level of its own, and this formation has also been trape-zoid. It could be recognized by means of founda-tion-walls and portions of vertical walls. West of zone A a building surface was fragmentarily pre-served. In zone A we see the truly sacral area, in the form either of a court or of a building. Here stood a concentration of cult assemblages. In the remaining zone B the floor surfaces were at a lower level than in zone A. Secondary rebuildings and demolitions, however, make the situation unclear, even where the masonry is still existent in zone B. In this area there are no cult assemblages of the same substan-tial character as in zone A.

The central platform's inner structure

The core of the Temple-II platform is naturally first and foremost governed by the fact that it encapsu-lates the Temple-I platform. Above that it adds its own layers of fill, first a layer of rubble as a demo-lition level from the earlier temple, and above it sand. For a closer description reference should be made to the Main Section, sections 2A, 4 and 5.

It is natural that the layers of fill are thickest un-der zone A. At a point in this filling a circular stone-setting (plan 3:17) was excavated under the floor of zone A – a sub-construction built of stone and plas-ter, with large plaster slabs as a bottom layer, or as a relic from the rubble layer in which it was built (figs. 126-127). Stratigraphically it thus lay above

Fig. 126. Temple II, cen-tral platform, central por-tion, from N. Circular sto-ne-setting in the inner substance of the platform, stratigraphically secon-dary in relation to the chamber of Temple I (1958).

107

Fig. 127. Temple II, central platform, central portion, from above, from W. As fig. 126 (1958).

Fig. 128. Temple II, central platform, bull's head and copper fitments in interior of platform, from above, from S (1955).

Fig. 129. Temple II, central platform, alabaster vessel in interior of platform, *in situ* (1958).

the Temple-I floor, and clearly secondary in relation to it. Consequently it must belong to Temple II, and can best be interpreted as a stonelined pit or a stone footing, a basis for a vertical object of unknown nature.

This "core" is much less interesting than the original, and we could let it go with recording it as a levelling-layer for Temple II's new floor-level, forming a well-founded boundary between Temples I and II.

However, there occurs in it a particular group of finds which we vaguely define as hoardings of "deposited" cult-objects. There has already been occasion to mention this phenomenon in connection with the northeast corner of zone A, but we will here pay it further attention, first and foremost on account of a noteworthy piece of sculpture in the round – a copper bull's head (fig. 698).

This object was found in 1955 together with a large quantity of deposited copper fitments (figs.

128 and 707) (see below, p. 265). The find was made at approximately level 1.00, i.e. about ½ m under Temple II's floor, which had here been broken up. It was interpreted by the excavator as buried from Temple II's floor, but no evidence of the existence of a pit was recorded. It lay spread out in the sand over an expanse of about 1 × 1½ m, the copper fitments in several layers. This quite considerable spreading could support a view that the objects were laid down during the construction of the Temple-II platform.

The documentation given here for the place of discovery (fig. 707) is based on a reconstruction, but must in the main be regarded as correct.

With regard to the objects discovered in the northeast corner of zone A, it is impossible to define the circumstances of discovery more precisely, apart from their distribution around and in the framed opening in the flagging here. The excavators suggested a plundering disturbance. The objects comprised copper, lapis lazuli, alabaster vessels and statuettes of copper – a figure of a bird and of a man. It is known that the bird was found just north of the opening, and the man to the north within it (see below, fig. 695).

As another representative assemblage of finds with an association with the "core" of Temple II there should be added still another alabaster vessel (517.AIR) (fig. 129 and 761), found together with a number of copper plates (517.AIY) (see below, p. 260). It was found at a considerable depth, at level 1.61, i.e. a little deeper than the floor-level of Temple I, but at a point where this was broken up. The vessel lay in two heaps of sherds, about 70 cm from each other, and no signs were observed of any digging down from the Temple-II floor. Moreover, the alabaster vessel (517.AIR) could be joined to a sherd (517.B) from the assemblage in the northeast corner. Still another two copper plates (517.AHM) were found close to the alabaster vessel at level 1.58. They lay a few cm behind the Main Section, which registers no sign of a pit (see below, p. 260).

5. Temple II. The Oval Platform

The dominating feature of the architecture of Temple II is an immense oval platform, which nevertheless seems not to have been completed to the eastward (fig. 4). It forms the base on which stands the central platform.

Like the central platform, this platform too is bounded by terrace walls, but because of the varying levels of the territory around the temple the walling varies in height. A change in level is particularly conspicuous in the south-west, where an original deep depression is still retained unfilled, and the oval wall is constructed to conform to it. Thus there is a depression in front of the wall, which has here deep foundations and is built to the height determined for the surface of the platform. At one end of the depression the pool is established.

The surface of the oval platform is kept horizontal, a necessary precondition for the uniform bedding of the central platform, which can be directly read off from the uniformity of the base-measurements along the terrace walls.

If one regards the oval platform as a closed plan, then its main axis lies east-west, but it is not a single concept, as it shows two terrace-wall building phases, IIa and IIb. It is of a considerable size. In its latest form it has measured 58 m across, while its longitudinal axis in the established western half has been about 40 m.

From the point of view of the history of the building, we have reason to believe that this platform followed a tradition from an older platform, connected with Temple I, but that platform is not so well attested in the form of terrace walls. The evidence for continuity which characterizes the central platforms of Temples I and II should therefore be extended to apply also to the oval platforms.

In the high southwesterly terrace wall ways of access can be seen, in the form of well-preserved stairways, belonging to wall IIa. The surface of the oval platform in the south and west has also been utilized, as is evidenced by the placing there of small cult-assemblages. To the east and the west the oval platform has moreover been specially structured to take account of the flanking structures there.

The oval platform's earlier terrace wall

This wall (plan 3:31), with its curving course to the south-west and its original height of about 3½ m fully preserved, stands as one of the most impressive remains of the temple. An advancement of the subsequent wall (41) and a filling-up of the space between them provided good conditions for its preservation. We are thereby provided with knowledge, not only of the actual oval wall, but also of a stretch of wall (32) built onto it at its eastern end. Thereby the impression is given of a sunk "forecourt" in front of the oval wall.

The stratigraphy of the wall is shown in the Main Section, in sections 26A and 27C, and in two sections not previously mentioned, 26C and 27A. Only the Main Section cuts the wall at a right-angle. None of the sections record the absolute bottom of the wall, which, however, is known from a single sondage.

In the Main Section the wall appears in association with a stairway built onto it (N and O) and a massive excavation of the subsoil (10). In section 26A it appears (D) in association with a later well-shaft (C) built onto the outer face, while behind the wall can be seen the same excavation as in the Main Section. Here the face of the wall shows at approximately level 3.00 a set-back running horizontally. In section 27C this situation is repeated, but instead of the well there appears a stairway (C) which, for its full length, is built sideways onto the wall. On account of the diagonal direction of the section two steps can be seen.

Section 26C is quite short, running from the face of the wall to the well-shaft and ending at a random depth. The oval wall (B) appears with its set-back outer face. Above it can be seen a fragment of walling (A) belonging to Temple III's terrace wall,

Fig. 130. Temple II, oval platform in south, from E. Terrace wall IIa on right and IIb on left. In background on an earth-pedestal can be seen Temple III's well, and below it an earlier oval-wall, fig. 80 (1958).

and opposite it a fragment (C) from the same temple's well-shaft. The layers shown vary between occupation deposits (10 and 7), a possible drift-sand layer (9), a layer of fill (6), building-layers (4 and 5) probably from phase IIb, the foundation layer for Temple III (2) and the masonry remains already mentioned from this temple (A and C), the one of them with an excavation layer (1). The surface is that reached by previous excavation in Temple III's levels.

Section 27A cuts across the west end of the wall, so that the stratigraphy on both sides of the wall can be seen, but considerable parts of the interpretation of the section concern special problems which can first be dealt with in other contexts. The layers behind the wall begin at the bottom with the probable subsoil (15), at about level 3.60. Above this can be seen the "clay core" (14 and 17), and above this again the layers of fill in and around the pool stairway, one of them being a building-layer (12), and the upper one (11) perhaps a demolition layer. Here, too, there occurs a wall-foundation (D), which has borne the southern edge of the pool stairway, and, higher up, secondary pool-walling (C). The oval wall itself (A), here without the set-back, is preserved right up to the crown.

A completely different sequence of layers is naturally found in front of the wall, but here it is

marked by a double complication, partly local walling (B) of typical Temple-II type, partly by secondary demolition of this walling in connection with local rebuilding. This walling, of large shaped limestone ashlars, probably belongs to phase IIb, plan 3:43-44, the later oval terrace wall, but it is built up against the earlier one (A) and has an angled course. The section cuts this walling in just such a way that the three northernmost ashlars lie in the length of the section, while the two southernmost, which are set the one above the other, are seen in cross-section (fig. 14).

It is clear that the walling (B) has been demolished. It seems to have stood approximately on the subsoil, and above it is a large layer (3) which marks the filling-up of the robber trench. To judge by this layer the upper edge of the walling has stood at a considerable height.

The layers to the left of the robber-trench (3) must then be fill for the oval platform IIb, cf. the various plans, in particular plan 3.

After this stratigraphical excursus we can describe the wall (31) with its architectural peculiarities (figs. 130-133). It runs in a fairly straight line facing south, but in the neighbourhood of the well it bends and continues in a northwesterly direction, until it ends at the southern edge of the pool stairway. In the east it ends at a transverse terrace wall

Fig. 131. Temple II, oval platform in south, from W. Terrace wall IIa on left and IIb on right. In background obtuse-angled terrace wall built onto the IIa-wall (1958).

Fig. 132. Temple II, oval platform in south, from SW. Oval-wall IIb in front, IIa behind, and the Temple-III well between the two walls (1959).

113

Fig. 133. Temple II, oval platform in south-west, from W. All phases of the temple are represented. In foreground upper parts of walling framing the pool with the pool stairway on left. Behind them the oval-wall IIb, turning at an angle at the edge of the stair, consisting of an ashlar wall on right and a wall of smaller stones on left. Behind this again, the oval-wall IIa with its sideways-built stairway. In background centre can be seen the exposed southern terrace wall of Temple Ia, including its SW-corner. On right remains of Temple III with ruins of well (1960).

Fig. 134. Temple II, oval platform in south, from W. Oval-wall IIa and upper part of frontal stairway (1957).

Fig. 135. Temple II, oval platform in south, from S. Oval-wall IIa and frontal stairway. In foreground oval-wall IIb (1958).

Fig. 136. Temple II, oval platform in south, from WSW. Oval-wall IIa and frontal stairway (1958).

Fig. 137. Temple II, oval platform in south, from S. Change of earth composition in frontal stairway (1960).

Fig. 138. Temple II, oval platform in south-east, from above, from N. Bottom left, oval-wall IIa. With built-on obtuse-angled wall, outer face visible, terrace wall. In the earth-face is the layering left by stone-robbery; the blocks below were placed there provisionally during the excavation (1958).

Fig. 139. Temple II, oval platform in south-east, from W. Outer face of obtuse-angled terrace wall built onto oval-wall IIa. Earth-face in background (1958).

Fig. 140. Temple II, oval platform in south-east, from SE. Rear side of angled wall from figs. 138-139. In background oval-wall IIa. To left, two blocks *in situ* from oval-wall IIb (1958).

Fig. 141. Temple II, oval platform in south-east, from S. Oval-wall IIa with built-on angled wall and wall crack. Up on the platform the course of a local curved terrace wall, cf. fig. 32 (1958).

(32). Both ends of the oval wall are characterized by disturbances caused by rebuildings, but otherwise it is well preserved, apart from damage to the upper rim between the well and the frontal stairway, caused by removal of earth by bulldozing.

The wall consists of two parts, a high lower portion and a low upper portion, set back in relation to the lower. This gives a characteristic profile to the wall-face, in the form of a 15-20 cm wide ledge or bevel. Its character as a terrace wall is shown in the smooth front face, which is furthermore coated with plaster, while the reverse side is raw and unworked. The plaster coat of the front face is only well-preserved part of the way down, to levels about 4.15-4.30, presumably a marking of the wall's latest phase of use. Just above this line of division there comes a large original break between the well and the frontal stairway (fig. 131). The top of the wall is at level 2.20, its bottom at 5.70, at least in a sondage near the frontal stairway. The wall was thus standing in the subsoil-water. It was built of the local stone set in gypsum-plaster.

The frontal stairway (33) was placed in the middle of the south-facing stretch of wall, at a somewhat oblique angle (figs. 134-136). It was built of the same material as the wall, and coated with plaster on all visible surfaces. The plaster coating stopped at the same height as on the wall.

The stairway consisted of nine steps leading down to a damaged foot. Because of the possible presence of foundation-offerings its inner structure was excavated in its full depth, but built up again on completion of the investigation. It consisted of two side-walls flanking a core of sand. The walls were about 55 cm thick, with their base at level 5.50. The stairway was first built after the oval wall had been raised and coated with plaster, also over the area where the stairway joined it. The core of the stairway showed three layers of sand, the upper one containing clay, the next of loose sand and the lowest of hard, compacted sand. In the loose sand there occurred intrusions of dark soil, some of them long with a circular cross-section, up to 10 cm in diameter, some of peculiar shapes, one of which was bent at an angle, about ½ m in length, 30 cm at its broadest point and 10 cm at its thickest (fig. 137). These dark patches presumably derive from pieces of wood embedded in the sand. Potsherds and bones were also found.

Onto the eastern end of the oval wall there was built a local terrace wall (32), 1 ½ m high, which in turn bends in an obtuse angle (figs. 138-139). It has an irregular reverse side, but is coated with plaster on the front, though not along the lower edge (figs. 140-141). It is of the local stone set in plaster, but is only partly preserved, the southern end being bro-

Fig. 142. Temple II, oval platform in south, from S. Oval-wall IIa with stone rings at its foot, enclosing pottery ovens (1957).

Fig. 143. Temple II, oval platform in south, from above, from S. As fig. 142 (1957).

ken off in a slanting line which ends in total demolition. The general picture shows that this is the result of stone-robbery. A large excavation has cut the wall away, and it is its close proximity to the oval wall of IIb that has sealed its fate. The ashlars of the IIb wall have here been completely plundered.

In the remaining piece of the angled wall (32) we can see a terracing which has delimited a sunk area in front of the oval wall (31). It should be remembered that the area east of this locality shows an original rise of ground, and that there were therefore differences in level to be adjusted. The building of the IIb oval wall and its later destruction by stone-robbers prevents us from determining more accurately the nature of the limited sunk area.

The angled wall has its top at level 3.10, but this has not been enough to complete the terracing. The shortage has apparently been made up by the building of still another angled wall (34). Its base is at level 3.17, but it is poorly preserved. Such parallel terrace walls, at intervals from each other to form several steps, are also known from the walls surrounding the pool.

At the east end of the oval wall still another terrace wall (35) was found, but this time up on the oval platform itself (fig. 32). It is built of stone and plaster, but in a remarkable undulating course. It starts from the oval wall, and is broken off at the other end; its southern side is plastered, while its northern side is entirely irregular. It has its base at the same level as the previously mentioned wall (34), and is preserved to about half a metre's height. We are not able to interpret this wall's architectural purpose, nor its con-

Fig. 144. Temple II, oval platform in south, from E. Detail of pottery oven in stone ring as figs. 142-143 (1957).

nection with the constructional history of the temple. Its connection with the oval wall was obscured by a preliminary trial trench, but it was probably built secondarily onto the oval wall. At the other end it passes and terminates an apparent continuation of walling belonging to Temple Ib, but the associations here are not satisfactorily worked out.

About ½ m west of the frontal stairway there were found at the foot of the oval wall at level 4.97 two stone rings (36 and 37) in which pottery ovens had been placed (figs. 142-144), see below, p. 231.

Fig. 145. Temple II, oval platform in south-west, from NW. Temple-well, partly collapsed. Bottom left, oval-wall IIa. The round well-shaft belongs to phase IIb, at the bottom a square well-shaft belonging to oval-wall IIa (1957).

Fig. 146. Temple II, oval platform in south-west, from SW. Oval-wall IIa with built-on side-stairway to temple-well. Behind the oval-wall, Temple-I stairways and pool stairway. In background Temple II's central platform (1957).

Fig. 147. Temple II, oval platform in south-west, from SSE. Oval-wall IIa with well-stairway. At bottom Temple-III well-shaft (1957).

Fig. 148. Temple II, oval platform in west, from S. Oval-wall IIa on right and IIb on left. In front of the IIb wall can be seen a rectangular platform with stone pillars (1957).

At the place where the oval wall bends it passes the temple-well (38). As has been stated earlier, this well also functioned later, its well-shaft being built upwards when it was incorporated in an extension of the oval platform, phase IIb. But originally the well lay at the foot of the oval wall, framed by a square well-head measuring about 1 x 1 m (fig. 145). Its level is only approximately known as about 4.75, so that the well-shaft had not far to go to reach water-level. For technical reasons the shaft could not be investigated more closely, but it was also square, with walls constructed of long flat stones.

Down to this well from the crown of the oval wall led a long, sideways-built stairway (39), built in the same technique as the wall itself (figs. 146-147, 74). It was well-preserved and ended at the bottom in a heap of stones below the level of the well-head, cf. plan 1:30. With its 15 surviving steps it descends for 3 m. One of the upper steps differs from the rest in having twice as large an upper surface.

The oval wall itself ends, after a final 2½-m stretch, in a large breach at the pool stairway. It is a sloping break running 2 m down from the wall-top, and is undoubtedly the result of local reconstruction. The oval wall has certainly originally been connected with the pool stairway in its full height. This point coincides with a change in direction of the pool stairway, which here turns in a very obtuse angle.

The association of the oval wall with Temple II in the history of the building is at least not contradicted by its stratigraphical associations. That this needs to be said is due to its divergence from the building technique otherwise characteristically used for Temple II - the cut ashlars. It can perhaps be said that, for example, section 27C, with its excavation for the building, cf. layers 11-17, comes very close to a proof for a view that the oval wall cannot be other than an early Temple-II construction. Other weighty arguments can, however, also be adduced.

Firstly, the oval wall IIa encloses and covers the two stairways of Temple I in the southwest sector, and is therefore clearly later than these. Secondly, the crown of the wall, which is preserved for long stretches, shows clearly that it delimits a surface at level 2.20, and this level coincides with the base of the central platform of Temple II. Thirdly, there are found, on the oval platform formed by the wall and at the summit-height of the wall, several structures which stand upon the remains of a plaster floor. Admittedly this floor has never been systematically exposed over any large areas, but it appears as a layer at the appropriate level in every relevant section.

The oval wall IIa continues, in its second half, in a similarly curved course in the west (40) at the other side of the pool stairway (fig. 148). Here, however, the wall is standing on much higher ground and is consequently of more modest height. The wall is badly preserved and was only followed for a distance of about 17 m.

The wall does not form a simple continuing stretch, for its investigated portion ends in a stairway and a little oval structure, which will be described below. The main stretch south of this structure consists of large and smaller stones, mortared with fine-grained white plaster. On its western side the wall is coated with plaster, while its east side is irregularly constructed, which justifies the interpretation of a terrace wall. At the southern end it terminates in a disordered condition, without any full contact with the northern edge of the pool stairway, presumably as a consequence of local reconstruction.

The stratigraphy around this wall is illustrated by *section 22* (D), which cannot, however, give an unequivocal statement of its placing in the constructional history of the temple. The stratification to the west is not extensive enough clearly to distinguish the various phases. A change in soil character above the wall in section 22 suggests that it has been higher, though hardly more than a short metre high. It is founded on the clay core, which must be considered older. In this situation we must resort to the expedient of defining the wall as a continuation of the high oval-wall (31) south of the pool stairway. Its course, and the similarity in construction of the two, support this attribution to the oval-wall IIa. It is made to some degree more likely by the fact that this wall, too, has a later successor lying about 2 m further to the west.

North of the little oval structure the wall (40) continues as a short projection sticking out from the north end of the structure and consisting of fairly small, partly shaped pieces of limestone set in white plaster. This portion of walling is broken off after a run of only 0.75 m, and at this point our knowledge of the oval wall IIa ends.

The oval platform's later terrace wall

Like its predecessor this oval wall also consists of two halves, meeting at the pool stairway (plan 3). Presumably partly in order to bring the prominent southern and southwestern portions of this wall into stylistic harmony with the central platform, they were now also built of large cut limestone blocks (figs. 131-132, 149-150). The building-material ensured that this wall, too, did not remain un-

Fig. 149. Temple II, oval platform in south, from W. Oval-wall IIb, partly demolished, outer face. Behind it, wall IIa with frontal stairway (1958).

robbed, though an impressive ruin has been left. The northwestern portion was also renewed, though less ostentatiously.

The southwestern curve (41) of the oval wall IIb only appears stratigraphically in the Main Section (P), where it stands with its base at level 6.50, in other words deep below the water-table. It stands here as a terrace wall, with smooth outer face and raw rear face. Layers of sediment and/or fill occupy the interval between the two oval walls (N and P). In front of wall IIb can be seen sedimentary layers, the upper ones, however, representing layers filling up a robber trench.

With a base at level 6.50 and a top partially appearing at about level 2.00 we have here before us a wall at least 4½ m high. It is built of large blocks in horizontal bands or courses, and they are mortared with grey-white or grey-brown plaster. Various building methods are employed, where the stones may be laid in alternate bands as pairs of "stretchers" or alone as "headers" (fig. 151). But they may also be placed in regular courses, like a two-stone wall, of large flat blocks of uniform size.

An almost complete robbery has removed the eastern end of the wall, leaving only two deep-lying lonely blocks. The robber-excavation can be seen in a nearby wall of earth on an excavation photograph (fig. 152). In a large concave breach of

the wall's upper portion another robber situation is portrayed, similarly marked out on a wall of earth (fig. 153). The robber hole has been of such an extent that there has been room at the bottom for a whole row of blocks, torn loose but left (fig. 154).

The outer face of the wall is characterized by close fitting of the blocks and by elegant surface treatment, though showing weathering in places (figs. 149, 155). In addition to walling in this technique there are also found fragments of a wall of smaller stones, a superstructure which displays a plastered face (fig. 150). In this one can see either a deliberate change of style or else a secondary addition in connection with reconstruction.

A single stone in an upper course may give the maximum height of the wall at level 1.92. Analogous to the earlier oval-wall this wall too should have had a frontal stairway, but of this no trace survives.

The termination of the wall in the area of the pool is complicated, and marked by rebuildings which have repeatedly modified the architecture – a situation which probably cannot be fully unravelled and to some degree must be described in connection with the following chapter on the pool.

As a commencing point we can take a joint between the stones of the oval wall running vertically

Fig. 150. Temple II, oval platform in south, from SE. Outer face of oval-wall IIb (1958).

Fig. 151. Temple II, oval platform in south, from E. Broken-off edge from demolition at east end of wall-course of oval-wall IIb. On right, temple-well from Temple III, resting on earth-pedestal (1958).

Fig. 152. Temple II, oval platform in south, from W. Oval-wall IIb, rear side. In the earth-face behind can be seen large layerings from the robbery of the wall. On left, oval-wall IIa (1958).

5.40 m south of the flanks of the pool stairway (fig. 156). From here the wall continues in two directions, the one a continuing course on a sharp curve (42), the other a cross-wall (43). Onto the cross-wall there is built still another wall (44). All three walls are deeply founded, and at least two of them (43 and 44) appear to have been considerably demolished (fig. 157).

We interpret these three wallings as contemporary with the building of the main portion (41). They can have functioned as a terraced termination to the oval platform at its junction with the pool-area. They represent a first phase in this architectural formation.

The cross-wall (43), according to this interpretation, forms the actual termination of the oval wall in a right-angled turn. It is partially preserved, in two courses with its outer face to the north, and it is built onto the earlier oval wall (31). As it thus delimits the oval platform, it must be assumed to have had the same height as the oval wall (41). Onto it another wall (44) has been built at an obtuse angle; it is only preserved in a single course, and its outer surface is clearly facing west. In its full height it would mask the older oval-wall and its stairway. One could thus say that the oval wall (41) terminates here in a double bend.

Both walls (43 and 44) have the same base level at about 5.00, and must have been about 3 m high. In their capacity as termination of the oval wall they have at the same time formed a delimitation of the eastern edge of the pool, but they have been demolished in connection with later changes of construction. They figure in section 27A with massive traces of a secondary filling-up after demolition.

The third stretch of wall (42) can be seen to continue from the above-mentioned wall-joint, though only in one course (fig. 156). It is particularly the rear side of this wall which has been exposed, while the finely cut front face could only be observed in places under a secondary wall (45) built above it. The wall (42) continues the course of the oval wall (41) as a slightly lowered course exclusively of "headers", and curves in a very sharp swing to end at the termination of the earlier oval-wall. It is probably only to a minor degree demolished, insofar as its top level of about 5.00 is seen to coincide with the bottom level of the other two walls (43 and 44); in other words, the curved wall (42) forms the front edge of a terrace which has the other two as rear edge. This little terrace is in reality part of the setting of the pool, and it was taken out of use by later changes of construction, which reduced the area of the pool. At the same time the wall (42) is a continuation of the oval wall (41) in a curve from the wall-joint to its junction with the pool stairway. This junction again takes place at the point where the pool stairway changes direction.

As support for this interpretation we possess still another characteristic reconstructional feature. The curved wall (42) is over-built by a secondary wall of smaller stones (45), slightly displaced and now turning in obtuse-angled bends (fig. 133). So far as can be seen, this secondary wall both continues the oval wall and forms the eastern edge of the pool. It begins at the wall-joint and ends at the same point as its predecessor. It must belong to a final phase in the constructional history of the pool.

For practical reasons we defer the continued discussion of this walling until the next chapter, and content ourselves here with the conclusion that the oval-wall IIb had in this area a special elaboration and shows signs of reconstructions. These reconstructions can have been occasioned by the fact that the framing of the pool in the course of time de-

Fig. 153. Temple II, oval platform in south, from NE. Oval-wall IIb, rear side with robber-intrusion in the wall and robbery-layering in the earth-face behind (1958).

Fig. 154. Temple II, oval platform in south, from E. Oval-wall IIb, rear side. Pulled-out stone blocks are *in situ* (1958).

Fig. 155. Temple II, oval platform in south-west, from S. Oval-wall IIb, outer face with locally built-on walling. Behind it, upper edge of walls framing pool and oval-wall IIa. Beyond these the west portion of the oval platform with continuing course of oval-walls, though partially demolished (1959).

Fig. 156. Temple II, oval platform in south-west, from SW. Oval-wall IIb with wall-joint and change of material from ashlars to smaller stones (1959).

Fig. 157. Temple II, oval platform in south-west, from SE. Deeply-founded walling between oval-walls IIa on right and IIb on left. Older transition zone between oval platform and pool. The north wall of the pool can be glimpsed as three blocks standing on edge in a row behind the small-stone portion of wall IIb (1959).

Fig. 158. Temple II, oval platform in west, from SW. Outer face of demolished oval-wall IIb with platform for stone pillars and remains of others in foreland. Behind lies oval-wall IIa. In foreground the northern margin of the pool. The earth-face in the background forms section 21 (1960).

Fig. 159. Temple II, oval platform in west, from N. Oval-wall IIb with platform for stone pillars. In foreground a possible threshold-stone. In background the pool and oval-wall IIb (1959).

Fig. 160. Temple II, oval platform in west, from E. In foreground stone-set drain in platform. In background rear sides of oval-walls IIa and IIb (1957).

Fig. 161. Temple II, oval platform in west, from S. Oval-walls IIa and IIb and drain. The earth-face in background to right bears remains of Temple III's western terrace wall. In foreground surviving steps down to the pool (1959).

manded continuously increased height, presumably to keep pace with growing accumulation outside.

These accumulations are impressively demonstrated by relatively high-lying additions built onto the face of the oval wall south of the pool, where the walls of a little room stand out from the wall, as it were half way up its face (plan 6:59, fig. 155).

In this feature, and in the weathering of the outer face (fig. 150), we can see evidence of a long-lasting period of use for the building which is characterized by the IIb oval wall. It is in the light of this long duration that we should perhaps view the small upper portions built of smaller stones instead of ashlars. One can moreover observe a beginning tendency for the wall to bulge. As it furthermore had a predecessor (IIa), there is here strong reason to allot a long life to Temple II.

Regarding the question of ascribing the oval wall to Temple II, this is based on the fact that Temple III can scarcely come into consideration. The oval wall stands in a reasonable relationship in level to the base of Temple II's central platform, whereas a ½ m difference in level must be reckoned with in relation to the base of the Temple-III platform. In addition attention should be called to the constructional history of the well, which is known to have been built to function in relation both to our oval platform IIb

and to Temple III, but with a separate building phase for each, cf. the next section. This is qualified evidence for the oval wall being older than Temple III.

The oval-wall IIb now continues north of the pool in a course parallel to wall IIa (plans 3 & 5). It has also been of modest height, and it is badly demolished, in places indeed completely absent (fig. 158). This wall (46-48) has been moved outwards by about 2½ m in relation to its predecessor (figs. 4, 148), and is regarded as later in date, insofar as it apparently demolishes the western edge of the earlier wall's oval structure. The admittedly not particularly informative stratigraphy at least does not contradict this interpretation, cf. sections 21 (F) and 22 (C). At the point of the latter section the wall forms a rear edge for a rectangular platform which is built onto the front face of the wall, cf. section 22 (A and B).

The wall is of quite heterogeneous construction, probably as a result of local reconstructions (plan 3). Over a long stretch (46) it is described as built of large and smaller stones set in clay, with an irregular eastern side and a trued-up western face. In places it also contains smaller limestone ashlars. It changes direction several times in more or less accentuated bends, and its base level slopes slightly downwards from north to south. As a datum point for a determination of the original surface at the foot of the wall we can use the plaster floor of the rectangular platform. It lies a few cm above the base of the wall, almost at level 3.30. If the top of the wall is assumed to have been level with the surface of the oval platform, then it has been about a metre high. A single large, finely shaped limestone block a little to the north of the rectangular platform may be interpreted as a possible surviving threshold-stone from an opening in the wall (fig. 159).

Thereafter comes a piece of walling (47), which is not described. It runs from the southeast corner of the rectangular platform as far as a cross-wall (49) (fig. 160). It is more deeply founded, resulting in it being preserved to a height of 60 cm. Here it runs above an earlier structure, a large double base or plinth block described under Temple I. The east side of the wall is particularly regular, and the structural peculiarities point to find circumstances which have not been elucidated.

Where it ends there was found a continuation (48), which runs onward to the edge of the pool (fig. 161). This piece of walling consists of three large cut stone blocks which are relatively deeply founded. A straight western edge suggests a front face. It remained unexplained why this stretch of wall differed, both technically and in its deep placing, from the rest of wall IIb.

The cross-wall (49) lies in continuation of an older wall with the same course, which has already been described under Temple I (figs. 82, 160). We can here add that the older stretch of wall is overlain both by wall IIa and by IIb. It was only preserved in a single course and was founded on the "clay core", cf. section 25, dealt with in the next chapter. The later cross-wall (49), which is curved, is without a description, but it seems to be built in one with the wall (47) from which it runs. As to its function nothing can be deduced with certainty.

The continuation of the oval wall IIb in the northwest and north is shown on plan 5. The first portion (1) ends blind; the next portion (2) is built of stone, with clay and plaster as mortar. The plaster in particular occurred in large horizontal sheets. The wall was in places preserved in up to 60 cm's height, and had a north-facing front, while the rear ran out into

large layers of plaster, the extent of which can be seen to effect in the Main Section and in section 30, while section 31, which is described below, only showed deep diggings in the probable position of the wall.

From the Main Section we see that the walling in question (A) is represented by a large sheet of light brownish plaster with stones and plaster fragments, lying at a level which agrees with the base of Temple II's central platform. This sheet is of greatest thickness at the course of the wall, but runs out both fore and back. The exposed rear extension to the south shows a broken edge.

In section 30, which does not fully cut across the course of the wall (A), occurs something most resembling the remains of a double wall of stones in clay with a flat plaster surface between. The rear extension to the south shows a broken edge. None of the sections shows the vertical front of the wall. Thus there are also unexplained aberrant circumstances in connection with this part of the IIb oval wall.

With regard to the placing of the whole of the northwest half of the oval wall within the temple's constructional history, we must again, and particularly, point to the real continuation of the line of the high oval wall (41) in the south (plan 3). To this can be added its secondary relationship with the oval wall IIa. Moreover, its foreland is characterized by stone pillars, some rising quite high, which point to a late situation. For stratigraphical reasons we have no reason to involve Temple III in our consideration, except insofar as its base level can be claimed to have put the whole complex underground, and thereby to have sealed it as a late phase of Temple II.

On the oval platform and in its western foreland there occurs a series of special structures. We have already mentioned an oval and a rectangular structure. In the following section these special small architectural features will be described, with the exception of structures with relation to the pool and the pool stairway, which will first be dealt with in the next chapter, as these features comprise a single unity.

The oval platform´s floor-level and its foreland

On the oval platform's southern portion, above the oval wall IIa and west of the frontal stairway, there appeared a peculiar altar-construction (plan 3:50). The structure's connection with Temple II is very clear: it stands on the floor of the platform a little distance from the foot of the central platform, and

it is secondarily overlain by Temple III, the terrace wall of which passes closely over it.

It consists of two parts, a relatively intact structure and a portion which has been demolished and buried (fig. 162). The structure is almost 3 m long and contains a central portion in the shape of a rec-

Fig. 162. Temple II, oval platform in south, from S. Remains of altar on floor level above oval-wall IIa (1955).

tangular platform with a damaged south end. It measures about 1 × 1½ m and has been almost 60 cm high. Its outer sides consist of large flat limestone slabs, standing on edge, with finely cut outer faces. The interior of this platform is filled with a mass of stones, plaster and fragments of gypsum, and in this there is embedded near one of the sides a massive upright-standing stone block of cylindrical form, in such a way that its plaster-coated upper surface is at a level with that of the platform. It has a diameter of 65 cm and a hewn area on the eastern side, running vertically down the stone.

On both of the longer sides of the platform masonry has been built on, to the west in the shape of a stepped buttress of plaster, stone and gypsum fragments (fig. 163). The uppermost step almost reached the surface of the platform. The addition to the east consisted of a shaped block of stone and a more loosely built-up portion in continuation of the block. The block had a concave eastern side, while the built-up portion was covered by a slab, in which an angled groove had been cut (fig. 162).

In a pit below this structure there was found still another cylindrical block of the same dimensions as that embedded in the platform (fig. 164). Its upper end had, however, a somewhat larger diameter, and

here in addition a raised edge running around the block and partly covered by plaster (fig. 165). The structure seems thus to have been remodelled, with the pious burial of the one cylinder. Its original appearance is thereby made difficult to establish. The slab with the angled groove, mentioned above, was not lying *in situ*. The block with the concavely curved eastern side could perhaps suggest an original twin-construction, the one part of which had been buried on the spot. In a reconstruction it was decided, however, to place the two cylinders the one above the other (fig. 166).

This altar's individual stratigraphy, as far as concerns the disposal of the discarded element, is illustrated by *section 20*, which is drawn at an angle (fig. 164). Here can be seen the pit (4), with the discarded stone cylinder (1). At the top level of the pit we note layers of plaster (3 and 5), presumably remains of plaster floors on Temple II's oval platform. Under these come layers of fill, which are followed by the older "clay-core" (10 and 11).

On the western area of the oval platform, north of the pool, the following structures are found: a detached fragment of walling (51), an oval structure in connection with wall IIa, a rectangular structure associated with wall IIb, and, in front of the latter wall, isolated occurrences of worked stones, which can in the main be interpreted as having served cult purposes.

The oval structure (52) has been about 6 m long and about 4 m broad, lying with its longer axis on the course of the oval wall (fig. 167). At its southern end there was in addition found a stairway leading up onto the oval platform. The oval structure had a floor at level 2.80, in other words at least ½ m under the assumed floor-level of the oval platform. It has thereby given the impression of a little sunk yard, to which there can have been access via the demolished western side. By this interpretation the western half of the wall around the yard would at the same time have functioned as a part of the terrace wall of the oval platform, forming a bulge in it.

The surrounding walling still rises, in spite of demolition, a little above the floor, and consists of large and smaller stones set in clay. This wall (52), however, surrounds an inner walling (53), surviving in three pieces and forming likewise an oval figure. It has used the same building technique as the outer walling. The northern portion of the inner walling overlies the outer, so that the inner oval must be assumed to be later in date than the outer.

Within the inner oval figure remains of the floor (54) survived, a thin layer of white fine-grained plaster. In places 3-4 layers could be seen, one above the other. Between the two wallings in the southeastern area flat stone slabs formed a paving (55) serving as a foundation for a stretch of plaster flooring.

The stairway (56) consisted of stone and stone slabs laid in white fine-grained plaster (fig. 168). It was 0.75 m wide, and the three surviving steps rose a half-metre upwards. Above the uppermost step lay a heap of stones as a foundation for the succeeding steps. The south side of the stairway showed traces of a wall.

South-west of the stairway and at right-angles to the oval wall IIa (40) there was preserved a short piece of walling (57) of stones and clay, while a similar piece (58) could also be seen north-west of the stairway, apparently with a south-turned face. It was built in one with the oval wall IIb and on the whole gave the impression of being secondary in relation to the oval structure here described.

A sondage was dug down from the plaster floor in the oval structure to virgin soil, in actuality from level 2.86 to 3.59. It registered six man-made layers – from top downwards: 1) 6 cm of plaster as floor of the structure, consisting of four thin plaster layers, 2) 12 cm of stone as foundation for the plaster floor, consisting of large flat limestone slabs, 3) 24 cm of grey sand with fragments of plaster, as fill for the oval platform, 4) a 4 cm thick heterogeneous layer of fragments of gypsum, plaster or powdery sandy

clay, the whole layer resembling a broken-up floor, 5) 10 cm yellow-grey sand, and 6) 17 cm grey clayey sand as the "clay core". Particularly the fourth layer, which occurred at level 3.28, gives grounds for a belief that there is here a level with connection to Temple I, but scarcely acknowledged. We draw attention to a related occurrence in section 22 (21) and reiterate that the western sector here dealt with has only been systematically dug to virgin soil along the soil walls of the sections.

The rectangular platform (59) in front of the foot of the oval wall IIb measures about 2 × 3½ m, and forms a little low terrace, on which there were placed two stone pilasters up against the oval wall and a third pillar in the middle of the platform and thus free on all four sides (figs. 148, 169).

As a frame around the platform there had been built a wall with relatively deep-founded foundations of large and smaller stones set in clay (fig. 170). Above ground-surface more chosen, slab-like stones had been employed, so that the frame was more or less flush with a floor of light fine-grained plaster on the surface of the platform. Along the east side the oval wall IIb formed a higher backdrop.

The two flanking stone pilasters on the platform are highly complex architectural miniatures. The southern one (60) points upwards on an early excavation photograph, which tells us of a protruding, though broken off, top, which has later disappeared. The whole block was later taken to pieces, and the following features appeared (fig. 171): Concealed beneath the plaster floor was a bevelled foundation-stone with a rectangular hole. In this, held by plaster, was inserted a long slim limestone pillar of rectangular cross-section, standing vertically and preserved to a length of about 1 m (figs. 172-174). Its foot was cut as a tenon which fitted into the hole in the foundation-stone. The protruding top mentioned above is in reality a part of this stone, which thus has been still longer. This stone pillar was built up on all four sides with stones, fragments and plaster, and coated with plaster on all sides, including the top. This built-up top surface lay at level 2.23, and the built-up block has thus risen 95 cm above the platform-floor at level 3.28. Out of its top surface protruded the rest of the stone pillar.

When the surrounding masonry was removed this "core" of stone was revealed as a damaged piece of stone, which may give the reason for the masonry support.

The northern stone pillar (61) provided an exact parallel to the one just described (figs. 175, 169). The built-up portion was 1.02 m high, and up from it projected the broken-off remains of the inner block for a further 30 cm in height. It was not further investigated.

Fig. 163. Temple II, oval platform in south, from W. As fig. 162 (1957).

Fig. 164. Temple II, oval platform in south, from E. As fig. 162, with buried cylindrical stone block (1957).

Fig. 165. Temple II, oval platform in south, from E. As fig. 164, with exposed cylindrical stone block (1957).

Fig. 166. Temple II, oval platform in south, from S. Buried cylindrical stone block placed on top of the corresponding block *in situ* (1958).

Fig. 167. Temple II, oval platform in west, from N. Little oval structure in association with oval-wall IIa. On right, oval-wall IIb (1960).

Fig. 168. Temple II, oval platform in west, from SW. Stair in oval-wall IIa by little oval structure. In background drain from Temple II. At top, western terrace wall of Temple III (1960).

Fig. 169. Temple II, oval platform in west, from SW. Platform with stone pillars at foot of oval-wall IIb. Behind it can be seen oval-wall IIa with little oval structure (1959).

Fig. 170. Temple II, oval platform in west, from above, from N. Platform with stone pillars, partly exposed (1957).

137

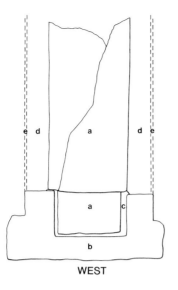
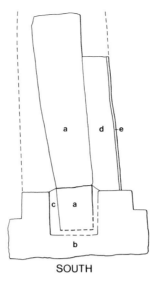

WEST   SOUTH

Fig. 171. Temple II, oval platform in west. Elevations of southern stone pillar, from W, cf. fig. 173 and from S, cf. fig. 174. a) limestone pillar, b) foundation stone, c) plaster, d) secondary masonry of rubble, stones and plaster, e) plaster coating. 1:20.

Fig. 172. Temple II, oval platform in west, from above from NW. Southern stone pillar partly peeled of masonry. A slim interior pillar in a foundation-block (1961).

The upper part of these two stone pillars may also have been surrounded by masonry with the object of making them more like the central pillar (62), which was one single massive block of light fine-grained limestone (figs. 176-177). This block had at the bottom two narrow bevelled ledges, after which follows a roughly cut foundation portion (figs. 174, 178). It is well-preserved, about 1.25 m high, and its upper surface reveals an irregular depression with remains of plaster (fig. 170). It can

therefore be assumed that it has served as a plinth for some unknown object.

On the free floor-surface of the platform, between the central block and the oval wall, there had been in addition inserted two connecting cross-walls (63), preserved in one course and consisting of stones set in clay. They rose 10-15 cm above the floor.

On the open ground in front of the oval wall IIb (fig. 158) there were found, at depths which can

Fig. 173. Temple II, oval platform in west, from W. As fig. 172. Behind, outer plastered face of oval-wall IIa. At top, Temple III's west wall (1961).

Fig. 174. Temple II, oval platform in west, from S. Southern stone pillar. Platform excavated in depth (1961).

Fig. 175. Temple II, oval platform in west, from N. Northern stone pillar (1959).

only justify an association with Temple II, other occurrences of finely cut limestone or remains of such, four in all. The first (64) was a rectangular foundation-block, badly hacked and with its southern end completely hacked away (fig. 179). It had a 35-cm deep rectangular hole in the middle. The second (65) was a rectangular block with a depression about 2 cm deep worn in the centre. The third (66) had been removed from its original position, but in its dimensions and with its carved-out hole offered an exact parallel to the first object (64) (fig. 180). The fourth object was in principle a parallel to the central pillar on the little platform. It was only exposed and measured-in as it projected from a section wall, cf. section 21 (E) (fig. 158). It was a massive standing-stone with double ledges at the bottom. Its upper surface had been cut away.

Discoveries of worked stone blocks were also made by the northern edge of the oval platform (plan 5). Thus close behind the Main Section there was found an extremely remarkable worked stone altar (3) (fig. 181). Its stratigraphical placing coincides with the level for the oval wall IIb in the Main Section (A). The stone block, whose measurements were 1.85 × 1.40 × 0.35 m, possessed a tenon to fit into a wall, probably the oval wall of Temple IIb. Its under side was roughly cut, whereas its upper side and edges were in contrast finely cut, its upper side

being indeed polished so that all tool-marks had disappeared. Along the three edges a groove of ½-1 cm's depth had been pricked out.

A little to the east of this stone block and at a similar depth a circular base-stone (4) was found. It was 40 cm thick and badly hacked on the periphery. In the centre it had an irregular four-sided hole, going all the way through. According to the registration it was found in a secondary position, but the reasons for this conclusion are not further elaborated.

Up on the oval platform in the north-east there were finally found two parallel walls, cf. *section 31* with accompanying plan (figs. 182-183). The walls (B and C) were 3 m long and consisted of stones set in clay. The two opposing wall-faces were smooth-finished, while the other sides were roughly built. Between the walls, at the bottom there was a burnt layer with many burnt bones, though in the upper part of the layer the bones were only partly burnt, or not at all. The same layer lay in heaps outside the walls.

Section 31 shows this situation. The walls (B and C) stand at a level flush with the oval platform of Temple II, and the stratigraphy of the burnt layers (8 and 9) is shown. The site seems to be cult-determined, and with it is associated a group of objects which is not met with elsewhere, small button-like

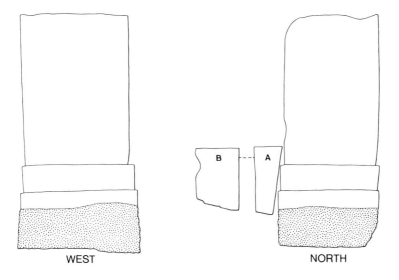

WEST   NORTH

Fig. 176. Temple II, oval platform in west, from W and N. Elevations of central stone pillar. A, wedge; B, oval-wall IIb. 1:20.

Fig. 177. Temple II, oval platform in west, from NW. Central stone pillar (1961).

discs of fired clay with seal-impressions stamped on one side (see figs. 783-788).

Otherwise section 31 is dominated by a large monotonous sand-layer (4), which makes difficult a separation of the upper temple-levels. An original section of the foot of the tell-surface here runs out at level 2.00, while the subsoil (6) appears at level 3.30. Masonry (A) in the extreme north has been already mentioned under Temple I. An excavation (12) in the extreme south indicates the robbery of Temple III's terrace wall. Another excavation (2) down from the surface suggests perhaps the removal of masonry at the Temple-III level. A third excavation (3) lies on the line of oval wall IIb's course in the north, and should perhaps be interpreted accordingly.

We have herewith described the whole of the western half of Temple II's oval platform, insofar as its terrace walls and its utilization are concerned. As far as we know it, it shows a bipartite constructional history, characterized by an expansion of the

Fig. 178. Temple II, oval platform in west, from NW. Stone pillars on rectangular platform at foot of oval-wall IIb (1960).

Fig. 179. Temple II, oval platform in west, foreland, from N. Blocks in front of oval-wall IIb (1960).

Fig. 180. Temple II, oval platform in west, foreland, from E. Blocks in front of oval-wall IIb (1960).

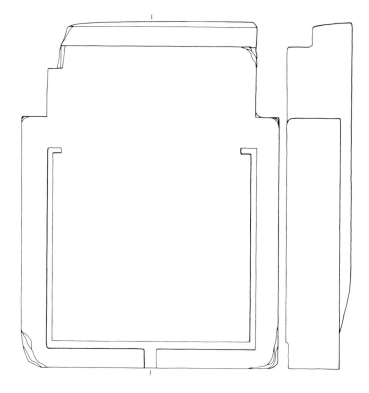

Fig. 181. Temple II, oval platform in north. Elevation of altar stone. 1:20.

platform. It had high walls in the south and southwest, low in the west and north. The younger oval platform, with its 58 m's width, is a very expansive construction, and it shows also signs of building activity in the shape of various altar-like structures, most prominently in the west. The area in the north, however, has not been intensively investigated, while in the south we must reckon with severe secondary disturbances. On the other hand, the expansion of the platform in the south occasioned a filling which left the terrace wall of the older phase, wall IIa, beautifully preserved. The southwest corner of the oval platform is furthermore, and decisively, affected by the presence there of the pool and its stairway, which will be described in chapter 6.

Where the sections contain relevant evidence, it appears that the oval platform was covered by layers deposited at the time of Temple III's construction.

Fig. 182. Temple II, oval platform in north, from E. Parallel walls on platform (1960).

Fig. 183. Temple II, oval platform in north, from SE. As fig. 182 (1960).

Fig. 184. Temple II, oval platform in west, from E. Drain from Temple II's western terrace-wall, here robbed. Drain-stone with channel bottom left. Overlying can be seen the rear side of Temple III's western terrace wall (1955).

The oval platform's inner structures

Temple II's oval platform has presumably in both its phases kept much the same surface level, which can best be defined from the fully preserved terrace wall IIa, the top of which lies at level 2.20 (plan 3). The absolutely highest known level on terrace wall IIb is 1.92.

Within this oval platform there are embedded a well-shaft (38) leading to the temple-well in phase IIb, a drain (67) in the west leading from the central platform, and secondary masonry in the south-east. This last-mentioned masonry is, however, much later in date than the temple buildings, cf. chapter 9.

When the later phase of the oval platform totally covered the temple-well, it was necessary to construct a well-shaft leading up to the new ground-surface (fig. 145). Phase IIb of the well appears as such a shaft, constructed of five round cast drums, set one above the other. They do not reach all the way up, the last metre being missing. The uppermost drum is moreover in fragments. The reason for this is a new reconstruction when the well was adapted for the needs of Temple III.

The drums in the well's phase IIb are fashioned as large rings of stone and fragments of plaster cemented with white plaster. They were built on the spot, one by one. They have a rectangular cross-section and are of varying heights. The following heights have been measured: about 25, 30, 50, 45 and 25 cm. Their thickness is about 50 cm, thickest at the bottom. They are joined together with plaster and smoothly plastered on the inner sides, more roughly on the outer.

In this way a slightly oval well-shaft was formed, with a diameter of between 1.30 and 1.45 m. On the inner side there were three vertical rows of holes to facilitate descent into the well.

To achieve continuity with the four-sided well from Temple IIa it was necessary to build the well-shaft quite close to the IIa oval-wall, at a distance of only 0.25 m.

Section 26B is drawn as an eastwest section through the well, though only as far as level 4.00. We see here the five drums, both in cross-section (C and D1-H1) and with their curved inner sides, projected in on the vertical section (D-H). In the eastern cross-section (C) the division into drums is not shown.

Section 26B contains layers which suggest that the well-drums were constructed in a building-pit (5). The pit breaks through man-made deposits (8) in front of wall IIa. Another layer (6) is possibly re-deposited from the pit. A layer interpreted as wind-blown sand (7) separates the two layers (6 and 8). In section 26C identical layers (8-10) occur, and here there is in addition another building level (3) of yellow plaster.

The upper part of the stratification in section 26B must presumably be understood as belonging to the Temple-III reconstruction, cf. below, chapter 8. This reconstruction we picture as a huge collar surrounding the well-shaft (A and B) at the top, the lowest of a new set of large-scale drums.

As a structure within the oval platform there was found in the west a drain (67) from the central platform. It is laid at precisely the same place as that where Temple I had earlier had a drain, and for the first four metres it therefore overlies the earlier structure, after which it turns off to the NNW, and was here followed for 17 m. It is not known how it ends.

The drain began immediately at the foot of the former terrace wall (5) (fig. 184). Undisturbed by the otherwise total robbery of that wall the gutter-stone (68) for receiving the down-run still stood *in situ*, with its weathered surface at the base level of the wall. It was a square-cut limestone block with a carved channel 17 cm deep. It presupposes a down-running channel in the wall, and such a one still survives on the opposite side of the temple (2) (fig. 90). After the gutter-stone came a section of gutter with covering-stones in place, after which the gutter changed direction and gradually assumed larger dimensions in the form of broader and broader channelling. It was built of smaller stones at the sides, and roofed with larger flat stone slabs; it was mortared with clay.

This stretch of drain appears in section 22 as a four-sided pipe (F) with its bottom at level 3.00. Water-laid layers (33) appear at the bottom. Here the sides are built of stones in plaster. The furthest excavated end of the channel to the north figures in section 21 (H). Here the bottom level is further lowered, so that run-off was ensured. The sections show also clearly that this drain was laid in an excavation in the oval platform. The upper level of this excavation reveals at the same time the surface of the oval platform of Temple II, which is otherwise not all too clearly indicated.

6. Temple II. The Pool

As a specially sacred feature of the Barbar temple a chamber with cult-attributes, build around a fresh-water spring, stands forth, with only minor deface-ment. It lay to the south-west of the oval platform, and was sunk down in the subsoil water, the actual level of which was measured at level 5.62, or 2.74 m above sea-level. Thus it was built above the as-sumed spring.

An important aspect of the whole picture lies in the fact that this pool was connected with the cen-tral portions of the temple by a stairway of real size and of imposing architecture. Its upper part was, however, badly demolished. Both the pool and the stairway were built of cut limestone blocks, and only masonry added at a later date gives a less im-posing impression.

The pool

The pool chamber was 4-5 m wide and about 6 m long (plan 6). In the condition in which it was found, representing a situation late in the building-history of the temple, it was connected with the front edge of oval-wall IIb (fig. 185).

Its lower portion showed a division into two halves, of approximately equal size, a western (1) and an eastern (2), insofar as a terracing occasioned a considerable difference in level, the western room being much deeper than the eastern.

The western room formed the pool proper, and measured about 4 × 2½ m. It appeared as an inte-gral work of architecture, with framing walls of a uniform construction. While the north, south and west walls were of the same height, with their up-per edges at approximately level 3.50 (if we ignore later additions and breaches), the east wall was only a terraced division between the east and the west room.

The west room had no floor. The deepest bottom level measured for the pool was close to 7.00, or al-most 1½ m under present water-level. The bottom levels of the walls varied between 6.60 and 6.80.

The end-wall (3) was almost 4 m long and pre-served to a height of 3.25 m (fig. 186). This wall can also stand as representative for the adjoining north and south walls. The building technique is charac-terized by seven courses of stone blocks, each one of a different height. The two lowest courses were each formed of three immense "stretchers", after which follow four alternating courses, which are finished off at the top by a framing seventh course of large flat slabs standing on edge.

On the third course there occurs a horizontal line which must mark the water-level. In that course there also occurred an opening (4) through the wall, about 20 × 20 cm in size, with its bottom level at 5.58. It marks the placing of a stone-set water-chan-nel which could be followed for 50 cm in a westerly direction. Another smaller hole in the fourth course is only a small niche, possibly for lighting purposes.

The south wall (5) in the western room was about 2.75 m long and a good 3 m high, built up in seven courses (fig. 187). It had in addition a secondary up-per wall in a different technique, stones and lime-stone blocks mortared with clay. In the south wall there were two openings for channels (6 and 7), one at each end.

The western opening (6) was set deep, in the sec-ond course, and the channel was constructed of ashlars on all sides. It was 43 cm high, with its bot-tom at level 6.23. From here the channel ran south for the first 30 cm, after which it changed direction towards the south-west. The eastern opening (7) stretched over the second, third and fourth courses, and was 126 cm high and about 30 cm wide. The in-side of the channel was built of ashlars. It had its bottom level at 6.22, and the direction of the chan-nel was towards the south-east. Inside, towards the bottom, there were found in the second course two holes, one on either side, about 11 × 18 cm in size and at least 30 cm deep (fig. 188). They have per-haps served as placement for a sluice-gate.

The north wall (8) was an exact parallel to the west wall, likewise in seven courses, but partly damaged, and partly, too, with remains of a sec-

Fig. 185. Temple II, pool, from NE. In foreground the portal step in partly demolished pool stairway, flanked by portal-foundation. The pool shown with natural subsoil-water level (1959).

Fig. 186. Temple II, pool, from E. Western wall in west chamber, with lowered subsoil-water level (1960).

Fig. 187. Temple II, pool, from N. South wall in west chamber, with lowered subsoil-water level (1960).

Fig. 188. Temple II, pool, from N. SE-corner of south wall in west chamber with channel-opening (1960).

149

Fig. 189. Temple II, pool, from S. North wall in west chamber, with lowered subsoil-water level (1960).

Fig. 190. Temple II, pool, from SE. North wall in west chamber with natural subsoil-water level. Vertical rebate in the wall at the chamber's NE-corner (1959).

Fig. 191. Temple II, pool, from SE. NW-corner in west chamber with channel-opening. Lowered subsoil-water level (1960).

ondary upper wall in a different technique (fig. 189). This wall, which continues directly into the stairway-wall, was about 2.75 m long, measured to a vertical groove in the fourth and fifth course above the second step of the stair (fig. 190). The wall was a good 3 m high, not counting the remains of the upper wall. The damaged portion gives us an insight into the construction, as it shows a filling of stones at the back of the wall-blocks. A little niche in the 6th-7th courses by the northwest corner may have served for lighting purposes.

Also in this wall there was an opening (9) for a channel (fig. 191). It was 120 cm high, 45 cm wide and had its bottom level at 6.28. It stretched over the second, third and fourth courses, and was made narrower at the bottom, but only in the outermost ashlar. The inside of the channel was built of ashlars. The channel ran towards the north-west.

All these openings for channels must represent a system of inflow or outflow, but only in one case has a continuation of a channel been excavated, namely about 3 m south-east of the southeasterly opening (58).

The 3-m long east wall (10) of the west room is, as a partition wall, at the same time the west wall of the east room (2), which lies at a higher level (fig. 192). It is therefore not continued upwards, but forms a "terrace wall". This wall consists of two

courses of large blocks (11 and 12). Both blocks in the upper course have been specially fashioned on the upper surface. The one block (11) has raised edges at each end, the interval between these raised edges forming a threshold about 80 cm wide, which is worn down about 5 cm in the middle. The other block (12) is provided with a channel running its full length, 12 cm wide and 10 cm deep (fig. 193). The actual block is 54 cm high and stands on a block from the bottom course which was about 30 cm high. The east wall has thus had a bottom level corresponding to that of the south wall.

The eastern wall then continues, to form the second lowest step of the stairway, which is 1½ m wide and connects the east wall with the north wall.

In the water-filled west room cult-objects were found, in the form of a well-like basin and a specially formed stone vessel. Both objects were placed so that they could be administered from the east wall.

The basin (13) consisted of two immense semicircular drums, each carved in one piece out of a large block of stone (figs. 194-195). They were placed the one above the other, though the upper one was slightly displaced. The lower drum, which describes a larger part of a circle than the upper, stood *in situ*. It was almost ½ m in height and, with its base level at 6.87, stood at the absolute bottom of

Fig. 192. Temple II, pool, from W. East wall in west chamber, with lowered subsoil-water level. Behind it, the east chamber (1960).

Fig. 193. Temple II, pool, from S. Part of east wall in west chamber, with lowered subsoil-water level. Lower part of pool stairway (1960).

Fig. 194. Temple II, pool, from NW. Basin in west chamber, with lowered subsoil-water level (1960).

Fig. 195. Temple II, pool, from above, top SE. Basin in west chamber, with lowered subsoil-water level (1960).

153

Fig. 196. Temple II, pool, from NW. Stone vessel in west chamber, with lowered subsoil-water level (1960).

the structure. Its inside diameter was 115 cm, it had absolutely vertical sides, and it was placed up against the east wall. The upper drum was 70 cm high. Its inner side was not completely vertical, the upper edge being provided along the inner edge with a bevel running all the way round. As it comprises a lesser segment of a circle it has not had connection at both ends with the east wall in the same way as the lower drum.

It must be assumed that there has been access to this basin from the east room by way of the threshold-like block (11). By the north side of the basin there had been placed on the floor of the pool a block of stone (14) cut in two steps which may have facilitated operation from this side.

In the space between this block and the lowest step of the stair a high plinth has been constructed up against the east wall, on which stood a stone vessel (15) (figs. 196-197). The plinth was built up of stone blocks measuring ½ × ½ m across the top. The lower block was 64 cm high and stood with its base at level 6.92, while the upper block was 40 cm high but pushed a little out of place. The whole plinth was therefore 104 cm high, and upon it stood a stone jar, 40 cm high and with an inner diameter of 35 cm (fig. 198). Like the basin, it was not completely circular, but had a flattened side designed to allow it to be placed against the east wall. Here the

rim of the vessel was slightly damaged. With its 12-cm-thick bottom it was a heavy vessel, and it was indeed meant to function hydrotechnically, as can be seen from the three four-sided holes cut through the side of the jar just above its base. These holes would lie at about level 5.70, while the rim of the jar was at level 5.48. The holes would thus allow water to run into the jar.

The two lowest steps of the pool stairway projected into this west room. In front of the bottom step there were two shaped blocks on the bottom of the pool, apparently to form a standing-place at the end of the stairway. One of these blocks (16) lay sloping and has probably slid out of place. The other (17) also sloped, but nevertheless projected in under the bottom step.

The east room (2) is of a more diffuse shape, being both narrowed by the pool stairway and reconstructed. As reconstructed it measures only a little over 2 × 2 m, but in the northeast corner it runs out into a point which wedges itself in between the stair and the oval-wall IIb.

Section 25 shows the stratigraphy, from an arbitrarily excavated surface, which, however, at the southern end is almost identical with the original surface of the site before excavation. We are here beyond the foot of the tell, cf. sections 28 and 29, described below, which are cut in close proximity. Sec-

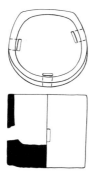

tion 25 also only goes down to an equally arbitrary excavation depth. It cuts slightly diagonally from the south wall of the east room, across and close to its floor level and on over the pool stairway's 6th and 7th steps to the northern edge of the east room, or stairway and thereafter into the lowest deposits in the oval platform north of the pool. It thereby throws light on a whole series of problems, partly architectural and partly concerning the subsoil. At the same time we get information on the layers filling up the pool. This last-named situation is of importance for an understanding of further connections of a wider significance.

The south wall (A-D) of the east room stands in section 25 as quadrupally terraced, and one of these terrace walls (B) can be seen to have been higher, cf.

the plaster layer and the overlying layer (6 and 5). The uppermost wall (A) has naturally also been higher. The two lower walls (C and D), on the other hand, may stand in the original height of the final phase. The terracing, as such, is rather the product of successive reconstructions. One of the walls (C) is in fact a direct continuation of the course of the south wall described in connection with the west room.

The stairway and the walls edging it (F-H) also figure in the section, the stairway with two steps on account of the diagonal direction of the section. Under one of the steps (F) a foundation block for the step can be seen. To the right of the northern stairway-wall (H) the subsoil (20) occurs at level 3.80-4.00, but it is dug away in a metre's depth further in towards the pool. This digging-away (16 and 19) should stratigraphically be associated with Temple I's level, and this situation can lend support to our theory of an older pool, earlier than the one found. Above the subsoil follow layers of clay and upon them the remains of a wall (I) belonging to Temple I, cf. plan 1 (37). It is described above as overlain both by oval-walls IIa and IIb.

The layers filling up the pool are of especial interest. The downward-sloping lines between the layers can be immediately read as signs of a deliberate filling, not of secondary plundering. And indeed the excellent state of preservation of the

155

Fig. 199. Temple II, pool, from NW. East chamber, with natural subsoil-water level (1959).

Fig. 200. Temple II, pool, from S. Lower part of pool stairway with edge-stones and north wall (1960).

Fig. 201. Temple II, pool, from NW. South wall and secondary east wall in east chamber (1959).

buried structure had already given support to that interpretation. Moreover, all objects found in the layers are completely free of later intrusions. The upper layers are more or less clean layers of sand (2, 4 and 7), the lowest (9) on the contrary is full of building fragments, large and small mixed with each other, probably coming from a light "destruction" of the upper edges of the structure.

We can with reasonable certainty conclude from these features that the pool has been taken out of use and deliberately covered over, and, as we have seen from the west room, this has been done not without a degree of piety towards the physical manifestations of the cult. Moreover, as the pool shows a complete connection with Temple II, these events must have taken place in connection with the transition to Temple III.

We can at this point turn directly to the east room (2) of the pool, which will first be described in its final form. As far as the floor level is concerned, it gives the impression of having been broken up, since the muddy layer excavated at the bottom of the room can scarcely have formed a floor (figs. 192, 199). We must assume that a floor-level has been removed, and this assumption is supported by the fact that three floor-slabs actually occur *in situ*, two at the western edge (18 and 19) and one by the eastern wall (20). These did not, however, lie at the

same level. A difference in height of ½ m suggests that the floor has been laid in several steps. The two slabs at the western edge have in that case formed the lowest step of the floor, standing partly under water. The higher step of the floor is only represented by one slab, but the excavation photograph apparently shows the impress of another slab at the same level on the south wall of the room, in a western continuation (fig. 199).

Access to this floor should presumably be looked for via the south edge of the pool stairway, which is admittedly partly broken up, but a surviving block (21) with a markedly horizontal surface offers a possible entry-stage (fig. 200). The block has a transverse groove cut in its surface. A single step south of the block would have provided a convenient descent to a floor in the east room.

The south edge of the pool stairway has thus provided a northern limit to the east room. Its western edge is identical with the east wall of the west room (10-12). It cannot be determined whether there has been a dividing wall between the two rooms, for example standing upon the block with the channel (12). The threshold-like block (11) in any case indicates an opening out to the basin (13) in the west room.

The south wall (22) of the east room is a very complex piece of architecture. The terraced outline

157

Fig. 202. Temple II, pool, from above, from W. Terraced south wall in east chamber. In background secondary east wall = oval-wall IIb (1959).

of this wall is shown in section 25 (A-D), but, as it was not dismantled out of consideration for the monument, we know but little of the inner structure of this 2.25-m broad complex of masonry.

The wall is a little over 2.25 m long, and consists of four different wallings (23-26) in a rising succession (figs. 201-202).

The lowest, a piece of walling about 1½ m high (23), consists of three courses of large limestone blocks with accurately fitted front sides. It may be a secondary addition as part of a reconstruction, as the wall is directly applied to the south wall (5) which is known from the west room, without integral bonding-blocks. Nor do its courses show any accord with the courses of this south wall. The upper edge of the wall forms a narrow cistern-like channel in against the next wall. Section 25 indicates a stone paving here.

The next stretch of walling (24) was only exposed in two courses of its outer face, the uppermost consisting of flat slabs standing on edge. As we have said, it forms a continuation of the south wall (5) of the west room. Its upper edge was coated with plaster of a grey-white coarse-grained type, in a layer about 1 cm thick, cf. section 25 (6).

The third piece of walling (25) was built of small stones set in clay, but clearly partly demolished. Its front face was coated with 1-2 cm of grey-white

plaster. The wall must have originally been carried up to the base of the next wall, cf. section 25 (5).

The fourth and highest section of walling (26) consisted of large and smaller stones, set in a mortar of clay-mixed sand. Here both sides of the wall were excavated, and the northern side appeared as a well-smoothed face, while the southern was irregular as on a terracing wall.

The east wall (27) we have already met, in its capacity as a secondary component of the terrace wall of the oval platform in phase IIb. Here, however, it is of immediate interest only in its capacity as east wall in the east room of the pool. It is built of small stones, only held together by sand-mixed clay, though in its upper parts by plaster-mixed clay.

The wall runs from the main course of the oval wall IIb (C), and ends at the oval wall IIa (B). On the way it makes two obtuse-angled changes of direction, and it takes its place as east wall in the room here described at the southern change of direction. Here it is built in one with the east room's south wall. The rest of the wall runs in two straight stretches of 2½ and 1½ m's length. It, too, is formed as a terrace wall.

This quite damaged east wall rests upon underlying masonry (28), which comes into sight as a ledge between the two changes of direction. Under it comes masonry (29), which is only present as two large blocks standing on edge, and apparently forms a lower covering of the east wall.

The east wall as here described gives the room a curious shape, but this feature is possibly based on an original version and thereby an expression of a reconstruction based on tradition. For in addition to the masonry here described there appears a wall (31) embedded in the floor. It can indicate an older and larger original version of the east room. It is, however, difficult to gain a clear picture of this, particularly because the compact south wall (23-26) can cover connecting links and because demolitions can obscure the picture. Moreover an excavation-area which here assumes a key-position, namely the area south of the south wall, was not excavated in depth.

In the last chapter the opinion was expressed that the oval-wall IIb in its initial form reached its connection with the pool-area by being turned in a right-angled corner (30) inward to meet the oval-wall IIa, which furthermore was screened off. From this corner the oval-wall IIb was in its final form carried onward as a secondary wall of small stones, which at the same time forms the east wall (27) in the pool's east room (fig. 156).

This wall (27) is seen to be underlain by a row of blocks (31) of which only the rear sides could be exposed (fig. 157). We know only of one course. They form at one and the same time a delimitation of a room (32) with its back wall in the right-angled course of oval-wall IIb (30) and a direct continuation of the main course from the south-west of oval-wall IIb.

Because of our limited knowledge of this somewhat inaccessible excavating area we can give no logically consistent picture of the transition between the oval wall and the pool, as viewed from an imaginary perspective from the south at the foot of the oval wall. Originally there should have been low-lying ground in front of the foot of the wall, and at least the south wall around the pool should have been visible, but we have no knowledge of a southern face of this walling. The continual accumulation of drift-sand is also a factor, shown by the fact that the room (59) built onto the oval wall IIb lies high up.

The latest secondary additions at the pool also bear witness to a phase of the constructional history when the sanding-up of oval-wall IIb was far advanced. A piece of walling so late as the uppermost (26) in the south wall of the pool we have had to interpret as a terrace wall facing inwards towards the pool. The comparative levels of the oval-wall IIb and of this walling (26) could suggest that, at the time when the wall (26) was built, only the uppermost metre of the oval wall still stood free.

For the final situation the upper walls around the pool must also be taken into consideration. They are admittedly not fully preserved, but on the south side there could nevertheless be exposed a fairly intact portion (33) above the pool's west room. It consists of large and smaller stones mixed with cut limestone blocks and mortared with sandy clay. It has presumably continued all the way round, since at the northwest corner a fragment of similar walling occurred, built of large and smaller stones set in clay. These walls can be seen to have raised the pool-walls by a further metre, but they may also represent a fencing wall around the roofed pool.

We can admittedly not directly prove that the pool has had a roof, but we consider it somewhat inconceivable that it stood open. The whole idea with the stairway, which in its lower course runs in a shaft down below the surrounding ground-surface, supports the picture of a roof, while pieces of wood from a putative roof were in fact found at the bottom of the pool.

This spring, with its double-chamber and its clear architectural connection with Temple II, has naturally served special cult-functions, must indeed have been a particularly sacred place within the structure. When it was demolished, special consideration was given to the most vital parts of the complex. It is perhaps worth pointing out that it is sited outside the oval platform, and is only integrated as part of the architectural whole by the medium of the grand pool stairway.

The pool stairway

In a 15-m long flight a "processional stairway" leads down from the central platform to the bottom of the pool (plan 6). It has been an exceptionally monumental structure, with a width of about 1.75 m and with steps about 0.25 m high, framed between flanking walls or side-slabs. But it is only partly preserved (figs. 203-204).

With the known average heights the complete stairway must have had about 30 steps, if we adopt the chosen reconstruction-model which takes the stairway up to the top of the platform-wall. These 30 steps have then taken us about 7 m upwards in vertical distance from the bottom of the pool, cf. *section 33.*

159

Fig. 203. Temple II, pool stairway, from NE. The full, but partly demolished, flight. In foreground the side-slabs of the stair and the flanking stones at the foot of Temple II's west wall, here totally demolished. In middle distance the portal-step and remains of portal. In background the pool (1959).

Fig. 204. Temple II, pool stairway, from W. The full, but partly demolished, flight. In foreground the pool and lower surviving portion of stairway. In middle distance the portal-step. In background the stairway's side-slabs and the flanking stones at the foot of Temple II's west wall, here totally demolished. At top, Temple II's platform. On right oval-walls IIa and b (1959).

Fig. 205. Temple II, pool stairway, from SW. Lower surviving flight with lowered subsoil-water level (1960).

Fig. 206. Temple II, pool stairway, from S. Detail of steps (1959).

161

Fig. 207. Temple II, pool stairway, from N. Portal-step. Behind it, against the side-slab, can be seen a broken-off portal-pillar, floor-slabs and secondary walling. On left, rear side of upper part of oval-wall IIa (1957).

Fig. 208. Temple II, pool stairway, from above from S. Detail of cast plaster container under stairway (1959).

Fig. 209. Temple II, pool stairway, from SW. Detail of demolished stair-section between the lower surviving flight and the portal-step. On left the oval platform in west with exposed drain and, above it, Temple III's west wall, and at top Temple II's central platform (1959).

Fig. 210. Temple II, pool stairway, from W. Detail of upper flight of stairway from portal-step to west wall of Temple II, here demolished. In background Temple II's central platform. On right, oval-wall IIa. Bottom right, projecting part of oval-wall IIb (1958).

Fig. 211. Temple II, pool stairway, from NW. Side-slabs after preliminary exposure. Besides and between the flanking stones a drain from Temple II. In layers behind are traces of robbery of Temple II's west wall. Upper left, remains Temple II's platform (1955).

Among the unique architectural features of this stairway is the fact that in its course it changes direction in a very obtuse angle in order to meet the central platform's wall at a right-angle. Where it turns, it is probable that it has had a "landing" in the form of a step in double width. This agrees well with the distance-relationships between the 8th and 18th steps.

The stairway has had part of its course above ground-surface and part below, insofar as the ground-surface is established by the oval platform and by its foreland. Where it passes below ground-level it has had a portal. In addition it was flanked, at the foot of the central platform, by a double row of large limestone plinths, cf. section 33 and plan 6.

These plinths, eight in number, were placed in pairs, six north of the stairway and two south. All of them were provided with four-sided double holes in the top to hold standards or cult figures. Of the portal there survive the foundation-stone and fragments of its vertical columns. In addition there was found beneath the stairway a built-up cylindrical tube.

The lowest portion of the stairway is preserved completely intact for eight steps (34-41), and a close-up photograph gives a good impression of the accuracy with which the work has been carried out, with the result that the steps have not moved by so much as a millimetre, though some of them are cracked through and through (figs. 205, 200, 204, 206).

The lowest step (34) rests upon a foundation-block. It has stood under water, which has resulted in severe wear during use. This attrition takes the form of a trough-like hollow, about 12 cm deep, 130 cm long and 35 cm wide. The stone is worn almost halfway through. The second step (35), too, has stood under water and is worn halfway through. The hollow measures 135×30 cm and is 15 cm deep. The third step (36) slopes slightly forward and down, but is only a little worn. The fourth to the eighth steps (37-41) are all above water-level and not worn in the same way.

These eight steps increase gradually in width from about 145 to 175 cm, the last being the normal width of the stairway. From section 25 (F) we know that at least some of these steps stand upon foundation-blocks. Two further steps, the 9th and 10th, though removed, can be directly traced, as a step-shaped impression in white plaster was left by them on the north wall of the stairway.

Fig. 212. Temple II, pool stairway, from NW. Detail of side-slabs, as fig. 211 but more deeply excavated. In foreground, portal-foundation (1957).

Higher up the course of the stair still another step (42) survived. It is – hardly by chance – precisely the "portal-step" (fig. 207). This step, section 33 (18), bears a groove to accommodate the next stone. This allows the insertion of a "landing" of two steps' size, just where the stairway changes direction, the 11th and 12th steps on section 33.

There were no further steps surviving, but the side-stringers in towards the central platform show that their course has continued upwards. This course is reconstructed to fit with the assumed height of the terrace wall, which is only known from the northeast portion. The stair can naturally also have been led in through a recessed access-zone in the platform. The earth under the portal-step was specially searched for possible foundation-inscriptions.

Exactly halfway between the end-wall of the pool and the terrace wall of the central platform, both of them natural reference points for the detailed layout of the whole structure, there was found an underground construction (43 and section 33:O). It was a cylindrical hole cast in grey-white plaster (fig. 208). It had no bottom and was 45 cm deep. At the top it was reinforced by a packing of stones. The construction was broken off at the top by the step that once lay above it. One may see in this one of the indication-marks of a technical nature, which must

have been an unavoidable prerequisite for an architectural project of the scale of the Barbar temple. Another possibility would be that it was a container for some perishable foundation offering.

The stairway has had flanking side-walls or side-stringers. The northern wall is simply a continuation of the north wall of the pool. The walls of the stairway fall into several stages, basically governed by the stairway's double character, respectively as a stairwell below ground-surface and as a freestanding stairway above.

The correspondence between a vertical groove in the north wall above the 2nd step, which has already been described, and the channel in a block (12) set on edge on the east wall of the west chamber may not be fortuitous. On the basis of the evidence found one could deduce a division of the pool with a partition-wall and a door. The groove is marked on section 33 (F).

After the groove the north wall gradually also becomes the wall of the stairway, which is led down, as into a shaft, through the oval platform; but this part of the north wall is only surviving as far as the "landing" at the 11th and 12th steps, and then only in the form of the lower wall-face, cf. section 33. The "landing" is at the same time the point where the oval walls from the south are consistently joined to the pool-structure, and where the stairwell is so

Fig. 213. Temple II, pool stairway, from S. Side-slabs after preliminary exposure. In background, Temple III's west wall and Temple II's west wall, partly exposed (1955).

deep that the wall must have stood in a man's height.

The southern stairway-wall begins at the bottom in the form of an edging in towards the east room of the pool, formed of a large block (21) which has already been described. After that comes a demolished section, but level with the lost 9th and 10th steps there is once more a surviving block, which ends at the "landing".

From this point the actual stairway-walls were no longer preserved, but instead there was, completely or partially preserved, a rough foundation (44) of larger and smaller stones set in plaster or in plaster-mixed clay (fig. 209). We must, however, assume from the data available that this stage ends where the stairway reaches ground-level at the 18th step, the portal-step (42). In other words, the portal has been erected at the point where the descent through the oval platform commenced.

The last stage is now the stretch from the portal to the central platform (fig. 210). Here the stair has the form of a free-standing stairway, fully visible above the surface, and here the walls also duly change their form to that of side-stringers (45), the lower part of which is well-preserved for a stretch of 4-5 m

(fig. 211). Thus the stairway now stands as an architectural block on the surface of the oval platform, cf. section 33.

The stones forming the side-stringers are set slightly sloping. The bottom of the stringers had to conform to the surface of the oval platform, and two features of the material as found are interesting. Firstly, the preserved portion of the stringers has been demolished down to a level corresponding to the bottom of Temple III's western terrace wall, the course of which cuts through the stringers. Secondly, the stringers stop precisely at the point where the line of the face of Temple II's terrace wall has passed across their course.

From these two features we can draw two conclusions, first that the stairway has been joined to the Temple-II wall, which at this point has been completely removed by stone-robbery, and secondly that the stairway has been broken off to make room for the Temple-III wall. The whole stairway-structure was thereby taken out of function. This situation agrees well with the stratigraphy of the pool, section 25, where we reached an exactly parallel interpretation of the final stage of the structure. It was eliminated with the building of Temple III.

Fig. 214. Temple II, pool stairway, from E. Flanking stones north of stairway. At bottom, masonry on west edge of Temple II's platform. Upper right, Temple III's west wall. Upper left, portal-step and portal-foundations (1959).

The actual side-stringers (45) are put together of large and small flat limestone slabs, which form a tile-like covering for the wall. This wall is built up in light grey-white plaster, and plaster-films on the upper edges indicate further units going higher, which now are lost (fig. 212). Under the wall lay a rough founding of stones in clay, and this foundation (46) continued at a gradually falling level, but was only preserved along the northern stringer. Under the structure there were found, as described earlier, remains of a similar primary structure. In it a smaller type of slab was used.

For this part of the stairway we have use of three sections. *Section 24* is a cross-section through the east end of the stairway. There can be seen from this, that the inner part of the stairway between the stringers (C and D) has been filled up with a very solid layer of plaster fragments (1), which has formed a very stable structure (fig. 78). The bottom level of the layer forms a horizontal band of plaster. Under a filling-layer (2) of clay-mixed sand there follows an earlier plaster-level (3), flanked by foundation-stones (E and F) for side-walls. We are clearly dealing with an earlier structure, which we have associated with Temple I, and which probably has had the form of a low ramp. It is underlain by the earliest feature, the "clay core" (4-5).

Section 27C touches at its north end one side of the stairway. Thus only the southern side-stringer (B) is here visible, with a layer of plaster fragments (1) and layers of fill (2 and 3), which further down give place to the previously mentioned older structure with stringer-slabs (F) on a foundation-stone (E). Just at this point the assumed ramp has, built onto it, a shaft-staircase (D) which further establishes an association with Temple Ia.

Section 27D runs along the south edge of the stairway and cuts through the portal-step (A). The layer of plaster fragments (1) is present here in a way that requires us to interpret the layer as disturbed by a local robbery, cf. also the vertical dividing line between the two upper layers (1 and 2) and the large stone block (B) from Temple III's terrace wall. This block lies by the outer face of that wall, slightly *ex situ*.

We have projected the outline of the stairway in from section 33, and thereby it is shown how the stratigraphy follows the structure's descending course towards the west. We have the plaster-fragment layer (1 and 6), the sandy filling (3 and 8), the clay core (4 and 9) and the subsoil (5). A cross-section in front of the portal-step is shown in an excavation photograph (fig. 210).

To the architectural complex of the free-standing stairway belong in addition the eight flanking foun-

Fig. 215. Temple II, pool stairway, from W. Detail of flanking stone with carved representations of human figures (1955).

dation-blocks (47-54) at the eastern end, and the portal (55-56) at the western end. The blocks stand in a double row just in front of the terrace wall (figs. 211, 213-214, 146). They must be understood as partly sunk plinths, which results in their base levels varying considerably, between 2.45 and 2.75. Their upper-surface levels show much less variation, between 2.05 and 2.18 in the case of the six northern stones, while the two southern stand a little deeper. This surface-level must be in agreement with the base-level of the terrace wall, while in addition the surfaces are in several cases more or less weathered, which must be seen as evidence of prolonged use. Between the two northern pairs of blocks runs a covered channel, which has already been described.

These plinths have been fashioned with varying regularity and varying dimensions. They all have rectangular holes across the longer axis of the stones, even in one case (48) a third, much smaller hole on the east side. The depth of the holes also varies, but is on average about 15 cm. Only one stone (49) has holes 20 cm deep.

The six northern blocks are characterized by uniform regular fashioning on all sides, though one of them (51) is very weathered, and moreover shaped with a ledge along the eastern side in its whole length. Another (52) has a specially fashioned south hole, the eastern side of the hole rising in an 8-cm high ledge, measured from the bottom. A third (47) has on its west side a portrayal of human figures carved in its surface (fig. 215). A fourth (48) has weathered sides and surface.

The two southern blocks are only really regularly fashioned along the western sides and the upper surfaces, which are somewhat weathered.

On excavation of these plinth-stones it was discovered that three of them (48, 53 and 54) possessed holes with a filling consisting of wood, copper and bitumen, remains from the sheathing of wooden objects which had been mounted in them (figs. 216-217) (see below, p. 270-274). About the nature of these objects many guesses have been made, ranging from major sculpture to standards bearing emblems.

It has been mentioned already that, at the point where the stairway descended below ground-level, it was flanked by a portal (fig. 210). The in-

Fig. 216. Temple II, pool stairway, from above from E. Detail of remains in hole in flanking stone (1955).

Fig. 217. Temple II, pool stairway, from S. Detail of remains in holes in flanking stones. A heap of copper sheeting between stones (1955).

Fig. 218. Temple II, pool stairway, from S. Portal-foundation north of stairway (1957).

Fig. 219. Temple II, pool stairway, from E. Portal-pillar south of stairway, set in plaster in foundation. On right, side-slab to stairway and portal-step (1957).

Fig. 220. Temple II, pool stairway, from N. Secondary wall south of stairway. On left, portal-step and portal-pillar (1958).

side width of this was 3.33 m, its height is unknown. Its foundations (55 and 56) were found on both sides of the "portal-step", and in both of them rested the remains of the portal's vertical columns. The distance between the step and the column is not the same on both sides, but the foundations are at the same depth.

This portal naturally emphasizes the special importance of the stairway as a processional route between temple areas of the utmost sanctity.

The northern portal-foundation (55) consists of a large four-sided block of stone, the lower half of which is roughly shaped (figs. 218, 212). On three sides there is a cut ledge. It is almost ½ m high, and has a hole cut for a four-sided column, about 30 × 45 cm across. The lowest part of the column is still *in situ.*

The southern portal-foundation (56) has the column preserved to a length of 1½ m (fig. 207). It has a cross-sectional measurement of 30 × 55 cm, and its foot is set in a foundation of stone and plaster (fig. 219).

Approximately at the level of the portal-step this column was surrounded by horizontal limestone slabs, 10-15 cm thick, presumably the remains of a floor. Running out from the southwest corner of the column there is a stretch of walling (57), about 4 m long, which ends abruptly in the west (figs. 210, 220). On its way it describes an obtuse-angled bend. It is built of stone, plaster-fragments and limestone blocks set in plaster and clay. It crosses a cut-away section of oval-wall IIa, and must in general be regarded as a late addition. This piece of walling figures on section 27A (C).

The southwestern foreland

South of the pool a fairly small area in front of oval-wall IIb was excavated to an arbitrarily chosen depth. Here there appeared a portion of an underground water-channel and the remains of a room built onto the oval wall. Other masonry was exposed west of the upper edge of the pool, and in addition two trial trenches were dug in a westerly direction. Their stratigraphy is given in sections 28 and 29. Only in section 29 did the trench go down to the subsoil.

The water-channel (58) issues from the southeastern hole (7) in the wall of the pool, but was not

Fig. 221. Temple II, south-west foreland by pool, from above from E. Partly exposed channel from pool (1959).

Fig. 222. Temple II, south-west foreland by west edge of pool, from N. Walling above pool (1959).

further investigated (fig. 221). Its sides could be seen, however, to have been built of cut limestone blocks, roofed with split stone slabs 10-20 cm thick. Its base-depth was not determined, but to judge by the opening in the chamber-wall the channel was almost in a man's height, about 1½ m.

The room (59) south of the pool is obliquely four-sided and has the oval wall IIb as its rear wall (fig. 155). Uniform walls of stones set in clay form the other sides. They were preserved in almost a metre's height. The room measures about 3 × 3½ m, and on the inner side of the south wall a 1-cm thick layer of grey-brown plaster could be seen. The remains of a darkened plaster coating occurred also on the inner side of the western wall. A hard layer of grey-brown clay, which was not dug through, formed a floor at level 3.45. With the breaking down of the upper parts of the wall the room had been filled with clay mixed with stones.

Section 28 started from this room, and cuts through the upper layers in a westerly direction, being only dug down to an arbitrarily chosen depth. On the other hand, it starts from the original surface, and the actual thickness of the layers at this point can be derived from section 29.

In section 28 the south and west walls (A and B) of the room appear, as well as the demolition layer and the floor-layer (3 and 4). The section also records high-lying masonry remains, such as a heap of stones (11), probably from a demolished wall, and a wall-foundation (C). In addition there are remains of a building (D and E) embedded in the latest layer (8). It is thus later in date than the room described above. Its wall (D) is of stones mortared with clay, and its inner wall is plastered. From the lower edge of the wall there extends a narrow strip of floor (E) of clay-mixed plaster, and large fragments of this floor can also be seen 4-6 m further west.

Above the western upper edge of the pool there occurred high-lying masonry, consisting of three sections (plan 6:60-62) (fig. 222). It is, however, not certain that it has an association with the pool, as it may be of later date. The masonry forms a quite large block (60) of very light grey-brown plaster mixed with stones, and across its northern end could be seen a low up-standing edge of grey-brown plaster as though left by a demolished partition-wall. Along the western side the block is edged by a wall (61) of large and smaller stones in clay-mixed sand. Another fragment of wall (62) consisted of stones mortared with very light grey-brown plaster, and coated on both sides with a layer of plaster 1-2 cm thick.

Section 29 brings this masonry into stratigraphical context as high-lying. For the section begins in fact from this masonry (8). It cuts down from the original surface before excavation commenced all the way to the subsoil, and has already been described in connection with Temple I. We cannot, admittedly, draw any well-defined dividing line between deposits from Temples I and II, but it is assumed that masonry above the Temple-I walls (19 and 27) belongs to Temple II, the uppermost perhaps to Temple III.

Most conspicuous in section 29 is a stretch of walling (12), parallel to the one already described (8). It is of stones set in clay, and it is coated with grey plaster on the eastern side. Level with the base of the wall is a plaster floor (10). Under it can be seen an isolated cut limestone block (14) and a heap of stones (16). The block lay on a level with the upper edge of the pool.

In the middle of the section there appears the lowest course (4) of a wall, made of stones set in clay. Finally, attention can be drawn to a quite large stone-set surface (3) uppermost in the west end of the section, and under it a wall (6), bent at an angle and also of stones set in clay. It surrounds a stone-setting (6) at a slightly lower level, probably a floor-foundation.

Sections 28 and 29 thus reveal a succession of layers, about 2 m thick, outside the temple-area proper. It contains traces of buildings, and both Temple I and Temple II have left levels, as the objects found also demonstrate. In the uppermost layer we can assume a Temple-III level.

7. Temple II. The Eastern Court

On the eastern side of the temple lay a large oval structure in the shape of a walled court. A ramp connected the court with the central platform (plan 7, fig. 223). Several building phases can be distinguished in both the court and the ramp, while we have in addition in the eastern area both water-channel systems and remains of buildings.

The Eastern Court

The latest phase of this feature was exposed in 1955 by following the walling along both sides. In 1956 the interior area thus delimited was specially investigated. Excavation was, however, only taken down to the subsoil in a trench, one metre wide, along the oval's longer axis. Systematic area-excavation outside the oval was not undertaken, but only trial trenches.

Section 10, a longitudinal section through the oval, runs between the oval's walls in the east and in the west (A). It spans from a dug-away surface to the subsoil (22), which here in some places lies

Fig. 223. Temple II, Eastern Court, from NE. Oval structure with earlier inner structure. In background, ramp to Temple II's east wall (1956).

Fig. 224. Temple II, Eastern Court, from W. As fig. 223. In foreground, end of ramp (1956).

higher than is usual. In the dug-away surface we can see in the west the outline of a large sondage from 1955, and in the east that of the trial trench along the wall from the same year.

In the stratigraphy three periods are clearly distinguished, with the oval as the latest link in a constructional sequence.

Above the subsoil we can see deposits (20 and 21), which are the only representatives in the section of the earliest period. The area exposed by excavation contains in places building remains which can be attributed to this period.

The middle period figures more prominently, partly with a plaster floor (16 and 17), partly with a walling (15), which is part of a south wall of a little almost circular central structure. In addition, the remains of a wall (C) rise from the floor-level, and at the western end there is a step (B), both seen in cross-section. The wall-remains represent a circular court, later demolished, and the step is the extreme end of the ramp.

Also belonging to this period is a thick covering layer of a dark powdery substance (12), and in this can be seen here and there remains of successive plaster floors (13). Larger stones scattered in the layer presumably signify demolished masonry, and indeed on the exposed area fragments of masonry

could be seen. At the eastern end a plaster channel (26) had been fashioned.

The latest period is marked by the ends of the oval wall (A), standing in the section with their bases relatively high in the strata, and quite clearly above the powdery layer (12). In the section the upper layers (1-8) therefore represent the deposits that can be associated with the oval court. It has no plaster floor.

In the excavated area (plan 7) the oldest building-remains only appear as deeply founded formations of greyish yellow plaster remains (1), sometimes incorporating stones. They are attributed to the earliest period of the section.

By contrast, the middle period presents itself in the exposed area with coherent building-remains and defined by a plaster floor (2) (fig. 224). This floor extended over the whole of the western half of the area excavated, was uneven and stony, and sloped down from north to south. It consisted of greyish, strongly granular plaster, in a layer up to 10 cm thick. On this floor there was built a little ring-shaped structure (3), consisting of the remains of an irregular circle of stone walling set in white fine-grained plaster, and with a plaster floor inside. To the west a little rectangular platform (4) had been built onto it, a cast block of plaster with, on its

Fig. 225. Temple II, Eastern Court, from SW. Drainage channel by oval wall (1956).

upper surface, the impressions left by three large, but now missing, stone blocks.

Similarly set in the plaster floor there were the remains of a wall (5) which described a quarter of a circle ringing the central structure (3 and 4) just described. Here can perhaps be seen the remains of a circular court-wall as a predecessor to the oval wall. For there was also found the impression (6) in the floor of a continuation of the wall in the north-west and a surviving wall-fragment (7). Here this northern half-circle ends with a plaster step (8) set in the floor, which forms the beginning of the phase of the ramp belonging to this period.

As the complex here described was gradually covered with further deposits it presumably had to be reconstructed. We find remains of new floors (9) which partly cover the rectangular platform (4), cf. also section 10 (13); new stretches of wall are more

or less underlain by the dark powdery layer (12) in section 10. To these secondary walls can be reckoned a wall-fragment (10) in the north-west, another fragment (11) close by, and a longer curved stretch of wall (12) in the south-west. It seems possible to bring them all into association with the original circular-court walls (5-7).

The remaining masonry within the area investigated comprises a straight stretch of wall (13) in the south-east, a drainage-channel (14) in the extreme east, and a pit (15) in the south-east. It is possible that these features also concern the middle period, while a block (16) placed in the stretch of wall can be better understood in relation to the latest period.

The drainage-channel (14) is fashioned of grey plaster and cemented together with remains of the floor (9) (fig. 225). It is 10-15 cm deep and 5-10 cm wide, with irregular walls and bottom. It is cer-

Fig. 226. Temple II, Eastern Court, from N. Plaster pit in connection with drain (1957).

Fig. 227. Temple II, Eastern Court, from N. Inner side of oval wall in southwest (1956).

Fig. 228. Temple II, Eastern Court, from NE. Cast plaster block in south side (1956).

tainly cracked at the top, and must originally have formed a closed drain-pipe system, presumably in connection with the pit (15), which lay under the oval wall. On excavation it appeared as completely enclosed, and only the crack above a short stretch of the channel was visible. First when it was uncovered could it be seen how the short channel ran into a round cistern-shaped pit, about 7 cm above the bottom of the cistern (fig. 226). Both cistern and channel were fashioned of greyish plaster, and the cistern was full of a black powdery mass.

The latest period manifests itself as the walled oval court. The wall (17) is fairly well preserved, and a large breach in the south-east is probably the result of stone-robbery. The little opening in the north-east, on the other hand, was not registered by the first survey in 1955. The wall is built of stones set in a yellowish plaster mass and is coated with the same plaster on both sides. The lowest courses consist of long roughly square stones, on which a wall of smaller stones has been built (fig. 227).

This wall forms a somewhat oblique oval, with maximum length of 15 m and breadth of 9 m. The bottom level of the wall varies between limits of almost ½ m. It is best preserved in the north-west, where it is a metre high. The width of the wall also varies, and the inner side of the wall is only rarely vertical.

The whole of this wall rests upon the grey-black powdery layer, and is thereby distinguished from the other structural remains, which must be assumed demolished to give place to the oval court. It is therefore not unreasonable to associate the block (16) with the oval wall (fig. 228). This block is four-sided and constructed in plaster. It stands above the grey-black layer and is shattered at the top, but even in that condition it rises high in the court formed by the oval wall.

The interpretation of the Eastern Court must be based on the dark powdery layers which are very conspicuous, not just inside the court but also outside, as described in chapter 2 in relation to sections 12 and 13, where the layers are characterised as dark grey and charcoal-coloured. They are probably ashy remains from the cooking over a fire of the animals sacrificed at the temple. The table-like constructions (4 and 16) related both to the oval and the earlier round phase of the court probably served for the cutting up of the animals. One may also refer to the many beakers found in this area.

Sections 12-13, and section 14, which will be described below, are our main witnesses to the utilization of the temple's eastern foreland. The method of extensive excavation employed precludes us from giving a more detailed picture of the utilization of this area.

The ramp

The ramp from the central platform led to the western end of both the oval and the earlier round structure (plan 7). The ramp was also accessible from the north by way of a cobbled road, at least in its final phase.

Section 11 is a cross-section through this ramp, and it shows a distinct stratification, revealing several reconstructions in the form of raising of the ground-level with new surfacing. The section is limited by the side-walls of the ramp, and it starts at the uppermost ramp-flooring found, but is not dug down to subsoil. The stratigraphy is characterized by layers of fill separated by floor levels.

Sand (9) with strips of powder forms the lowest layer recorded. Above it come clay-like fill (8) and a floor-level (7) of plaster. This is framed between the lower thick side-walls (11). This is the ramp in an early version with a breadth of 2½ m.

This older ramp is overlain with sandy fill (6) which, however, at the bottom contains a level of large split stones, certainly a separate floor-phase. At the same time the side-walls are built higher, though in a less massive technique (11). The new ramp is about 2 m broad. The sandy fill-layer (6) is covered with a plaster floor (5), above which new layers of fill are added (2-4). The latest plaster floor forms the surface layer (1).

As we have here a cross-section of a structure with a sloping course, we cannot use section 11 directly for a correlation with the building-phases of the court. For this a longitudinal section would have been better suited.

In plan the ramp appears in its two main phases, the lower one broader (plan 7:18), the upper one narrower (19). The upper ramp is about 8 m long and 2 m broad, and is covered by a stony plaster-floor (fig. 229). It is, however, damaged at both ends, the west end by a stone-robber hole, and the east end by a removal of the surface. Both disturbances reveal details of the inner structure. Of the lower ramp only the protruding edges can be seen, and both of these have been partly demolished (fig. 230).

In its final form the upper ramp has functioned in connection with the oval court, the ends of the wall of which turn in over the ramp's edges. From there the ramp rises with over ½ m in towards Temple II's terrace wall with which it is directly bonded (fig. 231).

Fig. 229. Temple II, Eastern Court, from E. Upper ramp to Temple II's eastern terrace wall, several surface-phases exposed (1957).

Fig. 230. Temples I and II,
Eastern Court, from
WSW. Upper and lower
ramps. Side view of
south edge of ramp-
walling (1957).

Fig. 231. Temple II, Eastern Court, from N. Detail
of upper ramp in connec-
tion with Temple II's eastern terrace wall, with terrace wall of Temple Ib beneath it. The surface of
the end of the ramp is
damaged (1957).

Fig. 232. Temple II, Eastern Court, from E. The upper ramp in the course of preliminary exposure, in foreground with attached oval walls. In background, Temple II's eastern terrace wall with built-on special structure of large blocks south of ramp (1956).

Here there also appears, on the south side of the ramp and in against the terrace wall, a special added structure (20). It stands as a half-demolished fragment of masonry in Temple-II style, consisting of cut limestone blocks. An early excavation-photograph gives an impression of this structure's relationship to the constructional complex (fig. 232). The stone-robbery prevents us from obtaining a clear conception of its original form, apart from a trapezoid ground-plan. But, taking into account the distance from the floor level of Temple II to the surface of the ramp, it is necessary to assume a stairway or a continuation of the ramp. Consequently we consider it likely that the built-on structure is the remains of such an access way.

The latest ramp-surface is at the same time connected with the surrounding countryside by a cobbled roadway (21) (fig. 233). It comes in from the north and joins the ramp at its eastern end, the road-bed itself being raised. It has allowed access to the temple for, for example, animals to be sacrificed. It was built up in several courses of stones and plaster, and had a quite well-preserved surface, paved with flat stones and pieces of plaster in the same way as the ramp. The road is about 1½ m broad and

was followed for 9 m of its length. An attempt to find it 6 m further north was unsuccessful. The road is cut by section 12 (J).

While the upper ramp thus shows a clear connection with Temple II, our documentation is inadequate to sustain a synchronization of the underlying floor-levels in the ramp with specific parts of the structures under the level of the oval court, though a connection between the step (8) at the east end of the ramp and the circular court does seem to be obvious. A series of indirect conclusions can, however be drawn, which concern in particular the lower ramp and its place in the temple sequence.

As has been said, the lower ramp is badly damaged, but its southern side-wall can nevertheless be followed for a stretch of more than 5 m (fig. 230). At its western end it disappears under the structure (20) built onto Temple II. Section 11 shows locally a bottom-level at 2.88 and a top-level at 2.55. Already during the excavation it was recognized that the bottom level of the lower ramp generally followed the same level as the foot of the terrace wall of Temple Ib. During the cleaning-up of the stone-robber hole (18) there was also found a plaster floor at the bottom (fig. 234). It is un-

Fig. 233. Temple II, Eastern Court, from S. Roadway joining upper ramp. In foreground, part of ramp-surface. In background, blocks from Temple III's eastern terrace wall (1961).

Fig. 234. Temples I and II, Eastern Court, from above, N at top. Surface of lower ramp bonded with Temple Ib's eastern terrace wall, on left, overlain by Temple II's eastern terrace wall on extreme left. At top, parts of upper ramp, at bottom, blocks belonging to structure built onto Temple II's terrace wall (1957).

Fig. 235. Temple II, eastern foreland, from above from NE. Water-channel with cleaning-hole (1961).

Fig. 236. Temple II, eastern foreland, from W. Water-channel, exterior (1960).

doubtedly the surface-floor of the lower ramp which here appears and is clearly joined to the Ib terrace wall. This floor lay here at about 2.20, or a good half-metre above the base of the Ib terrace wall. From this point we can follow the downward slope of the ramp towards the court, though it is broken off before it reaches it.

We see in these circumstances evidence that the ramp, and therefore the structures to the east, had roots in the Temple-I period, and refer to the earliest period under the circular court as supplementary stratigraphical observations. Close to and south of the ramp there was also found a layer of pottery beakers (figs. 282-283) which are characteristic of Temple I's foundation offerings, cf. section 13 (10). They lay at level 3.00 and were embedded in dark grey charcoal-coloured powder. It should be noted here that a clay beaker, though of another type (fig. 504-513), forms a distinct category among the finds from the excavations in the oval court (see below, p. 238).

As the ramp, too, was excavated by means of trenches following the walls, we are unable to illustrate its stratigraphical placing, but it should be recorded that, on the south side of the lower ramp, there was found a floor-like plaster layer near the foot of the ramp, at about level 2.70.

It is improbable that the lower ramp has been connected to the circular court. The ramp-step (8) has already a surface-level which lies higher than that known from section 11 for the lower ramp. The situation should have been the opposite. We therefore believe that the circular court and the ramp-step are, instead, constructed to fit in with the lowest level in the upper ramp, and thereby belong to an early phase of Temple II. A determination of this level must be a matter of opinion. The denuded east end of the earlier ramp shows two possibilities, which are also recorded in section 11, a paving (22) of split stone in yellowish plaster, and a plaster floor (23).

All the constituents of the structures in the east studied here belong, in other words, to Temple II, with the sole exceptions of the lower ramp and the quite unimpressive building-remains (1). On the other hand, these bear witness to a related situation already in the time of Temple I.

Water-channels

Under the north side of the lower ramp it was possible to excavate 1½ m of a drain (24), covered by flat stones (plan 7). It runs in under the ramp, and almost at right-angles to the east wall of the temple-terrace. It was not investigated further, but must from its position be interpreted as a Temple-I feature.

In the same area there also appeared traces of a later drain from the time of Temple II, but it is only recorded in section 13 (C). It ran in from the west, from Temple II's terrace wall, obliquely into the section, where it is seen to consist of stones set in plaster and larger covering stones at a level just under the foot of the Temple-II wall. This drain, too, was not further investigated.

An underground water-channel of a man's height (25) was on the other hand investigated (figs. 235-236). It can be seen in section 12 (K) and 13 (F) and has already been mentioned in chapter 2. The channel is built up with walls of fairly small stones and roofed with large flat stones, all held together with yellow plaster. From section 12 we also know of its stone-set base with a carved-out central channel. A missing roof-stone may reveal a cleaning-hole. This Temple-II channel is overlain by the oval wall, and is therefore older than that structure.

The southeast foreland

South of the oval court a cross-shaped trial trench was dug, in order to acquire a minimum of information concerning the southeastern foreland.

From the cruciform trial trench comes *section 14*, which stretches from the oval court's wall (A) for 16½ m in a southerly direction, only interrupted by an unexcavated block of earth in the middle. It goes down to subsoil and shows in part the original ground-surface of the foot of the tell in this sector.

The subsoil (13) runs downhill towards the south, where, as in other places on the outskirts of the temple area, it drops below level 4.00. The section shows a layering typical for the eastern area, with thick deposits of dark powdery material, cf. sections 12 and 13, but differs in containing a quantity of remains of buildings, of which the lower (I, J and L) should be attributed to Temple I, and the remainder to Temple II.

8. Temple III

The latest Barbar temple has been an imposing edifice, but it was severely plundered by stone-robbers, so that there were only modest traces remaining, if we leave out of account the quantities of fill from its platform (plan 8).

The ruins present themselves in a fashion which demonstrates both a continuity and a discontinuity in relation to Temple II. Where Temple II clearly retained basic ideas from Temple I, Temple III disassociates itself.

The clearest case of continuity shows itself naturally in the retention of the same site, expressed in the construction of a new central platform, which completely covers the platform of Temple II. A special sign of continuity is shown in the continued use of the temple-well, which is adapted to the new architecture. Signs of discontinuity, on the other hand, present themselves in the changed ground-plan.

The trapezoid central platform is replaced by a square one, the oval platform is covered over, together with the pool and the Eastern Court.

We know nothing of the buildings which have stood upon Temple III. Thus its interpretation as a temple must rest upon general considerations: it is raised directly above Temple II, and it retains a high central platform as the kernel of the structure. Moreover, it is enlightening that the temple-builders, who began by demolishing important parts of Temple II, nevertheless did so with due reverence. They seem thereby to act in accordance with the spirit of the place. There are also special features which point towards the temple-interpretation. We can point to the retention, in the new structure, of the well, and to the placing of large blocks of cut stone with four-sided excisions in front of the north wall of Temple III.

The walls and the well

We must picture to ourselves Temple III, at the time when the stone-robbery started, standing as an immense ruin of the temple platform. With the removal of putative remains of buildings upon the platform and of the surrounding terrace walls the site was reduced to the gravel mound with which Glob was confronted in 1954. We can also see how the robbers came into contact with parts of Temple II, and bit further into the tell, demolishing vital parts of temple II in part or totally.

The remains of Temple III are thus fragments of the footing of the terrace walls, left behind on all four sides, but without connection between them. These walls have originally formed an edifice measuring about 38 × 38 m in the shape of a square platform, oriented to the cardinal points of the compass. They have an average base level of 1.50 on a generally spread layer of fill which buries Temple II, and they have surrounded the masses of fill which comprised the platform, and which are only documented in the Main Section and in early excavation photographs.

We shall now take in turn the surviving fragments of these walls, beginning with the western portion of wall (1), which is relatively well preserved, insofar as it stands, exceptionally, in its full width and in several courses. It therefore gives us our best information on the building technique used.

The wall, which is 3½ m broad, is a shell-wall, where most care has been devoted to the outer face (figs. 237-238). It is built up systematically with the use of roughly shaped limestone blocks, which nevertheless are finely cut on the outer sides. In all the joints can be seen a mortaring of fine-grained grey-brown plaster, and in places a block has been replaced by masonry consisting of smaller stones cemented together with plaster (fig. 239).

The interior of the wall consists of enormous quantities of light brown fine-grained plaster, mixed with large and small stones and cut blocks (fig. 240). The back of the wall is also coated with plaster.

According to a description, a continuation of this walling overlay the pool stairway at the time when

Fig. 237. Temple III, western terrace wall, from W. Outer face (1959).

Fig. 238. Temple III, western terrace wall, from NW. Outer face (1959).

Fig. 239. Temple III, western terrace wall, from W. Detail of outer face (1959).

Fig. 240. Temple III, western terrace wall, from N. Body of wall, outer face to right (1959).

Fig. 241. Temples II and III, northern terrace walls, from S. In front, Temple-II wall, badly demolished with plaster surfaces sticking up along the northern edge and in contact with building layers of granulated plaster from Temple III behind them. Extreme rear, the Temple-III wall, badly demolished (1960).

Fig. 242. Temple III, northern terrace wall, from SE. Westernmost large foundation-block north of the wall, which cannot be seen (1960).

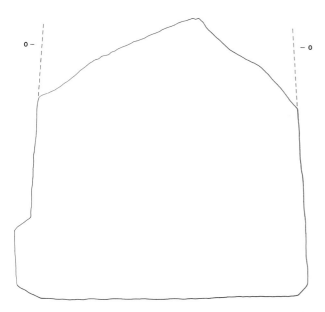

Fig. 243. Temple III. Elevation of foundation-block, northern side, as fig. 242. 1:20.

the wall was excavated, and section 7B (2) shows a part of this overlying portion. It had been partly demolished here, and section 7B (1) shows the outline of the robber-excavation. There was also found, *ex situ* on the stairway itself, one of the large stone blocks from the wall. Moreover, the demolition of the side-slabs of the stairway down to the level of the bottom of the Temple-III wall can bear witness to the situation, that the building of the west wall of Temple III cancels out the stairway as a connecting link to the pool, and thereby sets the pool out of function.

The stratigraphy of the west wall points in the same direction. Section 21 (J) and section 22 (H and G) show the section of the wall here described as lying high in the sequence of layers, while from the foot of the wall there extends a thick covering layer, which completely overlies the Temple-II levels, in this case the oval platform with its structures.

In the north only a central piece (2) of the wall had survived, and therefore it is first and foremost the layers from the stone-robber trenches that appear in the sections here, cf. sections 30 (2) and 31 (12). A special layer in section 30 (1) can moreover be interpreted as a demolition disturbance in the Temple-III level, where some large structure can have been removed. The underlying layer in section 30 (3) is evidence of the covering-up of the Temple-II levels.

At the north end of the Main Section the place in the sequence of the wall-section here described (C) can be seen. It has an intact rear face. As a poor reflection of a layer better preserved elsewhere in the north-east we can also note here a building-level from the construction of Temple III (fig. 241). It consists of light grey-brown coarse-grained plaster, cf.

Main Section (15), and has been deposited between the Temple-III wall (C) and the Temple-II wall (D). We shall return to this layer in connection with the following piece of wall.

About 2 m in front of the original face of this northern wall there stood two large cut limestone blocks which, with their holes in the top, must have served as plinths. They are extremely monumental, particularly the westernmost (3), which, with its dimensions of 1½ × 1½ × 1½ m is the largest single block in the whole temple-complex (figs. 242-244). It has moreover once been taller, since the top has been severely hacked to pieces, though not more so than to allow two square hollows cut in the top still to be seen.

The block is in the shape of a truncated pyramid and completely evenly finished on the outer sides, though with a footing-portion which is rough and irregular in treatment. The footing is shaped with a ledge on the south and east sides.

The eastern block (4) is somewhat smaller but is also more badly damaged (fig. 245). It has had three hollows. It is presumably not unreasonable to assume a flanking function for these blocks, but a widespread disturbance in the Main Section (1a) prevents us from identifying the actual structure which they flanked, presumably a stairway.

Of the course of the eastern wall (5) half is recognizable, though in a badly broken-up condition, partly as patches of connected masonry, partly as isolated limestone blocks, some of which lie *ex situ* east of the wall. It is built of cut limestone blocks and large and small fragments laid in excessive amounts of plaster. Right at the north we can see two large facing-blocks *in situ*.

Section 18 cuts this wall at its northern end. It was specially positioned in order to study the stratigraphical placing of the wall (A), the inner side of which was preserved. Here the eastern edge of the layer (1) left by the stone-robbery reveals the location of the wall's original outer face, and thereby established a wall-breadth of 3½ m. This layer-edge is also in fine line with the two facing blocks already mentioned. Finally, the section also shows the above-mentioned building-layer of grey-brown coarse-grained plaster (3).

East of the wall there can be seen yet another stretch of wall (plan 8:6) surviving in a length of 2½ m. It lies at a higher level than the rest of the masonry.

The east wall is also cut by section 12 (F), but at a point where it is almost entirely demolished. On the other hand the building-layer of coarse-grained plaster is strongly represented, overlying parts of Temple II which were already demolished, as described in chapter 2.

The continuing course of the east wall is cut in the south by section 13. But here the wall has been com-

Fig. 244. Temple III, outer face of large foundation-block as fig. 242, from N (1960).

Fig. 245. Temple III, northern terrace wall, from SE. Easternmost large foundation-block north of the wall, which cannot be seen.

Fig. 246. Temple III, SW-corner of terrace wall, from NW. The earth-face is section 27C. On right, oval-wall IIa, rear side (1957).

Fig. 247. Temple III, lower part of temple-well, from E. Bonded with southern terrace wall, which overlies oval-wall IIa. Well-drum on earth-pedestal (1958).

Fig. 248. Temple III, lower part of temple-well, from SE. Overlying oval-wall IIa (1957).

Fig. 249. Temple III, lower part of temple-well, from SE. Detail of bondage with wall (1957).

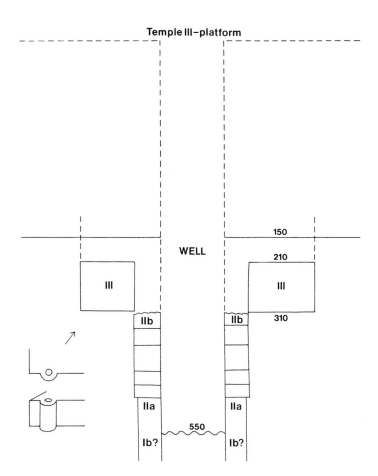

Fig. 250. Temples II and III. Reconstruction of well-phases. 1:50. In left corner, Temple III-well.

pletely removed, and only a robber-layer (1) filled with fragments bears witness to the wall's original presence.

The south wall (7) was gone, apart from its southwest corner (fig. 246). But here we are so fortunate that the inner corner is preserved, and thereby datum-points are in fact secured for all four walls. The terrace can be documented precisely.

To this southwest corner (7) the temple-well is also attached. The masonry appears on section 26A (C) as a cross-section through the south wall and on section 27C (A) as a longitudinal section of the west wall. On section 26A can be seen the remains of the wall bonded with the masonry of the well, cemented downward from the foot of the wall. In addition the wall and the masonry of the well are cut by section 26C (A and C).

In all three sections, the underlying layer of fill covering the Temple II horizon is seen, cf. section 26A (8), section 26C (2) and section 27C (9).

The temple-well is built onto this wall, and positioned above the phase of the well that was constructed in association with oval-wall IIb (fig. 247). The new well has projected outwards as a semicircular apse from the face of the wall, and presumably been continued upwards, so that the well was directly accessible from the surface of Temple III's platform.

This quite impressive construction has been carried out with masonry drums just as in the case of

the phase-IIb well, only much larger. The lowest drum is fairly intact, but it has also been covered over, since it lies ½ m under the foot of the wall (fig. 248). It has a diameter of about 5 m. On the plan can be seen the terrace wall (7), the remains of a well-drum (8) built into the terrace wall, and the well-preserved lowest well-drum (9); it is 1 m high and similarly built into the terrace wall.

The lowest drum (9) swings inwards in a circle – here shown dotted – under the next-lowest (8). The remains of this drum establishes contact with the bottom of the terrace wall by means of a side-patch with an upward-sloping baseline (figs. 247, 249). Approximately where this side-patch ends its upward course the front-face of the terrace wall, with its established width of 3½ m, must have been built on. This patching must thus have been invisible. The corresponding situation seen from within, with the masonry of the drum bonded to the base of the higher-lying terrace wall, is shown in section 26A (C). An excavation photograph even shows a cavity to the left of the sunk drum-masonry (fig. 74).

The lower drum also reveals a remarkably well-preserved outer face. The plastering stands with fresh strokes in the material. According to our interpretation it has also been buried, and its outer side covered. The inner side is broken up.

The plan also demonstrates the two older phases of the well (10 and 11), constructed respectively for

Fig. 251. In the background, surviving portion of Temple-III's platform with horizontal stratification of sterile fill. In the foreground cult arrangements on Temple II floor, from NE. Slab, plan 3:20, erected in its foundation groove, plan 3:21 (1955).

the oval-walls IIb and IIa. The IIa well-phase may go directly back to a Temple-I well, or indirectly to one in the immediate neighbourhood.

Section 26B (A and B) shows the well-masonry from Temple III, overlying the previous well-phase. Its inside is filled with layers of fragments (2 and 3) from the destruction of the well.

A reconstructional section gives a connected picture of the total building-history of the well, which is particularly interesting as illustrating a special aspect of the general segmentation of the temple constructions (fig. 250).

This well was cleaned out in the Islamic period, and from this period there comes a large collection of pottery, found lying in the layers that filled the surviving part of the well-shaft (Frifelt 2001).

As has been said, it is only the footings of Temple III's terrace wall that are preserved. The masses of earth that the walls held together, the "fill" of the platform, appear in the Main Section (1).

Already the breadth of the wall suggests that we are dealing with very high walls, and the masses of

fill, insofar as they are undisturbed, confirm this impression. The Main Section shows that the masses of fill are roughly divided into horizontal levels by layers containing plaster (figs. 15, 251). In this circumstance we can see stages both in the construction of the wall and in the accompanying filling of the interior of the platform. As none of the plaster layers can be interpreted as floors, we are forced to the conclusion that the actual floor-level of Temple III has lain above the tell-surface existing in 1954, and must therefore be regarded as demolished. This gives a minimum height for the platform as 4 m, and it has thereby reached double the height of Temple II's platform.

Concerning the organization of this platform we are for good reasons precluded from knowing anything at all, except that the demolition of the surface level bears witness to building material worthy of considerable effort and expense. It must be left to the eye of the imagination to see Temple III, with its large and high platform, rising impressively above the flat surrounding landscape.

9. Islamic Masonry

During the excavation there was observed, particularly in the south, masonry which was clearly shown, both by the stratigraphy and by the objects accompanying it, to be very much later in date than the temple (plan 8). This masonry, however, has its place in a description of the history of the Barbar temple, as a relic of the time when the temple was subjected to comprehensive and systematic stone-robbery.

This robbery has left traces, not merely in the Islamic pottery from the filled-in temple-well, but also in the numerous discoveries of the same pottery in the immense robber-trenches and pits which were dug to plunder the temple's solid masonry of its cut stone (Frifelt 2001; see also chapter 15).

Less prevalent but nevertheless present is Sassanian pottery, and here the finds of pottery are supplemented by fragments of a life-size stone statue of a human being, found on the east side of the temple (see chapter 16). The least one can say is therefore that the site has also been utilized in some way in late pre-Islamic times.

The masonry here described is concentrated on the southern edge of the tell (figs. 252-253), where there ran, parallel with each other but at various heights, three walls which were worth robbing, terrace wall IIb from Temple II's oval platform, the terrace wall from the same temple's central platform, and the terrace wall of Temple III. These three walls contained enormous quantities of cut stone blocks.

Fig. 252. Islamic masonry at foot of tell in south, from NE. In foreground, oval-wall IIa, in background, projecting portion of oval-wall IIb (1958).

Fig. 253. Islamic masonry
at foot of tell in south,
from NW (1958).

In order to plunder these walls it was necessary to dig both wide and deep trenches, and they assumed such a scale that the half-filled hollows left in the area invited building during or after the period of the robbery.

Only isolated remains of this building activity have been excavated, and this only to the degree necessitated by our own excavations. The walls which occur must be taken to be foundations. They are built of stones set in clay with lumps of plaster. One wall-remnant (12) can be seen to come from a rectangular corner-portion of a house. Another (14) survives as a fairly long stretch of walling. The third remnant (13) comes from a round tower, which has had a diameter of 4½ m.

The accompanying Islamic pottery can also be seen to underlie the masonry described, but here we are also down in the stone-robber trenches. In its turn the masonry is overlain by the foot of the tell, covered by more than metre-thick layers of earth. Under the wall-corner could moreover be seen an isolated torn-away block from the plundering.

We have here only paid attention to the southern edge of the tell, but both the same pottery and the same outlines of the robber-excavations can be seen everywhere on the tell. In the study of the Barbar temple these robber-trenches have been most useful, as negative impressions of vanished architecture. They are often just as accurately aligned as archaeological wall-following trenches. Where, however, stone-robbery reached such a scale that large built-up areas were obliterated, as for example in the southwest corner of Temple II's central platform, the work of the robbers rather lacks this positive aspect.

10. The Northeast Temple

In the northeastern border-area of the Barbar temple's large tell lay a smaller and lower tell, only separated from the larger by a hollow of 10-20 m's breadth (fig. 254, plan 9). This second tell only rose about 2 m above the surrounding land, and its total extent was 40-50 m. It was particularly characterized by a summit plateau, a good metre in height and over 20 m across, which formed the central area of the tell. Very near the edge of this separate top-plateau could be seen traces of an almost filled-in stone-robber trench, where a slight hollow ran. It was several metres wide and four-sided in its course, but it was almost without depth.

Preliminary investigations of this tell in 1956 and 1961 revealed that it covered a large, but fatally plundered, edifice of the Barbar temple's period. In contrast to the Barbar temple, the investigated portions of this structure showed no sign of any building-history in several stages. The considered interpretation therefore concludes that we have here the remains of a homogeneous construction, the ruins of which can best be understood as the remains of an impressive double terrace, two platforms one above the other. The upper platform has supported a very large building, of which, however, not a single stone remains. With this interpretation the site accords with the Barbar temple as an independent neighbour-temple.

The first investigation took place in the period 25th January to 27th March 1956. It only comprised the upper central portion of the tell, the summit plateau. This limitation naturally hampered the in-

Fig. 254. Northeast Temple, tell from N. In background the Barbar-temple's large tell (1954).

terpretation at that date of the character of the site (cf. Harald Andersen 1956 p. 175-188). The reworking here thus contains a number of reinterpretations in relation to the preliminary publication. The excavator – Harald Andersen – could nevertheless accurately determine the nature of the building-elements in the area involved, and record the upper part of the stratigraphy in exemplary fashion. The basic material for an understanding of the upper platform of the structure is thus available.

It had been a very systematic excavation, consistently carried out by the quadrant method (plan 10). Two trial trenches had been laid out in a cross over the area chosen for investigation, giving a north-south and an eastwest section. After that, the southeast quadrant had been excavated in its entirety, and the other quadrants in chosen sections, directed by the wall-courses found. A well-defined "base-level" was found over the whole area, in the form of a massive foundation layer of stones and plaster. It was upon this that the upper platform had been erected. This layer formed in principle the bottom limit of the excavation, but in itself lay well above the subsoil.

Andersen and Mortensen made later – in 1961 – a short investigation of the southeastern portion of the tell, in the form of three short sections. They produced evidence, admittedly to a restricted extent, concerning the lower part of the structure, which according to our interpretation should be understood as a separate platform.

The following description is divided into a stratigraphic and an architectural section, and, in order to facilitate understanding of the former, it may be briefly stated here that the structure of the upper platform reveals four well-defined main elements: the foundation-layer (plan 10:A), two wall-courses (B and C) based upon this layer, and a large pit (D) in the centre. Like the foundation, the two wall-courses had square ground-plans. They stood in the edge-zone of the foundation, and formed an inner wall (B) and an outer wall (C), the one square lying within the other. The inner wall has formed a foundation-wall for a building on the upper platform, while the outer wall was a terrace wall around this platform. The pit in the centre, however, was dug down to the very bottom of the tell, and thus broke through the foundation-layer. Thus there has originally been a centrally-placed building, the distinctive feature of which was a deep cavity within the terraced temple-structure. This building has been totally razed by stone-robbery.

The lower platform, too, must have been surrounded by a terrace wall, but this is only insecurely documented.

Finally, it should be noted that the coordination system of measurement is peculiar to this tell, but that levelling follows the same principle and datum point as was used in the Barbar temple. Levels given can thus be directly compared, being given positively downwards from a zero-point 8.36 m above sea-level.

Stratigraphy

The stratigraphy of the tell is, on account of the sequence of excavation, best known for the upper part, i.e. from the surface of the tell down to the foundation-layer (A) of the upper platform.

Sections 34 and 35, along the main axes of the coordination system, record the layers here observed and the four structural elements already named (A-D). In addition, the layers observed during the later excavation of 1961, which lay along other axes, have been projected in upon these two sections. They show the stratigraphy in the lower platform.

Thus *section 34* shows, in an eastwest cross-section and in a length of 36½ m, the robbed tell with its subsoil (1) at level 3.70 at the centre of the tell. This original ground-level falls steeply in the area of the eastern edge of the tell, and therefore suggests that a natural rise of ground has characterized the building-site. The surface of the tell falls in low terraces from a highest point in the centre. In the west the surface of the edge of the tell is missing. The top plateau, around the edge of which a slight

depression could be observed before excavation, stretches from point -12 m to point +12 m. The depression was the result of a stone-robber trench (B), then almost completely filled in.

A clear division through the layering of the tell is shown in the massive foundation-layer (A), fashioned of stones and plaster. It shows a local subsidence in the east, but at both ends the original edge of the layer is preserved. With an extent of almost 24 m, it has carried the upper platform.

Under the foundation layer can be noted a layer of sand (3) above slightly clay-mixed sand (2). This sand-layer (3) thus forms the fill in the lower platform. In the east a related layer of sand (4) must be regarded as a continuation, and out here in the eastern end of the section the layer ends in a disturbance (F). This disturbance consists of a layer left by a stone-robber trench, 1 m wide and 1½ m deep, where an original terrace wall has presumably been broken up. On its inner side the trench is accompanied by a robber-level (10) with abandoned cut lime-

Fig. 255. Northeast Temple, detail of earth-face = section 34 (22-23), from S. Plaster levels in fill between outer and inner walls in upper platform. On right, filling of robber-trench from inner wall; on left, likewise for outer wall. A little piece of the rear side of the wall survives (1956).

stone blocks. The evidence presented here forms the main basis for the theory of the existence of the lower platform, but the situation has not been investigated further by means of larger-scale area-excavation.

The remainder of the stratigraphy involves the layers above the foundation-layer, and it is marked by massive disturbances (B and C), which reflect robber-trenches. In contrast to the above-mentioned trench (F) we have here well-supported general features. The trenches ran around the tell in a four-sided course, and only went down to the foundation-layer. They have contained continuous walling, the courses of which could be seen, after area-clearance, as the impressions of an inner wall (B) and an outer wall (C).

In addition there was the central area, marked by a large robber-hole (D), which in section 34 is only excavated to the level of the foundation-layer, but which continued through a breach in this layer down to the bottom of the tell, cf. section 35.

Where the stratigraphy was untouched by the disturbing trench-layers, layers of sand and gravel with hard plaster-bound levels were characteristic of the stratigraphy between the inner walls (B), and similarly layers of sand and gravel with plaster lev-

els between the inner and outer walls (B and C) (fig. 255). All these layers (15-23) are to all appearances *in situ* as part of the construction; they form fill-layers in the upper platform, around which the outer wall (C) had originally stood as a terrace wall. A vertical remnant of this wall (C1) can still be seen with a bit of the rear of the wall in the western disturbance. The horizontally divided strata in this platform are moreover a feature which can be compared with the filling of the third Barbar temple.

The double-sided disturbance-layers (B and D) here shown give us thus a picture of the plundering of a wall embedded in the upper platform and of a centrally-placed structure, unknown to us in details, which was so deeply founded that it went down to the bottom of the tell. The surrounding disturbance (B) has contained a foundation-wall for a building which has stood upon a lost floor-level above the surface of the tell.

The layers left by the robbery of the outer walls (C) are characteristically one-sided; only their rear-sides stood clearly recognizable. The layers were filled with plaster fragments and chips of limestone, and these heaps of stone lay moreover in such a way that their lowest levels more or less corresponded to the level of the foundation-layer (A). This is a circumstance that suggests that the face of the robbed wall had been free of earth at the time of demolition, but not its reverse-side, where the robber-layers are clearly marked, where indeed bits of the wall in places remain behind. There are thus here circumstances of discovery which would particularly characterize a plundered terrace wall.

The upper platform deduced from the section has, as has been said, stood upon the foundation-layer (A), the edge of which, outside the terrace wall (C), which was originally about 1 m broad, must have been freely accessible as a "sidewalk", narrow in the east but broad in the west. The foundation-layer itself ended, both in the east and the west, in a stone-set edge, so carefully laid that we must assume it to have been visible. It has formed a low ledge at the transition between the upper and the lower platforms.

In section 34 can also be seen at the west end above the foundation-layer a large block of wall (E) which had fallen outwards, and at the east end just outside the foundation-layer are abandoned limestone blocks. On the surface of the lower platform in the east there was an isolated layer of plaster (G) on a foundation of broken stone.

Section 35, a north-south cross-section through the tell in a length of 40 m, is a close parallel to section 34, and attention will therefore only be drawn to chosen features.

In the few places where the subsoil (1) is recorded as appearing there is some uncertainty about the accuracy of the identification.

At the south end of the section can be seen a change in the nature of the soil (3), the only large irregularity in the stratigraphy of the area, a layer of sand containing many stones. It can be interpreted as a demolition-layer, and as a possible parallel to the eastern stone-robber trench (F) in section 34. The distance in section 35 between the disturbance (3) and the calculated original edge of the foundation-layer (A) agrees with the corresponding relationship in section 34. Thus the terrace wall of the lower platform can have stood here.

The foundation-layer (A) appears in section 35 with broken-off edges at both ends. The outer edge was chopped away, so that the measurement across the layer was reduced to 19 m, as compared with the intact length in section 34 of 24 m.

Furthermore, the central pit (D) has here been excavated to the bottom. Thus an impression can here be obtained of this disturbance seen in cross-section and to its full depth. With its considerable contents of broken stone, wall-fragments and cut blocks, the robber-hole gives emphatic evidence of a lost structural feature.

The remaining stratification and the large disturbances (B and C) are features practically identical with those appearing in section 34. Of special peculiarities we can only point to specific layers or the outlines of pits (8, 10 and 16) and to a small excavation (E) in the south end of the section and a block of walling there (F), the relationship of which to the structural complex remained unexplained. It lay somewhat far out and high up in comparison with the remaining parts of the building.

The architecture

The course of the excavation had the result that it is particularly the upper part of the tell that can be regarded as well-investigated (plan 10). The following detailed descriptions can be given of the four main elements already named (A-D) in the upper platform. They have already been clearly indicated in the stratigraphy.

The foundation-layer (A) formed a continuous base-surface for the upper platform, though with a large hole in the middle. It had a very horizontal surface, apart from a subsidence in the north-east, full of cracks. The surface-level lay at about 2.30, and the layer was 25-30 cm thick. It consisted of stones set in quantities of plaster, but the edge was broken up at most places. Its original straight course could, however, be seen at three points, namely in the middle of the east and west sides and at the eastern end of the south side (figs. 256-258).

This edge showed itself here to be formed of cut limestone blocks as though forming a low dais. From east to west the foundation-layer measured almost 24 m, and it has presumably been the same in the north-south direction. As the whole of the northern edge was broken up, it can only be claimed that the north-south measurement was in excess of 21 m, which was its greatest measurable extent.

The foundation-layer has formed a square of 24 × 24 m, laid out rather obliquely by the cardinal points of the compass. On this foundation traces were found of two walls, each forming a square, the one within the other, and placed asymmetrically upon the foundation-layer.

The inner wall (B) only appeared as an uneven mortar-coated impression in the foundation-layer, since this wall had everywhere been plundered to

Fig. 256. Northeast Temple, southeast quadrant, from SE. Foundation layer with impressions of inner and outer walls, and surviving remains of outer wall. In foreground surviving edge-portion of foundation layer (1956).

the last stone (figs. 256, 259-260). In sections 34 and 35 can be seen the outlines of the robber-trenches, which all start at the surface of the tell. This total plundering suggests a high quality for the lost building-material, and a number of impressions of stones in the impress of the foot of the wall in the foundation-layer confirm this. They reveal the original presence of large cut limestone ashlars.

The impress of the wall shows that it has been about 1½ m broad, and that the wall has had a ground-plan of 15 × 15 m in outside measurement. This vanished wall formed the foundation for a building which had crowned the upper platform.

The outer wall (C) also showed itself as an impress in the foundation-layer, but here there were preserved in addition at three places remains of the vertical walling (C1), though only of the back of the walls (figs. 256, 259-260). These three places lay in the middle of the western side, in the southeastern corner and at the north end of the east side. For this wall, too, sections 34 and 35 showed the corresponding robbery layers (C), or at least their inner sides. At all four places in the two sections they were filled with fragments and chippings. To judge

by the impressions this wall had also contained cut limestone blocks, especially along its outer face.

As the plan shows, this impression of the wall in the foundation-layer was far from universally present, since the underlying foundation-layer was often torn up together with the wall. This wall also followed a square ground-plan, about 19 × 19 m in outer measurement. It had been on average about 1 m broad, leaving an interval of about 1½ m dividing the two walls (B and C) from each other.

The surviving remains of the outer wall rose to a maximum height of 1 m above the foundation-layer (fig. 261). They were remains of the reverse-side, consisting of irregularly shaped blocks and local stones mortared with plaster, a material without value to the stone-robbers. The actual reverse-side was coated with plaster, a feature which we also saw in the terrace wall of Temple III. The resemblance can be taken further, insofar as our wall here seems similarly to have been a shell-wall with an ashlar-built outer face. The excavator noted further a striking similarity between the building technique and particularly the surface-finishing, as compared with the Temple-III wall.

Fig. 257. Northeast Temple, west end of eastwest section-trench, from W. Foundation layer with part of edging preserved in foreground, and fallen block of wall behind, cf. section 34 (E) (1956).

As a terrace wall around the upper platform, now demolished, there could be seen in the trenches (C) in sections 34 and 35 layers of fragments from the demolition, left behind in large heaps. They lay outside the wall's original position at a level which approximated that of the foundation-layer.

In the southeastern quadrant the foundation-layer was completely cleared. Here it could be seen that the whole area inside the inner wall (B) had been in use when newly laid. For well-preserved impressions of human footprints and handprints were found there (figs. 262-263), in addition to impressions of mats made of Z-twisted cords crossed by and interlaced with some sort of reeds (fig. 264). These impressions indicate that this surface had never thereafter been trodden and worn down. It had been covered as a stage in the building-construction, by the masses of fill within the overlying upper platform.

The foundation-layer's surface in the narrow edge-zone in the south-east – outside the outer wall (C) – is in contrast so characterized by weathering that we must conclude that it had been uncovered for a considerable period. On the other hand the parallel section of the foundation-layer's surface

between the two walls (B and C) showed no corresponding signs of weathering. This circumstance agrees well with the interpretation of the outer wall as a terrace wall, the outer face of which alone has stood free.

In the edge-zone in the middle of the west side, outside the outer wall (C), the surface of the foundation-layer is also not especially worn, but in contrast to the situation in the south-east this edge-zone in the west was of considerable width, so that one may well imagine that this broad terrace was utilized in some way or other that involved a roof or a covering.

The pit (D) in the centre of the structure is documented in sections 34 and 35 as the remains of a large robber-hole. It starts at the surface of the tell, breaks through the foundation-layer on its way, and first stops at the subsoil about 1½ m under the foundation-layer. This robber-hole can be regarded as the secondary trace of what was probably the most important feature of the site. Here there has been placed a deeply sunk structure, but our knowledge of its nature is unfortunately strictly limited. We do not even know the full extent of the hole, which stands vaguely in the survey plan at the foundation-level as a hole running east-west with a length of 5-6 m and a width of 1-2 m. The contents of this hole are only observed in the section-trenches, and, so far as the lower part under the foundation-layer is concerned, only in the north-south trench, i.e. in an excavation-sector 1 m wide. Here the lower part proved to contain, among other things, finely cut limestone blocks, lying *ex situ* in a compact demolition-layer.

On a basis of these observations it can be assumed that in the central hole there had stood an underground stone-built chamber of almost shaft-like character. Despite the immense degree of destruction, the situation invites a continued investigation, particularly because other structures from Bahrain give a possibility of interpretation which is highly relevant: the well-temples from Umm as-Sujur near Diraz, see Appendix 5. The type of structure found there would fit well into the hole in the Barbar site. If the central object in our double-terrace has indeed been such a well, then we are dealing with a structure which in principle should be identifiable even in demolished condition. The chamber has in that case formed the frame around the well and the stairway down to it. In the Diraz site this staircase was furthermore L-shaped.

This special feature of the Northeast Temple has lain in the centre of the building, the outlines of which are drawn by the foundation-wall (B), and which has stood upon the upper platform. It has naturally had a floor-level, but this has been the first victim of the stone-robbers, together with the building and its foundation-wall.

Fig. 258. Northeast Temple, portion of southeast quadrant, from N. Foundation layer with surviving edge-portion and limestone blocks *ex situ* (1956).

Fig. 259. Northeast Temple, portion of southeast quadrant, from S. Foundation layer with impressions of inner and outer walls, and surviving portion of outer wall in SE-corner (1956).

Fig. 260. Northeast Temple, southeast quadrant, from SW. Foundation layer with impressions of walls and preserved portion of outer wall; behind this an unexcavated baulk of earth. In background stone blocks *ex situ* (1956).

Fig. 261. Northeast Temple, portion of southeast quadrant, from NW. Surviving portion of outer wall with plaster-coated rear side (1956).

Fig. 262. Northeast Temple, foot-impressions in foundation layer within the inner wall (1956).

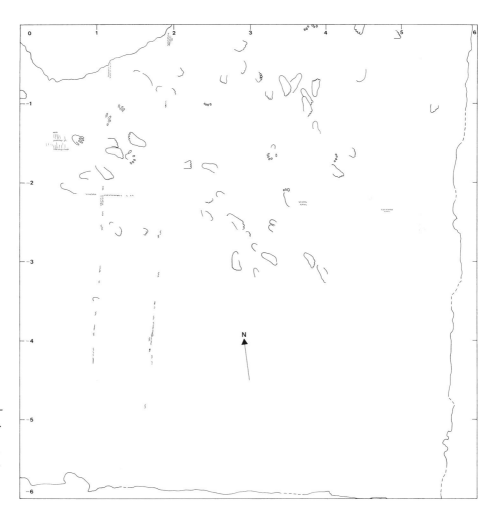

Fig. 263. Northeast Temple, southeast quadrant. Human footprints and handprints and impressions of mats in the surface of the foundation layer.

207

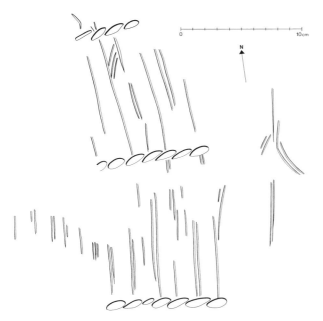

Fig. 264. Impression of mat; detail of fig. 263.

We can thus now describe the upper platform as standing upon the foundation-layer (A), surrounded by a terrace wall (C), and filled up inside. The foundation-layer has had an edge-zone which was freely accessible as a "sidewalk" of varying width. With its painstakingly stone-set edge the foundation-layer has formed a large low dais in front of the platform. With this interpretation the inner wall (B) is the foundation of a large building on the platform. Concerning the heart of this building, which was destroyed by stone-robbery in the central pit (D), we can as yet only speculate.

The upper platform has thus formed a terraced edifice standing upon the foundation-layer as a base measuring 24 × 24 m; upon this stood the actual platform measuring 19 × 19 m and about 2 m in height, and upon this again a building measuring 15 × 15 m, but of unknown height. Of the walls and floor of this building nothing remains.

The subsequent investigation in 1961 can add to this a lower platform in a double-terraced structure. It is only known through stratigraphical observations, without the support of area-excavation. Sections 34 and 35 showed layers which could be interpreted as the fill within a platform, and the outlines of stone-robberies which more or less clearly indicated the original presence of a surrounding terrace wall, cf. section 34 (F) and section 35 (3).

With these observations a new dimension is added to our conception of the original character of the site, a lower platform which bears the upper. The central structure (D) was carried down through this lower platform, of the ground-plan of which we cannot speak with certainty. But the platform has – at least in the east – been a minimum of 2 m high, and has here set a step which projects about 11 m forward in relation to the edge of the upper platform's foundation-layer. It possibly does the same in the south. These measurements support a view that the lower platform may have been twice as large across as the upper one. And this begins to indicate a structure which in extent bears comparison with the third Barbar-temple (fig. 265). It has merely lain at a lower ground-level. Of other points of resemblance with that temple may be mentioned the square ground-plans, the estimated total height of the structures, the similarity of the building techniques, and much else.

However limited our knowledge of the Northeast Temple, its structural peculiarities and its close proximity to the Barbar temple give reason for our interpretation of it as a separate temple-structure. It seems to be contemporary with the third Barbar-temple, and the conception of a double-temple thus takes form.

The Northeast Temple must in its day have stood more or less freely accessible for stone-robbery, and this has therefore followed a particularly destructive course, a fate which it shares with its large neighbour to the south-west.

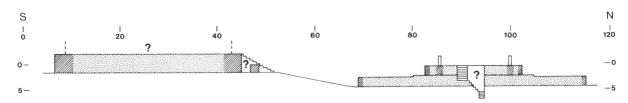

Fig. 265. Northeast Temple and Temple III, idealized reconstruction-section projected in on same axis. Temple III, left, with a hypothetical stairway on northern side and a completely unknown upper building. The Northeast temple, right, with hypothetical symmetry in the construction of the double platform; reconstructed with a well-shrine of Umm as-Sujur type, i.e. with an L-shaped shaft-stairway down to a well in the centre of the temple.

208

11. Pottery and the Dating of the Temple Phases

The first tentative attempts to date the Barbar temple placed its beginning in the early 3rd millennium BC (Glob 1954a; Bibby 1996; Mortensen 1971a-b). Larsen's comparisons of pottery from Barbar and Qala'at al-Bahrain with Mesopotamian material, however, pushed the beginning of the temple sequence into the end of the 3rd millennium BC (Larsen 1983).

Further studies in the ceramic material from Qala'at al-Bahrain, Barbar and Failaka led to a greater understanding of the chronological relations between the Barbar temple phases and the period system based on Qala'at al-Bahrain and thereby also to a more detailed comprehension of the chronological relations between the Gulf and Mesopotamia (Mortensen 1986; Højlund 1986, 1987; Højlund & Andersen 1994, 1997). The results presented in the following are based on a re-evaluation of all the finds excavated at Barbar and represent a revision of earlier published contributions (fig. 266).

The examination of the architecture and stratigraphy of the Barbar temple, presented in the preceding chapters, has led to the separation of five temple phases, Ia-b, IIa-b and III, in chronological sequence. A dating of these architectural phases is not without its problems. Firstly, this is because the phases were not all clearly distinguished in the field, but are at least partly the result of a review of the documentation from the excavation (cf. chapter 1). So, during excavation, trenches and excavation layers often cut through several temple phases, laterally or vertically and at a time when the excavators did not have full understanding of their internal connections. Secondly, the fact that the pottery was generally excavated in layers of 1-2 m thickness, obviously hampers chronological studies.

In the following, the temple phases will be dated, primarily by comparing selected assemblages of pottery found in distinct relation to their structures (fig. 267) with the pottery sequences based on Excavation 520 and Excavation 519 at Qala'at al-Bahrain (cf. *Qala'at 1* and *Qala'at 2*) and on Tell F3 and Tell F6

at Failaka in Kuwait (Højlund 1987). This is fairly straightforward with respect to Temple phases Ia and IIa-b, whereas phases Ib and III have remained more elusive. Apart from pottery, other finds and evidence will be adduced where relevant.

By far the majority of the pottery found at the Barbar temple is locally produced and belongs to the East Arabian late 3rd and early 2nd millennium pottery tradition named *the Barbar tradition* after the Barbar temple site, where it was first identified (Bibby 1996 p. 53). Only a few sherds can be referred to the other contemporary pottery traditions that have been identified at Qala'at al-Bahrain (cf. *Qala'at 1* p. 73ff): the Mesopotamian tradition and the Umm an-Nar tradition. The so-called Eastern traditions, i.e. pottery imported from the Indo-Iranian area, seem hardly to be represented.

In the following, description of pottery shapes and wares will be minimized; instead, reference will be made when possible to contemporaneous pottery types defined on the basis of material from Qala'at al-Bahrain (*Qala'at 1-2*) and Tell F3 and Tell F6 on Failaka (Højlund 1987).

It may therefore be expedient to recapitulate that the pottery from **Qala'at al-Bahrain** has been divided into **types B1-B75** in the local Barbar tradition (cf. *Qala'at 1* p. 75-101), **types M1-M27** in the Mesopotamian tradition (cf. *Qala'at 1* p. 102-110), and **types U1-U12** in the Umm an-Nar tradition (cf. *Qala'at 1* p. 111-117).

Likewise, the pottery from Failaka has been divided into **Failaka types 1-53** in the Barbar tradition (Højlund 1987 p. 13-55) and **Failaka types 54-100** in the Mesopotamian tradition (Højlund 1987 p. 56-99).

Reference is also made to four ware types defined on the basis of the Qala'at al-Bahrain material (*Qala'at 1* p. 101, reprinted below). Besides, a fifth ware type is introduced, which is characteristic of a number of Mesopotamian-inspired shapes found in Temple I contexts.

Ware type 1. Heavily tempered with sand and yellowish-white calcium carbonate particles ("halos"),

Mesopotamia	BC	Failaka	Barbar Temples	Qala'at al-Bahrain
Old Babylonian	1700	3A		
	1800			
Isin-Larsa		2B	ARU	
	1900	2A	III? NE-Temple ARP	IIc
	2000	1	IIb	IIb
Ur III			IIa	
			Ib — AHN + AOT	IIa
			Ia — ADY + AIM / ADZ?	
	2100			Ib
Late Akkadian				Ia
	2200			

Fig. 266. Chronological chart for Barbar temples I-III and the Northeast temple.

probably fragmented sea shells. The grains of sand are mainly almost transparent (quartz?) and strongly rounded. The calcium carbonate particles appear at the surface as irregularly rounded spots with a diameter of usually 0.05-0.3 cm, sharply defined in relation to the clay matrix in which they are embedded. In the centre of the spot there is usually a cavity. In the core of the sherd, the particles have a smaller diameter than at the surface, but retain the central cavity. There is clear lamination in the fabric. This seems to consist of innumerable thin flakes cemented together, but partially separated by very small, long and narrow cavities. The pattern of cavities reveals the pressure applied to the wall of the pot during the shaping process. A slip has normally been applied to the outside of the pot and the inside of the neck.

The colour of the ware varies from red, over light-brown to grey in Qala'at al-Bahrain period Ia, gradually changing to almost exclusively red in period Ib and II. Sections through sherds often show dramatic colour changes within the same sherd from red to grey, indicating poor control over the firing atmosphere.

Ware type 1 has been used only in the production of hand-made pottery, and it corresponds with Failaka A- and B-ware (*Failaka 2* p. 103, figs. 447-448).

Ware type 2. Medium- to low-tempered with mainly transparent sand grains; a few calcium carbonate particles occur occasionally. A slip has normally been applied to the outside of the pot and the inside of the neck. The colours are homogeneous and generally paler and more yellowish than in ware 1 and vary from red over light brown to yellow.

Ware type 2 has mainly been used in the production of hand-made vessels. A number of vessels of this ware are, however, wheel-made, and the fabric

of these vessels tends to have a finer temper. Ware type 2 corresponds to Failaka C-ware (*Failaka 2* p. 103-105, fig. 449).

Ware type 3. Well-fired, hard ware. Fine-grained clay matrix without a sand temper, but with some scattered sharp-edged hard pieces of deep red material (ochre?) 1-2 mm in size and sometimes a few "halos" (see ware type 1). That the ware actually contains ochre, as originally suggested by Mackay (1929 p. 24-25), has been confirmed by modern analysis (*Failaka 2* p. 106). The fabric is often broken into small, thin flakes parallel to the surface in a manner which cannot be observed in other wares. The colour is light red and uniform on both the outer and the inner surface and in the fabric section. There are often traces of red slip.

Ware type 3 has been employed only for hand-made vessels with rims of type B73 and perhaps also B74, and it corresponds to Failaka H-ware (*Failaka 2* p. 106, fig. 454).

Ware type 4. Heavily tempered with a white angular material, identified as calcite. The colour varies around grey, grey to cream, and grey to red. Ware type 4 has been used only in the production of neckless hand-made vessels with rims of types B10-B12.

Ware type 5. Light-red sand-tempered ware with yellowish-white slip. Ware type 5 has been used only in the production of wheel-made vessels.

During excavation of the Barbar temple, the pottery and other finds were collected from areas numbered with Roman letters by each year (e.g. area XII 1957, cf. figs. 6-13) and from each area from horizontal layers. Rim and base sherds were consistently kept, as well as other diagnostic sherds e.g. painted sherds, whereas common body sherds were normally discarded. Artefacts are numbered with letters following the registration number of the Barbar Temple (517) or the Northeast Temple (681).

A number of type series, especially useful for dating purposes, were described for Qala'at al-Bahrain, where the types in each series gradually replace each other in time (*Qala'at 1* p. 130). These type series can now be further refined with the evidence from Barbar. The development of neck-vessel rims from type B1,[1] through B2 to B3 was already clear on the basis of Qala'at al-Bahrain, with types B4-6 being later (*Qala'at 1* fig. 391). This picture has now been further substantiated. It is also clear that the late development of the shape of the triangular rim is parallel to that which has been described for Failaka (Højlund 1987 fig. 458, type 1A-H).

[1] This type series is probably inspired by the Mesopotamian type M1 (*Qala'at 1* figs. 240-242).

210

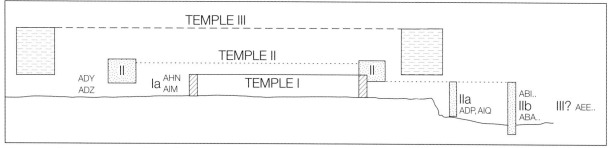

Fig. 267. Schematic section through the platforms of the Barbar temples I-III with important pottery contexts indicated.

Similarly, the development of the hole-mouth vessel rim types B13-19 can be followed both at Qala'at al-Bahrain (*Qala'at 1* figs. 392 and 715) and at Barbar.

Central to the following exposition will then be a series of pottery assemblages which can be shown on stratigraphical and architectural grounds to follow each other in time (fig. 266-267). When these assemblages of pottery are compared, they show a clear typological development, parallel to that identified for periods Ib, IIa, IIb and IIc at Qala'at al-

Bahrain, but more detailed. The comparisons will especially be based on typological details of the triangular neck-vessel rims and hole-mouth rims.

Apart from the close typological similarities between pottery from Barbar, Qala'at al-Bahrain and Failaka – similarities that are here interpreted as evidence of contemporaneity – there are also systematic differences in presence/absence of particular functional categories of pottery, which will be dealt with along other lines in the concluding chapter.

Temple I

Pottery from several contexts must be considered in an attempt to give a dating of the first phase of the temple, Ia: the clay level at the bottom of the central temple platform, the fill above this clay level, the floor of the platform and layers accumulated outside the platform.

No pottery assemblages can be safely assigned to the second phase of the temple, Ib.

Beakers from the clay level of Temple Ia

The first temple on the site of Barbar was constructed upon virgin sand. Between the retaining walls of the central temple platform was placed a thick layer of clay (Main Section: 64), and this layer contained a number of finds that are interpreted as offerings. The clay layer was also recognized outside the platform (cf. above, p. 24), and here finds were made of the same type.

The finds from the clay layer consisted of nearly 100 pottery beakers, besides a few examples of a low pottery bowl or plate, and some objects in other materials, metals and stone, described below (p. 255 and 315). The locations of some of these finds are marked with their registration numbers on plan 1, and a small group of beakers can be seen lying *in situ* in figs. 86 and 268. The finds do not, however, give very useful dating evidence.

The beakers have a conical to slightly flaring upper part and a low hollow foot (517.ACY, fig. 269; 517.DI, fig. 270; 517.CS, fig. 271) (fig. 272) (Lombard 1999, cat.no. 119-122). A few beakers have a more cylindrical body (fig. 273). The height of the beakers varies from 8.9 to 14.3 cm (Σ 37, M 11 cm), and the rim diameter varies from 7 to 8.9 cm. Rim and base edge are often horizontally cut. They are handmade in one piece, often with coarse scraping marks on the surface. The ware belongs to type 1 (cf. p. 209).

The height (= thickness) of the solid part of the foot normally varies from 0.5 to 3 cm, with a typical value of 1 cm, but a few beakers are more solid with a thickness of, for example, 4.7 cm (517.AJE) (fig. 274), cf. also fig. 314.

Two beakers deviate by being thicker-walled and more clumsily shaped (517.AIX) (fig. 275).

The Barbar beakers have previously been described as a variant of the Mesopotamian solid-footed goblet (Mortensen 1971a p. 395), which is a type fossil of the Early Dynastic I period in Mesopotamia (Nissen 1970 pl. 104, type 1; Moon 1987 nos. 97-197). With recent improvements in

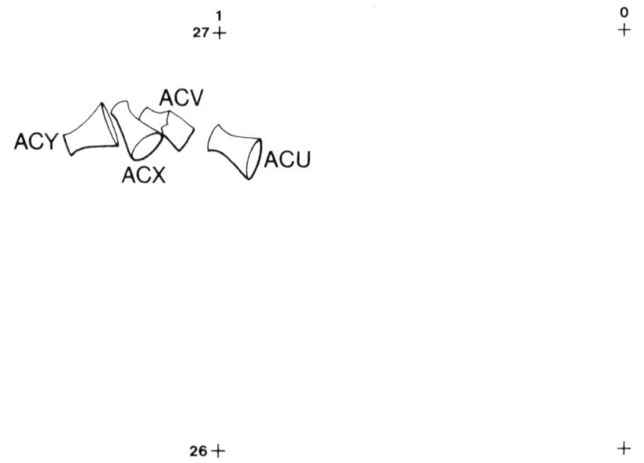

Fig. 268. Pottery beakers lying in situ in clay core of Temple I, from S, cf. fig. 86.

Bahraini chronology it is clear that more than half a millennium separates the Early Dynastic I period from the Barbar temple, and the alleged similarities can therefore have no chronological relevance (Mortensen 1986).

Only a few fragments of this type of beaker have been found at Qala'at al-Bahrain, three of them from period Ia and IIa contexts, a dating too wide to be useful for dating Temple I (*Qala'at 1* type B26, p. 85 and 132).

Besides these beakers, a low bowl found in just a few specimens should be mentioned (fig. 276). It is made in ware of type 1 and in the same coarse style as the beakers, and has the same cutting of the rim as these.

A special thin-walled beaker with a separately manufactured and attached base (figs. 277-280) has been found in three assemblages from the southeastern part of the temple, one from area III-IV 1958 (517.AJT) and one from area IX 1959 (517.ALX), both from the clay core, and one from area VII 1960, embedded in ashy layers above subsoil, cf. section 13, layer 10 (517.AOG). The same three assemblages feature a special upper part of a beaker with a vertical side (often with vertical scraping-marks) and a slightly everted rim part (often with horizontal smoothing) (figs. 281-283), that may go together with this special beaker base.

Besides, a few straight simple jar rims (figs. 284-285) may go with some small flat bases (figs. 286-287). A red-slipped simple neck is decorated with a plum-red chevron line (fig. 288) (cf. Ibrahim 1982 fig. 39). All in ware type 1.

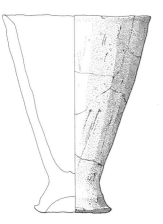

Fig. 269. 1:2.

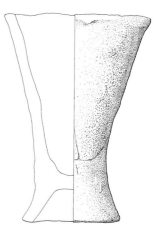

Fig. 270. 1:2.

Fig. 271. 1:2.

Fig. 272. Collection of beakers
from the clay level of Temple I.

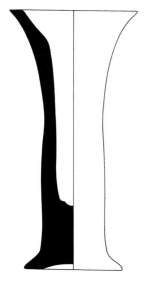

Fig. 273. 1:2.

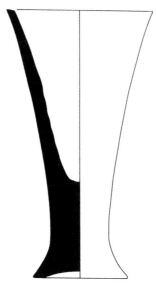

Fig. 274. 1:2.

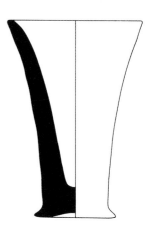

Fig. 275. 1:2.

Figs. 269-288. Pottery from the clay level of Temple Ia.

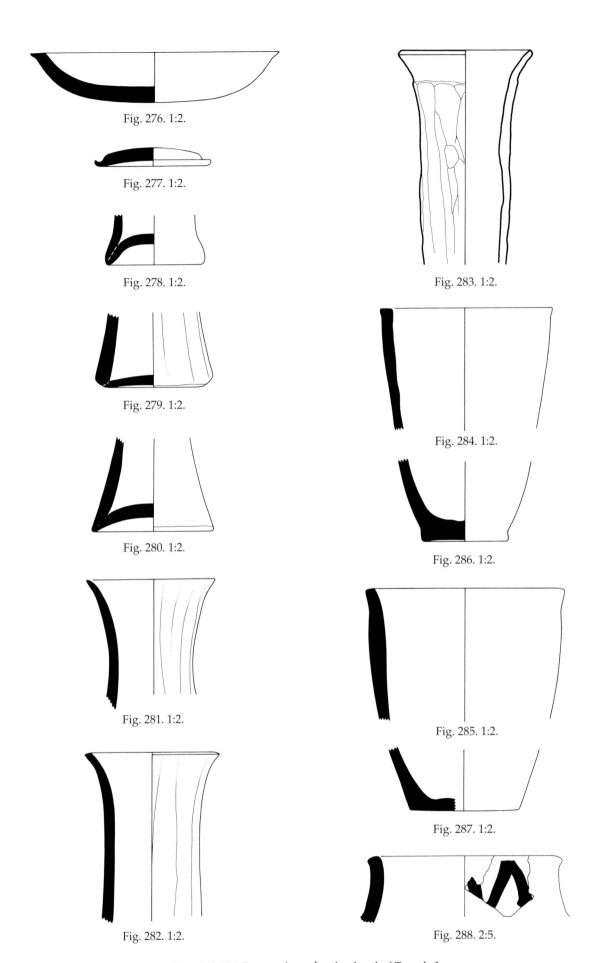

Fig. 276. 1:2.

Fig. 277. 1:2.

Fig. 278. 1:2.

Fig. 279. 1:2.

Fig. 280. 1:2.

Fig. 281. 1:2.

Fig. 282. 1:2.

Fig. 283. 1:2.

Fig. 284. 1:2.

Fig. 286. 1:2.

Fig. 285. 1:2.

Fig. 287. 1:2.

Fig. 288. 2:5.

Figs. 269-288. Pottery from the clay level of Temple Ia.

The fill of the Temple Ia platform

The finds from the fill of the platform of Temple Ia, heaped on top of the clay level, are not useful for dating purposes. Such fill could have been brought in from a variety of contexts and might therefore have provided a useful *terminus post quem* dating for the construction of the platform, were it not for the possibility of intrusions dug down from the floor of the platform. The upper part of a necked vessel in ware type 1 may be such an intrusion (517.AJM) (fig. 289). It has a triangular rim and a round knob applied to the upper shoulder (type B75).

Some large collections of pottery are flawed by the possibility that they contain material also from outside the platform. Besides, the platform fill contained only few, scattered sherds, compared to the quantitites encountered immediately outside of the platform.

The floor of the Temple Ia platform

The pottery assemblages from the floor of the platform at level c. 1.50 are not very useful for dating purposes either, since the floor was utilized in both Temple Ia and Temple Ib, and there is no way of knowing to which phase a particular assemblage belongs. Furthermore, the floor of Temple II lies only c. 1 m above that of Temple I, and the possibility of intrusions from Temple II levels into those of Temple I is obvious.

Finds from outside the Temple Ia platform

Outside the platform large quantitites of pottery were found, probably refuse from activities carried out either at the top of the platform or in the area around the platform.

Area XII 1957, lying 7-12 m north of the platform (fig. 9), has produced a sequence of two layers of the oldest pottery found at the site of the Barbar temple. From the bottom layer of 1 m thickness, level c. 3.50-2.50, directly above sterile sand (cf. the Main Section), comes a collection of pottery (517.ADZ). The section reveals horizontal, rather thin layers, apparently accumulated gradually.

All sherds belong to the Barbar tradition and are in ware of type 1, apart from two side-sherds possibly belonging to the Mesopotamian tradition, and one side-sherd in a hard, fine, red ware with a dense and smooth surface, probably belonging in the Umm an-Nar tradition (same general size and shape as types U5-7, cf. *Qala'at 1* p. 113).

Characteristic are many neck-vessel rims with either a simple, rounded rim of type B1 or a slightly drawn-out lip of type B2 (cf. *Qala'at 1* p. 75), in two

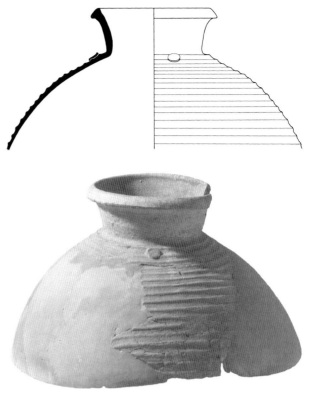

Fig. 289. 1:5.

cases combined with a sharp ridge on the upper shoulder followed by a chain-ridge decoration of the small variety of type B55B (figs. 290-299). Fig. 300 shows a fragment of the upper shoulder with a sharp ridge and three chain ridges of the small variety of type B55B. The corresponding base has probably been a ring-base with a chain-ridged belly of type B37 (figs. 301-302). A complete jar of this type is known from Qala'at al-Bahrain (*Qala'at 1* fig. 104) and from a burial at Shakhoura (Daems et al. 2001 fig. 5). A fragment of the upper shoulder of a vessel like this with a ridge that has flaked off and a chain ridge shows a vertical ridge of type B75 (fig. 303). There are also many simple, thin rims from hole-mouth vessels, of types B13-15 (figs. 304-313). Besides, a beaker (fig. 314), ovens of types B44-46 (figs. 315-318) and a large vessel of type B20 (fig. 319) should be mentioned.

The assemblage can be compared to period Ib pottery at Qala'at al-Bahrain (cf. *Qala'at 1* figs. 388-89, 460-610), but the absence of hole-mouth vessel rims in ware type 4 (types B10-B12) suggests a late part of period Ib. The complete pot from Qala'at al-Bahrain referred to above was found in Excavation 520, trench 92-98, level 22, which has been assigned a date of period Ib or IIa (*Qala'at 1* fig. 104, section C).

From the layer above, level c. 2.50-1.50, comes a slightly different collection of pottery (517.ADY). Again, the section reveals horizontal, rather thin layers, apparently accumulated gradually.

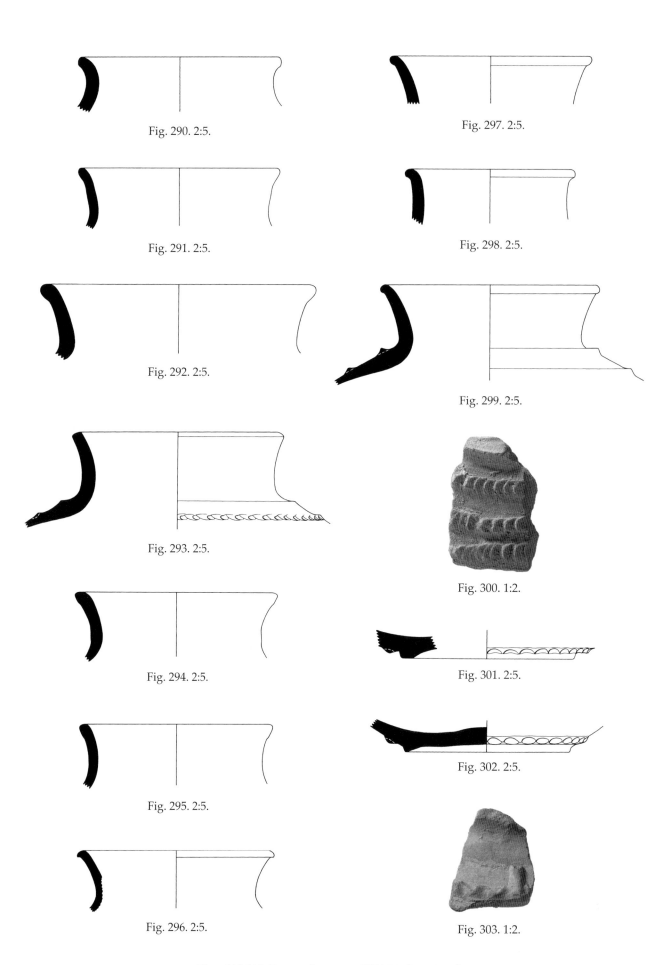

Fig. 290. 2:5.

Fig. 291. 2:5.

Fig. 292. 2:5.

Fig. 293. 2:5.

Fig. 294. 2:5.

Fig. 295. 2:5.

Fig. 296. 2:5.

Fig. 297. 2:5.

Fig. 298. 2:5.

Fig. 299. 2:5.

Fig. 300. 1:2.

Fig. 301. 2:5.

Fig. 302. 2:5.

Fig. 303. 1:2.

Figs. 290-319. Pottery from area XII 1957 (517.ADZ).

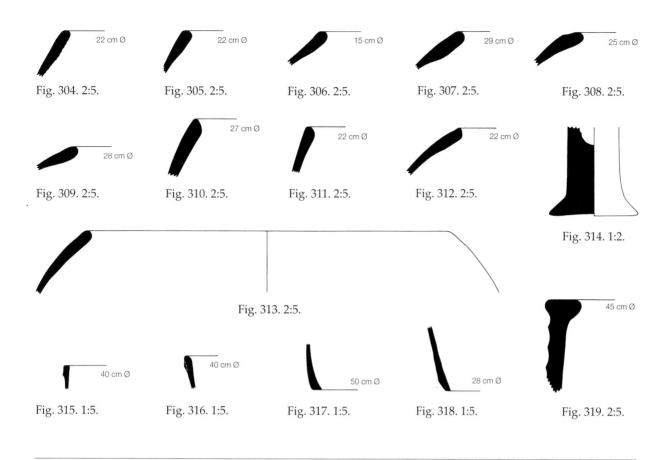

Fig. 304. 2:5.

Fig. 305. 2:5.

Fig. 306. 2:5.

Fig. 307. 2:5.

Fig. 308. 2:5.

Fig. 309. 2:5.

Fig. 310. 2:5.

Fig. 311. 2:5.

Fig. 312. 2:5.

Fig. 314. 1:2.

Fig. 313. 2:5.

Fig. 315. 1:5.

Fig. 316. 1:5.

Fig. 317. 1:5.

Fig. 318. 1:5.

Fig. 319. 2:5.

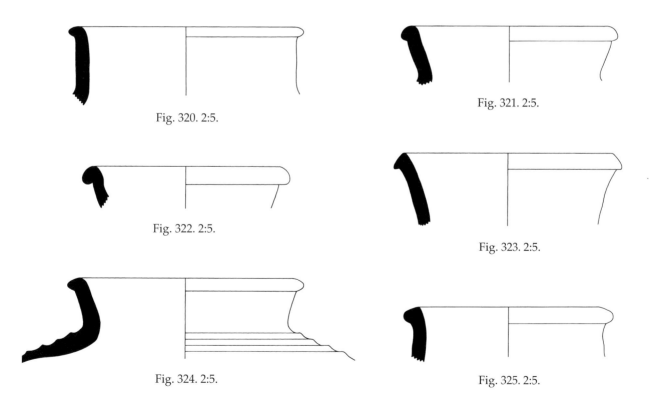

Fig. 320. 2:5.

Fig. 321. 2:5.

Fig. 322. 2:5.

Fig. 323. 2:5.

Fig. 324. 2:5.

Fig. 325. 2:5.

Figs. 320-338. Pottery from area XII 1957 (517.ADY).

217

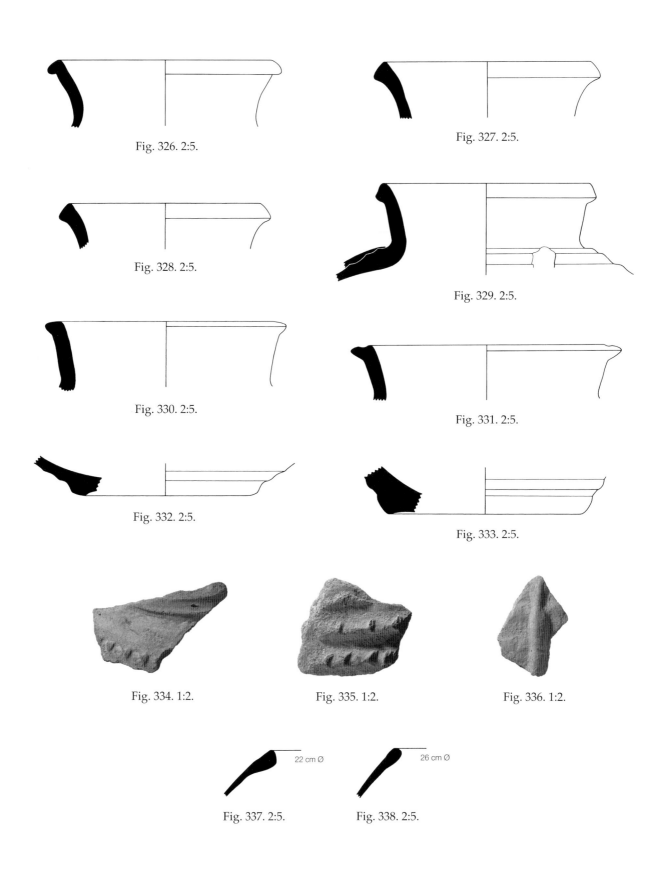

Fig. 326. 2:5.

Fig. 327. 2:5.

Fig. 328. 2:5.

Fig. 329. 2:5.

Fig. 330. 2:5.

Fig. 331. 2:5.

Fig. 332. 2:5.

Fig. 333. 2:5.

Fig. 334. 1:2.

Fig. 335. 1:2.

Fig. 336. 1:2.

22 cm Ø

26 cm Ø

Fig. 337. 2:5.

Fig. 338. 2:5.

Figs. 320-338. Pottery from area XII 1957 (517.ADY).

The pottery belongs in the Barbar tradition and is made in ware of type 1. Characteristic are many neck-vessel rims with a clearly drawn-out lip, others are shaped like a small triangle, and two have an almost horizontal upper side (figs. 320-331). Two neck-vessel rims are combined with horizontal ridges on the shoulder, and of these one has furthermore an applied vertical ridge of type B75 (figs. 324 and 329). The corresponding base has probably been a ring-base with ridged belly of type B38 (figs. 332-333); chain-ridged sherds of the small variety (type B55B), however, still occur (figs. 334-335). Another ridged shoulder sherd has an applied vertical ridge of type B75 (fig. 336). Two hole-mouth vessel rims of type B15-16 occur (figs. 337-338). Finally, a Mesopotamian shoulder fragment with a rope-decorated ridge in ware type 5 should be mentioned.

This pottery represents a typological development of the above-described assemblage ADZ, and it can be compared with pottery from period IIa at Qala'at al-Bahrain (*Qala'at 1* figs. 388-89, 546-610; Højlund 1986 fig. 55).

In *area III 1958*, a number of pottery assemblages were excavated. This area encompasses the northeastern part of the Temple Ia platform, and the material presented here comes from the extreme northern part of the area, i.e. from the narrow space immediately outside the platform wall, from the level of the platform floor, level c. 1.50, to virgin soil, level c. 3.50.

One of the many collections from this area contained material from the deepest levels in front of the platform wall (517.AIM), including the pottery illustrated in figs. 339-348, which show the same variations of neck-vessel rims as ADY, described above. The ware belongs to type 1.

However, by far the majority of the pottery from this part of area III is typologically later, which can be illustrated by the assemblage 517.AHN (figs. 349-366). The pottery falls in the Barbar tradition and is made in ware of type 1. Characteristic are triangular neck-vessel rims, and of these one has a ridged shoulder with an applied vertical ridge of type B75 (fig. 356). The corresponding base has probably been a ring-base with ridged belly of type B38 (fig. 358). Hole-mouth rims are both of the simple, thin variety of types B13-15 (figs. 359-364) and of the slightly thicker type B16 (fig. 365); one is ridged (fig. 364). A bowl is present (fig. 366).

This pottery represents a typological development of the above-described assemblages ADY/AIM, but, still, it finds its best parallels in period IIa at Qala'at al-Bahrain (cf. *Qala'at 1* figs. 388-89, 546-610).

From *area XV 1960*, encompassing a narrow area on both sides of the southern wall of the Temple Ia

platform, from the level of the platform floor, level c. 1.50, to subsoil, level c. 3.50, comes an assemblage (517.AOT) rather similar to the above-described AHN.

The pottery falls in the Barbar tradition and is made in ware of type 1. Characteristic are triangular neck-vessel rims, and of these one has a ridged shoulder (figs. 367-375). Four fragments of ridged shoulders have further applied ridges of type B75: two have 1 vertical ridge, one has 2 vertical ridges and one has 2 vertical-wavy ridges (figs. 376-379). The corresponding bases have probably been of type B38, a ring-base with ridged belly (fig. 380). A slightly bevelled rim on a splaying neck has a plumred slip (type B9) (fig. 381)(cf. Ibrahim 1982 fig. 39). Hole-mouth rims are both of the simple, thin variety of types B13-15 (figs. 382-384) and of the slightly thicker type B16 (figs. 385-390). Besides, a fragment of a plain bowl rim in the Mesopotamian tradition (type M13) and a shoulder fragment in fine, red Umm an-Nar ware with a black painted line (type U3) (fig. 391) may be mentioned.

An early stray find. A Jemdat Nasr sherd (517.APS) was found c. 20 m north of the platform, in area III 1960, 1-2 m below the surface, in mixed layers with pottery belonging to all phases of the temple. The sherd (fig. 392) "... belongs to the transition between the body and the shoulder of a large, wheel-made jar, painted in black and plum-red. On the lower part of the body is a horizontal metope-decoration: a wide area filled in with black cross-hatching, limited by narrow black and red bands. On the transition between the body and shoulder of the jar there is a slightly incised groove, along which a horizontal black band runs on the shoulder of the jar. Inside this band the space is filled out with red paint. The core is reddish buff, tempered with fine sand, and the clay contains a large quantity of mica." The sherd "... undoubtedly comes from an imported jar of late Jamdat Nasr type." (Mortensen 1971a p. 395).

The sherd must be considered a stray find, hundreds of years earlier than the first temple (Mortensen 1971a p. 395), but it testifies, together with two complete Jemdat Nasr pots found in a grave at Hamad Town (Vine 1993 p. 16), to a human presence in Bahrain in the early 3rd millennium BC and perhaps also to an early interest in the area of Barbar.

A pre-temple spout. Only a single piece of pottery found in area X 1960, can be shown to stratigraphically ante-date Temple I, a pottery spout (517.AQG, fig. 393), found in the sand layer below the clay layer below the terrace wall of Temple I (plan 1:4-5). The adjacent section 24 shows the sand layer (6) and the clay layers (4-5) in question. The spout is rather clumsily shaped in a sand-tempered pinkish-

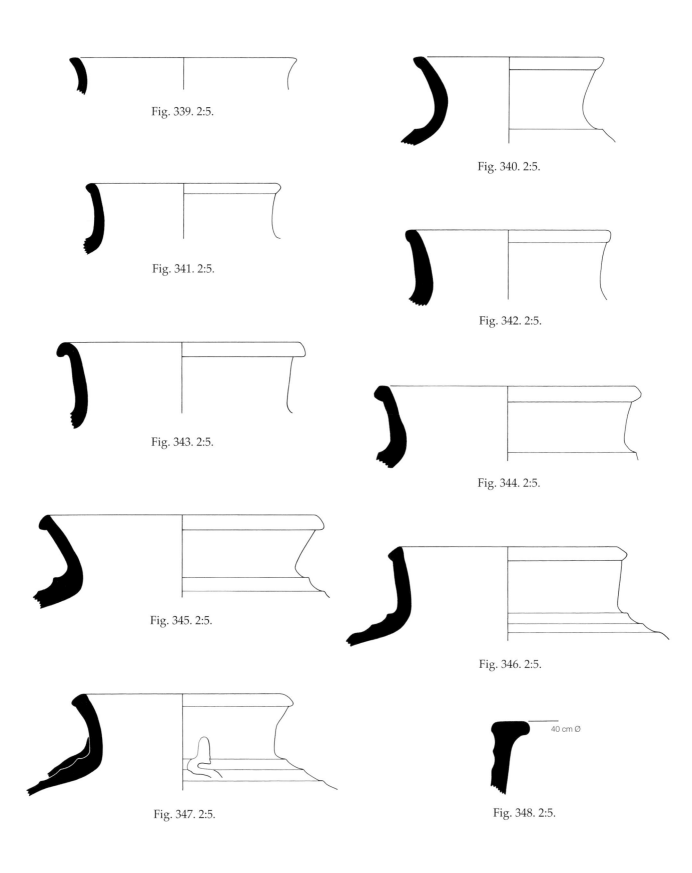

Fig. 339. 2:5.

Fig. 340. 2:5.

Fig. 341. 2:5.

Fig. 342. 2:5.

Fig. 343. 2:5.

Fig. 344. 2:5.

Fig. 345. 2:5.

Fig. 346. 2:5.

40 cm Ø

Fig. 347. 2:5.

Fig. 348. 2:5.

Figs. 339-348. Pottery from area III 1958 (517.AIM).

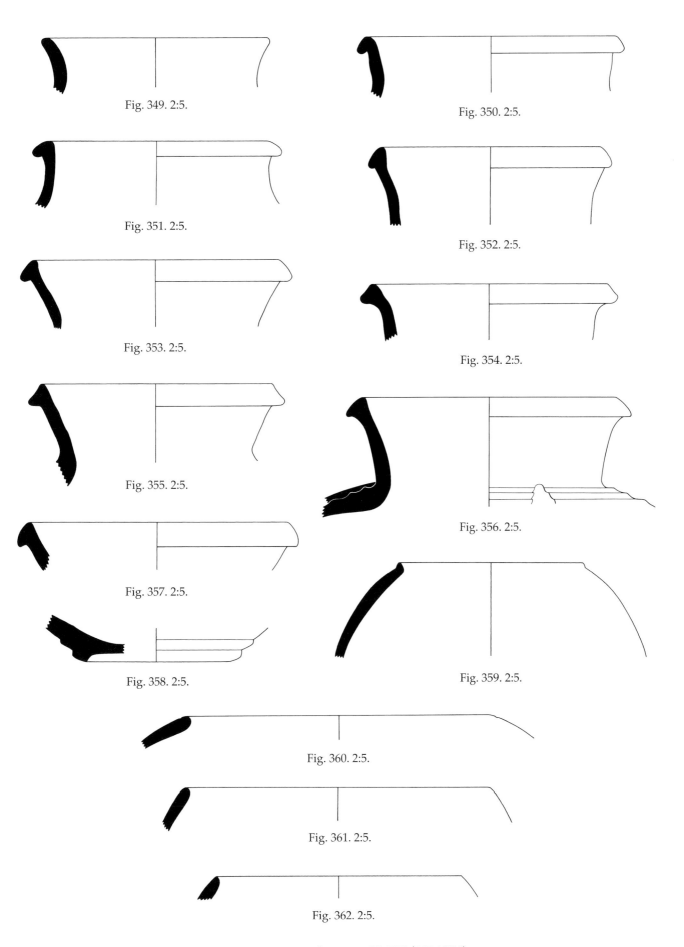

Fig. 349. 2:5.

Fig. 350. 2:5.

Fig. 351. 2:5.

Fig. 352. 2:5.

Fig. 353. 2:5.

Fig. 354. 2:5.

Fig. 355. 2:5.

Fig. 356. 2:5.

Fig. 357. 2:5.

Fig. 358. 2:5.

Fig. 359. 2:5.

Fig. 360. 2:5.

Fig. 361. 2:5.

Fig. 362. 2:5.

Figs. 349-366. Pottery from area III 1958 (517.AHN).

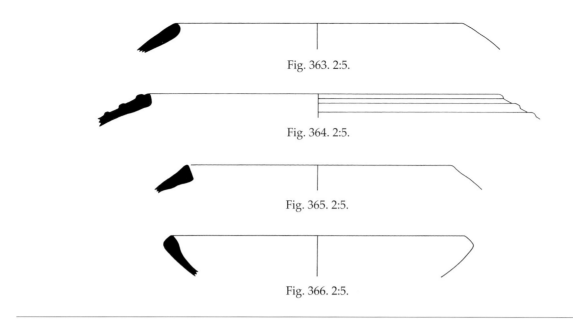

Fig. 363. 2:5.

Fig. 364. 2:5.

Fig. 365. 2:5.

Fig. 366. 2:5.

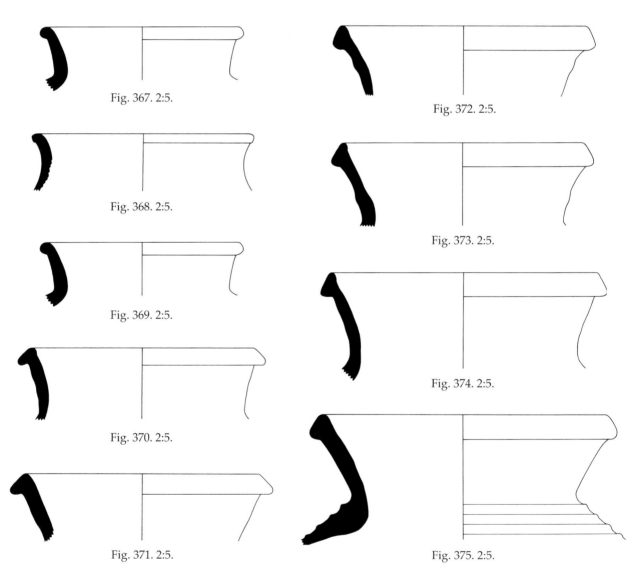

Fig. 367. 2:5.

Fig. 368. 2:5.

Fig. 369. 2:5.

Fig. 370. 2:5.

Fig. 371. 2:5.

Fig. 372. 2:5.

Fig. 373. 2:5.

Fig. 374. 2:5.

Fig. 375. 2:5.

Figs. 367-391. Pottery from area XV 1960 (517.AOT).

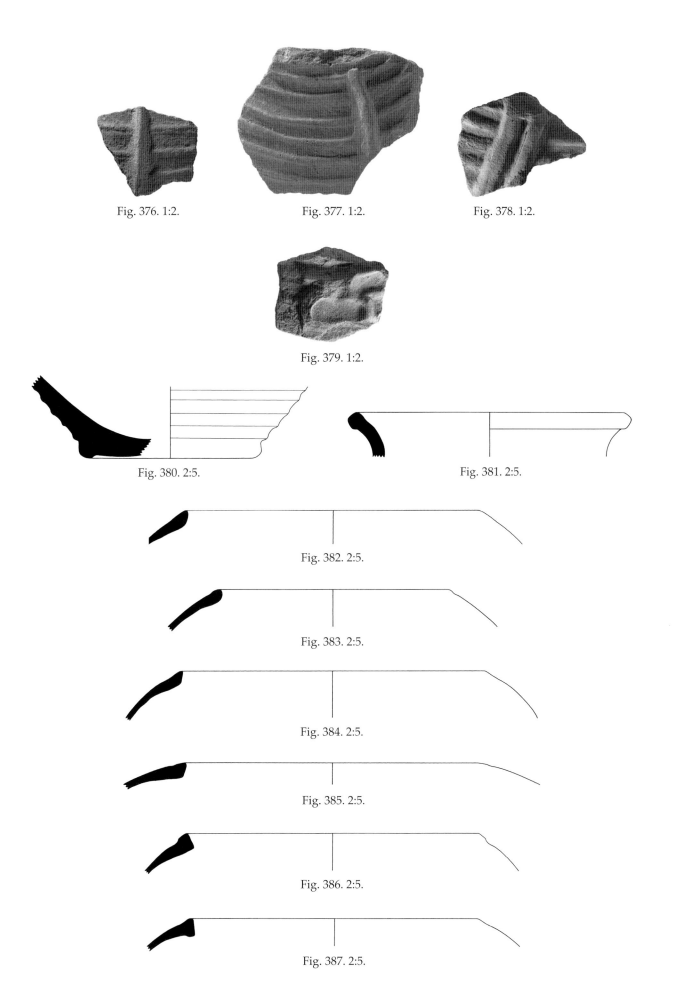

Fig. 376. 1:2.

Fig. 377. 1:2.

Fig. 378. 1:2.

Fig. 379. 1:2.

Fig. 380. 2:5.

Fig. 381. 2:5.

Fig. 382. 2:5.

Fig. 383. 2:5.

Fig. 384. 2:5.

Fig. 385. 2:5.

Fig. 386. 2:5.

Fig. 387. 2:5.

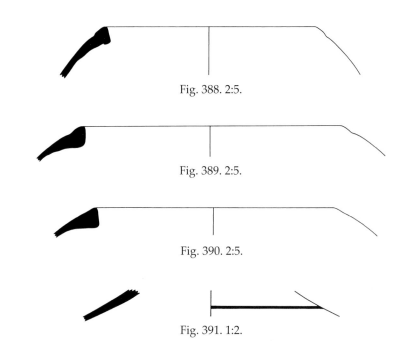

Fig. 388. 2:5.

Fig. 389. 2:5.

Fig. 390. 2:5.

Fig. 391. 1:2.

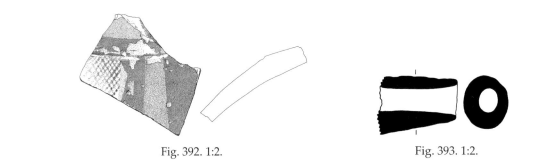

Fig. 392. 1:2.

Fig. 393. 1:2.

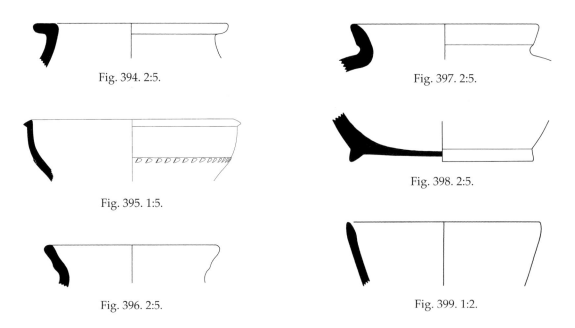

Fig. 394. 2:5.

Fig. 397. 2:5.

Fig. 395. 1:5.

Fig. 398. 2:5.

Fig. 396. 2:5.

Fig. 399. 1:2.

Figs. 394-407. Mesopotamian pottery from Temple Ia.

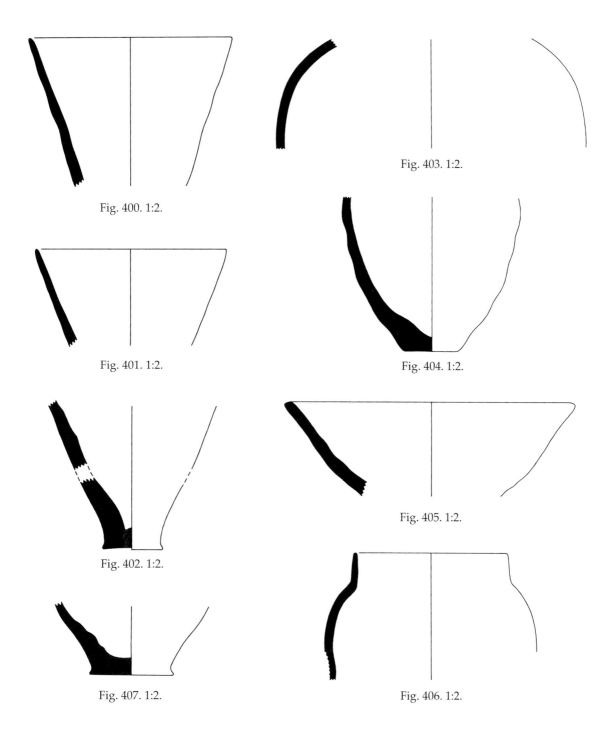

Fig. 400. 1:2.

Fig. 401. 1:2.

Fig. 402. 1:2.

Fig. 407. 1:2.

Fig. 403. 1:2.

Fig. 404. 1:2.

Fig. 405. 1:2.

Fig. 406. 1:2.

brown ware with a buff surface very similar to ware type 5 (cf. above, p. 210). Spouts occur in the Barbar pottery tradition, but are very different, cf. type B52, and this specimen has more resemblance to Mesopotamian spouts from the Early Dynastic-Akkadian period.

Finds from the "room" inside the platform

From the "room" in the southwestern corner of the Temple Ia platform (cf. p. 63) comes an assemblage (517.AOS), very similar to the above-described AOT, showing that the use of this "room" was related to Temple Ia.

Mesopotamian pottery from Temple Ia

Apart from a few sherds mentioned above, only a little Mesopotamian pottery was found in Temple Ia contexts (517.AJT, fig. 394; AOG, fig. 395; AMB, fig. 396; ALX, figs. 397-402). The ware varies from light yellow to light green or light reddish, and it is tempered with fine sand.

Of special interest are some sherds of simple shapes in ware type 5, made rather clumsily on the fast wheel (517.ALV, figs. 403-405; AMB, fig. 406; ALX, fig. 407). The ware and the string-cut base are paralleled in period I at Qala'at al-Bahrain (*Qala'at 1* figs. 151-2, 418, 469-70) and may be evidence of a

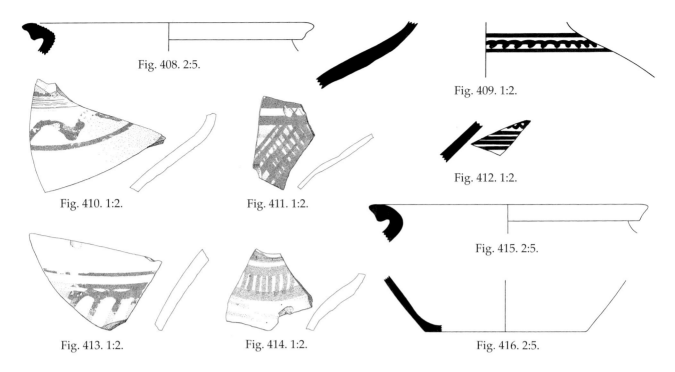

Fig. 408. 2:5.

Fig. 409. 1:2.

Fig. 412. 1:2.

Fig. 410. 1:2.

Fig. 411. 1:2.

Fig. 415. 2:5.

Fig. 413. 1:2.

Fig. 414. 1:2.

Fig. 416. 2:5.

Figs. 408-416. Umm an-Nar pottery from Temple Ia.

hitherto little known, early local imitation of Mesopotamian imports using the fast wheel.

Umm an-Nar pottery from Temple Ia

Apart from the sherd mentioned above (fig. 391), two Umm an-Nar sherds were found in Temple Ia contexts, a rim (517.ALX, fig. 408) and a side-sherd without any decoration preserved. Besides, a small number of black-on-red Umm an-Nar side-sherds were found in undatable contexts (517.ALV, fig. 409; AEN, fig. 410; APN, fig. 411; AEX, fig. 412; AEO, fig. 413; AEO, fig. 414), as well as a fragment of a rim (517.ABM, fig. 415) and a base (517.EY, fig. 416).

Temple Ib

The second phase of Temple I, Ib, is well-attested from its southern and eastern platform walls (plan 1:12), which represented an enlargement of the central platform of Temple Ia, but unfortunately the excavation produced no pottery assemblages that can be said with certainty to have accumulated outside these walls, and no other assemblages of sufficient quality can safely be related to Temple Ib. It has, therefore, not been possible to date this phase of the temple in terms of pottery chronology.

Summary of Temple Ia

Not all the finds mentioned above have proved particularly useful for dating Temple Ia, e.g. the finds from the bottom clay layer of the temple platform, from the upper fill of the platform, and from the floor of the platform. Instead, a dating must proceed from an evaluation of the above-described collections of pottery found in the immediate and the near vicinity of the platform and accumulated on the same level of sterile sand upon which the platform was built.

There can be no doubt that the pottery accumulated in the immediate vicinity of the platform, i.e. immediately in front of the platform walls (AIM, AHN and AOT), represents refuse discarded from activities taking place on top of, or around, the platform and therefore dating to the period in which the platform was in use (fig. 267).

It is less certain if the same applies to the pottery (ADZ) accumulated in the near vicinity of the platform, 7-12 m north of it, and on the same layer of sand on which the platform was erected. It is possible that there are here levels which pre-date the temple.

Three different phases of pottery development can then be described, in which the relation of the first to Temple Ia is uncertain, but in which the two following phases are contemporaneous with the temple: 1) ADZ, 2) ADY and AIM, and 3) AHN and AOT, beginning in late period Ib and continuing well into period IIa, according to the Qala'at al-Bahrain chronology (fig. 266).

Temple IIa

The floor of Temple II is situated c. 1 m above the floor of Temple I, at level c. 0.50, but this floor was used in both Temple IIa and IIb, and the pottery assemblages found there are, thus, not particularly useful for dating the first phase of Temple II. Furthermore, there are many disturbances of this level from the time of the construction of Temple III and, much later, from the demolition of the temple in Islamic time.

Of prime importance are, however, assemblages of pottery collected south of the central platform, at the foot of the oval terrace wall, which defines Temple IIa (plan 3:31). The pottery found here, between levels c. 4.00 and 5.00, cf. the Main Section, must have accumulated during the time when this phase of the temple was in use. In the following, two assemblages from this area will be described (fig. 267). All sherds belong in the Barbar tradition, and ware of type 1 predominates by far, with only a few sherds of type 2 present.

The assemblage 517.ADP, from *area IV 1957*, is characterized by many hole-mouth rims without ridges on the shoulder of type B16 (figs. 417-426) and one thick hole-mouth rim with ridges on the shoulder of type B17 (fig. 427); furthermore, a yellow-slipped bowl rim (fig. 428) and two neck-vessel rims with a triangular rim (type B3) (figs. 429-430).

The assemblage 517.AIQ, from the northern part of *area VIII 1958*, is characterized by many hole-mouth rims without ridges on the shoulder of type B16 (figs. 431-435), plus a single hole-mouth rim with ridges of type B17 (fig. 436), and many sherds of neck-vessels with triangular rims of type B3 (figs.

437-444) and probably a corresponding ridged base of type B38 (fig. 445). Two neck-vessel rims stand out, perhaps related to type B9 (figs. 446-447). Besides, solid pithos rims occur (figs. 448-450) and a neck vessel with a round rim, possibly of type B35.

From the fill of the *staircase* built against the oval terrace wall (plan 3:33) come a few hole-mouth rims of type B16 (517.ANQ, figs. 451-452), which may give a *terminus post quem* dating for the staircase and the oval terrace wall.

To the left of the staircase, in *area IV 1957*, immediately in front of the Temple IIa oval terrace wall, were two circular stone settings (plan 3:36-37) (figs. 142-144, 453), probably made to stabilize pottery ovens (cf. Killich et al. 1991 p. 129, fig. 22), of which several were found in fragments: two in the western circle, being a lower (517.AGQ, fig. 454) and an upper (517.AGP, fig. 455), and two in the eastern circle; one of which has been reconstructed (517.ADL-M) (fig. 456), and the other having a base diameter of c. 50 cm (517.ADK). Besides, a few sherds (517.ADM, etc.) of other types were found in and between the stone circles (figs. 457-462).

Summary of Temple IIa

The pottery found accumulated in front of the oval terrace wall of Temple IIa presents typologically an advanced stage in relation to that of Temple Ia. It has similarities to pottery from both period IIa and IIb at Qala'at al-Bahrain (cf. *Qala'at 1* figs. 546-663) and may therefore be placed at the transition between these two periods (fig. 266).

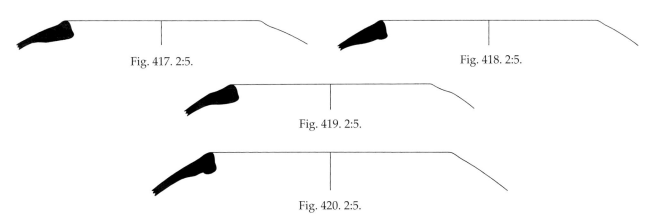

Fig. 417. 2:5.

Fig. 418. 2:5.

Fig. 419. 2:5.

Fig. 420. 2:5.

Figs. 417-430. Pottery from area IV 1957 (517.ADP).

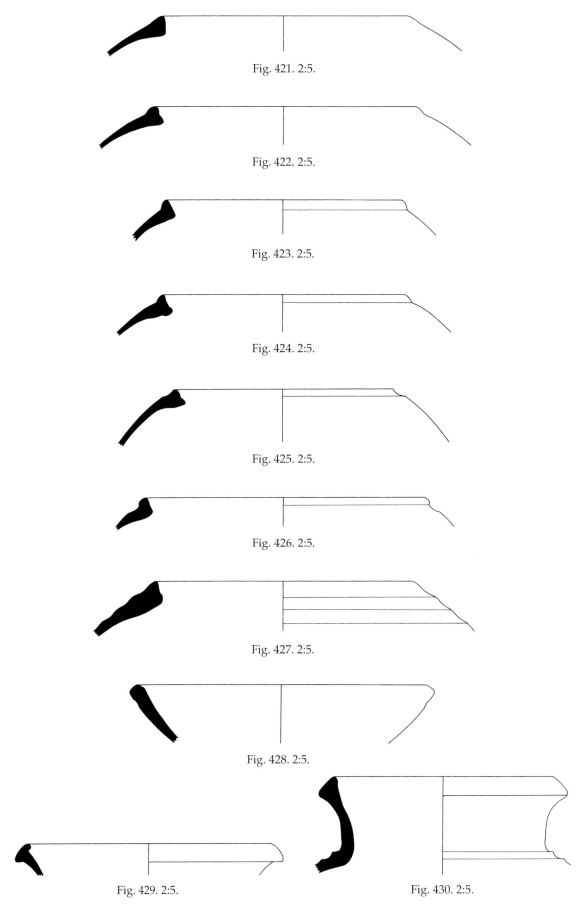

Fig. 421. 2:5.

Fig. 422. 2:5.

Fig. 423. 2:5.

Fig. 424. 2:5.

Fig. 425. 2:5.

Fig. 426. 2:5.

Fig. 427. 2:5.

Fig. 428. 2:5.

Fig. 429. 2:5.

Fig. 430. 2:5.

Figs. 417-430. Pottery from area IV 1957 (517.ADP).

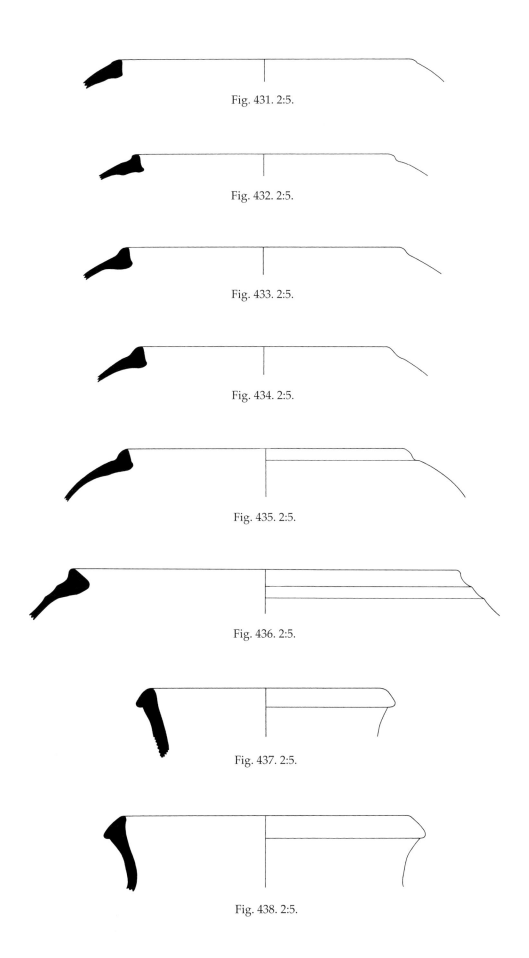

Fig. 431. 2:5.

Fig. 432. 2:5.

Fig. 433. 2:5.

Fig. 434. 2:5.

Fig. 435. 2:5.

Fig. 436. 2:5.

Fig. 437. 2:5.

Fig. 438. 2:5.

Figs. 431-450. Pottery from area VIII 1958 (517.AIQ).

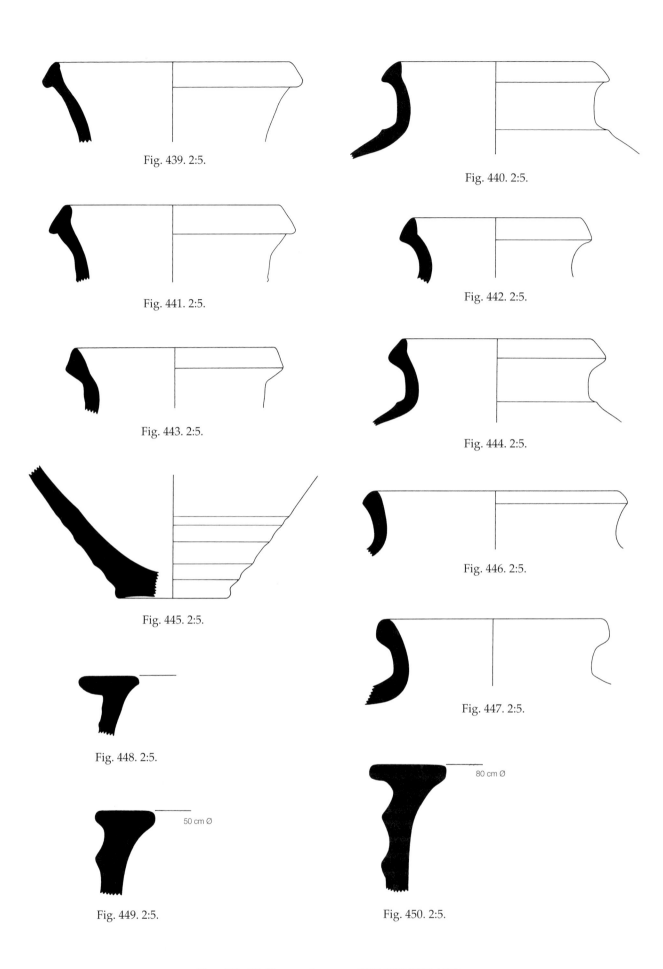

Fig. 439. 2:5.

Fig. 440. 2:5.

Fig. 441. 2:5.

Fig. 442. 2:5.

Fig. 443. 2:5.

Fig. 444. 2:5.

Fig. 445. 2:5.

Fig. 446. 2:5.

Fig. 447. 2:5.

Fig. 448. 2:5.

80 cm Ø

50 cm Ø

Fig. 449. 2:5.

Fig. 450. 2:5.

Figs. 431-450. Pottery from area VIII 1958 (517.AIQ).

Fig. 451. 2:5.

Fig. 452. 2:5.

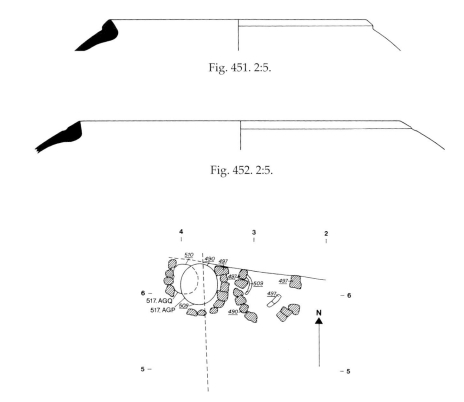

Fig. 453. Pottery ovens in stone rings in front of the Temple IIa oval terrace wall.

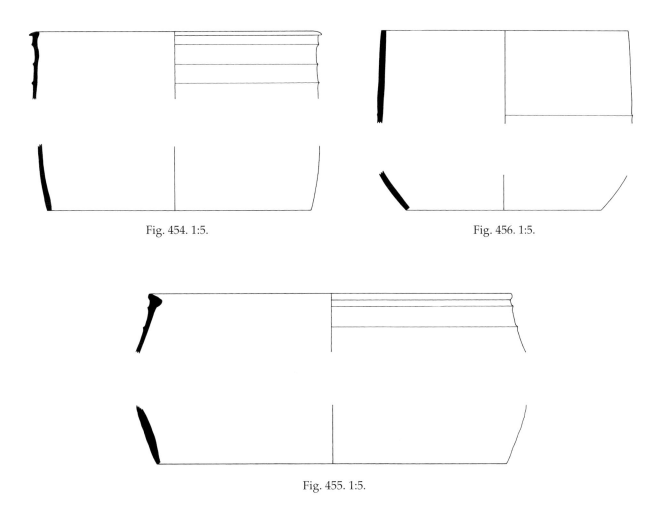

Fig. 454. 1:5.

Fig. 456. 1:5.

Fig. 455. 1:5.

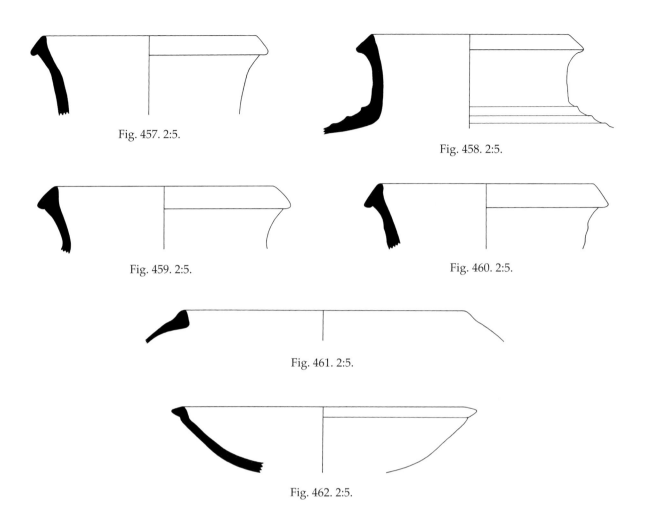

Fig. 457. 2:5.

Fig. 458. 2:5.

Fig. 459. 2:5.

Fig. 460. 2:5.

Fig. 461. 2:5.

Fig. 462. 2:5.

Temple IIb

Temple IIb, the second phase of Temple II, is defined by a new oval terrace wall, prominent towards the south as a tall retaining wall built of dressed ashlars (plan 3:41). Great quantities of pottery were accumulated in front of this wall, during the time when this phase of the temple was in use. The pottery presented in the following comes from area VIII 1957 and has been excavated in two layers, each of one metre thickness (cf. fig. 267). The pottery belongs in the Barbar tradition, and ware type 2 dominates over type 1.

From the *lower layer*, c. 5.00, the pottery assemblages (517.ABA, ABC, ABD, ADR) are characterized by neck-vessels with triangular rims with a tendency towards lower necks compared to Temple IIa, a few furnished with incised lines on the outer rim face (figs. 463-469). The first ridge on the shoulder is often clear and sharp, but the following ridges may be irregular and faint. Dark-painted, horizontal lines (instead of ridges) occur very rarely. Bases of type B40 are present, smooth or ridged (fig. 470), and simple flattened bases normally without ridges of type B43 (fig. 471). One neck-vessel rim stands out (fig. 472). Hole-mouth rims without ridges on the shoulder of type B16 are common (figs. 473-477), supplemented by a few ridged rims of type B17 (fig. 478) of the same thick variant as known in a few examples from Temple IIa (fig. 427 and 436). Besides, hole-mouth rims of type B18 occur for the first time (fig. 479). A number of rims similar to type B30, but here belonging to bowls rather than to plates, as is usual at Qala'at al-Bahrain, should be mentioned, normally with a yellow surface (figs. 480-483), along with large rims of type B34 (figs. 484-485). Fragments of ovens occur (figs. 486-487), and flat baking plates (fig. 488) of Failaka type 42 appear, cf. Højlund 1987 p. 48.

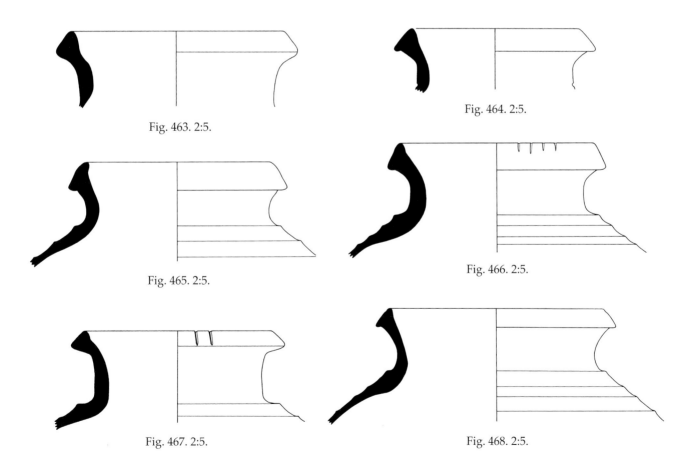

Fig. 463. 2:5.

Fig. 464. 2:5.

Fig. 465. 2:5.

Fig. 466. 2:5.

Fig. 467. 2:5.

Fig. 468. 2:5.

Figs. 463-488. Pottery from area VIII 1957, lower layer.

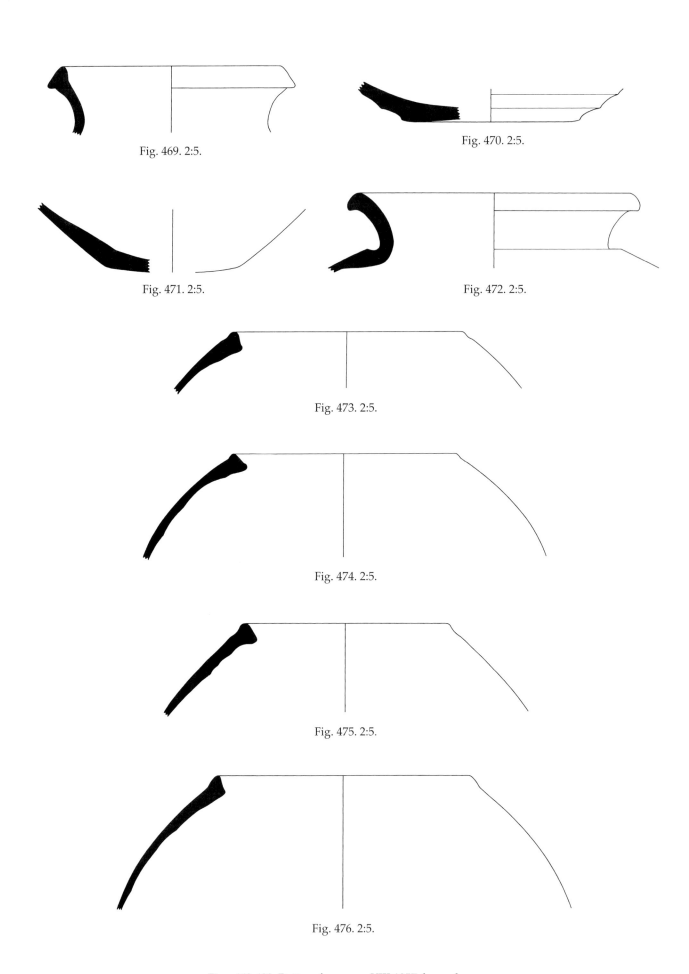

Fig. 469. 2:5.

Fig. 470. 2:5.

Fig. 471. 2:5.

Fig. 472. 2:5.

Fig. 473. 2:5.

Fig. 474. 2:5.

Fig. 475. 2:5.

Fig. 476. 2:5.

Figs. 463-488. Pottery from area VIII 1957, lower layer.

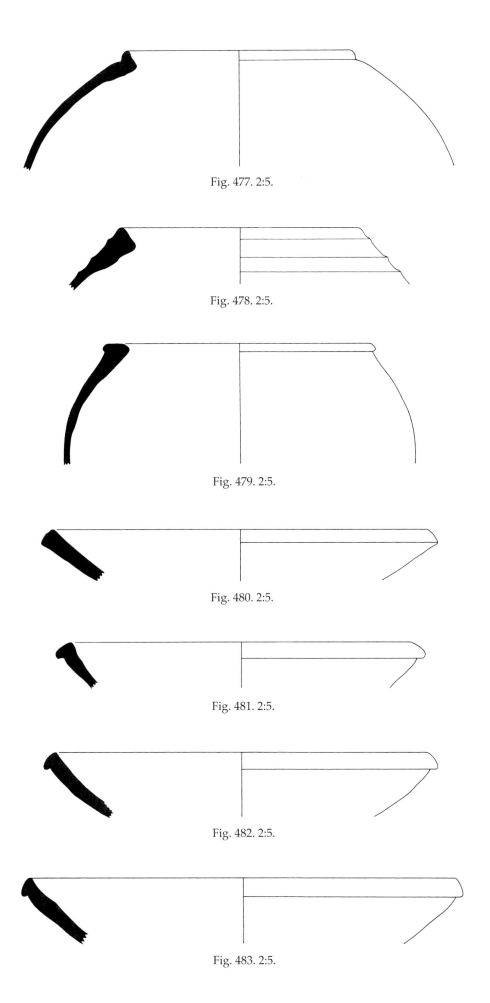

Fig. 477. 2:5.

Fig. 478. 2:5.

Fig. 479. 2:5.

Fig. 480. 2:5.

Fig. 481. 2:5.

Fig. 482. 2:5.

Fig. 483. 2:5.

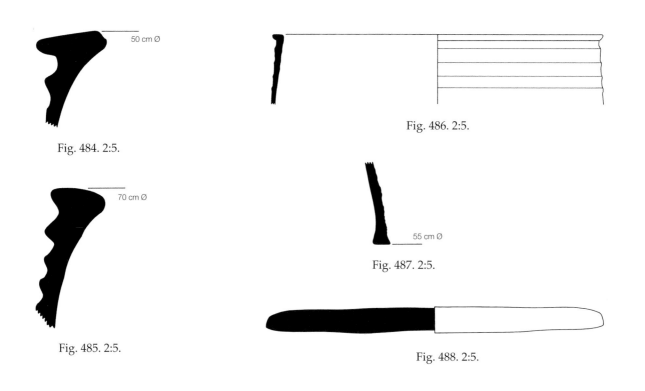

Fig. 484. 2:5.

50 cm Ø

Fig. 486. 2:5.

70 cm Ø

Fig. 485. 2:5.

Fig. 487. 2:5.

55 cm Ø

Fig. 488. 2:5.

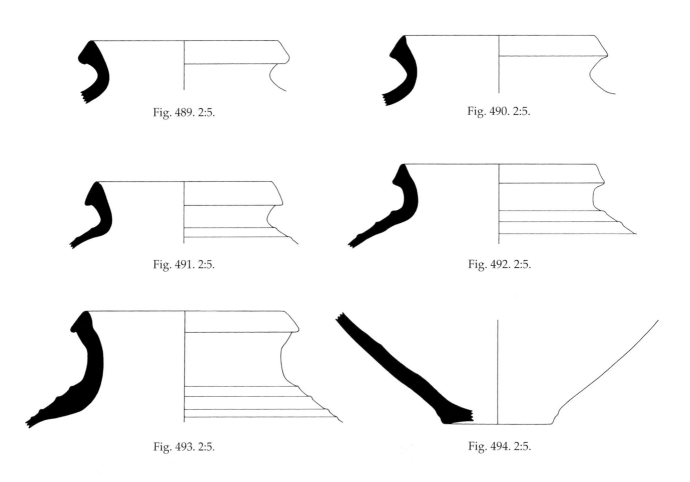

Fig. 489. 2:5.

Fig. 490. 2:5.

Fig. 491. 2:5.

Fig. 492. 2:5.

Fig. 493. 2:5.

Fig. 494. 2:5.

Figs. 489-503. Pottery from area VIII 1957, upper layer.

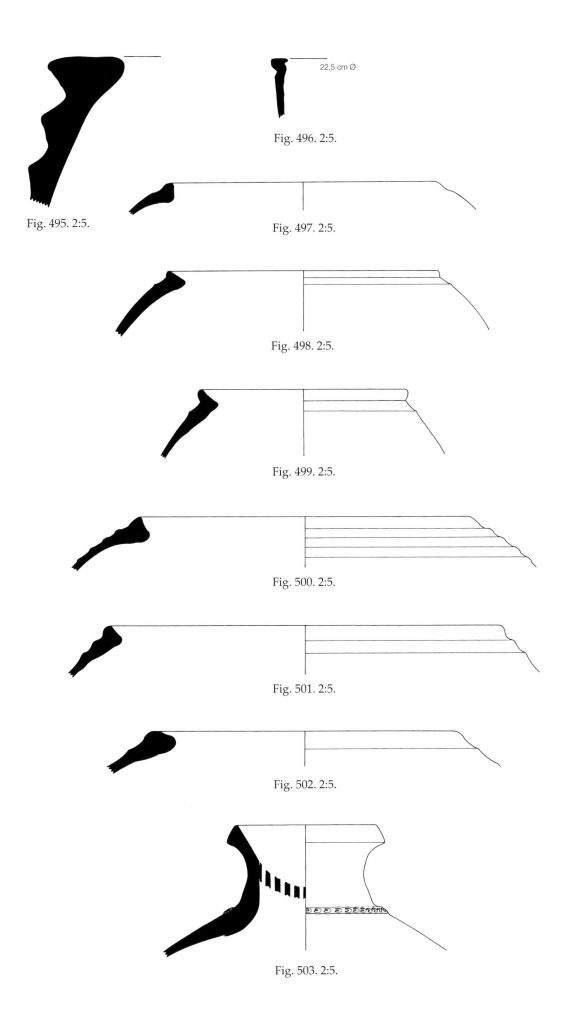

22,5 cm Ø

Fig. 495. 2:5.

Fig. 496. 2:5.

Fig. 497. 2:5.

Fig. 498. 2:5.

Fig. 499. 2:5.

Fig. 500. 2:5.

Fig. 501. 2:5.

Fig. 502. 2:5.

Fig. 503. 2:5.

From the *upper layer*, c. 3.00, come assemblages (517.ABI, ABJ, ABK, AEQ) with a close similarity to the pottery from the lower layer (figs. 489-503), though the neck-vessels with triangular rims tend to have even lower necks, and the ridged hole-mouth of type B18 has become much more common. Besides, a yellow-slipped sieve-necked jar of type B7 with c. 60 perforations and a stamp-impressed ridge must be mentioned (cf. *Qala'at 1* fig. 237).

In the court east of the central platform (plan 7), two main layers were isolated: a grey-black layer (section 10:12) with levels c. 2.60–2.20 and a grey layer (section 10:8) with levels c. 2.20-1.60. The pottery from both layers is very similar to that described above, but as a special feature the occurrence of many half-globular goblets must be mentioned. Like their predecessors, the conical beakers from Temple Ia, they are handmade with coarse scraping-marks on the surface. Figs. 504-508 were found in the grey-black layer (517.TQ, TH, XG, TM, VT), figs. 509-512 in the grey layer (517.YA, TL, TI, TK), whereas fig. 513 is from a mixed context (517.ZR). Two fragments of wheel-made vessels were also found, one red-slipped rim with a black stripe on the upper lip (517.ARF, fig. 514) and one simple, thin triangular rim of Failaka type 2A with a red slip on the lower neck, a cream slip on the upper neck and a black stripe on the upper rim (517.UD, fig. 515), as well as a triangular rim with an incised arrow (517.TN, fig. 516).

From mixed contexts another triangular rim with incisions (517.ANA, fig. 517) and a triangular rim with a branch motive incised on the shoulder with black painted stripes (517.AKC, fig. 518) should be mentioned (cf. Højlund 1987 p. 166).

A small number of *burial pot fragments* of type B73 in ware type 3 were found at the Barbar Temple, almost all in Temple IIb contexts. One came from a sand layer at the bottom of the pool (area XVI 1960, 517.AQE, fig. 519), 6 were found in and around the Eastern Court, from Temple IIb contexts (area I 1956, 517.TQ, fig. 520; area VI 1961, AQV, fig. 521; area IV 1960, AND, fig. 522; area VI 1960, ANO, fig. 523) and two came from mixed contexts in area I 1960 (517.ANA and AQJ, figs. 524-525).

A special *large variety* of this shape, but in ware type 1, is known in 4 fragments from 3, perhaps 4 different pots. The striation of the shoulder is exceptional and never seen on the normal burial pots. Two fragments came from Temple IIb contexts in area VI 1961, south of the Eastern Court (517.ARF, fig. 526; ASF, fig. 527), one was found, probably in a Temple IIb context, in area XIII 1957 (517.AED, fig. 528), and one stems from a mixed context in area II 1960 (517.ANB, fig. 529).

Finally, a few almost complete pots with uncer-tain dates can be mentioned; fig. 530 was found in 1955 by the eastern terrace wall of the central platform of Temple II, while figs. 531-534 were found in 1956 in the area south of the temple. A sherd decorated with opposing concentric semicircles found in an uncertain context north of the temple has disappeared, so it cannot be decided whether it belonged to a pot imported from the Wadi Suq culture of Oman (Frifelt 1975 p. 379. Mortensen 1986 p. 181) or whether it was a local imitation (cf. *Qala'at 1* p. 97, fig. 224).

Summary of Temple IIb

The pottery found accumulated in front of the oval terrace wall of Temple IIb presents a typologically advanced stage in relation to that of Temple IIa. It finds close parallels with pottery from period IIb at Qala'at al-Bahrain (cf. *Qala'at 1* figs. 611-663) and also some similarities with period 1 on Failaka (Højlund 1987 figs. 462-483). The lack of burial pot fragments in Temple IIa contexts and their marked presence in Temple IIb contexts echoes the picture seen at Qala'at al-Bahrain, where burial pot fragments are common in period IIb-c. The lack of burial pot fragments in Temple III contexts (see below) may be only apparent and due to the scarcity of deposits from this temple phase.

This chronology (fig. 266) is entirely compatible with the evidence from the stamp seals, the seal impressions and one C14 dating, as will be shown below.

A number of stamp seals and seal impressions found in Temple IIb contexts (cf. Kjærum below, p. 302-305) indicate a correlation between Temple IIb, Qala'at al-Bahrain period IIb-c and early Failaka.

Five stamp seals (517.AOU, AOV, AOX, APY, AQB, figs. 773-777) were found in the sand layer at the bottom of the pool which is structurally a part of Temple II, here in its last phase of use, Temple IIb. In this layer a small number of sherds were also found, e.g. a low-necked triangular rim, a hole-mouth rim of type B18 and a rim fragment of a grave pot of type B73 (fig. 519), all belonging in the normal Temple IIb pottery inventory.

The five seals are stylistically very homogeneous and belong to Kjærum's style 1A (see below, p. 303). Seals of this style date at Qala'at al-Bahrain to period IIb-c, and on Failaka they belong in the earliest levels.

A piece of unburned wood from the pool has been C14-dated and yielded 3600 ± 100 BP, calibrated to 1940 BC, and ± 1 stdv. 2120-1780 BC (Pearson & Stuiver 1993) (K-1576) (*Qala'at 1* p. 174). The wood (517.AON) lay in a sand layer in level c. 4.50 in area XVI 1960. Other wood samples from the same deposit have been analysed, cf. Tengberg in Appendix 2.

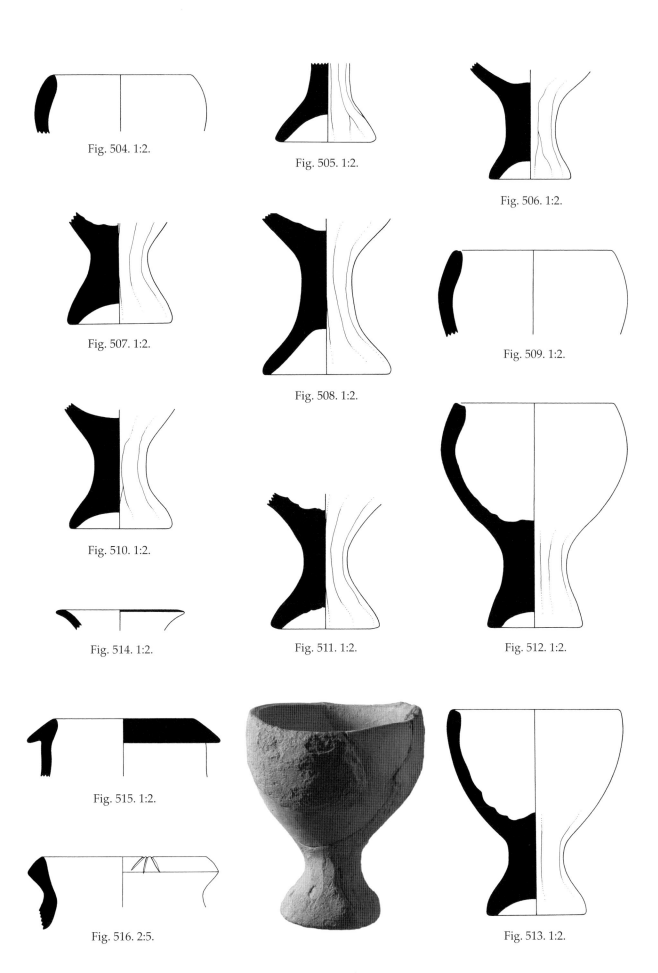

Fig. 504. 1:2.

Fig. 505. 1:2.

Fig. 506. 1:2.

Fig. 507. 1:2.

Fig. 508. 1:2.

Fig. 509. 1:2.

Fig. 510. 1:2.

Fig. 514. 1:2.

Fig. 511. 1:2.

Fig. 512. 1:2.

Fig. 515. 1:2.

Fig. 516. 2:5.

Fig. 513. 1:2.

Figs. 504-516. Pottery from the Eastern Court.

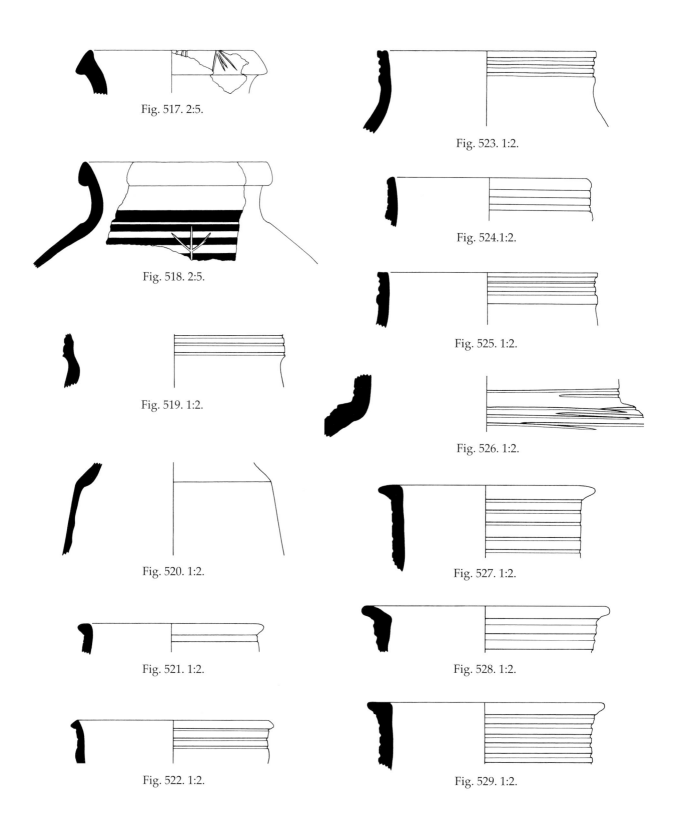

Fig. 517. 2:5.

Fig. 518. 2:5.

Fig. 519. 1:2.

Fig. 520. 1:2.

Fig. 521. 1:2.

Fig. 522. 1:2.

Fig. 523. 1:2.

Fig. 524.1:2.

Fig. 525. 1:2.

Fig. 526. 1:2.

Fig. 527. 1:2.

Fig. 528. 1:2.

Fig. 529. 1:2.

In the filling of the pool chamber, level c. 5.40, a seal-impressed potsherd was found (517.ALM, fig. 778). The sherd comes from the upper, ridged shoulder of a neck-vessel, which has undoubtedly had a triangular rim. The seal is stamped into a lump of clay placed on the ridged surface just before the transition to the neck (cf. *Qala'at 1* p. 177). The ware is type 1.

Besides, one stamp seal (517.AIS, fig. 781) belonging to Kjærum's style 1A (see below, p. 303) was found south of the oval terrace wall of Temple IIb, in area IX 1958, in an Islamic demolition layer at level c. 4.50. Apart from the Islamic intrusions, the pottery from this area is entirely of the Temple IIb variety, so this was probably also the context of this seal.

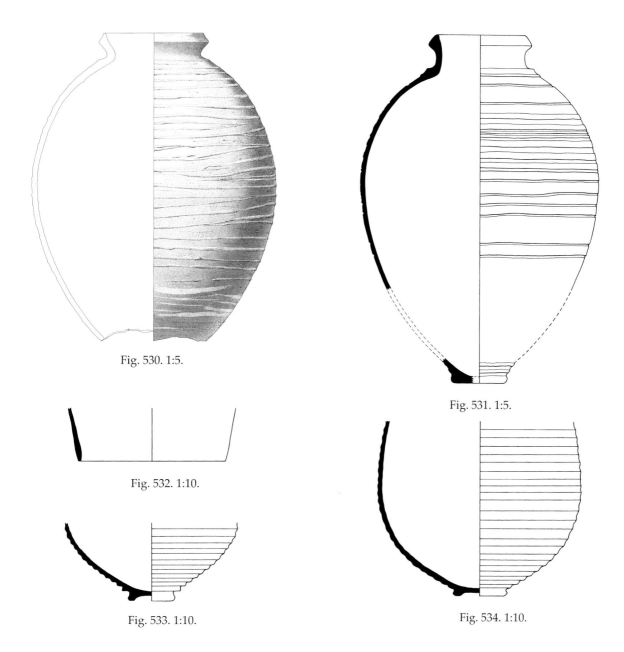

Fig. 530. 1:5.

Fig. 531. 1:5.

Fig. 532. 1:10.

Fig. 533. 1:10.

Fig. 534. 1:10.

Two fragments of a seal were found separately south of the temple, in the spoils from the excavation (517.AMQ/ANZ) (fig. 782). This seal also belongs to Kjærum's style 1A (see below, p. 303).

In the northern part of the temple, near two parallel walls in area III 1960, 6 seal-stamped tokens were found (517.ANR, ANS, ANT, ANU, ANV, ANX) (figs. 783-788). Generally, these seal impressions belong to Kjærum's style 1A (see below, p. 303-304). One of the tokens came from a fire layer between the two walls, which has been C14-dated. Charcoal of date palm (*Phoenix dactylifera L.*)

yielded 3630 ± 100 BP, calibrated to 1970 BC, and ± 1 stdv. 2140-1790 BC (Pearson & Stuiver 1993) (K-1775) (*Qala'at 1* p. 174). Unfortunately, the pottery from the layers between and around the two walls is mixed and contains material of Temple I, IIa and IIb variety.

From the adjacent area II 1960, stems another seal-impressed token (517.ANY, fig. 789), also with a general attribution to Kjærum's style 1A (see below, p. 303-304), but without any clear context in terms of either architecture or pottery.

Temple III

The huge retaining walls of the central platform of Temple III were almost completely removed during the demolition of the monument in Islamic time. The base of the platform walls was preserved at level c. 1.50, but during excavation no suitable pottery assemblages securely related to these sparse building remains were retrieved.

A number of areas cutting through levels related to the demolished platform walls have been examined for their pottery: area V 1955, area X 1957, area XVI 1957, area XVIII 1957, area II 1958, area V 1959, area VI 1960 and area VIII 1960. In general, the pottery assemblages from these contexts are small and mixed; many of the sherds have a general similarity to Temple IIb-pottery, but older material is also represented. Besides, there are sherds from the Islamic period in these levels, which led the excavators to conclude that the demolition of the monument for stone took place at that time. From this sparse material a secure dating of Temple III cannot be given.

Attention is, however, drawn to some finds in the southern part of the excavation which may perhaps give an indication of the date of Temple III, apart from the stratigraphic fact that it is later than Temple IIb. In the southernmost area excavated on the site, *area XIV 1957*, several assemblages of pottery occur (517. AEE, AEF, AEG, AEH), which is typologically later than the pottery related to Temple IIb. The assemblages were retrieved from level c. 3.00-5.00 (cf. fig. 267).

The pottery is characterized by a number of necks with triangular rims of the same types that occur with Temple IIb (figs. 535-543), but here accompanied by new variants of the triangular rim, for example with a more narrow triangle (cf. Failaka type 1B) (figs. 544-550) or with the rim edges drawn out (figs. 551-553). The hole-mouth rims are few, mostly similar to those of Temple IIb of types B16-17 (figs. 554-561) and type B18, one with a spout (figs. 562-563), but also with one rather similar to type B19 (fig. 564) and a new evenly thickened variant (fig. 565); besides, a few rims of normal pithoi (fig. 566), a large rim (cf. Failaka type 28) (fig. 567), bowls (figs. 568-570) and fragments of plates with finger impressions and three feet (Failaka type 44) (figs. 571-572) were found. In general, ware type 2 dominates well over type 1.

Similar pottery has been excavated at the nearby Northeast Temple and will be described below.

Summary of Temple III

The above-described assemblages are typologically advanced in relation to the pottery assemblages of Temple IIb, with some general parallels at Qala'at al-Bahrain in period IIb-c and some parallels in Failaka period 2A, especially in the new variants of the triangular rim.

As stated above, there is no definite stratigraphical relationship between these assemblages and the architectural remains of Temple III, nor to the pottery assemblages described above from the nearby area VIII 1957, which are related to Temple IIb. The upper stratigraphy of the temple site has simply been destroyed by demolition of the monument and by geological deflation of the mound. But the assemblages described above may perhaps be interpreted as evidence of a horizontal stratigraphy: Later material accumulated against the sloping side of the temple mound (fig. 267). As such the assemblages of area XIV 1957 may tentatively be related to Temple III.

In the extreme southwestern periphery of the temple, two long trenches were set out in 1961, areas I and IV, which both produced a small amount of even later material, perhaps lending support to the hypothesis of horizontal stratigraphy expressed above. It is not possible to relate these finds to the layers in sections 28-29.

The pottery from several assemblages found in the upper excavated level of *area I 1961* (517. AQQ, AQR, ARM) is rather homogeneous and can be referred to either the Barbar tradition or the Mesopotamian tradition.

The Barbar types consist of triangular rims of the tall and low smoothed variant (Failaka type 1G and 1H) (figs. 573-575), a wheel-made rounded-square rim with red stripes on a yellow slip (fig. 576), and two hole-mouth rims, one, fig. 577, related to fig. 565, the other, fig. 578, related to type B19; furthermore, rimmed plates (Failaka type 43) (figs. 579-583), a fragment of a plate with finger impressions and three feet (Failaka type 44) (figs. 584), and a side-sherd with a broad, red painted band on a light red slip. Fig. 585 is a unique sherd, wheelmade, and red-slipped on a light-red sand-tempered ware.

The Mesopotamian types consist of two broad-grooved, double-ribbed rims (Failaka type 55A) (figs. 586-587), a triple-ribbed rim (Failaka type

56) (fig. 588) and a fragment of a Kassite goblet (fig. 589).

Most of this pottery, the Barbar types as well as the Mesopotamian types, would fit well into period IIIa at Qala'at al-Bahrain (cf. *Qala'at 2* figs. 129-158) or period 3B on Failaka (cf. Højlund 1987 figs. 532-561), with the exception of the goblet fragment, which most likely belongs in period IIIb at Qala'at al-Bahrain.

The pottery from the upper excavated level of *area IV 1961* (517.ARA), is at least partly contemporaneous with that of area I. A number of sherds belonging in the Mesopotamian tradition have close parallels in period IIIa at Qala'at al-Bahrain or period 3B at Failaka: triple-ribbed rims (Failaka type 56) (figs. 590-593), bowls with slightly drawn-in rim, either without rim decoration or with multi-

grooved rim (Failaka type 67A and C) (figs. 594-595). Other sherds have parallels in period IIIb at Qala'at al-Bahrain and period 4A in Failaka: the slender, double-ribbed rim (Failaka type 55C) (fig. 596) and simple plain bowl rims (Failaka type 68) (figs. 597-599).

From the deeper levels of both area I and IV came earlier material, similar to that of Temple IIb and to the above-described pottery from area XIV 1957, which has been tentatively related to Temple III. This is probably the context of a stamp seal (517.ARE, fig. 780) found at the bottom of area IV, immediately below a floor in the middle of the area (section 28:E), but precise information about the pottery context is not available. This seal belongs in Kjærum's style 1B (see Kjærum below, p. 304).

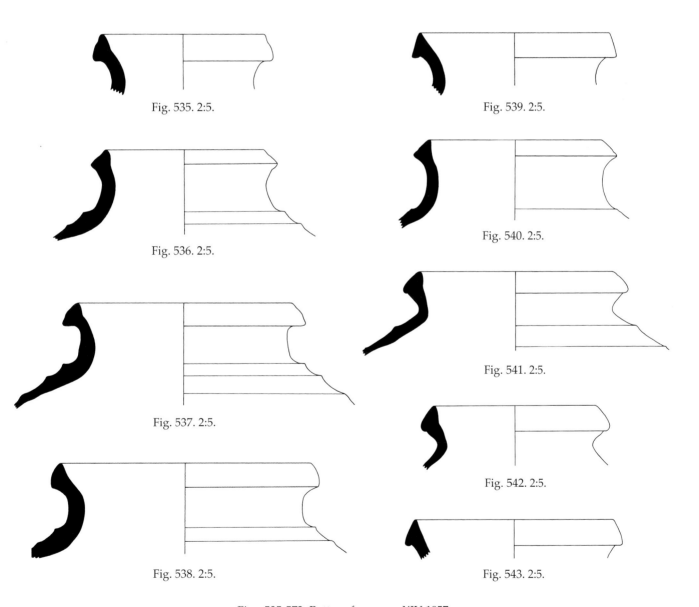

Fig. 535. 2:5.

Fig. 536. 2:5.

Fig. 537. 2:5.

Fig. 538. 2:5.

Fig. 539. 2:5.

Fig. 540. 2:5.

Fig. 541. 2:5.

Fig. 542. 2:5.

Fig. 543. 2:5.

Figs. 535-572. Pottery from area XIV 1957.

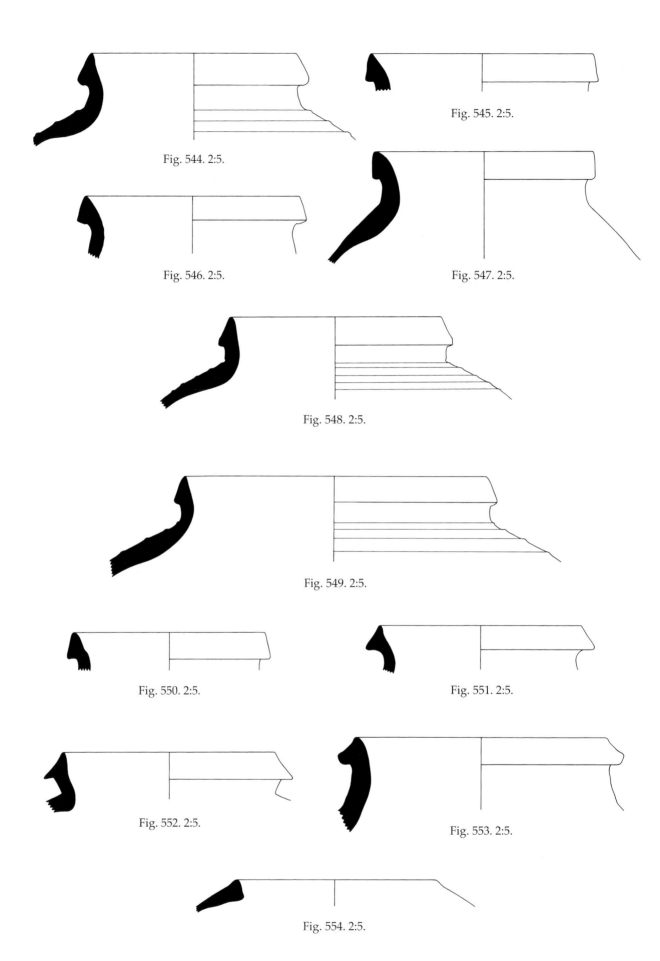

Fig. 544. 2:5.

Fig. 545. 2:5.

Fig. 546. 2:5.

Fig. 547. 2:5.

Fig. 548. 2:5.

Fig. 549. 2:5.

Fig. 550. 2:5.

Fig. 551. 2:5.

Fig. 552. 2:5.

Fig. 553. 2:5.

Fig. 554. 2:5.

Figs. 535-572. Pottery from area XIV 1957.

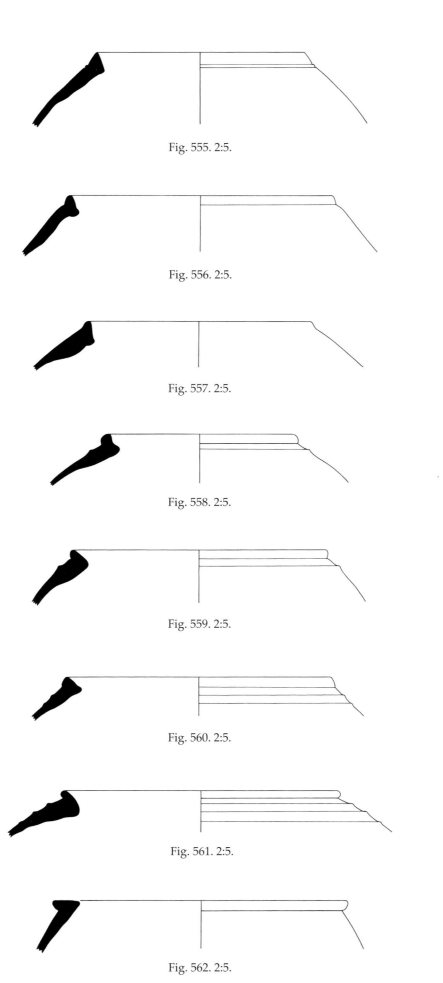

Fig. 555. 2:5.

Fig. 556. 2:5.

Fig. 557. 2:5.

Fig. 558. 2:5.

Fig. 559. 2:5.

Fig. 560. 2:5.

Fig. 561. 2:5.

Fig. 562. 2:5.

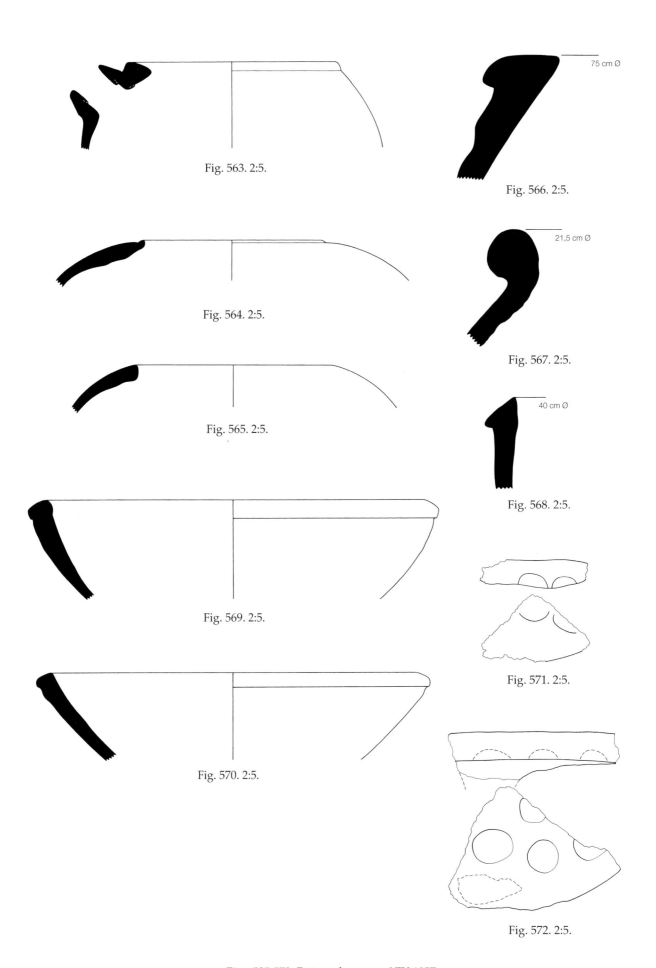

Fig. 563. 2:5.

75 cm Ø

Fig. 566. 2:5.

Fig. 564. 2:5.

21,5 cm Ø

Fig. 567. 2:5.

Fig. 565. 2:5.

40 cm Ø

Fig. 568. 2:5.

Fig. 569. 2:5.

Fig. 571. 2:5.

Fig. 570. 2:5.

Fig. 572. 2:5.

Figs. 535-572. Pottery from area XIV 1957.

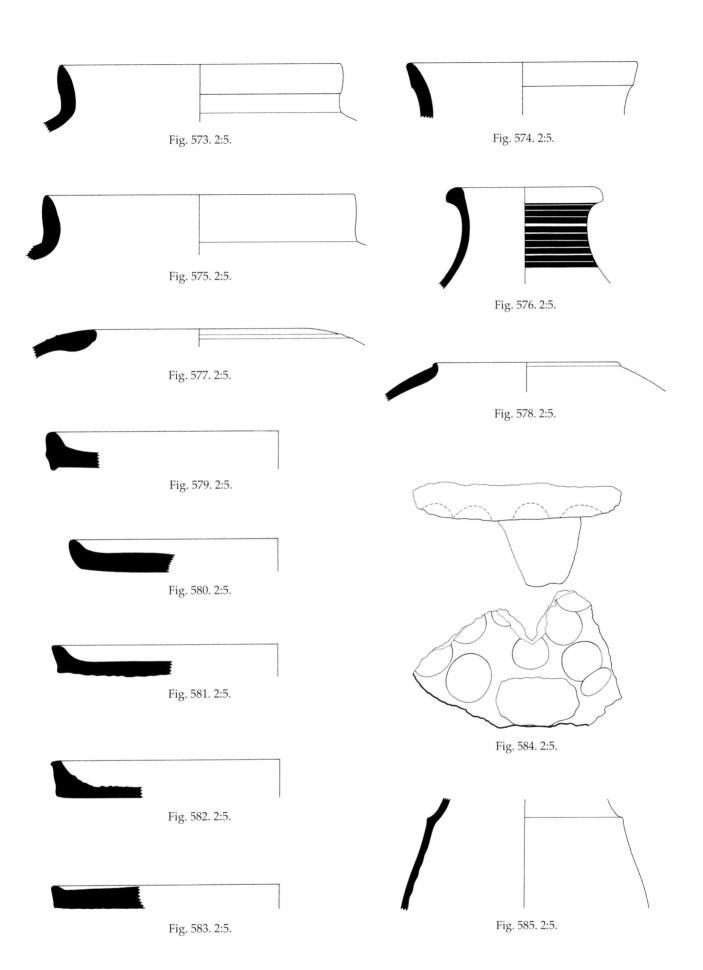

Fig. 573. 2:5.

Fig. 574. 2:5.

Fig. 575. 2:5.

Fig. 576. 2:5.

Fig. 577. 2:5.

Fig. 578. 2:5.

Fig. 579. 2:5.

Fig. 580. 2:5.

Fig. 581. 2:5.

Fig. 584. 2:5.

Fig. 582. 2:5.

Fig. 583. 2:5.

Fig. 585. 2:5.

Figs. 573-589. Pottery from area I 1961.

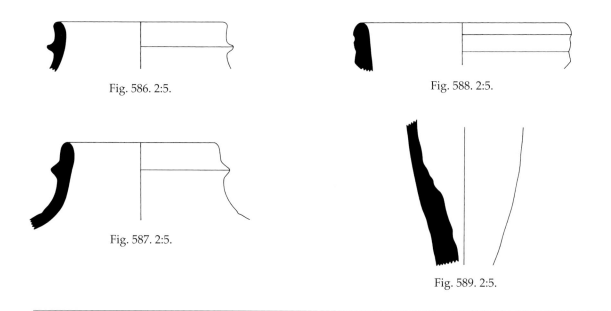

Fig. 586. 2:5.

Fig. 588. 2:5.

Fig. 587. 2:5.

Fig. 589. 2:5.

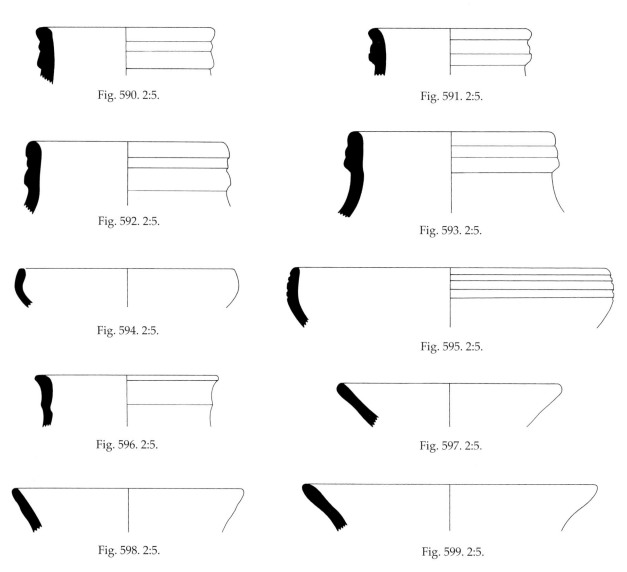

Fig. 590. 2:5.

Fig. 591. 2:5.

Fig. 592. 2:5.

Fig. 593. 2:5.

Fig. 594. 2:5.

Fig. 595. 2:5.

Fig. 596. 2:5.

Fig. 597. 2:5.

Fig. 598. 2:5.

Fig. 599. 2:5.

Figs. 590-599. Pottery from area IV 1961.

The Northeast Temple

The Northeast Temple lying 30 m to the north-east of the Barbar temple was almost completely demolished, leaving only a 24 × 24 m plastered level on which a central platform was originally erected.

During the uncovering of this plaster floor a number of potsherds were found, mostly triangular rims and hole-mouth rims (figs. 600-615), which have their closest parallels in an assemblage, described above, from the southernmost area at Barbar (figs. 535-572). A unique sherd in the Barbar Temple context, a black-on-red painted one (fig. 616), has parallels at Failaka (Højlund 1987 fig. 502).

A large assemblage of similar pottery (517.ARP) was found in a sounding outside the plastered platform floor (figs. 617-632). One notes especially the variants of the triangular rim with a more narrow triangle (cf. Failaka type 1B) (figs. 621-623). Ware type 2 dominates over type 1.

Another assemblage (517.ARU), also found in a sounding outside the plastered platform floor, is typologically later than ARP (figs. 633-656), as can be seen in the presence of a triangular rim with the rim edges drawn out (fig. 638) and many triangular rims with a more narrow triangle (cf. Failaka type 1B) (figs. 639-643) and even later variants of the triangular rim: the sharp type B4 (cf. Failaka type 1E) (fig. 644), the concave type B5 (fig. 645), the tall smoothed variant (cf. Failaka type 1G) (fig. 646) and

some heavy triangular rims on low necks (figs. 647-648). Several side-sherds had horizontal dark painted bands, like an imitation of the ridging (cf. *Qala'at 1* type B3, p. 664). The ware is almost exclusively of type 2.

No earlier or later pottery was found on the site of the Northeast Temple, apart from a sprinkle of Islamic sherds which can perhaps be related to the demolition of the building.

Summary of the NE Temple

The pottery from the NE Temple is not abundant – some scattered sherds and two good assemblages – and it has only sparse context information. However, the absence on the site of pottery that can be compared to that of the nearby Temples Ia, IIa and IIb, and the presence of pottery typologically later than that of Temple IIb, indicates that the NE Temple should be dated to the period following immediately after Temple IIb. This would make the NE Temple contemporary with Temple III, if the slim dating evidence for that Temple is to be trusted (fig. 266).

There are general parallels in Qala'at al-Bahrain period IIb-c and more specifically, the variation of the triangular rims relates assemblage ARP to Failaka period 2A and assemblage ARU to Failaka period 2B (fig. 266).

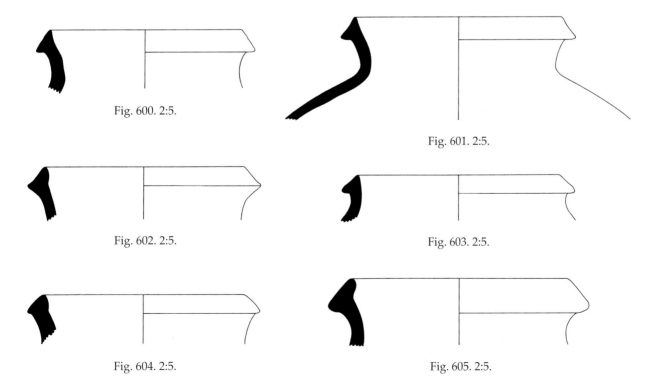

Fig. 600. 2:5.

Fig. 601. 2:5.

Fig. 602. 2:5.

Fig. 603. 2:5.

Fig. 604. 2:5.

Fig. 605. 2:5.

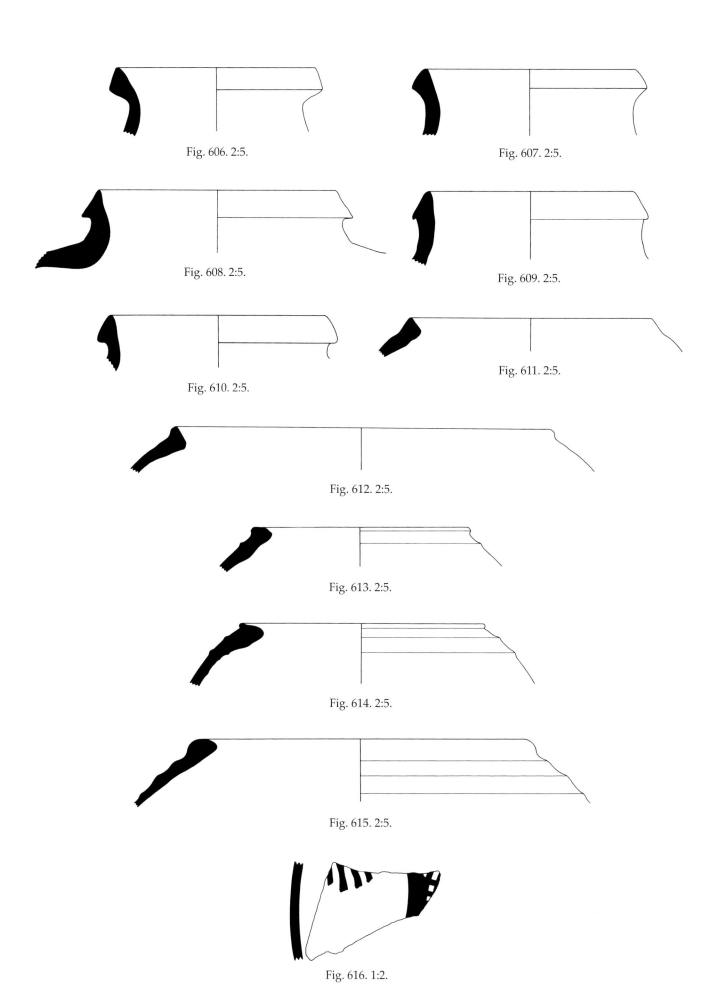

Fig. 606. 2:5.

Fig. 607. 2:5.

Fig. 608. 2:5.

Fig. 609. 2:5.

Fig. 610. 2:5.

Fig. 611. 2:5.

Fig. 612. 2:5.

Fig. 613. 2:5.

Fig. 614. 2:5.

Fig. 615. 2:5.

Fig. 616. 1:2.

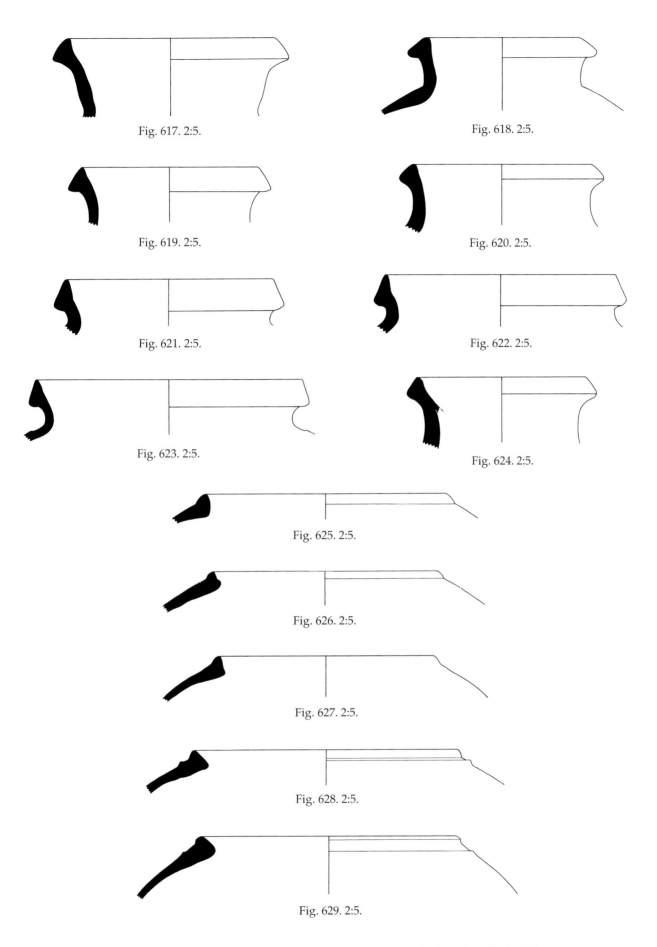

Fig. 617. 2:5.

Fig. 618. 2:5.

Fig. 619. 2:5.

Fig. 620. 2:5.

Fig. 621. 2:5.

Fig. 622. 2:5.

Fig. 623. 2:5.

Fig. 624. 2:5.

Fig. 625. 2:5.

Fig. 626. 2:5.

Fig. 627. 2:5.

Fig. 628. 2:5.

Fig. 629. 2:5.

Figs. 617-632. Assemblage of pottery from sounding outside platform floor (517.ARP).

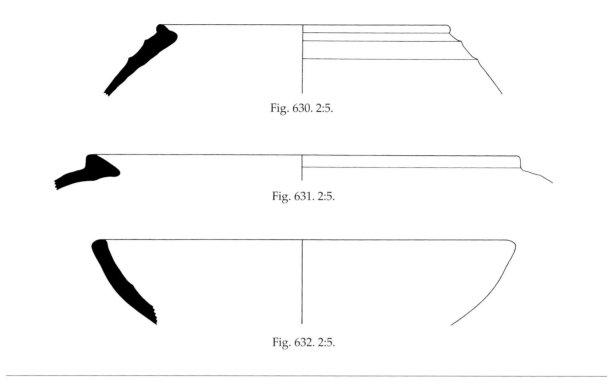

Fig. 630. 2:5.

Fig. 631. 2:5.

Fig. 632. 2:5.

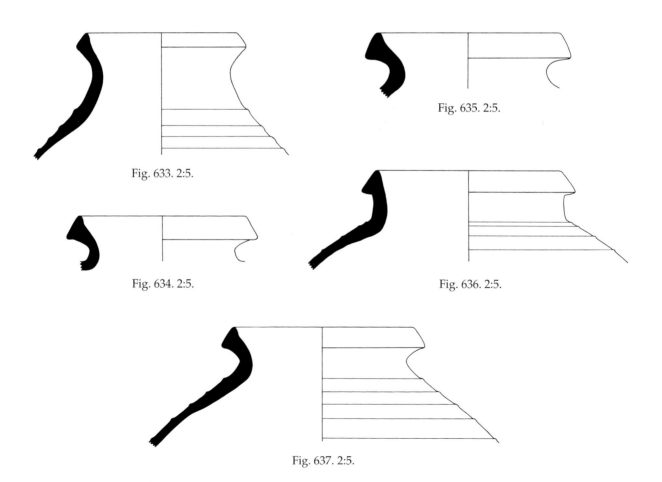

Fig. 633. 2:5.

Fig. 635. 2:5.

Fig. 634. 2:5.

Fig. 636. 2:5.

Fig. 637. 2:5.

Figs. 633-656. Assemblage of pottery from sounding outside platform floor (517.ARU).

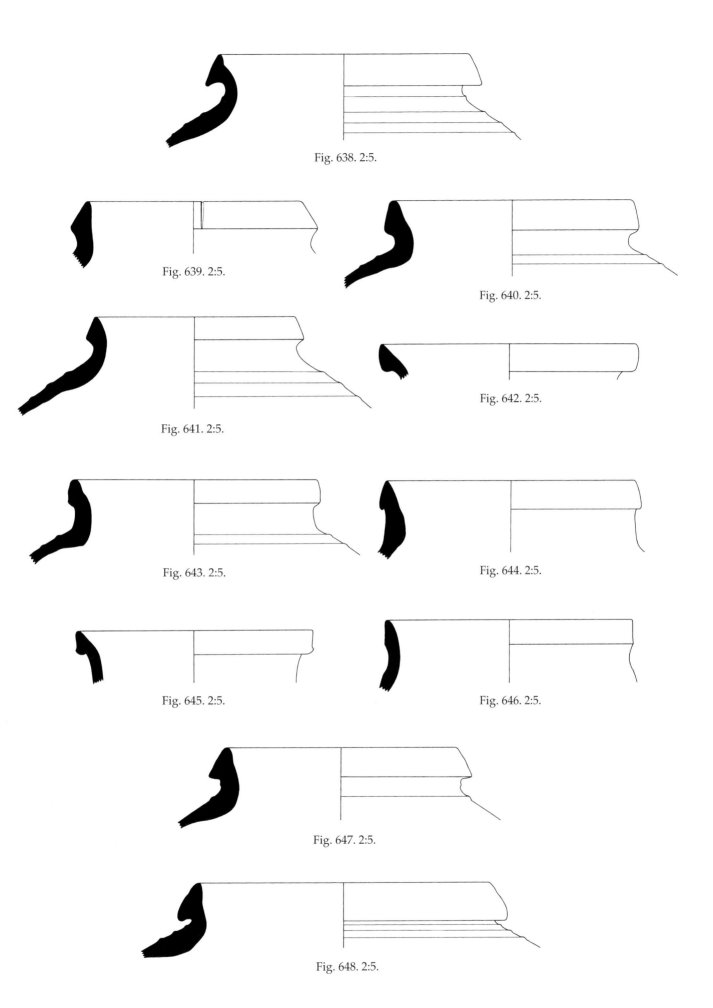

Fig. 638. 2:5.

Fig. 639. 2:5.

Fig. 640. 2:5.

Fig. 641. 2:5.

Fig. 642. 2:5.

Fig. 643. 2:5.

Fig. 644. 2:5.

Fig. 645. 2:5.

Fig. 646. 2:5.

Fig. 647. 2:5.

Fig. 648. 2:5.

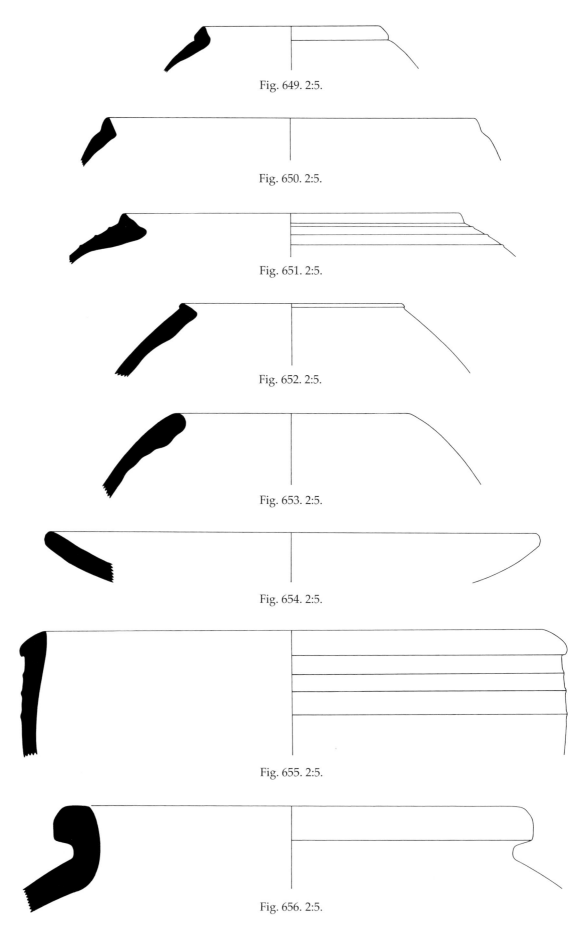

Fig. 649. 2:5.

Fig. 650. 2:5.

Fig. 651. 2:5.

Fig. 652. 2:5.

Fig. 653. 2:5.

Fig. 654. 2:5.

Fig. 655. 2:5.

Fig. 656. 2:5.

Figs. 633-656. Assemblage of pottery from sounding outside platform floor (517.ARU).

12. Copper and Copper Working

The copper objects

A large number of copper or copper alloy objects were found at the temple. In the clay level at the base of Temple Ia, a number of copper artefacts, some of them evidently only symbolic, were placed, apparently as offerings. But most of the metal found at the temple consisted of fragments of sheet, originally attached by nails to wooden structures. Fragments of crucibles and moulds show that copper was melted and worked at the temple.

All the copper objects found were heavily corroded. Most of the tools and objects were subsequently cleaned and conserved, whereas only a small part of the sheet and nails that make up the majority of the metal finds, has been treated. The original metal core of the object has often disappeared, and it may be difficult to establish the original surface. The smaller and thinner the object, the more often this is the case. It is therefore usually difficult to measure the original thickness of, for example, the metal sheet with any degree of certainty. The best-preserved fragments vary between 0.1 and 0.3 cm in thickness. Due to the high rate of corrosion, it may often be difficult to see the nail-holes punched through the sheet. Remains of broken nails still *in situ* may also merge with the corrosion layer. Because of the heavy corrosion, the length of the nails is given only approximately. As part of the corrosion process the copper material has become very fragile, so that most plates have broken up.

Most plates are flat or somewhat curved, whereas others seem to have been folded together in a haphazard manner. In a very few cases only it seems that a plate has been hammered into a specific shape, and these pieces are illustrated.

C. 75 analyses of copper-alloy objects from Barbar were made in 1960, using optical emission spectroscopy, by the *Arbeitsgemeinschaft für Metallurgie des Altertum* based in Stuttgart (Junghans, Sangmeister & Schröder 1960). The results are listed in Appendix 3.

In addition, c. 52 spectrographical and metallographical analyses of copper objects from Barbar were made by Dennis Heskel of the University of Utah on the initiative of Peder Mortensen. The samples were taken in 1980 – their positions are indicated on the drawings of the objects – and the report finished in 1984 (Heskel 1984[1]). The results of the analyses are listed in Appendix 4.

In the following, the copper objects will be briefly described within a few contextual groups each ending with some concluding remarks. For area designations reference is made to figs. 6-13.

Pre-Temple

Area XII 1957

Fragment of plate, 6 × 7 cm, c. 0.5 cm thick (517.ADZ).

Summary. This piece of plate is the only metal find from pre-Temple layers, and its function cannot be determined. It lacks any traces of nail-holes as are normal for the sheet metal from the temple phases.

The clay level of Temple Ia

Some of the metal objects found in the clay level related to Temple Ia, both inside and outside the platform walls, have their positions marked on plan 1.

1955

Copper vessel (517.CB) (fig. 657). Found together with gold band, 517.FF (fig. 809), at level 2.72, cf. section 5:17, black triangle. For spectrographic analysis, see Appendix 4.

---

[1] The assignment of metal objects to temple phases in Heskel's original report should be taken with reservation, as these have been revised since his samples were taken.

6 pieces of sheet, the largest being 9×13 cm, c. 100 cm² in all (517.FG). At level 2.90. For spectrographic analyses of two sheet fragments, see Appendix 3.

Irregular disc-shaped ingot, weight 0.884 kg (517.FH) (fig. 658). At level 2.90. For a spectrographic analysis, see Appendix 3.

Shaft-hole adze with damaged edge and socket (517.FI) (fig. 659) (cf. Deshayes 1960 pl. 30). At level 2.90. For a spectrographic analysis, see Appendix 3. A fragment of the socket of this adze was found later, see 517. AJI below, and has been spectrographically and metallographically analysed (fig. 664).

Area XII 1957

Crescent-shaped object with shaft-hole, possibly axe, clumsily made (517.AGR) (fig. 660). At level 3.20, i.e. at the transition between the clay level and the underlying sand. For a spectrographic analysis, see Appendix 3.

Socketed spearhead with flat blade; clumsily made, especially the transition between socket and blade (517.AGS) (fig. 661). At level 3.26, i.e. at the transition between the clay level and the underlying sand. For a metallographic and spectrographic analysis, see Appendix 4.

Area III 1958

Bun-shaped ingot, weight 1.15 kg (517.AIV) (fig. 662). At level 2.25.

Fragments of sheet, c. 80 cm² in all. For a metallographic and spectrographic analysis of a fragment (fig. 663), see Appendix 4. Two amorphous lumps, 40 cm² in all (517.AJH). At level 2.98.

Fragment of the socket of the shaft-hole adze described above under 517.FI (fig. 664). For a metallographic and spectrographic analysis, see Appendix 4. Rod, 5.8 cm long, with rectangular cross-section (fig. 665). For a metallographic and spectrographic analysis, see Appendix 4. Rod, 9 cm long, 0.4 cm in diameter. Sheet, c. 10×5 cm, 50 cm² in all, rolled into a 10.5 cm long rod with an oval, 1.2×1.6 cm cross-section. Sheet with punched holes, 50 cm². Other fragments of sheet, c. 260 cm² in all. One nail, 2 cm (517.AJI).

Area III/IV 1958

Cylinder made of rectangular sheet (517.AJN), c. 60 cm long. The overlap of the sheet was at least 3 cm, and the overlapping edges straight. The original di-

ameter of the cylinder is estimated at c. 10 cm, but when found it was somewhat compressed and damaged at one end. The cylinder appeared not to have been closed at either end. Originally mounted with nails on wood, traces of which were present. The sheet is broken in many pieces, c. 1100 cm² in all. 20 nails, of which 17 in situ, c. 2.5 cm long. Oriented N-S and located in the upper part of the clay level, at level 2.73.

Fragmented cylinder of sheet (517.AJO), c. 400 cm² in all. Originally mounted on wood with nails, 31 pieces, of which 10 in situ, c. 2.5 cm. Located about 20 cm west of 517.AJN, oriented in the same direction and at the same level.

Flat, rectangular sheet (517.AJQ) (fig. 666). At least 3 original edges preserved, two long sides and one short side, c. 50 punched holes, and c. 20 nails still in situ, 3 of them measuring 2.6-2.7 cm. Dimensions 14×60.5 cm, or c. 8470 cm², but some parts are missing. Uppermost in the clay level, at level 2.90.

Area III 1959, immediately north of Temple Ia

Socketed spearhead with broken point and flat blade (517.AKZ) (fig. 667); asymmetrical, clumsily made, especially the transition between socket and blade. 40 cm deep in the clay level.

Crescent-shaped object with shaft-hole, possible axe, clumsily made (517.ALB) (fig. 668). 50 cm deep in the clay level. For a metallographic and spectrographic analysis, see Appendix 4.

Socketed spearhead with long socket and fragmented, flat blade; the transition between socket and blade is clumsily made (517.ALC) (fig. 669). 40 cm deep in the clay level.

Possible knife made of flat sheet with folded edges in shaft segment (517.ALD) (fig. 670). 60 cm deep in the clay level. For a metallographic analysis, see Appendix 4.

Dagger with flat blade and tang with rectangular cross-section (517.ALL) (fig. 671). 50 cm deep in the clay level. For a metallographic analysis, see Appendix 4.

Fragments of sheet, c. 40 cm² in all. 2 nails, c. 2.5 cm (517.ALR).

Area VIII 1959

Quadrangular blade with 4 nail-holes and 1 rivet in place (517.ALO) (fig. 672). In clay level near subsoil.

Area XIII 1959

Fragment of sheet, 3 cm², with 1 punched hole (517.AMB).

Area XIV 1960

9 fragments of sheet with punched holes, c. 50 cm² in all (517.AOP).

Rattle (517.APT) (fig. 673) (cf. Woolley 1955 pl. 29: U.17879; Contenau, G. & R. Ghirshman 1935 pl. 28, Burial 105).

Summary. A number of weapons and other objects were found in the clay level at the base of Temple Ia: 3 socketed spearheads with flat blades, 1 broken shaft-hole adze, 1 fragment of the same shaft-hole axe, 2 crescent-shaped objects, possibly axes, 1 dagger with flat blade and tang, 1 possible knife, 1 quadrangular blade, 1 rattle, 1 copper vessel, 1 disc-shaped ingot, 1 bun-shaped ingot, 3 rods, 2 lumps; besides, a total area of 10603 cm² sheet metal, incl. 2 cylinders mounted with nails on wood and 1 rectangular sheet, 14 × 60.5 cm, having originally been attached by nails to wood, and 74 nails.

It is remarkable that several of the weapons are clumsily made. This goes for the two crescent-shaped, possible axes, a possible knife and all the spearheads, where the transition between the socket and the blade is awkwardly made. Besides, it is notable that all spearhead and knife/dagger blades are made of flat sheet and thus without any strengthening of the blade in the shape of a midrib or a rhomboid/lenticular cross-section. This clumsiness and lack of practical efficiency is all the more evident if comparison is made to a contemporaneous or slightly earlier find from Qala'at al-Bahrain, a 31 cm long, strong and well-made socketed spearhead with a midrib, dating to Qala'at al-Bahrain period Ib (*Qala'at 1* fig. 1855).

These weapons were hardly made for practical use, but were rather symbols intended as offerings to the gods, and as such they fall in line with the many pottery beakers found in the same clay layer and interpreted as remains of a sacrificial ceremony where libations were made. The rest of the objects may perhaps also be regarded as offerings or remains from an offering ceremony.

Fig. 657. 1:2.

Fig. 658. 1:2.

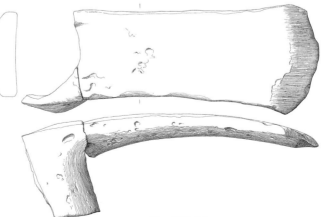

Fig. 659. 1:2.

257

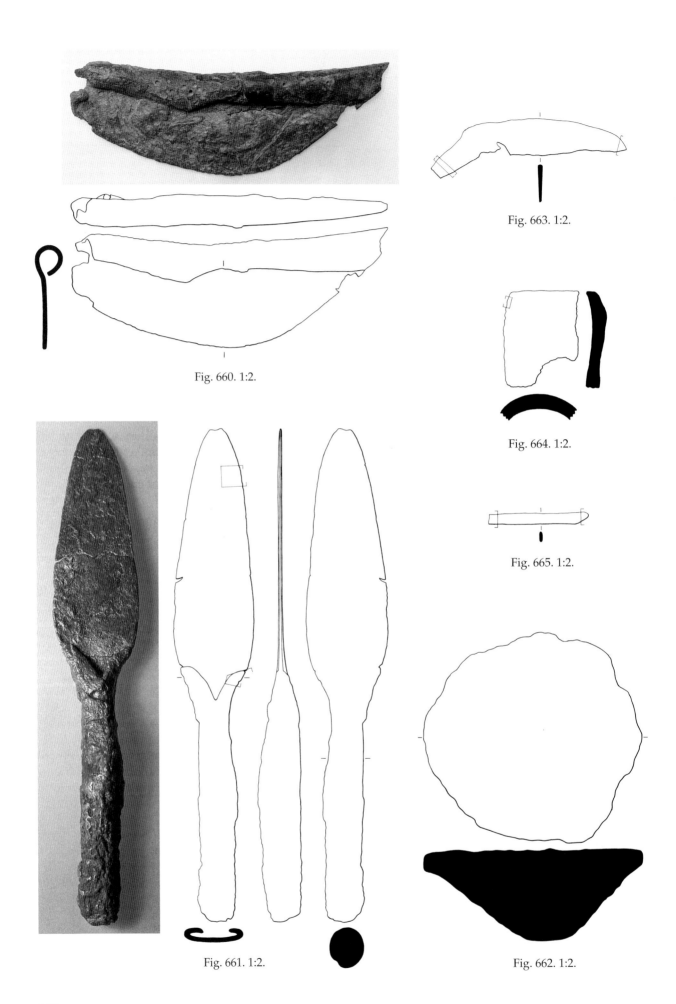

Fig. 660. 1:2.

Fig. 663. 1:2.

Fig. 664. 1:2.

Fig. 665. 1:2.

Fig. 661. 1:2.

Fig. 662. 1:2.

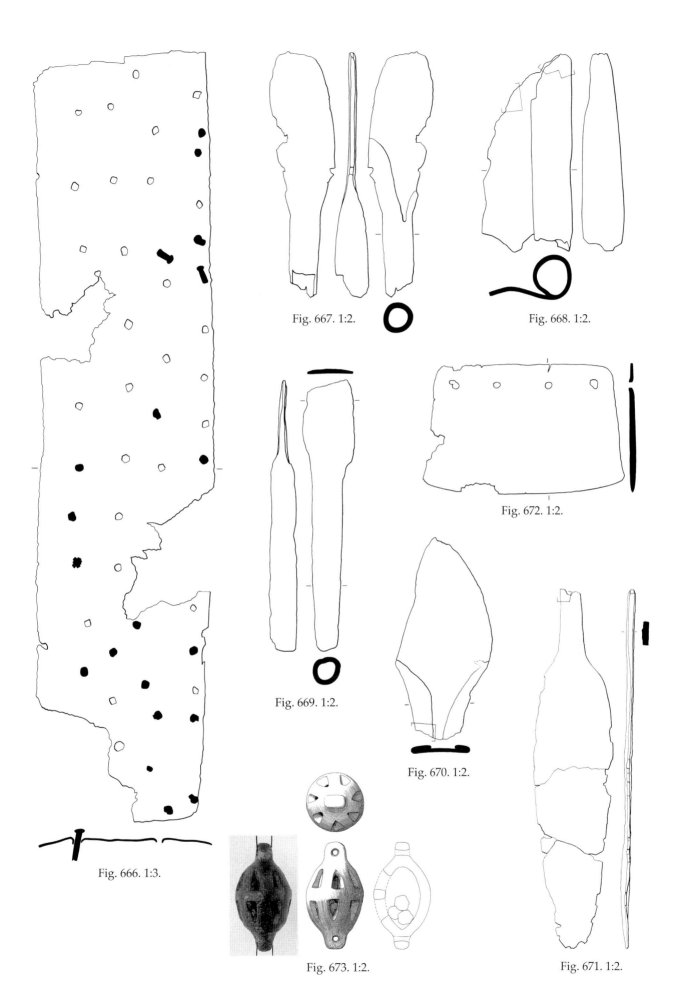

Fig. 667. 1:2.

Fig. 668. 1:2.

Fig. 669. 1:2.

Fig. 672. 1:2.

Fig. 666. 1:3.

Fig. 673. 1:2.

Fig. 670. 1:2.

Fig. 671. 1:2.

The fill of the Temple Ia platform

1955

Fragments of sheet with punched holes; the largest piece being 13 × 22 cm and folded, c. 420 cm² in all. 1 nail, c. 2.5 cm (517.DV).

Area V 1957

Sheet, c. 5 cm² (517.ACD).

Fragments of sheet, 65 cm² in all. Nail, 4.8 cm long with square cross-section, 0.5 cm thick (517.ACH).

Fragments of sheet with punched holes, c. 420 cm² in all. Four nails, 2.2-2.5 cm (517.ACI).

Fragments of sheet, 10 cm² in all. 1 fragment of ingot (fig. 674). For a metallographic and spectrographic analysis, see Appendix 4. 1 nail (517.ACL).

Fragments of sheet, 180 cm² in all. 3 nails, c. 2.5 cm (517.AJT).

Area III 1958

Fragment of sheet with two original edges and 1 nail *in situ*, 15 × 16 cm, 240 cm². Further fragments of sheet with punched holes and 1 nail *in situ*, 550 cm² in all (517.AHM). Found at level 1.58 at coordinate 24.30/-0.10.

Fragments of sheet with punched holes, the largest pieces being 8 × 13 cm and 16 × 20 cm, 1830 cm² in all. 9 nails *in situ*, 2.5-3.2 cm (517.AIY). Found together with sherds of a calcite jar (517.AIR) at level 1.61 at coordinate 24.40/-1.10, at a place where the floor of Temple I was broken through (see Casanova below, p. 285).

Fragments of sheet with punched holes, 120 cm² in all (517.AJA).

Area III-IV 1958

Fragments of sheet, 180 cm² in all. 3 nails, c. 2.5 cm (517.AJT).

Area IX 1959

Fragments of sheet, 30 cm² in all (517.ALX).

Area XIV 1960

2 fragments of bun-shaped ingots (figs. 675-676). For a metallographic analysis of fig. 676, see Appendix 4. Fragment of metal bar (fig. 677). Fragment of sheet, 6 cm². Nail, 2.3 cm (517.AOS).

Area XV 1960

Sheet fragment, 3 cm². Fragment of rod, 2 cm long, 0.2 cm diam (517.AQF).

Summary. A considerable number of metal sheet fragments, 4059 cm² in all, and 25 nails were found in the fill of the Temple Ia platform, besides 3 fragments of bun-shaped ingots, 1 fragment of a bar, and 1 rod.

These finds may have been accidentally incorporated into the fill of the temple platform, and the sheet fragments and nails, for example, could thus be remains from an earlier temple on the site. Alternatively, the material could have been deposited from the floor of Temple I: one lot of sheet fragments (517.AIY), and perhaps another lot as well (517.AHM), were found just below the floor of the platform at a place where the floor was disturbed.

Fig. 674. 1:2.

Fig. 675. 1:2.

Fig. 676. 1:2.

Fig. 677. 1:2.

The floor of Temple I

Area IV 1959

Nail, 2.8 cm (517.AMG); found in one of the pits in the southwestern part of the floor, plan 2:1.

Summary. The floor of Temple I produced surprisingly few finds of metal. Apparently, no accumulation of refuse on the floor had taken place.

Between floors of Temples I and II

Area III 1958

Fragments of sheet, 100 cm² in all. 1 rod with round cross-section (fig. 678). 1 nail, 3 cm (517.AHC).

4 fragments of bun-shaped ingots (figs. 679-682). For a metallographic analysis of fig. 682, see Appendix 4. Fragments of sheet, 70 cm² in all. 5 nails, 2-3 cm. 6 lumps (517.AHF).

Fragment of ingot (fig. 683). For a metallographic and spectrographic analysis, see Appendix 4 . Fragment, probably from ingot (fig. 684). For a metallographic and spectrographic analysis, see Appendix 4. Possible fish-hook (fig. 685). For a metallographic and spectrographic analysis, see Appendix 4. Possible chisel. For a metallographic and spectrographic analysis, see Appendix 4. 9 lumps and 1 nail, 3.5 cm (517.AHI).

Area IV 1958

3 lumps (517.AHK).

Area VII 1958

Fragment of rod, 5 cm long and rectangular in cross-section, one end being broken and the other having two prongs (fig. 686). For a metallographic and spectrographic analysis, see Appendix 4. Fragments of sheet, 9 cm² in all. 3 nails, 2-3 cm (517.AHD).

Fragments of sheet with punched holes, 50 cm². 5 lumps (517.AHJ).

Summary. Between the floors of Temple I and II were found 4 fragments of bun-shaped ingots, 2 fragments of ingots, 1 possible fish-hook, 1 possible chisel, 1 rod, 23 lumps, 229 cm² fragments of sheet and 10 nails. The finds may either be accidentally occurring in fill for the Temple II floor or have been dug down from the Temple II floor.

One large group of metal objects found between the floors of Temple I and Temple II has been treated separarately as the bull's head deposit, see below, p. 265.

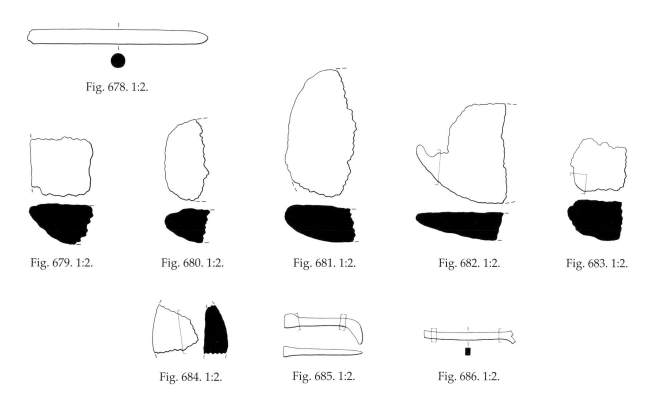

Fig. 678. 1:2.

Fig. 679. 1:2.   Fig. 680. 1:2.   Fig. 681. 1:2.   Fig. 682. 1:2.   Fig. 683. 1:2.

Fig. 684. 1:2.   Fig. 685. 1:2.   Fig. 686. 1:2.

261

The floor of Temple II

1955

Fragments of sheet with 3 nails *in situ*, 200 cm^2 in all. For a spectrographic analysis, see Appendix 4. 8 nails, 1 of c. 2.5 cm, 3 of c. 3 cm, 2 of c. 3.5 cm and 2 of 4.5 cm (517.BA). Between the channel and the framed area in the corner (plan 3:15-16).

Fragments of sheet with punched holes, 100 cm^2 in all. 3 nails c. 3.5 cm (517.BB). On the flagged floor south of the channel, plan 3:15.

Fragments of sheet with punched holes, 100 cm^2 (517.BC). On the flagged floor (plan 3:12) along the east wall (plan 3:1).

Fragments of sheet with punched holes and 15 nails *in situ*, 880 cm^2 in all, one of them being 15 × 19 cm, where 15 cm is the original width. This piece is corroded together with another piece, 8 × 13 cm. Two other pieces are also corroded together, 10 × 14 and 12 × 17 cm. A third piece consists of two pieces of sheet originally overlapping, 13 × 23 cm, with 7 nails *in situ* and 6 broken nails *in situ*, in 3 rows (fig. 687) (517.EF). Found in the channel, plan 3:15, but in secondary position and unlikely to be remains of a casing.

Fragments of sheet, 110 cm^2 in all. 13 nails, 1 of c. 5 cm, 5 of c. 4 cm, 6 of c. 3 cm, and 1 of c. 2 cm. 1 lump, 10 cm^2 (517.EI). Probably found on the flagged floor south of the double altars, plan 3:18.

Summary. Rather few finds of metal were made on the flagged floor of Temple II: c. 1390 cm^2 of fragments of sheet and 42 nails, besides 1 lump.

"Pit of offering"

1954

1 spike with round head and a square cross-section (fig. 688). For a spectrographic analysis, see Appendix 4. 64 nails, a few c. 2.5 cm, most 3-5 cm. 1 rod with square cross-section (fig. 689). For a metallographic and spectrographic analysis, see Appendix 4. 1 curved rod with round cross-section, possibly with a flattened end with an eye, needle? with broken-off point (fig. 690) (cf. Frifelt 1995 fig. 278). Metal fragment. For a spectrographic analysis, see Appendix 4. 5 lumps, 3 × 6 cm (517.A).
Fragments of sheet with punched holes and 4 nails *in situ*, 1025 cm^2 in all (517.C).
128 nails, a few 2.5 cm, most 3-4 cm, a few 5 cm (fig. 691). 1 lump, 10 cm^2 (517.J).

Fragments of sheet with punched holes and 10 nails *in situ*, 2330 cm^2 in all. Of these one band with at least two original long sides, 5-6 × 17 cm; 4 narrow, slightly irregular bands, 2 × 10 cm, 2 × 14 cm, 2.5 × 7 cm and 3.5 × 8 cm; 1 curved piece of sheet, 8 × 9.5 cm, with two nails *in situ* (fig. 692), 1 fragment, 11.5 × 12 cm with 3 rows of holes (fig. 693). For a spectrographic analysis, see Appendix 4. 2 loose nails. 2 lumps, 20 cm^2. For a spectrographic analysis, see Appendix 4 (517.L).

Bird (517.O) (fig. 694 and 695:2). For a photo of the bird before conservation, see Glob 1954a fig. 7. For a spectrographic analysis, see Appendix 3. The bird is made up of several pieces: the head- and neck-piece is joined to the body by sinking the neck into a rectangular hole in the body, the leg-piece was probably mounted in the same way. On the back of the bird a fragment of a rectangular piece is sitting in a rectangular hole (pers.comm. conservator Helle Strehle, March 2002).

Male figurine (517.P) (fig. 696 and 695:3). For a photo of the figurine before conservation, see Glob 1954a fig. 6. For a spectrographic analysis, see Appendix 3. The figurine was probably originally the handle of a mirror attached below its feet (Rao 1970 p. 218). The origin of this type is found in late 3rd or early 2nd millennium southern Uzbekistan and northern Afghanistan (Potts 1983b p. 131-132, and 1990, I, p. 205, note 84), though the Barbar piece could well have been locally made, influenced as it is also from Mesopotamia (During Caspers 1973a).

Curved rod with circular cross-section and one end flattened (fig. 697). For metallographic and spectrographic analysis, see Appendix 4 (517.Q).

Fragments of sheet, 35 cm^2 in all. 4 nails, c. 2 cm. 1 lump, 3 cm^2 (517.AX).

Summary. In the northeastern corner of the Temple II platform floor, between walls 8 and 9 on plan 3, an area was set off by a low framing (plan 3:16), named by the excavator in 1954 a "pit of offering" (Glob 1954a) From layers in and around this off-set area (fig. 695), a number of spectacular objects were found, vessels of alabaster/calcite, 2 lapis-lazuli beads, another object of lapis-lazuli, apart from the above-mentioned objects of copper: 1 bird, 1 male figurine, 1 spike, fragments of sheet, 3390 cm^2 in all, 212 nails, 3 rods, and 9 lumps.

The framed-off area may perhaps be interpreted as a receptory of temple equipment deposited there during the time of Temple IIa and/or IIb and perhaps disturbed during the demolition of the monument, either in connection with the building of Temple III or in Islamic times.

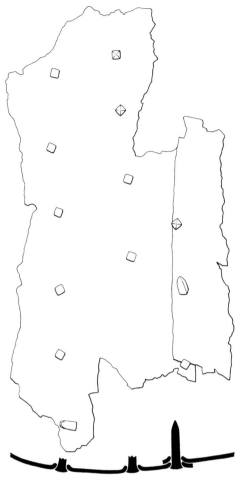

Fig. 687. 1:2.

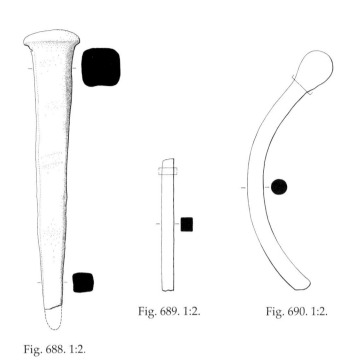

Fig. 688. 1:2.

Fig. 689. 1:2.

Fig. 690. 1:2.

Fig. 691. 1:2.

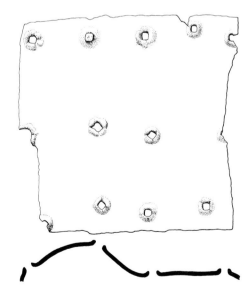

Fig. 693. 1:2.

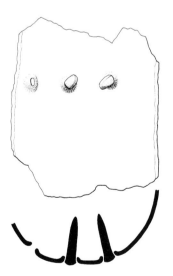

Fig. 692. 1:2.

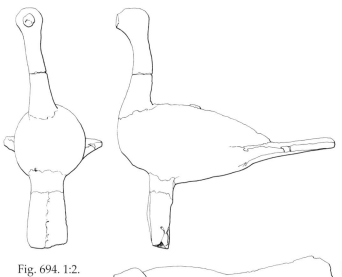

Fig. 694. 1:2.

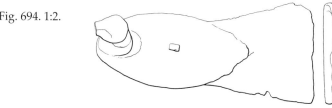

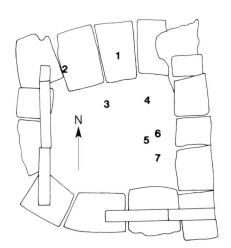

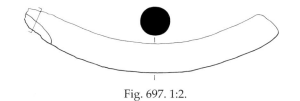

Fig. 697. 1:2.

Fig. 695. Sketch of framed-off area in the northeastern corner of the Temple II floor with finds plotted in: 1. Jar with lid of alabaster (fig. 762 and 765); 2. Copper bird (fig. 694); 3. Copper figurine (fig. 696); 4. Fragment of lapis-lazuli bead (fig. 815); 5. A linga-shaped amulet of lapis-lazuli (fig. 816); 6. Jar of calcite (fig. 764-765), sherd of jar of calcite (fig. 761), jar of alabaster/calcite with missing upper part (fig. 763 and 765) and five alabaster sherds (figs. 766-767); 7. Fragment of lapis-lazuli bead (fig. 815).

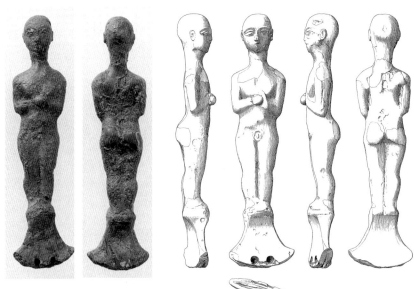

Fig. 696. 1:2.

The bull's head deposit

1955

Bull's head (517.FJ) (fig. 698). For two spectrographic analyses, see Appendix 3 and Prange 2001 Tab. 33 and 38. The bull's head has been compared to similar, Early Dynastic pieces from Ur, Khafajah, al-Ubaid and Tello (During Caspers 1971), but Mortensen has stressed the similarity in the curvature of the horns of the Barbar head to horns of bulls and bull men depicted on cylinder seals from the late Akkadian-Ur III periods (Mortensen 1986 p. 184).

Small, circular band (517.FN) (fig. 699). The diameter varies between 6.0 and 6.4 cm. The band is c. 3.2 cm wide and c. 23.5 cm long with an overlap of c. 3 cm, i.e. the circumference is c. 20.5 cm, c. 75 cm^2 in all. In the overlap zone there are two nails *in situ*, c. 1.5 cm, and one more nail opposite.

Small, circular band (517.FN). The diameter varies between 5.5 and 7 cm, and the circumference is c. 20.5 cm with no visible overlap. The band is 3.7-4.5 cm wide with 7 nails *in situ*, 6 of 2 cm and 1 of 3 cm, c. 84 cm^2 in all.

Large, circular band (517.FN) (fig. 700). The diameter varies between 15 and 17 cm. The band is 4.5 cm wide and c. 53.5 cm long, with an overlap of c. 9.5 cm, 240 cm^2 in all. It has 5 nails *in situ*, 3 of 2.5 cm and 2 of 3 cm. Besides, fragments of 3-4 large, circular bands, similar to the one described above. The bands are c. 4.5 cm wide and on one piece the diameter can be seen to vary between 15 and 20 cm; 800 cm^2 in all. 9 nails are *in situ*, 1 of 2 cm, 5 of 2.5 cm and 3 of 3 cm.

Fragments of sheet with punched holes, 8866 cm^2 in all (517.FN). The largest fragment measures 15.7 × 34 cm, and many other large fragments can be listed, measuring 6 × 18 cm, 9 × 14 cm, 11 × 12.5 cm, 11 × 13 cm, 11 × 16 cm, 12 × 12 cm, 12 × 13 cm, 12 × 16 cm, 13 × 14 cm, 13 × 17 cm, 13 × 21 cm, 14 × 14 cm, 14 × 17 cm, 14 × 18 cm and 14 × 22 cm. The shape of the fragments is normally flat, but other shapes occur, e.g. S-shape, L-shape, where the plates appear to have been ripped off. A few seem to have an original shape other than flat (fig. 701). Several plates are corroded together with others (fig. 702).

34 nails were found *in situ* in the sheet fragments, and those that were measurable comprised 1 of 1 cm, 11 of 1.5 cm, 5 of 2 cm, 6 of 2.5 cm and 1 of 3 cm. 60 loose nails were found with the sheet fragments, and of these 19 of 1.5 cm, 9 of 2 cm, 14 of 2.5 cm, 2 of

Fig. 698. 1:2.

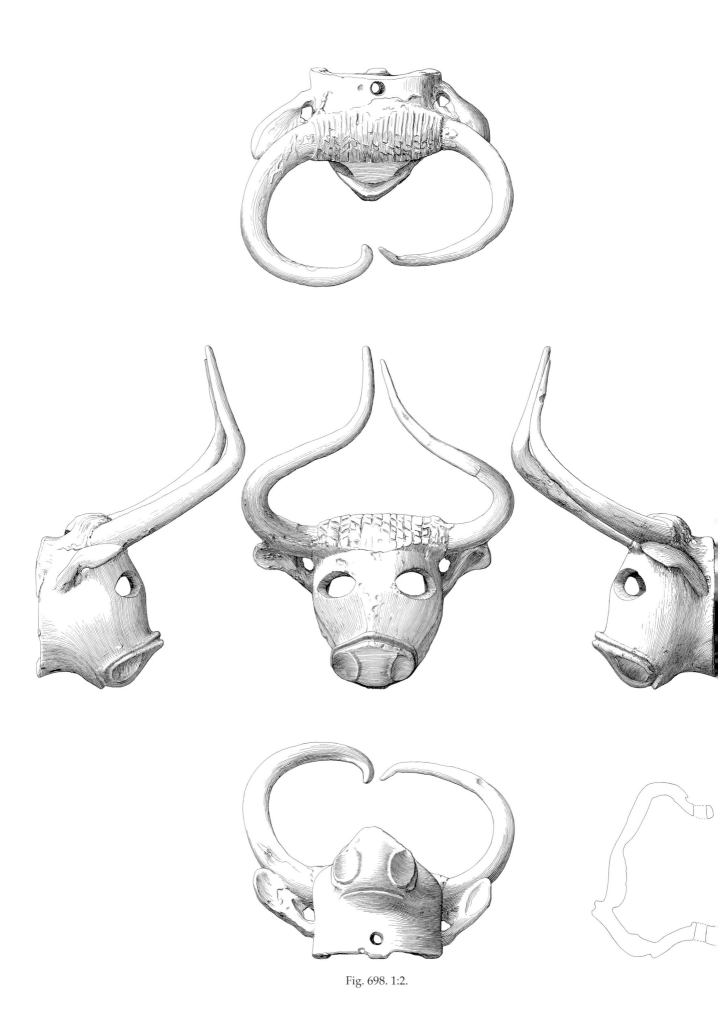

Fig. 698. 1:2.

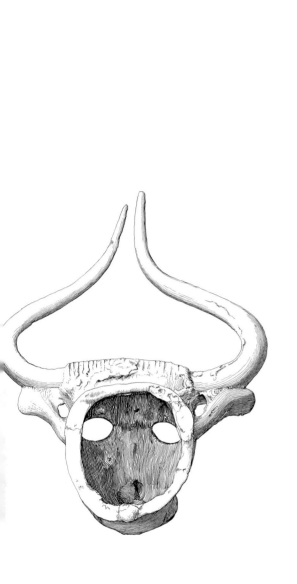

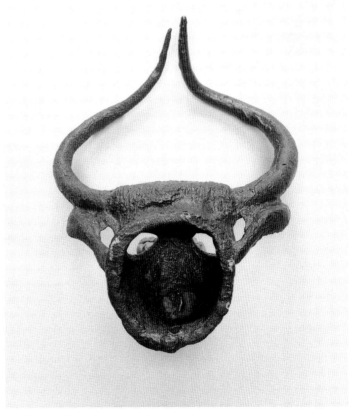

267

3 cm and 1 of 4 cm (figs. 703) (517.FN). For a metallographic and spectrographic analysis of one nail (fig. 704) with some sheet attached, see Appendix 4.

Chisel or fragment of sheet, rectangular cross-section (517.FN) (fig. 705). For a metallographic and spectrographic analysis, see Appendix 4.

Knife or fragment of sheet (517.FN) (fig. 706). For a metallographic and spectrographic analysis, see Appendix 4.

Summary. The bull's head was found with a substantial deposit of rectangular plates, two small and 4-5 large, circular bands below the Temple II floor of the central platform. It lay at approximately level 1.00, i.e. c. 0.5 m below the floor of Temple II and c. 0.5 m above the floor of Temple I, and in the corner between two Temple I walls in the northern part of the platform (fig. 707). The metal objects lay in sand within an area of c. 1.2 m². The excavator interpreted the deposit as buried from Temple II's floor, at a place where this had been broken up.

A sketch illustrates the position of the bull's head, the bands and the plates, some with the nails pointing up, some pointing down (fig. 707). The plates are generally c. 15 cm wide. The longest appear to have been c. 120 cm, whereas several are around 40-50 cm long. The measured area of the actual plates, retrieved from the deposit and described above, is 10065 cm², which is c. 3000 cm² more than can be seen on the sketch.

Glob suggested that the copper plates were originally attached to an object of wood on which the ox-head was mounted (1955 p. 191-192). Barnett proposed that such an object might be a lyre of the type found in the Royal Graves of Ur, which are decorated with a bull's head, and that the accompanying copper plates might have covered the sides of the sound box (1969 p. 101).

That related musical instruments were in fact known in Dilmun appears from contemporaneous stamp seals found on Failaka and referred to by Barnett (Kjærum 1983 nos. 267-268), and a few speculative deliberations may therefore be in order. The lyres depicted on these seals consist of two bulls, one large and one small, shaped not just with the bull's head, like the Sumerian type, but also with naturalistic neck, body and legs.

C. 10000 cm² of copper sheet have been preserved from the deposit, and this amount would have sufficed to cover the soundbox of such a lyre. If the length of one of the plates, 1.2 m, is indicative of the size of the largest bull's body, one would imagine that the extant bull's head would belong to the smallest bull, and that a larger bull's head is thus missing.

In this context it may be relevant to note that the 118 nails found in the bull's head deposit range from 1 to 4 cm in length and have a median value of 2 cm, which is significantly smaller than nails found elsewhere at Barbar, e.g. the area of the plinth-stones (see below), where the length ranges from 1.5 to 5 cm with a median value of 3 cm. It might be hypothetically suggested that the generally longer nails found in the plinth-stone area were suitable for attaching copper sheet to solid wooden statues (see below), whereas nails attaching metal sheet to a hollow sound box would have to be smaller.

The two small bands could have been mounts for the horizontal yoke of the lyre, but it is doubtful what function could be ascribed to the 4-5 large bands. In conclusion, the theory of a bull-headed lyre remains nothing more than an interesting and perhaps likely suggestion, for which there is only circumstantial evidence.

Besides, a possible knife and a possible chisel were found in the deposit.

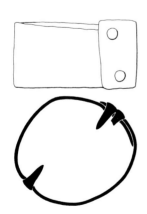

Fig. 699. 1:2.

Fig. 700. C. 1:2.

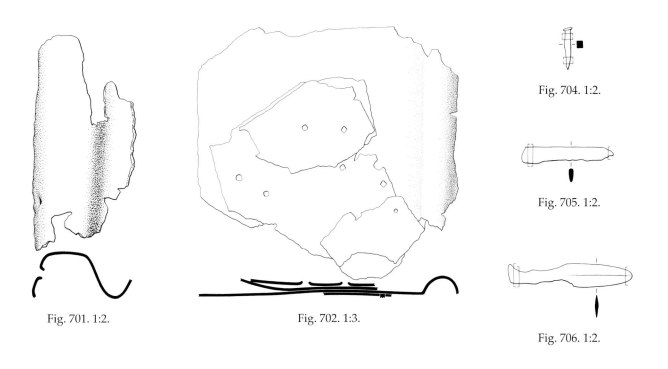

Fig. 701. 1:2.

Fig. 702. 1:3.

Fig. 704. 1:2.

Fig. 705. 1:2.

Fig. 706. 1:2.

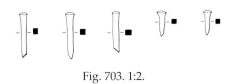

Fig. 703. 1:2.

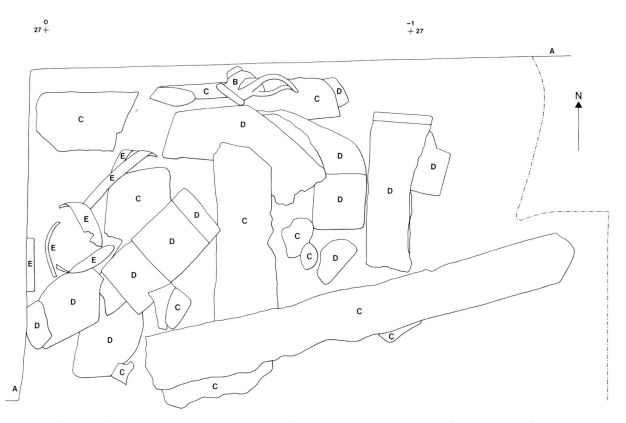

Fig. 707. The bull's head deposit. A: walls in Temple-I chamber (cf. plan 2:13); B: bull's head, C: metal sheeting in strips c. 15 cm broad, pierced with copper nails projecting upwards; D: same, with nails projecting downwards, E: metal band, 4-5 cm wide. 1:10.

269

Plinth-stones north of pool stair

1955

18 nails, 2.5-3.5 cm (517.CD). From holes in plinth-stone, plan 6:47.

Fragments of sheet, 80 cm² in all, and 15 nails, c. 2.5 cm (517.CF). By the plinth-stones.

Fragments of sheet, 12 cm² in all, and 3 nails, 2.6-3 cm (517.CG). From the cut holes in the plinth-stone, plan 6:48 (figs. 708-709).

Fragments of sheet, 60 cm² in all, and 14 nails, c. 2.5-3 cm (517.CH). From the eastern hole in plinth-stone, plan 6:48.

3 nails, 2.2, 3.5 and 3.5 cm, and two spikes (517.CI). From the plinth-stone, plan 6:48.

Fragments of sheet, 60 cm² in all, and 7 nails, c. 2.5 cm (517.CJ). From the southern hole in plinth-stone, plan 6:48.

Fragments of sheet, 30 cm² in all, and 3 nails, c. 2.5 cm (517.CK). From the northern hole in plinth-stone, plan 6:48.

Fragments of sheet, 180 cm² in all, 4 nails *in situ*, c. 2-2.5 cm, and 3 loose fragments of nails (517.EA). From the eastern hole in plinth-stone, plan 6:48. The metal sheet has been attached with nails to a cylindrical wooden object positioned in the cut hole in the plinth-stone. The metal was folded around the wood and has bent to form 2-3 cm wide facets (fig. 710).

Fragment of sheet, 9 × 25 cm, 225 cm² in all, with 9 nails *in situ* and 4 loose nails (517.EC). Consists of two slightly curved plates with an overlap with particularly many nails in the overlap zone (fig. 711). On the inner side remains of wood has been identified as a hardwood (Tengberg, see Appendix 2.

Area XII 1959

Fragments of sheet, 130 cm² in all, and 54 nails, ranging from 2.5-5.4 cm, with an average of 3.5 cm (517.AKR) (fig. 712). From clay around plinth-stone, plan 6:47-48.

Dagger blade, perhaps with midrib (517.ALJ). From clay level immediately below plinth-stones.

80-90 nails, 1.5-3 cm (517.AMA) (fig. 713). In clay level between plinth-stones.

Plinth-stones south of pool stair

1955

Fragments of sheet, 1270 cm² in all, with 30 nails *in situ* and 120 loose nails, 2-4 cm, most c. 3 cm (517.BV). Of these three fragments of sheet, 10 × 11 cm, 10 × 12 cm and 14 × 22 cm, are corroded together (fig. 714). On the inside, remains of wood, but no further identification possible (M. Tengberg pers. comm. 2002).

Fragments of sheet with punched holes (figs. 715-719). The largest pieces being 10 × 11 cm, 10 × 17 cm, 8 × 20 cm, 12 × 16 cm, 12 × 13 cm; 4200 cm² in all. Some plates were originally clearly overlapping (figs. 715-716); others were bent (fig. 718) or corroded together (fig. 719) after they had been removed from the wooden structure they originally covered. 58 nails *in situ* (2.2-3 cm), and 225 loose nails (2.5-3 cm, a few up to 3.5 cm) (517.FO). Found in a heap between plinth-stones, plan 6:53-54 (fig. 720:D).

Fragments of sheet, 170 cm² in all, with 7 nails *in situ* and 29 loose nails, 2.2-2.8 cm (517.FQ). Found in holes in plinth-stones, plan 6:53-54.

Fragments of sheet, 1100 cm² in all, with 63 nails *in situ* and 42 loose nails, 2-3 cm, most 2.5-3 cm. One piece of sheet, 8 × 12 cm, is curved and has particularly many (9) nails. Fragment of small dagger or arrowhead with broken tang (517.FR) (fig. 721).

Area I 1957

Fragments of sheet, c. 100 cm². For a spectrographic analysis, see Appendix 4. 28 nails (517.ZB). Especially between the plinth-stones, plan 6:53-54.

Fragments of sheet with punched holes, 120 cm² in all (517.ZC). Found between plinth-stones, plan 6:53-54, c. 15 cm below their surface.

Summary. A major concentration of metal sheet and nails was in the area of the plinth-stones flanking the staircase to the pool of Temple II. This is the only place at the temple where these metal finds can be shown to have been originally situated, since metal sheet and nails were found *in situ* in the holes of the plinth-stones, and it was clear that the sheet had been attached with the nails to wooden objects positioned in these holes. Remains of wood on the inside of metal sheet have in one case been identified as hardwood (cf. Tengberg in Appendix 2). The *in situ*-remains as well as the plates seen on fig. 720, must belong to Temple IIb, whereas it is uncertain if some of the metal found between the plinth-stones should be assigned to phase IIa.

North of the staircase, plinth-stone plan 6:48 has documented remains of sheet and nails in all three holes (figs. 708-709). In the northern hole one could observe an almost meeting tube of copper sheeting around the edge of the hole, a sleeve which stood to about 10 cm in height and had a diameter of about 20 cm. The copper was pierced through with copper nails in four rows, one above the other, with the points projecting inwards, c. 2 cm between each row. On the inner side of the sleeve there were remains of unburnt wood, and on both sides of the copper sheeting and in the bottom of the hole there was also bitumen. The sheeting stood at a slope as though it had been subjected to pressure. In the southern hole there were only a few remains of sheet, nails and bitumen, similar to those just described. In the eastern hole were a c. 13 cm high cylinder, c. 10 cm in diameter, with 4 rows of nails (517.EA) and traces of bitumen. The cylinder extended all the way to the bottom and was open-ended.

Besides, some nails were found in the holes of the plinth-stone plan 6:47 and further sheet and nails

come from the area around the plinth-stones north of the staircase.

All in all, north of the staircase around 777 cm² of metal sheet fragments were found, with 13 nails still in position and 124-134 loose nails. It can be noted that the nails found around the two northern plinth-stones in this area are larger than average.

South of the staircase, the northern hole in the plinth-stone 6:53 had remains of a sheet cylinder (fig. 720:A1) with nails, 18-20 cm in cross-section, with some bitumen (A3) and an unidentified material (A2).

Both holes in the plinth-stone plan 6:54 have remains of sheet cylinders (fig. 720:B1 and C1). They appear to have had similar cross-sections to the above mentioned, c. 18×20 cm, as well as traces of bitumen (3).

Between these two plinth-stones was a heap of metal sheet, where the outlines of at least 5 plates are sketched on the plan (cf. fig. 720:D). The plates are c. 13 cm wide and 35-43 cm long, and two of them are placed so that the nails point upwards, whereas the remaining three have their nails pointing downwards (cf. 517.FO and possibly BV). The

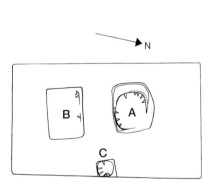

Fig. 708. Plinth-stone north of pool stairway, cf. plan 6 (48). A, northern hole; B, southern hole; C, eastern hole, all with remains of copper. 1:20.

Fig. 709. Plinth-stone north of pool stairway, cf. plan 6 (48).

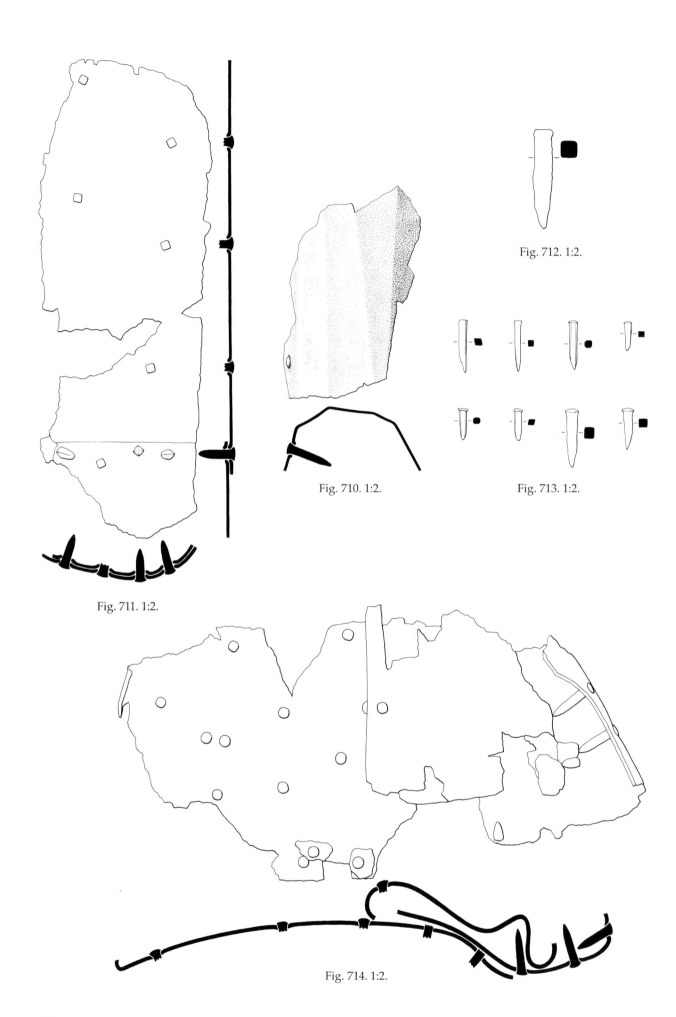

Fig. 712. 1:2.

Fig. 710. 1:2.

Fig. 713. 1:2.

Fig. 711. 1:2.

Fig. 714. 1:2.

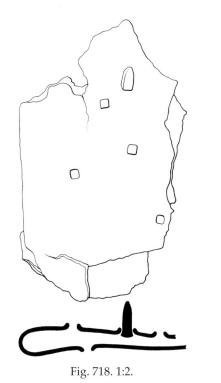

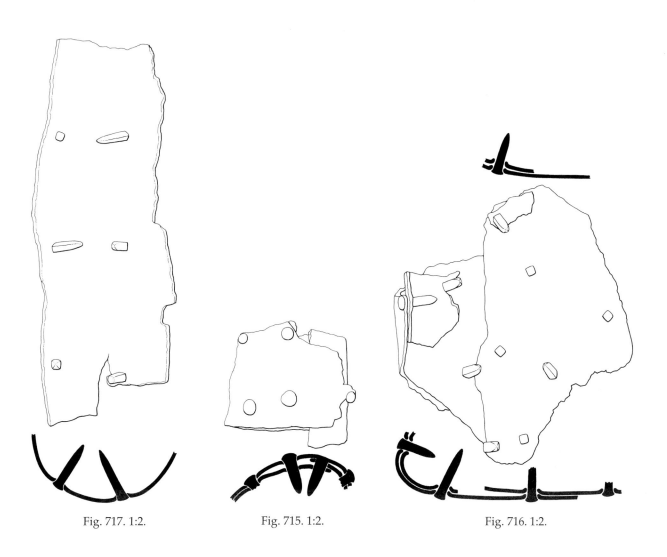

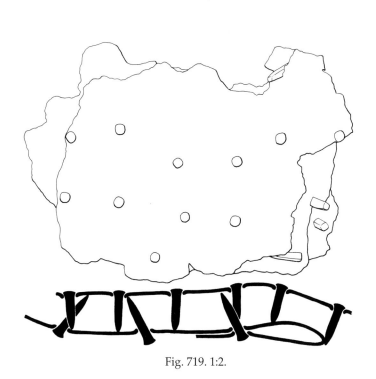

Fig. 717. 1:2.

Fig. 715. 1:2.

Fig. 716. 1:2.

Fig. 718. 1:2.

Fig. 719. 1:2.

273

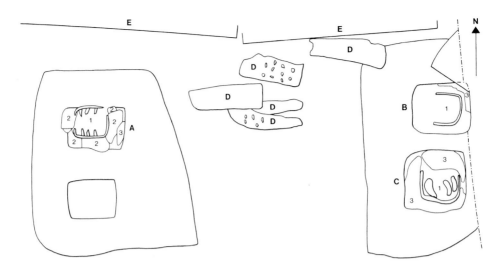

Fig. 720. Plinth-stones south of pool stairway, cf. plan 6 (53-54). A, hole with remains of copper (1), unknown material (2) and bitumen (3); B, hole with remains of copper (1) and bitumen (3); C, as B; D, sheets of copper, some with nails pointing upwards; E, stair strings. 1:20.

size of each of these plates would have been c. 500 cm², i.e. a total area of c. 2500 cm².

All in all, south of the staircase around 6960 cm² of metal sheet fragments were found and have been registered above, with 158 nails still in position and 444 loose nails.

From the position of the nails it can be concluded that the metal sheet was nailed onto the wooden objects before they were fixed with bitumen in the holes.

Nothing can be said with certainty about the copper-sheathed wooden objects positioned in these plinth-stones. "One can imagine bull-figures with their forelegs in the holes on one block and their hind legs in the rear block; or human forms standing with their legs in the holes, each on his own block." (Glob 1968 p. 60). "In the case of the block with the third hole it would be feasible to suppose that the figure held a staff or the like" (Glob 1955 p. 191). "On the side of one of these blocks two human figures were carved out ... There are two male figures, one with its arms arching downwards, the other with a hand lifted high, its fingers distended, and a bundle of rays in the other; these may be depictions of the wooden statues which, studded with copper nails, stood upon the stone blocks." (Glob 1968 p. 60) (cf. above, fig. 215).

Mortensen suggested instead that the staircase had been flanked by "a double row of wooden pillars" ... "coated with thin copper sheets." (1971a p. 394). A similar interpretation was put forward by During Caspers (1971 p. 220), who added that the pillars may have been crowned by cult emblems or shaped in such a way as to serve as a cult object.

Such objects may actually be represented on stamp seals (cf. Kjærum 1983 nos. 108-138).

In view of the shallow depth of the holes in the foundation blocks, c. 15-20 cm, it is evident that for reasons of stability such pillars could not possibly have been very tall, perhaps not more than around 1 metre.

The fact that the 8 plinth-stones occur in pair each having 4 holes with a certain internal distance, perhaps points in favour of a row of four-legged animals parallel to the staircase. The combination of four structural elements would add appreciably to the stability of the construction, their shallow depths of the holes taken into consideration. The extra, fifth hole in one of the rear stones (plan 6:48) could then be intended as a support for a particularly long tail.

It should be noted that one of the two similar, but much larger plinth-stones related to Temple III (plan 8:3-4) also has a third hole in the same position, and that this stone, placed up against the platform of Temple III, can be interpreted as a rear stone and a full parallel to the Temple II plinth-stone here described, plan 6:48.

A few other finds from the area of the plinth-stones may support the interpretation of animal or human sculptures: two pieces of very likely eye inlays of lapis lazuli (fig. 819), and some fragments of gold foil and two gold nails (figs. 810-813), that could have been used as decorative features on the faces of the sculpture. The use of the same technique for attaching sheet of both copper and gold with nails should be noted.

274

Eastern Court

1956

Fragments of sheet, some of which have punched holes, c. 440 cm² in all. 6 nails: 2 of 2.5 cm, 3 of 3 cm, 1 of 4 cm (517.GF, HU, JP, JQ, TC, TO, TR, TY, UA, UH, VH, XZ, YN).

Dagger with ellipsoid cross-section of the blade and a tang with rectangular cross-section (517.UB) (fig. 722).

Dagger with flat blade and tang with rectangular cross-section (517.YK) (fig. 723).

Area IV 1960

Flat knife blade with incised sign (517.AOY) (fig. 724).

Area VI 1961

Dagger with rhomboid cross-section (517.ARV) (fig. 725). For a metallographic and spectrographic analysis, see Appendix 4.

Bead (517.ARZ) (fig. 726). For a metallographic and spectrographic analysis, see Appendix 4.

Summary. From the Eastern Court and the area to the south of it come some fragments of sheet, 440 cm² in all, 6 nails, 3 daggers, 1 knife and 1 bead. The objects derive either from the two main layers of the court, datable to Temple IIb, or from contemporaneous layers south of the court. The large number of cutting instruments compared to other metal objects is remarkable for this area.

Refuse layers

Area VIII 1957

Fragments of sheet, 136 cm² in all, and 1 nail, 4 cm. Found in the lower layer, level c. 5.00, a Temple IIb context (517.ABA, ABC).

Area III 1958

Fragments of sheet, 300 cm² in all (517.AJC). South of the oval terrace wall of Temple IIb, in Temple IIb level.

Summary. In refuse layers south of the Temple IIb oval terrasse wall, scattered fragments of sheet, 436 cm² in all, and 1 nail were found.

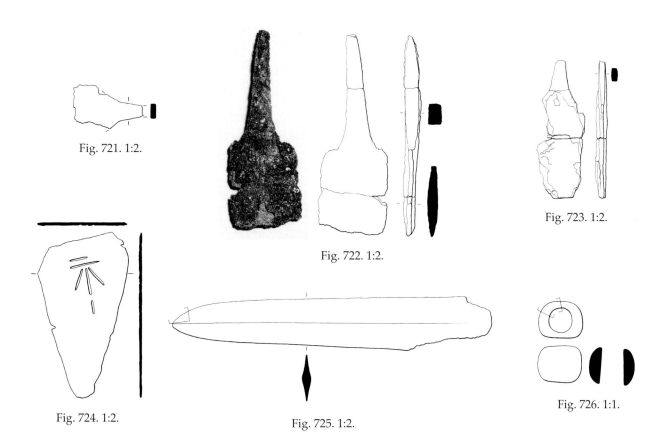

Fig. 721. 1:2.

Fig. 722. 1:2.

Fig. 723. 1:2.

Fig. 724. 1:2.

Fig. 725. 1:2.

Fig. 726. 1:1.

Nails in ashlar wall

Remains of 6 copper nails were observed (in 2000) on the outer face of 3 ashlars in the upper two courses of the southern oval terrasse wall belonging to Temple IIb (figs. 132 and 727). The nails were firmly embedded in the stone and must have fastened something, perhaps metal plates, to the outer façade of the oval wall. A search for more copper nails in the extant wall facings of the temple was fruitless.

Uncertain contexts

1954

Fragments of sheet, 50 cm² in all. Nail, 4.1 cm (fig. 728), for a metallographic and spectrographic analysis, see Appendix 4 (517.AP).

Fragments of sheet, 70 cm² in all. 4 nails, 2.5-3 cm (517.AQ).

Fragments of sheet, 160 cm² in all. 1 piece with many small holes, 13 × 17 cm. 4 nails, c. 2 cm. For a spectrographic analysis, see Appendix 4 (517.AY).

1955

Fragments of sheet with punched holes, 235 cm² in all, of which 1 band, 4.5 × 6 cm (517.AZ).

Fragments of sheet, 16 cm² in all. 11 nails, 3-4 cm (517.BD).

Fragments of sheet, 200 cm² in all (517.BE).

Curved rod with a circular cross-section (517.BF) (fig. 729). For a metallographic and spectrographic analysis, see Appendix 4.

Rod, 9.8 cm long, rounded point and flat top, square cross-section, 0.6 cm thick (517.BG).

Fragments of sheet, 180 cm² in all. 10 nails, 2-3 cm (517.BS).

Fragments of sheet, 30 cm² in all (517.BT).

Fragments of sheet with 5 nails *in situ*, 90 cm² in all, of which 1 piece shaped like fig. 732. 8 nails: 7 of 2-3 cm, 1 of 5 cm. Rod, 5.4 cm long, square in cross-section, 0.6 cm thick. (517.BU).

Fragments of sheet with punched holes, 100 cm² in all (517.CA).

Fragments of sheet, 70 cm² in all (517.CE). 4 nails, 2-3 cm.

Fragments of sheet with punched holes, 460 cm² in all, and 18 nails *in situ*. Of these one piece, 8 × 10 cm, with 2 nails *in situ* and 9 other holes or broken nails in two rows. Another piece, 6 × 23 cm, consists of two overlapping plates with 3 nails *in situ* and traces of 6 nails in the overlap zone. 20 loose nails, c. 2.5 cm (517.CL).

Fragments of sheet with punched holes, 30 cm² in all, and 3 nails *in situ* and 19 loose nails, 2-3.5 cm (517.CY).

8 nails, 2-4.5 cm (517.CZ).

Fragment of sheet with punched holes, 10.5 × 18 cm, 170 cm² in all (517.DS).

Fragments of sheet with punched holes, 100 cm² in all. For a spectrographic analysis, see Appendix 4. 8 nails, 3-4 cm (517.DT).

Fragments of sheet with punched holes, 1 piece ridged (fig. 730), 450 cm² in all. 2 nails, 3 and 4.5 cm (517.DU).

Rod, 9.2 cm long, round cross-section, one end is flat, the other broken (fig. 731). For a metallographic and spectrographic analysis, see Appendix 4. Fragments of sheet, 60 cm² in all. Nail 3.5 cm (517.DX).

Fragments of sheet, 95 cm² in all (517.DZ).

Fragments of sheet with punched holes, 1160 cm² in all. 15 nails *in situ*, 2-2.5 cm, and 28 loose nails, 2-3.5 cm. Two overlapping pieces of sheet are possibly hammered to shape (fig. 732) (517.EE).

Fragments of sheet with punched holes, 300 cm² in all, of which 1 piece 12 × 13 cm (517.EG-FM?).

Fragments of sheet, 120 cm² in all. 6 nails, 2-5 cm (517.EK).

Fragments of sheet, 220 cm² in all. 2 nails, 2.5 cm, and 2 lumps. One piece of sheet seems to have been shaped (fig. 733) (517.EL).

Fragments of sheet, 30 cm² in all (517.EN). Nail, 4 cm.

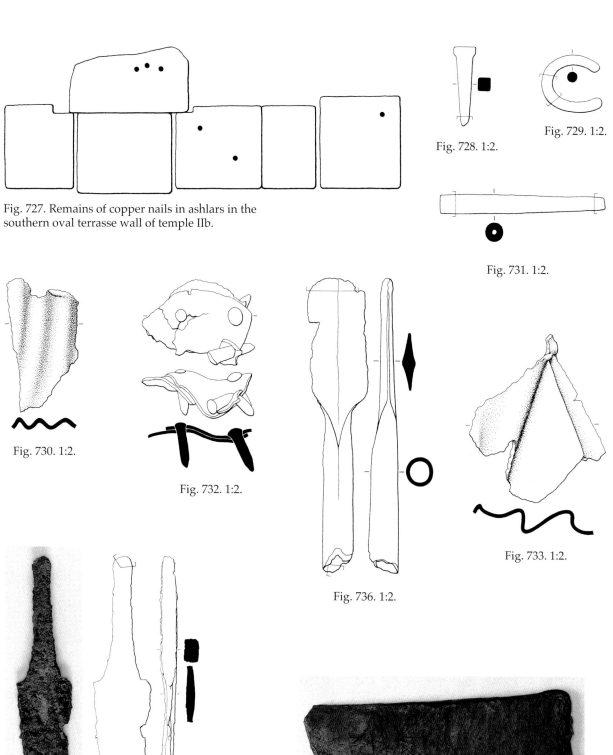

Fig. 727. Remains of copper nails in ashlars in the southern oval terrasse wall of temple IIb.

Fig. 728. 1:2.

Fig. 729. 1:2.

Fig. 731. 1:2.

Fig. 730. 1:2.

Fig. 732. 1:2.

Fig. 733. 1:2.

Fig. 736. 1:2.

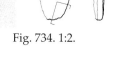

Fig. 734. 1:2.

Fig. 735. 1:2.

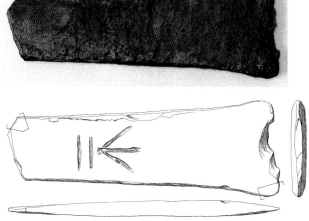

Fig. 737. 1:2.

Nail, 7 cm (517.EU).

Fragments of sheet punched with holes, 100 cm² in all (517.EY). 21 nails, 2.5-4 cm.

5 nails, 2-3 cm (517.EZ).

Dagger with ellipsoid cross-section of blade and rectangular tang cross section (517.FB) (fig. 734). For a metallographic and spectrographic analysis, see Appendix 4.

3 fragments of a rod with square cross-section (517.FD) (fig. 735). For a metallographic and spectrographic analysis, see Appendix 4.

Socketed spearhead with rhomboid section of blade and a facet at the transition from socket to blade, well-made specimen (517.FE) (fig. 736). For a metallographic and spectrographic analysis, see Appendix 3 and 4.

Flat axe with damaged edge and incised sign (517.YM) (fig. 737). Found in "stone-quarrying layer" by the east side of the temple. For a metallographic and spectrographic analysis, see Appendix 3 and 4. For a similar axe with a similar incised sign from Diraz, see Lombard & Kervran 1989 no. 39. Cf. also the sign on the clay tokens below, figs. 785-786 and 788-789, and incised signs on pottery from Failaka (Højlund 1987 fig. 712:k and l).

Area IX 1957

Fragments of sheet, 100 cm². 1 nail, 2.5 cm (517.ADS).

Area III 1958

3 fragments of bun-shaped ingots and 6 lumps (517.AHV) (figs. 738-739). For a metallographic and spectrographic analysis of fig. 739, see Appendix 4. Found north of the north wall of Temple I, in unspecified level, dating to Temple I or Temple IIa.

Rod, 9.4 cm long, 0.3 cm thick, one end rounded, the other broken, circular in cross-section (517.AIB) (fig. 740). For a metallographic and spectrographic analysis, see Appendix 4. According to the spectrographic analysis, this is probably an Islamic piece.

1960

Point of dagger or spear. For a spectrographic analysis, see Appendix 4. Surface find from south of temple (517. APG).

Year unknown

Curved handle with hexagonal cross-section and expanded ends (517.Sample 27) (fig. 741). For a metallographic and spectrographic analysis, see Appendix 4.

Fragment of sheet with two nails *in situ* and two more punched holes, 11 × 13 cm, 143 cm² in all (517.Sample 28). For a metallographic and spectrographic analysis, see Appendix 4.

Knife blade? (517.Sample 29) (fig. 742). For a metallographic and spectrographic analysis, see Appendix 4.

Nail, 2.5 cm (fig. 743). For a metallographic and spectrographic analysis, see Appendix 4 (517.AEB).

Fragments of sheet, c. 950 cm² in all, and c. 165 nails. A number of lots coming from the surface, from accidentally mixed lots, etc.

Summary. From uncertain contexts come 1 dagger, 1 knife blade?, 1 socketed spearhead, 1 point from dagger or spear, 1 flat axe, 1 handle, 3 fragments of bun-shaped ingots, 6 rods, 8 lumps, besides numerous fragments of sheet, c. 5689 cm² in all and 372 nails; the nails vary between 2 and 5 cm, most c. 3 cm.

The North-East Temple

Fragments of sheet, c. 8 cm² (681.G, H).

8 nails, 2.5-3.5 cm (681.H, BF, CZ, ER, EU). For spectrographic analysis of a nail (EU), see Appendix 4.

Curved rod (681.F).

Ring, 1.8 cm in diameter, semicircular in cross-section (681.DA) (fig. 744). Spectrographic analysis, see Appendix 4, indicates an Islamic date.

Fragment of ingot, 2 × 2.5 × 3 cm (681.G).

8 lumps, 2-4 cm in cross-section (681.AB, AG, AI, AM, DT, EG, EU, EY).

Summary. Only a few metal objects – 1 curved rod, 1 ring, 1 fragment of ingot, and 8 lumps, – were found at the North-East Temple, but they are in harmony with the metal finds from the Barbar Temple.

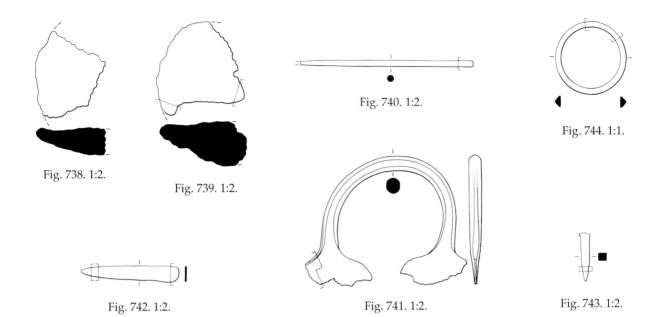

Fig. 738. 1:2.

Fig. 739. 1:2.

Fig. 740. 1:2.

Fig. 744. 1:1.

Fig. 742. 1:2.

Fig. 741. 1:2.

Fig. 743. 1:2.

Copper-working

There is evidence that copper-working took place at the site of the Barbar Temple in the shape of c. 50 fragments of crucibles and moulds. Half of the objects cannot be referred to any specific temple phase, but around 24 pieces can be dated to Temple IIb. They obviously continue a tradition for copper-working that is well-known from Qala'at al-Bahrain periods Ib-IIa (*Qala'at 1* p. 370-381).

The crucible and mould fragments were found spread over the entire site, with no clusterings in specific areas, and no other indications as to where the workshop was actually situated; no area had, for example, the amount of residue from the processing of copper that was found in the copper workshop in Excavation 520 at Qala'at al-Bahrain (*Qala'at 1* p. 378, 467-68).

Fragments of 4 rims and 28 side-sherds of *crucibles* derive from the site. The crucibles are very similar to the ones found in Excavation 520 at Qala'at al-Bahrain (*Qala'at 1* p. 370, figs. 1818-1831). Their diameters on 3 fragments are 13 cm (517.AHD, fig. 745), 14 cm (517.ASE, fig. 746) and 24 cm (517.ALV, fig. 747). These three fragments all have unspecific datings. The rims and side-sherds are made of baked clay, the ware tempered with some sand and a lot of straw. The outside colour is whitish-buff, but the section reddish and sometimes grey-black. The inner side is strongly marked by the high temperature in the crucible: Near the rim, the surface is normally only slightly vitrified, if at all, but moving away from the rim down into the crucible the layer of vitrification grows thicker and becomes dark grey or dark green, often stained green by oxidized copper particles or with a layer of green copper attached. The layer of vitrification was formed by the melting of the surface layer of the crucible at the high temperatures present within it with some reaction with the metal oxides and fuel ash within the crucible. The layer of vitrification may be quite thick and can be labelled as a crucible slag (Northover in *Qala'at 1* p. 374). The vitrification layer is rendered in black on the drawings. A crucible side-sherd from Temple IIb is illustrated in fig. 748 (517.ABK) and three more, without any specific dating, in figs. 749-751 (517.DB, EB, AKU).

Several pieces of crucible slag (517.AR, BR, ZA, AHR, AID, AIL) were analysed metallographically, see Appendix 4.

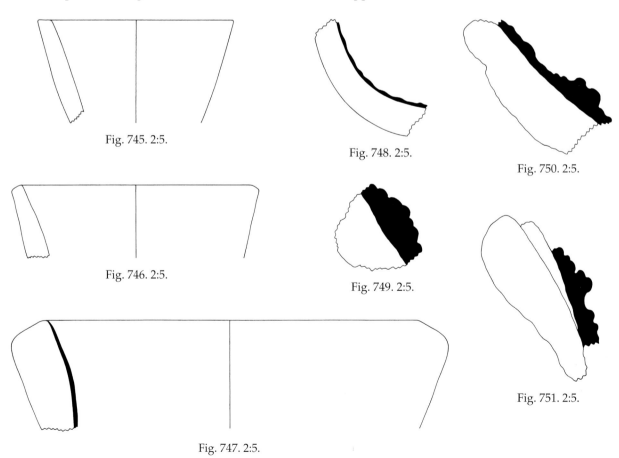

Fig. 745. 2:5.

Fig. 748. 2:5.

Fig. 750. 2:5.

Fig. 746. 2:5.

Fig. 749. 2:5.

Fig. 751. 2:5.

Fig. 747. 2:5.

8 fragments of *mould* rims and 10 side-sherds of moulds and 1 possible fragment of a mould cover were found on the site. The ware seems to be the same as that of the crucibles. The colour of the surface is whitish-buff, sometimes turned grey in the bottom of the moulds (indicated on the drawings by a brace). In the section the moulds are grey-black, probably because the organic temper has not been burnt out. On one mould fragment there are a few drops of copper, and some have perhaps a slight sintering of the surface.

All moulds are apparently four-sided and open, and most are very large, i.e. much larger than those found in Excavation 520 at Qala'at al-Bahrain dating in period Ib (*Qala'at 1* p. 375, figs. 1837-1842), but similar in size to the later ones found in Excavation 519 there (*Qala'at 2* p. 35, figs. 87-88). Two mould-rim fragments from Barbar are found in Temple IIb contexts, fig. 752 (517.ABB), the rest are without specific dating, figs. 753-754 (517.ARC), fig. 755 (517.ACA), and fig. 756 (517.ASD). One specimen, fig. 757, is divided into at least two compart-

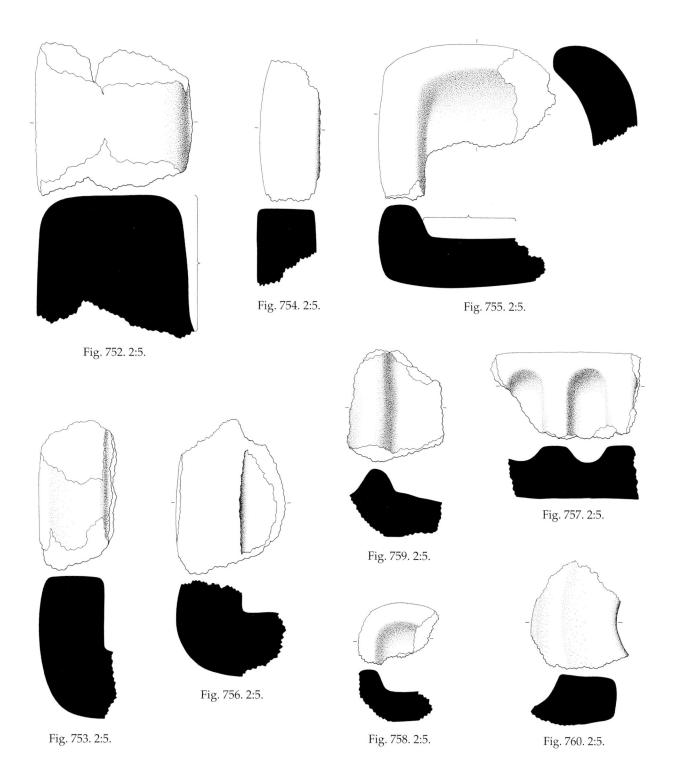

Fig. 754. 2:5.

Fig. 755. 2:5.

Fig. 752. 2:5.

Fig. 756. 2:5.

Fig. 753. 2:5.

Fig. 759. 2:5.

Fig. 757. 2:5.

Fig. 758. 2:5.

Fig. 760. 2:5.

281

ments (517.AOF); another one, fig. 758, has probably had the same shape (517.ZQ), and a third, fig. 759, has an inner partition wall (517.AOQ).

A possible fragment of a *mould cover*, fig. 760 (517.AEH), with an opening of 6 cm and the same ware and colour as the moulds, belongs to Temple IIb (cf. *Qala'at 1* p. 377, figs. 1848-1853).

Spectrographic analysis shows that the metal used at Barbar was copper containing a number of other elements present as impurities, notably arsenic and nickel. There are only two objects, the human figure (517.P, fig. 696) and an axe (517.YM, fig. 737), with more than 10% tin, that deserve the label bronze, and a small number of copper objects with medium-low tin, see Appendices 3-4 (Heskel 1984 p. 89-96. Prange 2001). A few objects made of copper and zinc have been referred to the Islamic period.

A number of other contemporaneous coppers from Bahrain have been analysed spectrographically (Prange 2001 p. 96, Tab. 33 and 38), and they follow the same pattern as do contemporary copper objects and ores from Oman (Prange 2001 p. 73, Tab. 32, 34, 36 and 39), from where metal was probably imported to Bahrain as bun-shaped ingots.

There does not seem to be any high correlation between the type of object and the kind of metal used to produce it (Heskel 1984 p. 94).

Most objects were formed by hammering and annealing a cast bar into final shape, and only a few objects appear to remain in their as cast state (Heskel 1984 p. 89). Only remains of open and quite large moulds have been found at Barbar, possibly designed for casting the metal plates used to make the sheet metal found in such large amounts on the site.

An experiment by Heskel trying to hammer a copper nail through a copper sheet demonstrated that the use of a pre-punched hole is sometimes necessary. The modern sheet used in the experiment had an average hardness of 104.5 VHN, and the nail used had an average hardness of 118.5 VHN (Heskel 1984 p. 3 and 45). Note, though, that the Barbar sheet and nails examined by Heskel have average hardnesses of 110 and 145 VHN (see Appendix 4).

The holes in the sheets are generally square (cf. fig. 666) and could well have been punched with tools similar to the spikes found on the site. The punching of the holes produced a raised edge around the hole (cf. fig. 666), and this edge is always on the inside face in relation to the position of the nails.

On smaller pieces of sheet the position of the nails may seem random, but on larger pieces a placement in rows may often be seen (cf. figs. 687 and 693). There is a tendency for more nails in zones of overlap. The most apparent fact is the large amount of nails, which cannot be warranted by any practical considerations, but must be subsumed under the notion of conspicuous consumption.

13. Alabaster and Calcite Vessels

by Michèle Casanova

Nine fragments of alabaster/calcite[1] vessels and three complete vessels were discovered in the area of the temple at Barbar. 5 sherds and 2 vessels are of alabaster (gypsum) and 4 fragments and 1 vase of calcite. The remains recovered can be associated with a total of ten individual vessels: four cylindrical vessels belonging to the Série IV (3 of calcite, 1 probably alabaster), 1 truncated cone bowl belonging to Série XV (of alabaster), 1 jar related to Type B (of calcite) and 2 cylindrical pyxes (in alabaster), as well as two pieces which can no longer be identified with certainty, due to their abraded state. The most remarkable are the 3 complete vessels discovered in the "Pit of offering" of Barbar Temple II, c. 2000 B.C. (fig. 266). The parallels refer to the typology of Early and Middle Bronze Age alabaster vessels from Mesopotamia, Iran and Central Asia established in Casanova 1991.

1954, "Pit of offering", Temple II

Sherd of jar of calcite (517.B) (figs. 761 and 695:6). The rest of the jar (517.AIR) was found 8-9 m towards the south-west, see below.

This vessel recalls those of the Série IV, specifically Variante IVa, which is the form with the greatest distribution. The form IVa is that of a vessel with a wide base and a concave body.

The Série IVa was in use in Western Asia from 2600 to 1800 B.C. (Casanova 1991: Série IVa p. 33 note 37, fig. 3 & pl. 3 no. 41). It is known from sites in Mesopotamia: Ur (Woolley 1934: pl. 177a, U 8949, PG/497, type 3, pl. 178c, U 7645 PG/1, type 4, pl. 241, types 3-4), Kish, and Tello; as well as Iran (Susa, Shahdad, Tepe Sialk), Afghanistan (Mundigak IV, 3 and southern Bactria), and Pakistan (Kulli). The form was also replicated in pottery as well as copper, and even bitumen at Susa.

The shape is known from sites in Egypt dating to either the end of the fourth (Naqada II) or the beginning of the third millennium (the Archaic Period): El Amrah, Kôm al-Ahmar, Abu Roash, Minshat Abu Omar (Aston 1994: no. 28 fig. 9 p. 80, p. 99, p. 101, Naqada I-Dyn. 1; Kroeper & Wildung 1994: p. 160-161, Tafel 43-44, Dyn. "0"). The Egyptian vessels were often decorated with an incised or excised cord pattern below the rim, familiar on contemporary Egyptian pottery (Aston 1994: p. 99; Casanova 1991: Série IVa p. 33 note 37; Cleyet-Merle & Vallet 1982: p. 120, no. 77 705 ff, p. 156, no. 58 197, p. 131, no. 56 493-56 495; Desroches-Noblecourt & Vercoutter 1981: p. 28-29, no. 27; El-Khouli 1978: pl. 9 no. 190-2, pl. 11 no. 253-74, pl. 13 no. 298-9, pl. 28 no. 630, pl. 29 no. 636-37, pl. 149 no. 253; Kroeper & Wildung 1994: no. 160/5 p. 160, 160/11 p. 161, Tafel 43-44, Dyn. "0"; Kroeper & Wildung 2000: Tafel 27-28, 31, 44, 49-50, 53).

Analogous vases, but generally squat and low, classified as Type IVa1, were found in Mesopotamia at Ur (Woolley 1934: pl. 241, type 1), Iran (at Tepe Hissar IIIC, Shahr-i Sokhta II-III) and in Afghanistan (Mundigak IV, 1-3 and southern Bactria). They all date to 2600 – 1800 B.C. (Casanova 1991: Type IVa1 p. 38 note 55).

Jar with lid of alabaster (517.BX) (figs. 762, 765 and 695:1. For a colour photo, see Lombard 1999 no. 115).

Beige gypsum with altered surface (due to variations in temperature and humidity).

Several scholars (Glob, Mortensen and Potts; cf. Potts 1983 notes 42-45, 51 p. 129-130) have proposed a comparison of this vessel with the circular pyxis Type 100 from Ur, described by Woolley (1934: p. 381, pl. 250): "with a lid (…) secured by strings passed through holes in the sides and tied over the top". There is, however, a contrast – rather than a similarity – in the form of the lids and their relation to the vessels. The piece from Ur is designed with a unique form whereby the lower outer edge of the

---

[1] Some of the vessels described below were subjected to X-ray diffraction analysis, by Henrik Friis of the Institute of Geology at the University of Aarhus. They have been identified as either alabaster (gypsum) or calcite. The analyses of gypsum contain only reflections of gypsum, revealing a very complete range with a high degree of uniformity, and no extraneous minerals. The two analyses of calcite show a very pure calcite. Only in 517.APU there is a small foreign reflection, probably quartz, probably representing some sand embedded in the calcite. Those vessels which were not analysed are identified as "alabaster/calcite".

lid fits into a groove cut into the outer edge of the rim of the vessel. The vessel from Barbar on the other hand has a lid (well known from Iron Age alabaster vessels) whereby the interior (lower) surface of the lid has a smaller diameter than the lid itself and is thus intended to fit snugly into the vessel. The decisive modification is thus in the lid and not the vessel – in contrast to the piece from Ur. Woolley remarked that this was the only piece of its kind found at Ur (and it may well be unique in antiquity). The vessel from Barbar, however, may be one of the first of its kind, and thus at the origin of a tradition.

There is a slightly different, but earlier, parallel for this piece, of Type H (Casanova 1991: Type H p. 44-45, note 81 p. 44), from Mundigak, identified by Casal as the fragment of a covered pyxis (MG. D., 97, period IV, 2). The jar from Barbar is completely cylindrical with a circular lid whereas the one from Mundigak is only cylindrical inside, the exterior surface having been cut to form an irregular pentagon (Casal 1961: p. 234, fig. 134 no. 15). Most of the archaeological material from Mundigak belongs to Period IV, dated to the first half of the third millennium during which period the site reached its maximum size.

Both the pieces from Ur and from Mundigak are decidedly earlier than the context of the Barbar temple, and different.

Jar with missing upper part of alabaster/calcite (517.BY) (figs. 763, 765 and 695:6).

This object is probably the same form as vessel 517.YL, assigned to Série IVc. The material is most probably alabaster (Casanova 1991: Série IVc p. 34 note 39, fig. 4 & pl. 4 no. 49).

Jar of calcite (517.YL) (figs. 764-765 and 695:6. For a colour photo, see Lombard 1999 no. 116).

This vessel should be assigned to the Série IVc, a vessel with a wide base and large hyperbolique body, i.e. cylindrical with concave sides. Série IVc is known from Western Asian contexts between 2600 and 1800 B.C. (Casanova 1991: Série IVc p. 34 note 39, fig. 4 & pl. 4 no. 49).

The form is known from Mesopotamia at Ur (Woolley 1934: pl. 241, types 5, 6, 7), Iran at Susa, Shahdad and Shahr-i Sokhta II-III (Ciarla 1981: fig. 1b, cylinder-cone) as well as Afghanistan and Pakistan (Khurab). The form is widely distributed in southern Bactria.

There are analogous forms from Egypt, dating from the end of the fourth millennium through the entire third millennium (Aston 1994: nos. 32-33, fig. 9 p. 80, p. 99, p. 103, Dyn. 1-4; Casanova 1991: Série IVc p. 34 note 39; El-Khouli 1978: pl. 12 no. 286, pl. 13 no. 297, pl. 23D no. 435, pl. 30 no. 691-93; Kroeper & Wildung 2000: Tafel 29, 54): Beit Allam, Kôm al-

Ahmar, Minshat Abu Omar as well as pieces made from other materials, green schist from Abu Roash (Desroches-Noblecourt & Vercoutter 1981: p. 35, no. 40 & 41, Archaic, Dyn. I).

Parallels in pottery (Egypt, Seistan, Shahr-i Sokhta) and copper (Susa) have the same form as the stone vessels of Série IVc. The Egyptian pottery vessels are, however, decorated with a wavy ledge handle or the fine rope groove below the rim: Abu Zeidan, Kawamil, Kôm al-Ahmar, Mazaideh, Tukh (Aston 1994: p. 99; Casanova 1991: Série IVc p. 34 note 40).

The exterior surface of a stone vessel of this series found at Byblos was decorated with scenes depicting offerings related to eternity (Jidejian 1971: fig. 16).

There is a vessel form close to the Série IVc with different proportions (the diameter being proportionally greater in comparison to the height), Type IVc1 (Casanova 1991: Type IVc1 p. 39-40 notes 57-61). This form is known from Shahr-i Sokhta II-III (Tosi 1969: fig. 40i, XXV, 9; Ciarla 1981: fig. 1b, cylinder-cone) in Iran, Turkmenistan (Ulug Depe and Altyn Depe), and Afghanistan (southern Bactria). These contexts suggest dates ca. 2300-1800 B.C.

Two rim-sherds, one base-sherd and two side sherds, all of alabaster (517.H) (figs. 766-767 and 695:6).

White and beige gypsum, surface degraded. These fragments appear to belong to a rimless cylindrical vessel. It is probably a variant of the same form as 517.BX, a circular pyxis.

1954, unknown location

Base sherd of alabaster (517.AV) (fig. 768). Found together with Temple IIb pottery.

White and beige gypsum. Severely abraded in a regular fashion. The interior is smooth.

Area VI, 1957

Side sherd of calcite (517.ACA) (fig. 769). Found with a few potsherds probably dating to Temple I or IIa. Translucent white with a patch of orange and ground exterior surface. There are traces of the manufacturing process, visible on the interior in the form of deep scratches describing a circular pattern, the results of the drilling process.

The body is very thick, appearing to belong to a globular jar. It could be a jar of Type B (Casanova 1991: Série B, Sous-types B1, B2 & B4, p. 42-43 notes 71-74), a form well known from the Royal Cemetery at Ur (Woolley 1934: pl. 176, U 11786 PG/11730, pl. 246, type 61b, pl. 177, U 8980 PG/511, pl. 246, type 62, pl. 247, type 72, pl. 249, types 90b & 91b). This type was manufactured and used between 2600 and 1800 B.C., and the example from the Barbar temple probably dates to the very end of the 3rd millennium.

Area III, 1958

Jar of calcite (517.AIR) (fig. 129 and 761). Found in a heap of sherds at 24.40/-1.10 at level 1.61, i.e. a little deeper than the floor-level of Temple I, but at a point where this was broken up. Found together with a number of copper plates (517.AIY), see above, p. 260. Another heap of sherds from the same jar lay about 70 cm toward the east. A sherd from the same jar (517.B) was found 8-9 m towards the north-east in the "Pit of offering" belonging to Temple II, see above.

Area VIII, 1959

Base sherd of alabaster (517.AMC) (fig. 770). Found in the spoils.

Translucent white gypsum. It appears to be a fragment of a cup in the form of a truncated cone, recalling Série XV. The form is known from Mari, Ur, Tepe Moussian, Susa and Shahr-i Sokhta (Casanova 1991: Série XV p. 37 note 50, Sous-type XVb fig. 11 no. 135 & pl. 10 no. 133).

Area II/III, 1960

Rim sherd of calcite (517.APU) (fig. 771). From undatable context.

Translucent veined white with a very fine vein of orange. There are scratches of abrasion (traces of the manufacturing and drilling process) on the interior and the exterior surfaces.

This broken fragment including part of the rim and the upper part of the body should probably be identified as one of the cylindrical vessels belonging to Série IV.

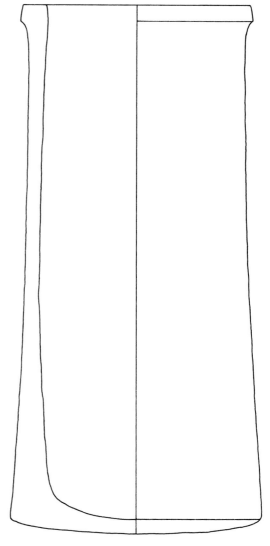

Fig. 761. 1:2.

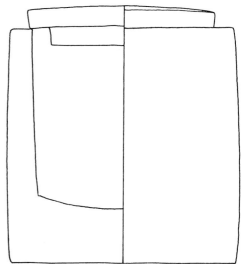

Fig. 762. 1:2.

Série IV is known from ca. 2600 to 1800 B.C. (Casanova 1991: Série IV p. 33-35, figs. 3-4, pl. 3-4).

Area IV, 1961

Lid sherd of alabaster (517.AQP) (fig. 772). Found in the spoils. White and beige gypsum.

General observations

The forms and materials of these vessels have parallels from Egypt to Iran and Central Asia dating to the third millennium and the beginning of the second millennium B.C. The actual character of the vessels and the place of manufacture remain the subject of debate. The earliest known examples of the forms close to Série IV are from Egypt, but manufacturing waste of such vessels reveals that they were also manufactured at e.g. Altyn-Depe in Central Asia. It is difficult to determine whether the form was typically Egyptian and consciously reproduced as such, or whether the individual forms did not bear any specific "identity" and were merely produced and exchanged because of a general aesthetic appeal.

Such vessels are generally found in temple and burial contexts rather than ordinary domestic ones. This implies a certain consciousness of a "special" character, which is matched by the limited number of forms which were all widely distributed.

The immediate question concerns the provenance of these vessels found at the Barbar Temple on Bahrain. The fact that there are analogous forms at Ur in Iraq gave rise to the idea that the vessels from the Barbar temple were Egyptian, having been traded from Egypt to Ur, and thence to the Gulf.

This idea was at least partly based on the earlier date for the Barbar Temple, when both the Barbar temple and the Royal cemetery at Ur were placed closer to the start of the third millennium B.C. than they are today.

Several vessels have a form which should be assigned to Série IV. Although the form itself is Egyptian in origin, these vessels would not appear to be Egyptian. The Egyptian parallels are older and Egyptian vessels of the second millennium are generally of a different form, although there are vessels close to the Série IV in Egypt and the Levant in the second millennium. The related forms in Egypt differ in having characteristically Egyptian features, unknown in Mesopotamia, Iran and Central Asia: the wavy ledge handles or the moulded cord below the rim (Casanova 1991: p. 47, 59-61).

A close study of the vessels from Ur suggests that they are not Egyptian (Reisner 1931: p. 200). Woolley noted that of the 103 stone vessel types at Ur, "the commonest [were] in white calcite, ranging from ordinary limestone to the finest stalagmitic calcite richly veined and beautifully coloured or to a plain translucent stone almost blue-white" (…) "The 'spill-vase' types 1-12 were always of calcite" (Woolley 1934: p. 379). This richly veined translucent calcite is common among the vessels of Iran and Central Asia. The vessels from Ur reveal influence of both Mesopotamian and Central Asian origin. The alabaster and calcite vessels from Ur mean that it is the only site in Mesopotamia which reveals such a close relationship to Central Asia (Casanova 1991: p. 50). All of the forms known from Susa are present, as well as a number of Central Asian forms unknown at Susa. The numerous prestige objects

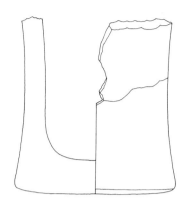

Fig. 763. 1:2.

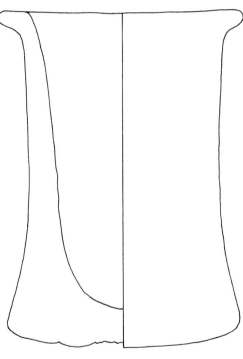

Fig. 764. 1:2.

found at Ur very frequently have a strong affinity to those found in Iran and Central Asia. Recalling that a site such as Ur was a major station on the route by which lapis lazuli moved from Central Asia to Egypt and the Levant; Ur would appear to have played an important role as a hub of trade and in-

fluence. It is probable that the objects from Iran, Afghanistan, and Pakistan were carried to Bahrain and then traded into southern Mesopotamia.

The vessels close to the Série IV discovered at Barbar would appear to belong to a tradition which – at this date – was more characteristic of Susa than of the

Fig. 765. Jar of calcite (517.YL), jar with lid of alabaster (517.BX) and jar with missing upper part (repaired) of alabaster/calcite (517.BY).

Iranian Plateau. D.T. Potts (1983: p. 130) has suggested that the vessels of the type found at Barbar might have been manufactured initially in southern Babylonia, and only subsequently in eastern Iran or Afghanistan. He has argued for an eastern Iranian workshop. The vessels from Central Asia – particularly those of Turkmenistan and Afghanistan – are generally squatter and not very tall (Casanova 1991:

38-40, 47, 50, 61). Although an Iranian manufacture is more probable, the possibility of an origin in Afghanistan or Turkmenistan cannot be excluded. The known third and early second millennium archaeological sites which had workshops producing alabaster and calcite vessels are Shahr-i Sokhta in Iran, Mundigak in Afghanistan, Altyn Depe in Turkmenistan, and Sarazm in Tadjikistan. There will probably also have been workshops at Susa, Tepe Hissar, and Shahdad in Iran. The date of the vessels found at the Barbar temple in Bahrain excludes sites such as Sarazm, which are much older (dating to the mid-fourth and early third millennia).

It is highly probable that the vessels found at the Barbar Temple at Bahrain were the products of a workshop in eastern Iran. Vessels similar to those of Bahrain belonging to the Série IV were recently recovered by the Iranian authorities. These apparently came from clandestine excavations near the city of Jiroft in the Kerman region in southeastern Iran. They came from the pillaging of cemeteries in the region, essentially those of Alaeddini, Kenar, Sandal, Riganbar, Mahtoutabad, and Nazmbad (Majidzadeh 2003: p. 13-19, 135 upper row, cylindrical vessel, 146 upper right, cylindrical vessel).

This type of alabaster/calcite vessel was widely distributed in Western Asia in the 3rd and 2nd millennia. It is generally considered to be a luxury product belonging to the network of exchange which was at once economic, political and symbolic.

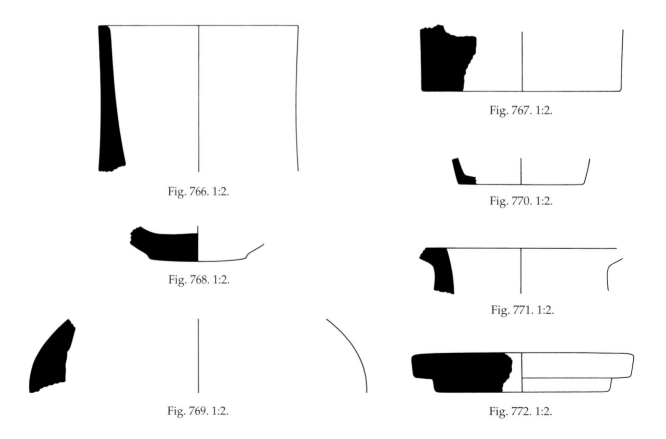

Fig. 766. 1:2.

Fig. 767. 1:2.

Fig. 770. 1:2.

Fig. 768. 1:2.

Fig. 771. 1:2.

Fig. 769. 1:2.

Fig. 772. 1:2.

14. Stamp Seals and Seal Impressions

by Poul Kjærum

Within the Barbar temple area, a total of 9 seals have been found, all of Dilmun type, 1 seal-impressed potsherd and 7 seal-impressed tokens. The seals are below numbered 1-5 and 7-10, the sealing no. 6, and the tokens nos. 11-17. Their provenance by area, level and pottery context, with period designation, is given in the catalogue.

With a few exceptions, the seals can be assigned to Temple phase IIb. Five seals (nos. 1-5) were found dispersed in the bottom sand layer in the pool of Temple IIb context (area XVI 1960, cf. fig. 12), while the sealing (no. 6) was recovered from overlying fill in the pool (area VI 1959, cf. fig. 11). No. 9 was found in Temple IIb context, no. 8 in Temple IIb or later context, no. 7 in uncertain context and no. 10 in unknown context.

As stated above, the seals are all of Dilmun type, as this was defined in 1994 (Kjærum 1994 p. 319ff), in its ordinary circular form and with the almost standardized reverse ornament consisting of three diametric grooves or fine lines over the boss. All are of form variant 2 (cf. below), apart from nos. 8 and 10 of variant 3 and variant 1, respectively. And all are glazed with a white or cream glaze, which is, however, slightly reddish or orange-coloured in seals nos. 1-5 from the pool – probably stained by ochre in the pool water.

Six stamp-sealed tokens (nos. 11-16) were found in the northern part of the temple, near two parallel walls in area III 1960 (cf. fig. 12). One of the tokens (no. 15) came from a fire layer between the two walls that has been radiocarbon-dated to 1970 BC (see above, p. 241). Unfortunately, the pottery from the layers between and around the two walls is mixed and contains material of Temple I, IIa and IIb variety. From the adjacent area II 1960 (cf. fig. 12), comes one further seal-impressed token (no. 17), but without any clear context in terms of either architecture or pottery.

The term "token" has here been used for the 7 circular clay pellets with seal impressions on one or two sides without any traces of attachment (nos. 11-17). The term was first used on this material by Crawford (1998), following Joshi and Parpola (1986 p. XXIX), while the term "bulla" was used by Beyer (1989).

If impressed only on one side the tokens are semi-spherical (nos. 11, 12, 13, 15, 17), if bifacial they are flat and the impressions are made with two different stamps (nos. 14, 16).

The style of the tokens indicates contemporaneity with the seals from the pool, and close parallels are found on Qala'at al-Bahrain (Kjærum 1994 no. 24, fig. 1749) and in Saar Settlement (Crawford 2001 p. 108 ff). Of special interest is the fact that among the 12 tokens from Saar Settlement, three were stamped with the same seals as five tokens from Barbar (cf. nos. 11-12 and 14-16).

Several proposals for the use of such tokens have been suggested based on the occurrence of similar phenomena elsewhere in the Middle East and India (cf. Crawford 1998 p. 53ff). Generally, most of these proposals point to some kind of administrative function, such as identification, authorization or receipt. In Bahrain, the material evidence is still weak, but the spread of tokens issued by the same person or institution to both the Barbar temple and several houses in the Saar Settlement point in the same direction.

Catalogue

The objects are designated by the registration number of the Barbar Temple excavation, 517, followed by three capital letters.

Colour determination of the seal body is, in cases where the seal is glazed, based on desquamated surfaces. The colour may have been changed by heat in connection with the glaze-firing.

With respect to motif descriptions, it will merely be remarked that they follow the orientation on the impression, though unfortunately impressions of nos. 1, 4 and 9 are missing. The description sequence is thus laterally reversed in relation to the original seal. Description of the obverse is limited to an underlining of special characteristics and discussion of specific figure forms of importance for the perception of the character of the motifs. Style, interpretation and comparative material are mostly treated under *Commentary*, with many references to the catalogue of stamp seals from Failaka (Kjærum 1983, abbreviated *Fai.cat.*)

Abbreviations

Disc profile: the appearance of the cross-section of the edge of the disc, defining the variations in the form of the Dilmun seals (Kjærum 1980 p. 14):
Variant 1: straight or convex.
Variant 2: slightly concave.
Variant 3: angular.
Variant 4: grooved.
D. obv.: diameter of the obverse, as a rule the maximum diameter of the seal.
D. boss: diameter of the boss perpendicular to the perforation.
T. h.: total height, measured from the obverse to the top of the boss.
Disc h.: height of the obverse disc, measured from the face to the top of the rim.
All dimensions are in mm.

Seals

1) 517.AOU, fig. 773 (Andersen 1986 p. 176, fig. 43 left; Al-Sindi 1999 no. 203).
Form variant 2. Grey steatite, white-glazed with an ochre tone.
D. obv. 22, d. boss 17, t. h. 10, disc h. 6.
Reverse: Three diagonal lines and four circles.
Obverse: Nude man standing within a vertical, rectangular construction interpreted as a shrine. The outline is carved as a broad, flat-bottomed, hatched line. In the middle of the vertical parts of the construction are two jar-like mouldings.
The man in the shrine is facing right and grasping the two jars. The shrine is flanked by a scorpion with claws downward (left), and a gazelle, regardant, facing the man.
Location: Area XVI, 1960. From sand layer on the bottom of the pool.

Commentary. A shrine motif of the same kind, but without the jars, occurs on several seals of Dilmun type and the closely related group 2A, of the same shape but without circles on the reverse (Kjærum 1983 p. 122), from Bahrain and Failaka in Kuwait.
Bahrain: On two seals, Al-Sindi 1999 no. 202 from an unknown location (incorrectly given as Barbar) and Al-Sindi 1999 no. 204 from Hamad Town, a garbed man stands in the shrine. The motif is otherwise without characterizing symbols, unless the flanking figures – a monkey-like figure but with claws, grasping the shrine, and a gazelle regardant – should be considered symbols (Al-Sindi 1999 no. 202). The shrine on a seal from Saar (Al-Sindi 1999 no. 205) is filled with symbols in the form of two bucrania, one above the other and over a cubic altar. The shrine is flanked by two sitting garbed men, grasping the structure.
Failaka: Six seals with shrine motif, in which in three cases there are only symbols. In Fai.cat.no.

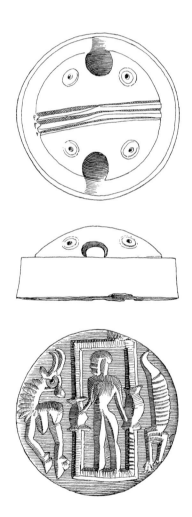

Fig. 773. Seal no. 1 (2:1 and 1:1).

51 these are a podium, two platforms and a sun circle, whereas the shrine of the other two is filled with tridents (Fai.cat.no. 52) and bidents (Fai.cat.no. 53) in discrete fields. These three shrines are respectively flanked by a garbed man and a bull-man (Fai.cat.no. 51), two garbed men (Fai.cat.no. 52), and a nude man facing an altar-like structure on the opposite side of the shrine (Fai.cat.no. 53).

Of the three remaining seals, one is, like the others mentioned above, a proper Dilmun seal (Fai.cat.no. 54), whilst two belong to group 2A (Fai.cat.nos. 303-304).

The shrine on Fai.cat.no. 54 stands on a podium and is characterized by a sun-ring in a crescent over the middle of the lintel. It is flanked by sitting garbed men grasping horned serpent monsters. The figure in the shrine is grasping the jambs, and in front of him is a vertical palm frond, which has been interpreted as the god Enzag's symbol (Butz 1983 p. 117-118; Nashef 1986 p. 345). Here it should be remarked that palm fronds are very common in many different contexts, which can hardly all relate to the god.

On the two seals of form group 2A, the lintel over the shrine is decorated with symbols: a rosette in a crescent on Fai.cat.no. 303, and a rosette symmetrically flanked by snakes and birds under an arc of three stars on Fai.cat.no. 304. The shrine's sacral character is further accentuated by two naked adorants – with only a ring around the waist – flanking a sun or star standard on an altar inside the shrine. The entire structure is finally flanked by adoring bull-men with raised hands and vertical palm fronds. All these symbols are well known from other contexts on the Dilmun seals, where they presumably characterize ritual and sacral motifs.

On the present seal the jars may be considered characteristic of the cella. Andersen has previously interpreted the seal as "Enki in his apsu", referring to Akkadian seal designs (Andersen 1986 p. 177; cf. also in general Collon 1987 p. 35). Here, among other comparative reproductions of the motif, the decoration on an apsu basin from the Temple of Ningirsu in Girsu from the Early Dynastic period (Black & Green 1992 fig. 114) should be adduced. The outside is here covered with reliefs of gods with gushing vases, the jets of which form vertical divisions between the figures, like the Akkadian renderings of Enki in the apsu (e.g. Collon 1987 figs. 105, 760).

The jar designs on the seal in question might well be simplified renderings of the gushing vases mentioned above, and the hatching of the frames, which is unique on Dilmun seals, an indication of the flowing water.

The gushing vase is a common symbol from early historic to Achaemenid times as a symbol of fertility and abundance. On the seal here it is supplemented in its own way by the scorpion along the lintel, which is likewise a fertility symbol. None of these symbols is, however, as said of the gushing vases, "a divine symbol in the sense that it represented a particular deity, but was a general attribute of certain divine and semi-divine figures, perhaps signifying fertility and abundance" (Black & Green 1992 p. 184; cf. also below, no. 4), and is thus not necessarily related to Enki.

Neither the gushing vase or an apsu has hitherto been recognized in the pictorial repertoire of Dilmun. Two motifs on Dilmun seals from Failaka (Fai.cat.nos. 101 and 171) must, however, be considered in this connection.

The motif on Fai.cat.no. 101 belongs to a small group interpreted as shrines standing on a platform (Fai.cat.nos. 62-66), but has been placed wrongly in the catalogue. The shrine is here reproduced as a rectangle, perpendicular to three diagonal wavy lines serving as its base, and is further filled out with parallel, vertical wavy lines. The shrine itself is flanked by antelope (or goat) protomes, with long curved horns, and in front of it stands a garbed man, who according to convention is shown lying down. That the motif stands for a water divinity of some kind seems evident, and it thus possibly represents the apsu.

The motif on Fai.cat.no. 171 is of a different nature, an altar scene with two opposing, seated, garbed men, one on each side of an altar and grasping a jar from which a plant of some kind emerges (incorrectly described in the catalogue as a "drinking-tube"). In front of, or presumably beside, each sitting man is an antelope or goat with raised forelegs. They have strongly curved horns, which quite uniquely depart from the neck and end over the muzzle.

From the altar depart three vertical, parallel wavy lines, where the one on the far right has pointed crests. The podium's or altar's upper contour line and the space up to the wavy lines are damaged, so whether these lines should symbolize water, as on Fai. cat. no. 101, or smoke, like the vertical wavy line over a stellate figure on an offering table (Fai.cat.no. 167), is uncertain. If the wavy lines symbolize water, it is natural to regard the jar with plant as a representation of a "jar of abundance".

Among Dilmun seals this is the only case where a plant sprouts from a jar, but the phenomenon is well known, i.a. from paintings in Zimri-Lim's palace in Mari and on seals (Black & Green 1992 figs. 16 and 115).

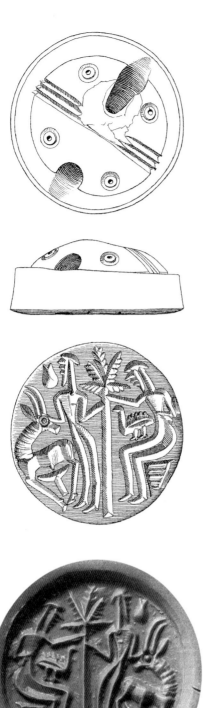

Fig. 774. Seal no. 2 (2:1 and 1:1).

2) **517.AQB**, fig. 774 (Mortensen 1971a, fig. 8: centre, Beyer 1989 no. 276; Al-Sindi 1999 no. 103).
Form variant 2. Grey steatite, white-glazed with ochre tone.
D. obv. 24, t. h. 10, d. boss 19, disc h. 6.
Reverse: Three diagonal lines and four circles.
Obverse: Central palm tree flanked by two nude men. The one on the left is seated on a stool with his left hand grasping the palm, the other hand by his waist; on (or above) his knees a bird. The man on the right faces outward, standing with his back to the palm, which he grasps with his right hand, holding a gazelle, regardant, by a horn with the left. In the field top right a jar, and a crescent staff between the legs of the gazelle.
Location: Area XVI, 1960. From sand layer at the bottom of the pool.

Commentary. Palm trees, in a relatively naturalistic rendering, are a central motif in a large number of Dilmun seals and two cylinder seals with motif in Dilmun style, one from Bahrain and one from Failaka, but in only a few specimens are they combined with human figures. Where only human figures occur, they are, unlike in the present seal, placed symmetrically, and are either seated and nude (Al-Sindi 1999 no. 101 from Saar; Fai.cat.no. 157) or standing and garbed (Fai.cat.nos. 155-156). They are usually facing the palm, grasping the trunk with one hand, with the other hand by the waist. In one case only, the standing men turn their backs to the palm and are holding gate symbols in their free hands (Fai.cat.no. 155).

On two of these seals (Fai.cat.nos. 156-157), the palms are standing on podia, and serpents are symmetrically incorporated in the motifs.

In a further two seals there is a single naked human figure, sitting and standing respectively, grasping the palm trunk and facing an antelope regardant. The latter grasps with his left hand a notched symbol (Crawford 2001, 1953:18, from Saar; Kjærum 1994, p. 332, no. 20, from Excavation 520 at Qala'at al-Bahrain).

On a seal from Failaka (Fai.cat.no. 162), a palm, standing centrally on a podium, is flanked by two human heads or masks, both facing right, with two gazelle protomes facing the palm and outermost two net podia. In a lower register a net podium is flanked by two goose-like birds. Similar masks are found on a sealing from the Saar temple (Crawford et al. 1997 no. 1612:10)

In the most common motif with a palm, this is flanked by gazelles or antelopes. It occurs on nine seals from Bahrain and one from Failaka.

The ruminants stand either directly opposite each other (Al-Sindi 1999 nos. 107-108 (= Kjærum 1994 no. 14, fig. 1739) and 112-113) or regardant but facing each other (Crawford 2001, Saar 1040:01 and

2051:06) and in the same posture, but pinioned (Al-Sindi 1999 nos. 104-105).

It is worth remarking that the palm, Al-Sindi 1999 no. 105, has an anthropomorphic character suggested by bent, man-like arms, departing from the lowest fronds of the palm's crown and gripping the ruminants by the neck. This phenomenon is known only from this one representation. It immediately reminds one of Anatolian representations of bull altars, where the bull is humanized by human arms originating from its breast reaching out to an offering table with food offerings in front of it (cf. Özgüç1965, pls. XII-XIV, figs. 35-40).

The motif on the seal Al-Sindi 1999 no. 72 departs from the others in that the static composition is replaced by a lively representation of lions attacking rampant antelopes nearest the tree.

From Failaka there is only a single fragment of a seal, apparently with the motif that is so popular on Bahrain with the palm flanked by ruminants (Fai. cat.no. 160), and another fragment with an antelope regardant by a palm standing on a podium (Fai.cat.no. 161). Finally, the palm on the seal Fai. cat.no. 159 is flanked by snakes, birds and sun circles.

Palms are also a part of three radial motifs, of which only one is truly radial with marked centre and a purely geometrical division of the circle by eight radii, whose motifs alternate in a fixed rhythm between antelope protomes and palms (Pic 1990 no. 20). On a seal from Saar with four radii only (Al-Sindi 1999 no. 258) one of the radii is a palm tree, while the three remaining are straight lines terminating in jars as also seen on a linear platform with birds flanking a palm frond (Fai.cat.no. 100). Finally the palms on the seal from Qala'at al-Bahrain are protruding obliquely from a platform terminating in crescents besides human figures with raised hands grasping crescents and bucrania (Kjærum 1994 fig. 1741 and p. 330).

The prominent position of the palm tree in the motifs, in some cases further accentuated by its position on a platform or podium, and its anthropomorphic character on one of them, indicates that the palm has had a religious or at least ritual meaning in line with cult objects like the standards topped with different celestial symbols (cf. also Kjærum 1994 p. 329ff, nos. 14 and 16). The pinioned animals, flanking some of the palms, may also be perceived as sacrificial (concerning pinioned animals cf. also Amiet 1986 p. 266). Finally, the admittedly unique motif with fish swimming along the periphery of the seal under the central motif may suggest a connection with the "vase of abundance" motif and thus the fertility cult, as possibly also the jars on the seal from Saar and Failaka mentioned above and one from Ur (Legrain 1951 no. 624). On the latter the quadrants between the radii are occupied by naked female figures. Two of these figures (in alternate quadrants) clasp their hands upon their breasts.

Chronology: The two seals with naturalistic palms from Qala'at al-Bahrain, nos. 14 and 16 (cf. above), were both found in layers belonging to period IIc, seal Qala'at al-Bahrain no. 20 in a layer belonging to period IIb/c (Kjærum 1994). The two Dilmun seals and the cylinder seal from Kuwait with human figures flanking a palm (Fai.cat.nos. 155, 157 and 373) were found in the oldest layers in Tell F6, which belong to the earliest occupation on the island, Failaka period 1, corresponding to Qala'at period IIb.

The remaining seals with this motif are from considerably later layers and have probably been rebedded.

3) 517.AOX, fig. 775 (Beyer 1989 no. 271; Al-Sindi 1999 no. 188).
Form variant 2. Grey steatite, white-glazed with an ochre tone.
D. obv. 21, d. boss 17, t. h. 10, disc h. 5. The seal was complete when found, but flaked slightly before the drawing could be made.
Reverse: Three diagonal lines and four circles.
Obverse: Circular motif consisting of a central, squarish, slightly rectangular podium drawn as five nested squares, surrounded by four scorpions along the sides, all facing in the same direction following the circle.
Location: Area XVI 1960. From sand layer on the bottom of the pool.

Commentary. Square or rectangular podia are relatively common on Dilmun seals, but none of them are more than double (Fai.cat.nos. 23, 166 and 296). The combination of scorpions, as a prominent component of motifs with podia, shrines and presumed temple representations, is, on the other hand, frequently met with. From Bahrain the combination was found of snakes and a scorpion over a square net podium (Al-Sindi 1999 no. 146), and on a seal from the Saar settlement (Crawford 2001 no. 2667:03) a seated man by a podium is grasping a huge scorpion. On Fai.cat.no. 60 the flanking scorpions are thus rendered to the full height of the seal, one on each side of a net rectangle, and on two seals scorpions are shown vertical and at the same size as the men (Fai.cat.nos. 69 and 95), and as on no. 1 above, where the shrine is flanked by a large scorpion and a gazelle, the shrine on Fai.cat.no. 59 is flanked by a large scorpion and a monkey. In large numbers the scorpion also appears in other constellations, which might indicate its symbolic meaning, thus where it, as in many instances, is linked to coitus scenes (cf. below, no. 10), perhaps in combination with the crab figure, as it respectively supplements (e.g. Al-Sindi 1999 no. 224 from Janabiya)

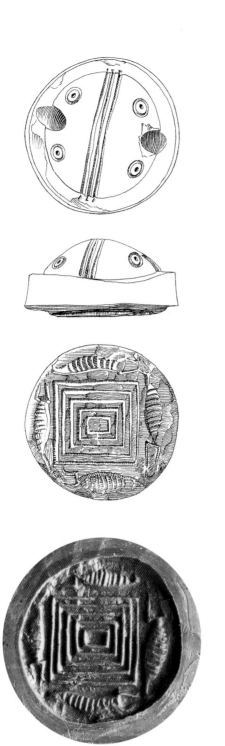

Fig. 775. Seal no. 3 (2:1 and 1:1).

and replaces (Kjærum 1994 p. 331, no. 18). Here the relation to fertility is clear. The same also seems to apply where the scorpion is part of the central motif flanked by bulls of the same size as the scorpion (Ibrahim 1982 fig. 50:5), or is placed before the chest of bulls (e.g. Fai.cat.no. 204) in the same way as palm fronds (cf. below, no. 8).

Some of these contexts then indicate that the scorpion in Dilmun in some cases relates to the fertility cult, as it does in certain periods of Mesopotamia (cf. Buchanan 1981 no. 458 and p. 200ff), but possibly also in other, undefined functions (Green & Black 1992 p. 160f).

4) 517.AOV, fig. 776 (Beyer 1989 no. 279; Al-Sindi 1999 no. 277).
Reverse and left side of the obverse have been knocked off.
Form variant 2. Grey steatite, glazed.
D. obv. 24, disc h. 6.
Reverse: Traces of three diagonal lines.
Obverse: Radial composition consisting of six antelope protomes (neck and head), all with profiled neck and two long, parallel, curved horns with strong protuberances. All are facing right. The intersection of the necks is the centre of the motif, which is not specially marked (cf. also nos. 5 and 7 with the same basic motif).
Location: Area XVI 1960. From sand layer on the bottom of the pool.

Commentary. The purely geometrical motif with radii consisting only of gazelle or antelope protomes is known in two further examples from the Barbar temple (nos. 5 and 7). From the Saar settlement the motif is reproduced with small variations on seals from building 3 (Crawford 2001 no. G17:18:02 = Al-Sindi 1999 no. 185) and building 35 (Crawford 2001 no. 7008:5). Related, but slightly deviant, variations of the motif also come from building 51, in which the protomes emanate from a central cross to form a swastika-like figure (Crawford 2001 no. 2535:01). It is further found on a sealing from house 50 (Ibid. no. 2570:11), where human figures occur in two opposing quadrants of the four present, while celestial symbols, rings with loops on the periphery, are found in the two others (cf. below, nos. 15-16). One motif, which is almost identical to that on seal no. 4, is also found on two seals from Failaka, where they were found in the earliest settlement layers in Tell F6 (Fai.cat.no. 1 and Beyer 1986 no. 176).

In a few radial motifs, protomes may be likened to cult objects in which protome radii alternate with crescent standards (Fai.cat.no. 3), or with net-square standards, which radiate from a sun rosette in the centre (Fai.cat.no. 16). Possibly the same ap-

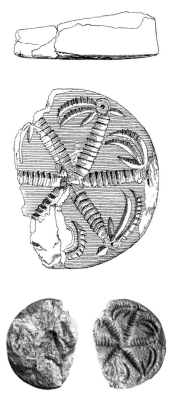

Fig. 776. Seal no. 4 (2:1 and 1:1).

Fig. 777. Seal no. 5 (2:1 and 1:1).

plies where protomes alternate with palms in seals from Failaka Tell F6 (Pic 1990 no. 20).

The cultic aspect is further accentuated where the radial motif is an obvious abstraction from cultic scenes by an altar, where the centre is a podium, from which protomes radiate from all corners (Fai.cat.no. 20) and the broad sides are the base for protruding cult symbols, adorants – sometimes raising rings and palm fronds (Fai.cat.nos. 23, 25, 26, 27) – and even gods with horned crowns raising palm fronds and podia (Fai.cat.no. 24).

The closest parallel from Bahrain to the last-mentioned group is the motif on a seal from Hamad Town (Al-Sindi 1999 no. 232). The centre is here, as on several examples, a net podium, but the protomes originate from three broad sides while a triple crescent protrudes from the fourth. Three stars both in the crescents and in the squares between the protomes surround the motif.

On Failaka these two groups – altar representations and pure radial motifs with protomes, perhaps alternating with cult objects – belong to the earliest Failaka settlement.

The radial motif with protomes has by Porada (1971 p. 335 and pl. 10, figs. 8-9) been compared to seals from Acemhüyük, which are so close to the seal from Barbar no. 5 that she states: "It seems most likely that a seal of Acemhüyük type reached Bahrain or Kuwait and was imitated or that one of

Fig. 778. Seal impression no. 6 (2:1 and 1:1).

the Gulf seals was brought to the west." The seal impression from Acemhüyük is from finds belonging to Shamsi-Adad's reign (c. 1800 BC). The comparison is convincing, although the protomes depict griffins and antelopes, respectively, and the testimony to relations between Dilmun and Syria has later been strengthened, through new studies and finds (Buchanan 1965 p. 207; Matthiae 1980 p. 14; Pettinato 1983; Kjærum 1986 p. 269ff; Potts 1986 p. 389ff; Collon 1996 p. 209 ff. Eidem & Højlund 1993 and 1997).

5) 517.APY, fig. 777 (Beyer 1989 no. 278; Mortensen 1971a, fig. 8: right; Porada 1971 pl. X, fig. 8; Al-Sindi 1999 no. 184).
Form variant 2. Steatite glazed.
D. obv. 23, t. h. 11, d. boss 18, disc h. 6.
Reverse: Three diagonal lines and four circles.
Obverse: Radial composition consisting of six protomes, three gazelle protomes with straight or slightly curved horns and three antelope protomes with long, curved horns. The five of them have two horns, which is the usual situation, while one protome (to the right) has one markedly curved horn only, which is rare (but cf. no. 7, below). The horns are smooth without protuberances, and the necks are profiled. All are facing right. In the quadrant between the two top gazelle protomes is a tree or palm frond. The centre of the motif is marked with a circle drilling, which forms the base of the necks.
Location: Area XVI, 1960. From sand layer on the bottom of the pool.

Commentary. The appearance of the horns characterizes two, possibly three, different variants within the antelope or goat family that are also found among the numerous animal representations on the seals.
For further commentaries, cf. no. 4.

Impression

6) 517.ALM, fig. 778 (Beyer 1989 p. 144 no. 259; Mortensen 1971 p. 385, fig. 1; Al-Sindi 1999 fig. 3).
Impression on a circular lump of clay attached on the upper shoulder of a ridged jar of Barbar type before firing (cf. above, p. 240).
D. of impression 22, d. of clay lump 28.
Motif: Nude man, with a helmet-like cap, standing between two antelopes, grasping them by their necks. The antelopes are shown in profile, with one horn only, regardant and looking outward. The horns are curved, with prominent protuberances. Between the legs of the left antelope a small vertical crescent.
Location: Area VI 1959. Found in the pool fill in level c. 5.40.
Commentary. A seal-impression in Dilmun style on the same type of vessel has been found at Qala'at al-Bahrain dating to Qala'at al-Bahrain period IIb (Kjærum 1994 p. 335, no. 22, fig. 1747). Further, Shakhoura grave 10 contained a chain-ridged pot with a seal-impression on the shoulder rendering a drinking-scene in Arabian Gulf style (Daems 2001 p. 173). For seal impressions on Dilmun pots and contemporaneous material outside Dilmun, cf. Beyer 1989 no. 259 and Kjærum 1994 p. 335, no. 22.

The Master of the Animals motif, as here with a man standing between as a rule symmetrically placed ruminants, commonly occurs in both Bahrain (Al-Sindi 1999 nos. 31-33 and 35 and Crawford 2001, 1580:01, building 203, and worn, unclear 6581:01 building 60) and Failaka (Fai.cat.nos. 212-217). One of these, from Hamad Town (Al-Sindi 1999 no. 35), is, like the impression here, in Proto-Dilmun style, and from Saar we have a seal with symmetrically placed ruminants with the same characteristic horn shape as here, likewise in Proto-Dilmun style (Crawford 2001 no. 6583:01, building 61).

Seals

7) 517.ALE, fig. 779 (Beyer 1989 no. 280; Al Khalifa 1986 p. 259, fig. 82; Al-Sindi 1999 no. 186).
Form variant 2. Grey steatite, glazed.
D. obv. 21, d. boss 17, t.h. 9, disc h. 5.
Reverse: Three diagonal lines and two of probably four circles.
Obverse: Radial motif comprising four antelope protomes, all facing right, with bent forelegs, profiled necks and long wavy horns. The legs are bent at a sharp angle and touch or cross the neck of the preceding protome. The protomes radiate crosswise and are joined in the centre by a small square, the sides of which form the baseline of the necks. In each quadrant are two or three only slightly curved crescents.
Location: Area VIII 1959 (cf. fig. 11), c. 2 m west of the western terrace wall of Temple III (plan 8:1) at level c. 2.25, in uncertain context.

Commentary. Forelegs are found only exceptionally in these pure protome motifs (Crawford 2001 no. G17:18:02), but are more common where the radii emanate from central podia. The legs are on these often shown in the same position as here (e.g. Fai.cat.nos. 26 and 28).
For further comments, cf. above, no. 4.

8) 517.ARE, fig. 780 (Beyer 1989 no. 269; Al-Sindi 1999 no. 149).
Form variant 3. Grey steatite, glazed.
D. obv. 17, d. boss 13, t.h. 8, disc h. 4.
Reverse: Three diagonal lines and four circles.
Obverse: A standing nude man, facing left, grasping a podium above the back of a bull also facing left. On the podium a crescent staff with a sun circle in the crescent. Along the chest of the bull is a palm frond. Before its head, along the periphery of the seal, a serpent. Opposite the serpent, a bird facing the crescent.
Location: Area IV 1961 (cf. fig. 13), below floor in the middle of the area. The pottery context is either Temple IIb or later.

Commentary. Two seals with a very similar motif and in the same style 1B were found on Failaka (Tell F3, Fai.cat.no. 70 and Tell F6, Fai.cat.no. 248). On both of them the podium is raised by a bull-man. Above the back of a bull and below, respectively, a sunflower and a sun circle in a crescent. On Fai. cat.no. 70 is, as here, a bird beside the crescent.

A further three seals show the same basic motif, one from Hamad Town (Al-Sindi 1999 no. 148, Proto-Dilmun style) and two from Failaka (Fai.cat.nos. 68-69 in style 1A). The podia are grasped here by one naked man and two garbed, respectively.

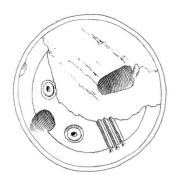

Fig. 779. Seal no. 7 (2:1 and 1:1).

Fig. 780. Seal no. 8 (2:1 and 1:1).

sent seal, interprets it as a shield "Only once do I know a shield to be used on a seal which also shows persons armed with what could be weapons. Otherwise, it is often held by a person who at the same time grasps a tree or is shown in some other action which is in no way aggressive or warlike or in need of the protection of a shield. For the shield as a ceremonial emblem used without immediate warlike connotation, we have to look beyond the Asiatic mainland to areas with which the Gulf people could have been in contact through their maritime connections."

A similar argument has been used against the shield theory and, with starting-point in the two seal motifs from Failaka (Fai.cat.nos. 75-76), the figure has been described as a "notched symbol" (Kjærum 1994 p. 333f). A seal motif from Saar (Crawford 2001 no. 5099:33), does, however, suggest that this figure form should be designated a shield. It is here combined with a spear, the point of which is visible in the middle of the bottom notch, while what may be the opposite end of the shaft is visible in the top notch. Here the spear is thus connected to the shield. It is, however, also apparent from the seal motif from Saar that the shield here, too, has had no protective function, but is of a symbolic nature. It is directed towards a scorpion with gazelle head, while the man standing on a podium turns towards a lion in front of him. The same applies to the other of the now many "shield representations" coming from Saar (Crawford 2001 1612:01, F18:33:15, 6580:04; ibid. 1997, 1920:01) and Bahrain in general (Al-Sindi 1999 nos. 155, 209-210, 213-214). On the seal in question (no. 9), it is also remarkable that the two spear-carrying men should share a shield, unless it, as suggested by Porada, has become "a ceremonial emblem" (1971 p. 337). The motif can thus be assigned to the same category as scenes by an altar (cf., for example, Fai.cat.nos. 68-76).

9) 517.AIS, fig. 781.
Form variant 2. Grey steatite, glazed.
D. obv. 26, d. boss 20, t.h. 12, disc h. 8.
Reverse: Three diagonal lines and four circles.
Obverse: Two opposed men grasping a notched symbol between them and each holding a spear behind his back. Above the notched symbol an eye-shaped device, below it a bird.
Location: Area IX 1958 (cf. fig. 10). South of the oval terrace wall of Temple IIb. From Temple IIb layers – level c. 3.00 – disturbed in Islamic times.

Commentary. The notched symbol is dealt with by Hallo and Buchanan (1965 p. 205) and later by Porada (1971 p. 337), who, in a discussion of the pre-

10) 517.ANZ & AMQ, fig. 782 (Beyer 1989 no. 268; Mortensen 1971a, p. 392, fig. 8: left; Porada 1971 pl. X, fig. 7; Andersen 1986 p. 176, fig. 43 right, Al-Sindi 1999 no. 222).
Form variant 1. Disc profile convex (worn). Grey steatite, glazed. Severely worn.
D. obv. 23, d. boss 17, h. boss 12, disc h. 8.
Reverse: Three diagonal lines and four circles.
Obverse: Standing nude, ityphallic man on the point of entering a nude woman with widely spread legs. She is grasping her toes with both hands and is drinking from a tube in a jar. He is facing right towards her and has one hand by his waist, the other grasping her right leg by the ankle. In field a scorpion behind the man's back, a foot sign behind the neck of the woman. Between them,

Fig. 781. Seal no. 9 (2:1 and 1:1).

centrally below the scene, a prominent star.
Location: Half of the seal was found in 1960 on the
surface south of the temple, the other half was later
in the same year found on the surface south-west of
the temple.

Commentary. This motif commonly occurs on Dilmun seals in Bahrain. A similar motif in respect of
both motif and style derives from Qala'at al-
Bahrain, on a Dilmun seal stratigraphically dated to
period IIb/c (Kjærum 1994 no. 18, fig. 1743, p. 331f).
The motif group is also presented and discussed in
its entirety by Buchanan (1981 p. 200ff). A few sup-

Fig. 782. Seal no. 10 (2:1 and 1:1).

plementary finds and/or publications of Dilmun seals with the same motif is mentioned below, with special emphasis on the supplementary figure forms that can symbolize the motif's character and meaning.

The scorpion that occurs in the motif on both the Qala'at seal and the one presented here occurs in the same context on a seal of Proto-Dilmun style from Janabiya (Al-Sindi 1999 no. 224), where it is abundantly supplemented by a crab figure. That this, like the scorpion, in one way or another symbolizes the nature of the motif is apparent from the fact that it can occur between the woman's legs, as a substitute for the man (Erlenmeyer & Erlenmeyer 1966 fig. 18). Of other supplementary animal figures, monkey and snakes occur (Al-Sindi 1999 no. 225 from Hamad Town) and turtle (Crawford 2001 p. 74 K16:29:08 from Saar Settlement).

On a fragment of a sealing from the Saar Settlement is an erotic scene with man and woman in usual position and a crescent above the woman's right thigh; no further demonstrable supplementary motifs (Crawford & Matthews 1997 16:10:03).

On a seal from the Saar Settlement is a variation over the same theme, here with two men, one of them phallic, holding a woman with widespread legs and raised arms above an offering table with slightly curved plate and feet with hooves (Crawford 2001, 4025:06).

Another variation is found on a stamp seal from Grave BII-7 at Karaneh that depicts *coitus a tergo* where both stand on a net podium, the woman bending over, drinking from a tube in a jar. Supplementary figures, an antelope and a sun symbol (Velde 1998 p. 250).

Tokens

11) 517.ANR, fig. 783.
D. 21, h. 10. Light brown clay.
Reverse: Hemispherical, plain, cracked.
Obverse: Zoomorphic boat-like construction consisting of two foreparts of bulls connected by their extremely long, slightly curved, merged "spine". They have bent forelegs with hooves touching the lower end of the outermost of five vertical ribbons below the middle of the spine. Between the two outermost protomes that make up the prows of the boat are four bull protomes on a baseline continuing as the prominent dewlap of the left and the right protome. The three protomes on each side face right and left respectively.
Location: Area III 1960, found in yellow sand from above or around the walls in the middle of the area (cf. section 31).

Commentary. Impressions from the same stamp are found on nos. 12 and 15. The former is rather eroded, but easily recognizable by the prominent cutting of the dewlap on protomes nos. 2 and 3 from the left. No. 15 is the best-preserved of all.

A token, stamped with the same seal, derives from the Saar settlement, house 224 (Crawford 2001 no. 5012:06). The motif on this token is very eroded or worn and difficult to decipher. Compared to the three Barbar tokens it is, however, unmistakably printed with the same seal. In spite of erosion, this is apparent from the characteristic deeply carved line separating the dewlap from the body on the first and second upright figure on the Saar sample as well as the three samples from Barbar mentioned. Faint traces of the outer protomes and the vertical ribbons below the "spine" are also recognizable on the Saar specimen when directly compared with the better-preserved impressions in question.

Though bulls are numerous on Dilmun seals, bull protomes are rare among the many protomes of ruminants, only known in a single case attached to a podium (Fai.cat.no. 174) and in a boat design on a bifacial seal from Sar El-Jisr, grave S-267.4 (Ibrahim 1982 fig. 49:1 and pl. 60:1 = Al-Sindi 1999 no. 268), which may be directly comparable to the motifs in question, though this boat is of a more prosaic type.

12) 517 ANT, fig. 784.
D. 20, h. 9.
Reverse: Hemispherical. Surface plain.
Obverse: Same impression as nos. 11 and 15. Eroded.
Location: Area III 1960, found in yellow sand c. ½ m east of walls in the middle of the area (cf. section 31).
Description and commentary: Cf. no. 11.

13) 517.ANV, fig. 785 (Beyer 1989 no. 286).
D. 21, h. 9. Colour light brown.
Reverse: Hemispherical. Surface plain. From the edge a horizontal hole, not carried through, the surface of which is eroded. No trace of impression in the hole.
Obverse: An emblem consisting of two laterally reversed bundles, one above the other, consisting of three separate lines at acute angles. Between the bundles, slightly displaced in relation to one another, four horizontal lines. Above them a canopy (cf. Fai.cat.no. 126).
Location: Area III 1960, found in yellow sand north of top of walls in the middle of the area (cf. section 31).

Commentary. At a quick glance the sign reminds one of fasces (Crawford 1998 p. 52) or, as formulated by

Fig. 783. Token no. 11. 1:1.

Fig. 785. Token no. 13. 1:1.

Fig. 784. Token no. 12. 1:1.

Beyer "an evocation of a bundle of cereal straw" (Beyer 1989 no. 286). But both "interpretations" must be rejected, since the lines in the two bundles, as mentioned above, are not coherent.

Beyer compares in the same publication the sign with the script-like signs on the seal Fai.cat.no. 45. It occurs on several seals, but deviates clearly from these by always consisting of two tridents, laterally reversed and separated by two lines. They are all in style 3 and are a part of a script-like arrangement.

In former publications the "canopy" is placed under the sign (Beyer 1989 nos. 284 and 286-88). As the only parallel is placed over the chief device (Fai.cat.no. 126), this rendering has been preferred. However the motif should be interpreted, the sign is so far unique, not being known either in context with other figures or separate, as here.

14) 517.ANX, fig. 786 (Beyer 1989 no. 285).
Bifacially stamped token
D. 21, h. 10. Ochre clay.
Impression 1: As no. 13.
Impression 2: Triple concentric circles around a central circular dot. Along the outer periphery of all three circles out-turned loops.
Location: Area III 1960, found in yellow sand c. 20 cm above top of and between the two walls in the middle of the area (cf. section 31).

Commentary. Oblique perforation from edge on impression 1. No traces of string. Tokens stamped with the same seal as impression 2 on this one and as no. 16:2 are found on a token in the Saar settlement building 53 (Crawford 2001 no. 2665:06) and building 224 (Ibid. 5500:27). Their diameter is very much the same as that of the token in question, just as the clay in no. 2665:06 (Ibid.) is in colour very close to that of the tokens from Barbar.

Fig. 786. Token no. 14 (2:1 and 1:1).

In addition, Saar building 50 has yielded a tag in which circles with loops occur as a secondary motif (Ibid. 2570:11). Finally, a seal from Al-Hajjar (Al-Sindi 1999 no. 193), in which the motif is bordered by a circle with loops, and a seal from Failaka Tell F6 (Fai.cat.no. 37) from layers belonging to Failaka period 1 (Højlund 1987 p. 107 ff and p. 138) should be mentioned.

301

Fig. 787. Token no. 15 (2:1 and 1:1).

Fig. 789. Token no. 17 (2:1 and 1:1).

15) 517.ANU, fig. 787 (Beyer 1989 no. 289).
Hemispherical.
D. 21, h. 10. Colour light brown.
Deep hole from under-edge, breaking lower part of the obverse surface; the hole is not carried through. Beyer describes the hole as a "stringhole", but its surface is eroded and thus without traces of a cord or other impression.
Obverse: Impression as no. 11 and no. 12. Extremely well preserved.
Location: Area III 1960, found in fire layer between two walls in the middle of the area (cf. section 31).
Commentary: Cf. no. 11.

Location: Area III 1960, found in yellow sand c. 1 m under the section top (cf. section 31).
Description and commentary: cf. no. 14.

17) 517.ANY, fig. 789 (Beyer 1989 no. 287).
D. 21, h. 8. Colour light brown.
Hemispherical.
Obverse: Impression as no. 13, 14:1, and 16:1.
Location: Area II 1960, found in yellow sand c. 1 m under the section top (section 30).
Description and commentary: cf. no. 13.

Conclusion

The Barbar temples and the two important settlements – Qala'at al-Bahrain and Saar – are all situated in the northern part of Bahrain, only a few kilometres apart. At a certain period they have all three functioned at the same time, and seals and seal impressions indicate a close relation and presumably a direct connection between these different sites. The testimony of the seals on contact between these sites and also with the early settlement on the island of Failaka in Kuwait, which must have originated in Bahrain and is roughly coeval with period IIb-c at Qala'at al-Bahrain, should be taken into account.

Qala'at al-Bahrain. At Qala'at al-Bahrain the earliest seals appear in period IIa, in the same period as

Fig. 788. Token no. 16. 1:1.

16) 517.ANS, fig. 788 (Beyer 1989 no. 284).
D. 21, h. 8. Ochre clay.
Impression 1: Same stamp as nos. 13, 14:1, and 17.
Impression 2: Same stamp as nos 14:2.
Impressions on both sides with the same stamps as no. 14: impression 1-2. Impression 1 further as nos. 13 and 17.

the town is fortified. In this period the form and style of the seals are completely dominated by the Arabian Gulf type. In the same period, seals of Dilmun type with motifs in an extremely varied style, called the Proto-Dilmun style, are developed, referring to the Arabian Gulf style, but also forward to the later Dilmun style, which is characteristic of period IIb-c (Kjærum 1994 p. 345ff).

In the Barbar temple no seals with motifs in either Arabian Gulf or Proto-Dilmun style have been found. But the latter is represented in the stamp on sherd no. 6 from the pool. This is, however, from a fill layer which can include sherds from an earlier epoch in the temple's history than the five seals from the bottom layer in the pool (nos. 1-5), which must all be referred to Temple IIb and were covered in its final phase, when the pool was filled in.

The five seals from the pool (nos. 1-5) and seals no. 7 (uncertain context) and no. 9 (from disturbed Temple IIb context) are all of form variant 2 with slightly concave disc profile like all mature Dilmun seals from Excavation 520 at Qala'at al-Bahrain dating to period IIb-c. Form variant 1, as Qala'at 520 no. 12 dating to period IIa, is represented at Barbar only by the severely worn seal no. 10 (out of context). Seals of form variant 3, like no. 8 at Barbar, have hitherto not been found at Qala'at al-Bahrain.

Stylistically, there seems to be a close parallelism between the seals from Qala'at al-Bahrain period IIb/c, which with a single exception (Qala'at 520 no. 12) are in style 1A like almost all the seals from Barbar, except no 8. The likeness is especially evident in the seals from the pool. Seals no. 9 and in particular no. 10 seem typologically slightly older, characterized by the more "naturalistic" faces and flat, broad rib cage of the human figures, approaching the style of the Proto-Dilmun seals such as the seals with the same motif from Janabiya (Al-Sindi 1999 no. 224) and the Saar settlement (Crawford 2001 K16:29:08).

The seal form with angled disc profile like seal no. 8 has no parallels at Qala'at al-Bahrain, nor is style 1B represented in the seals from here. In the stamp on the token Qala'at 520 no. 24 there is, however, a rosette form which occurs sporadically in style 1B and massively in style 2 (Kjærum 1994), but the style identification is uncertain, since decisive elements in the impression are unclear and should rather be assigned to style 1A.

As a whole, the seals thus indicate a clear parallel between the Barbar Temple IIb period and Qala'at al-Bahrain period IIb-c. The time relationship between the Barbar temple's earliest and its latest period and Qala'at al-Bahrain is, on the other hand, tenuously based on the seal finds.

Proto-Dilmun is indeed represented in both places, but only in a single specimen from each –

Barbar			
11	O		
12	O		
13		O	
14:1		O	
14:2			O
15	O		
16:1		O	
16:2			O
17		O	
Saar			
5012:06	O		
2665:06			O
5500:27			O

Tokens from the Barbar Temple and the Saar Settlement stamped with the same seals.

from Qala'at al-Bahrain in period IIa context, and in the Barbar temple from a fill layer that covers Temple IIb layers which can derive from an earlier phase in the temple. Barbar seal no. 8 in style 1B, found in a context belonging to Temple IIb or later, is stylistically and possibly also in context the latest seal in the structure, but has no parallels in Qala'at al-Bahrain.

Saar Settlement. A close contact between the Saar settlement and the Barbar temple is clearly documented by the presence in both complexes of several tokens stamped with the same matrix (cf. nos. 11-12, 14-15 and 16). In Saar these tokens are found in two houses, 53 and 224. Two of these tokens from Saar correspond in diameter, thickness and the colour of the clay to tokens from Barbar. Whether they were directly exchanged between the two sites, or both sites received them from the same outside source, is unknown. No tokens from Barbar have occurred in secure ceramic context, but token no. 15 was found in a layer of charcoal radiocarbon-dated to 1970 BC.

Here it should also be remarked that the central motif on two tokens from the Saar settlement (Crawford 2001 nos. 6539:01 and K16:53-02) from house 51 and house 60, respectively, is found again in the central motif on a token from Qala'at al-Bahrain from period IIb/c (Kjærum 1994 fig. 1749) and on a bitumen sealing from the same place belonging to period IIb (ibid. fig. 1748). Finally, the stamp on token no. 14, found again in Saar house 53 (Crawford 2001 no. 2665:06) and house 224 (ibid. 5500:27) also shows a formal resemblance to the motif on a Dilmun seal from the earliest settlement on Failaka (cf. above, no. 14, and below). The shape, style, motifs and figure forms of the seals are to a great extent common to the two places, which, however, is not necessarily evidence of direct contact, since these features are common to the entire Dilmun area within styles 1 and 2, although there are naturally individual differences even on presumably truly coeval seals belonging to the same stylistic group (compare for example, the human figures on nos. 1 and 2 with nos. 9 and 10).

The different elements of the seals indicate, as do the tokens, a high degree of coevality between the finds in Barbar Temple IIb and the Saar settlement.

The seals from the Saar settlement are in respect of morphology equally divided between seal variant 1 with straight or convex edge profile and variant 2 with concave edge profile, while variants 3-4 with angled or grooved edge profile occur in only three well-preserved specimens. In the Barbar temple there is one example of variants 1 and 3, while the remainder are of variant 2.

Style 1A is in both places the predominant one, and several motifs in this style occur in quite uniform execution (cf. nos. 2, 4-5, 7, and 9-10).

In both places both Arabian Gulf and Proto-Dilmun style occur, and style 1B, albeit much more rarely. How scarce Arabian Gulf and Proto-Dilmun style are in the Saar settlement is, however, still unknown "as some buildings have only been excavated down to the top of the occupation levels, some have been dug to the primary floor, and some have been completely explored" (Crawford 2001 p. 39ff). The earliest stages must therefore be underrepresented, but are known from houses in the northern part of the settlement in particular and from one in the centre (cf. ibid. p. 39 and above, no. 6).

Style 1B is the latest style represented in the Barbar temple (no. 8), while both this and style 2 are found in the Saar settlement in the form of both proper seals (Crawford 2001 nos. 2500:01, house 53 and 2109:01, house 56) and of sealings (Ibid. style 1B, building 56, nos. 2057:09, M16:33:07 and building 57, no. 2171:02; style 2 building 56, no. 2141:01). These occurrences are not numerous, true enough, but it is remarkable that both seals and sealings are concentrated in two contiguous houses (nos. 56-57) and a house lying opposite them (no. 53), of which it is stated that houses 53, 56 and 100 "appear to have been occupied after the neighbouring ones had fallen into ruins" (Crawford et al. 1997 p. 21). The settlement terminates in Saar period 4, which according to Carter (2001 p. 184) "... postdates the occupation of the North City Wall at Qala'at al-Bahrain, but shows development towards Højlund's Qala'at City IIF assemblage from the West Wall (Højlund 1994 fig. 395), towards ... Periods 2B and 3A at Failaka (Højlund 1987 p. 157ff). There is no firm evidence that Saar Period 4 extends into the Old Babylonian period...".

This would seem to be in good agreement with the fact that there are no seals of styles 1B and 2 from Qala'at al-Bahrain Excavation 520, where the settlement is interrupted in period IIc, while both styles occur both as seals and sealings in the latest-occupied houses at Saar.

Failaka. The first site to be settled on Failaka was Tell F6, comprising in its final form a temple, a big house and a few store-rooms and smaller buildings. This was followed by the establishment of a small civil town about 200 m west of Tell F6 designated Tell F3 (Failaka period 2). Both sites were founded during Qala'at al-Bahrain period IIb-c and were settled into Kassite times, but apparently with a break somewhere between Failaka periods 2 (Isin-Larsa) and period 3A (Old Babylonian) (Højlund 1987 p. 137 and 157ff and ibid. 1994 p. 475).

During the Danish excavations 366 stamp seals were found, of which 292 are seals of Dilmun type and 19 of related forms (Kjærum 1983). From later excavations in Tell F6 by a French expedition a further 26 seals have been published (Beyer 1986; Pic 1990).

The many seals from Failaka formed the basis of a classification of the stamp seals based on seal shape and motif style (Kjærum 1980). But the seal material from Failaka contains only a few seals of Arabian Gulf and Proto-Dilmun style, and the relative occurrence of the various seal variants is different in Bahrain and Failaka. In Bahrain form variants 1 and 2 make up more than 90% of all Dilmun seals, while the same variants on Failaka together make up hardly 50%, and variant 3 is here quite the dominant one, with about 40% of all Dilmun seals, whereas variants 3-4 together make up only around 5% in Bahrain.

The settlement on Failaka was not founded before Qala'at al-Bahrain period IIb-c (Højlund 1994 p. 474), which explains the scarcity of seals of Arabian Gulf and Proto Dilmun type on Failaka. The other differences mentioned above may be a result of the fact that apparently the traces of occupation in Bahrain are diminished in the late Isin-Larsa period, whereas occupation continues on Failaka into the early Old Babylonian period (fig. 266). During this period, form variants 3 and 4 and style IB and II, which are missing or badly represented in Bahrain, were developed in Failaka.

The stylistic differences find their clearest expression in a massive occurrence of seals in style 1A right from the early layers of both Tell F3 and F6, whereas styles 1B and 2 together make up about

20% of the total number of Dilmun seals from Failaka.

Four of the five seals from the pool share motif and style with Failaka seals (cf. nos. 1-2 and 4-5), which go back to the earliest settlement layers in Tell F6 and Tell F3 (Failaka periods 1 and 2A). The motif in Proto-Dilmun style on the potsherd (no. 6) has close parallels on Failaka, but there they are all in a typologically early Dilmun style 1A (Fai.cat. nos. 212-217).

On seals found outside the pool are found both the erotic motif (no. 10) on a fragmented seal (Fai.cat.no. 270) and notched symbols (shield devices) as on no. 9 on the seals Fai.cat.nos. 75-76, the latter belonging to the earliest building phase on Failaka.

Tokens are not known from Failaka, but the motif on a seal from the bottom layer of Tell F6 period 1 (Fai.cat.no. 37) is close to the impressions on tokens nos. 14 and 17 and several tokens from Saar (see above, no. 14).

Finally, parallels to the motif on seal no. 8, which is the only one in style 1B, are found on two seals (Fai.cat.nos. 70 and 248), both executed in the same style and with related motifs. The latter, from Tell F6, was found in layers belonging to Failaka period 2, just below the floor level in the "Palace" dated to Failaka period 3A.

15. Sasanian and Islamic Pottery

by Søren F. Andersen and Derek Kennet

More recent pottery was recovered in all trenches from layers overlying the Barbar temple. A large assemblage of predominantly 9th century AD pottery was found in the fill of a well (see plan 8:8-9) (Frifelt 2001 p. 13ff) and similar material was found in other scattered contexts together with some slightly earlier material and a few later sherds. The pottery presented here augments the well assemblage and emphasizes late pre-Islamic and Islamic activities at the site.

Sasanian and Early Islamic wares

Two groups of wares do not belong in either the 3rd – 2nd millennium or the 9th century AD assemblages. The first is a group of *alkaline-glazed pottery* and the second sherds in a very hard-fired fabric with lime grits. The alkaline-glazed pottery has a long tradition in Bahrain, for example it is commonly found at Qala'at al-Bahrain from layers dated to Period IVc/d (Højlund 1994 p. 221ff) until the middle Islamic occupation (Frifelt 2001 p. 104). A kiln-tripod (Frifelt 2001 p. 62) and a waster (Højlund 1994 p. 370) might indicate a production of glazed pottery at Bahrain in some periods, but the subject is still disputed.

The glazed carinated bowls (figs. 790-791) do not find well-dated parallels in Bahrain, but at Failaka the type is common in the Seleucid layers of the Hellenistic fortress (Hannestad 1983 p. 23, Bowls with flaring side and offset lip). The type may have continued in use and is common among the finds from the survey and excavations of the village of al-Qusur on Failaka (Patitucci & Uggeri 1984, form 1f, p. 187), which can be dated to the 8th century AD based on the absence of Samarra-horizon wares (see below).

The large, glazed fish-plate (fig. 792) with a thickened, overhanging rim is common in the late Parthian layers (Period Vd) at Qala'at al-Bahrain,

but the best published parallels are in a red-slipped ware (Højlund 1994, fig. 1552) and common ware (figs. 1614-1617). At the third century AD fortress at ed-Dur in Umm al-Qaiwain similar plates were found in glazed ware (Lecomte 1993, fig. 4-1), but not at nearby Kush, where only the later Sasanian and Islamic periods are represented (Kennet 1997 p. 296).

The bowl with a pronounced shoulder (fig. 793) has a good parallel from al-Qusur (Patitucci & Uggeri 1984, fig. 55:576), and the form seems to be without a long previous tradition in the Gulf-region. The concave base (fig. 794) also appears at al-Qusur (fig. 57.609), and so does the concave base illustrated in fig. 795, which is in a mustard-coloured fabric, the glaze of which has degenerated into an iridescent golden layer (Patitucci & Uggeri 1984, fig. 58:629). The illustrated example from al-Qusur is without the internal incised rings, a feature that is commonly found on bases from late Parthian layers at Qala'at al-Bahrain (Højlund 1994 p. 289), but not earlier. This indicates that this type of base was in use during most of the first millennium AD, with the incised rings being a relatively early feature.

A very *hard-fired fabric with lime grits* characterizes the other group of pottery. The colour varies from grey to brown or red, and the forms show significant variation. From the third century AD fortress at ed-Dur a grey, hard-fired ware is very well represented. It is divided into two groups, one of smaller vessels: *Thin grey ware* (*céramique grise mince*) and another of larger vessels: *Thick grey ware* (*céramique grise épaisse*). Similar wares have been noted in the Danish excavations at Qala´at al-Bahrain (S. F. Andersen 2001, p. 77ff). These wares are closely related, both in forms and fabric, to late Parthian wares from the settlement at ed-Dur, which might argue for a production at ed-Dur (Lecomte 1993 p. 200). Close parallels to the ed-Dur assemblage were also found at the Barbar Temple site. A simple outturned rim (fig. 796) is common in the Barbar assemblage: all examples being in a dark grey fabric (Munsell® 5YR 4/1), sometimes with a dark reddish grey core (Munsell® 5YR 4/2) with lime grits up to 3 mm in diameter. They find good parallels in the *Thin grey ware* from ed-Dur (Lecomte 1993, fig. 8:11), but the form is also well attested at various Sasanian sites on the Oman Peninsula, i.e. Jazirat al-Ghanam (de Cardi 1975, fig. 8:28-29), Kush (Kennet 2002B, Fig. 4: Type 81) and Khatt (Kennet 1998, fig. 5:11-12). However, these examples are in a brown or reddish fabric, which might reflect a slightly later date or a different place of production. The rim of a large vessel (fig. 797) in a similar hard-fired, grey fabric, finds its closest parallels at ed-Dur (Lecomte 1993, fig 8.5), but the form is also known from Jazirat al-Ghanam (de Cardi 1972, no. 24). This is the most common rim type amongst the larger vessels in the Barbar assemblage and is also seen in a brown fabric with a sandy texture (Munsell® 10 YR 5/6, yellowish brown with a red core, Munsell® 2,5 YR 4/6), which is close to the fabric from Jazirat al-Ghanam (de Cardi 1972 p. 306). A distinctive group of body sherds from storage vessels are also present. From the lower to the upper body they have raised bands, c. 1.5 cm. wide, running around the vessel. This feature is seen at Qala'at al-Bahrain in the late Parthian period on vessels in a very hard-fired black fabric and is abundant at ed-Dur (Højlund 1994 p. 288). At the late Sasanian site of Hajiabad in Fars Province the same feature is seen (Azarnoush 1994, fig. 185:o). In Bahrain this feature may continue until the ninth century AD or later, since a very large fragment in a hard-fired reddish fabric was recovered from the fill of the Barbar Well (Frifelt 2001, fig. 39).

All bases in the hard-fired ware are simple with a rough, flat underside (fig. 798). The external sides is facetted by scraping whilst the interior is marked with deep finger grooves. This form and type of manufacture are similar to those described on bases from Jazirat al-Ghanam (de Cardi 1972, no. 31) and from Khatt (Kennet 1998, cat. no. 19).

The rim with a triangular cross section in a dark red fabric (Munsell®10 R 3/6) is probably from a large bowl (fig. 799). The rim from a jug is made of a very similar fabric (fig. 800), though darker in colour (Munsell® 2.5 YR 4/2, weak red).

The decorated shoulder sherd from a jug is in the greyish fabric (fig. 801). The decoration is made of impressed triangles and incised lines, for which no exact parallels have been found. However, incised and impressed patterns are common in published Sasanian coarse wares from the Oman Peninsula. The decorative pattern on the neck of a larger storage vessel (fig. 802) is seen on vessels from Hajiabad (Azarnoush 1994, figs. 174f, 180y and 183a). The fabric of this sherd contains many black inclusions up to 2.5 mm in size. The rim of a jug (fig. 803) is of a similar fabric and both sherds have traces of a black slip or wash. These features are not seen in the

rest of the Barbar assemblage but are included in the general description of the Hajiabad material (Azarnoush 1994 p. 186f).

Abbasid and later wares

The ruby lustre bowl (fig. 804) and the glazed bowls and jar illustrated by Frifelt (2001, figs. 9, 10, 12, 13, 14, 16) belong to a group of glazed pottery known as the 'Samarra horizon'. This term refers to a technical revolution in Islamic ceramic production, believed to have been brought about by the response of Iraqi potters to Chinese imports. It includes the introduction of opacified lead and possibly tin glazes, polychrome decoration, and a new range of vessel forms including delicately shaped bowls with flaring rims (fig. 804). The clay of many of the classes suggests a manufacturing centre in southern Iraq, possibly in the vicinity of Basra (Mason & Keall 1991 p. 61).

The problem of the precise dating of the beginning of the Samarra horizon is slowly being resolved. A recent review incorporating evidence from a large-scale surface pottery collection at Samarra has proposed a dating based on analysis of historical evidence for the construction and abandonment of different parts of the 41 km-long site (Northedge 1996). The crucial points for dating the well-assemblage are al-Mu'tasim's attempt to establish a city at al-Qatul to the south of Samarra which was occupied for only one year in 835-6; the foundation of the new caliphal city of al-Mutawakkiliyya at the northern limits of the site in 859, which was abandoned ten days after al-Mutawakkil's assassination in 861; and the final end of large-scale occupation over most of the city which occurred between 885 and 895 (Northedge 1996 p. 231ff). The related pottery evidence is discussed by Northedge and Kennet (1994) and the dates are summarised in Table 1.

The white-glazed ware with cobalt decoration (Frifelt 2001, fig. 16) is therefore the earliest Abbasid ware in the well, and is indicative of early 9th century occupation. The Splashed wares are a later group, and indicate that occupation continued into the later 9th or 10th century (Frifelt 2001, figs. 9, 10).

One sherd illustrated by Frifelt (2001, fig. 11) appears to be considerably later than the rest of the assemblage. This seems to be a sherd of Monochrome Green Sgraffiato. The most important site for the dating of this type of pottery is Lashkari Bazar (Gardin 1963). Gardin's pottery group XIII-1 is very similar to the sherd illustrated by Frifelt (Gardin

Class	Date of introduction (and demise)
White-glazed ware with cobalt decoration	after 803-4, before 835-6, (out of use by 838?)
Plain opaque white glaze	after 835-6 and before 861
Splashed ware	after 835-6 and before 861
Monochrome lustre	after 885-895
Early sgraffiato	after 885-895

Table 1: Summary of the dating of the principle Samarra horizon classes (after Northedge and Kennet 1994).

1963, pl. XXVIII p. 525ff). Gardin dates XIII-1 to the early part of the period 1100 to 1220 AD (1963 p. 136), which has since become the accepted date for the introduction of this ware.

Similar classes occur at other sites such as Sirjan in Iran where 'Group 3 Type A Style I with monochrome glaze' is very similar to the sherd from the well (Morgan & Leatherby 1987 p. 73ff). Morgan and Leatherby's proposed date of 950 to 1050 for the Sirjan assemblage (*ibid.* p. 52) places the manufacture of Monochrome Green Sgraffiato 50 years before the date suggested by Gardin. However, Morgan and Leatherby's date is not based on very strong evidence. The pottery described as 'green glazed with abstract decoration' which was present in layers pre-dating the Mtumbwe Mkuu coin hoard of 1066 or later, may be monochrome sgraffiato (Horton *et al.* 1986 p. 116). In addition a sherd from layer 6 at Nzwani is associated with a C^{14} date of 920+/-50, which calibrates to 1030 to 1160 at 68.2% confidence (Wright 1992 p. 94). The evidence from East Africa might therefore suggest that Monochrome Green Sgraffiato was in circulation before the end of the 11th century AD.

Conclusion

Though the finds presented here cannot be associated with structures or stratified archaeological layers, they document activities at the Temple site from around the third century AD. A few sherds can be assigned to periods later than the ninth century AD and the fragment of Monochrome Green Sgraffiato from the well indicates that the well assemblage is not to be dated to one single episode, but as it is not yet possible to suggest a dating for the majority of the coarse wares, it is unclear what proportion of the well assemblage may be of the later period. However, the very limited number of sherds from

the site datable after the ninth century AD does not indicate a permanent occupation in this later period, but more likely represents domestic refuse either from the nearby village of Barbar or from farming activities in the surrounding gardens.

The pre-9th century AD pottery does not by itself give any clue to the nature of the site and the reason for reoccupying an area that had been abandoned since the 2nd millennium and the same is true of the 9th century AD material. The high proportion of glazed wares from the well led Frifelt to suggest that the assemblage is evidence of some degree of luxury and of possible direct links with Samarra (Frifelt 2001 p. 33). It should be noted that 'Samarra horizon' wares, although celebrated by art historians for their imagined luxury and links with the Caliphal court, actually appear to have been relatively cheap and very widely traded. This can be demonstrated by the fact that they occur on numerous small rural sites around the shores of the Gulf: for example Sasaki recently excavated the remains of a deflated temporary campsite at Hulaylah in Ras al-Khaimah (Sasaki 1995 Area A). The site consists of ash lenses, fire places, shells, sherds, glass, and fish bones with no stone walls or other evidence of structures (Sasaki 1995 p. 3-5, 18-20). Nonetheless, 'Samarra horizon' wares made up over 34% of the total Abbasid pottery assemblage from this site (calculated from Sasaki 1995 p. 8ff). A similar pattern can be observed from other rural sites in and around the Gulf. Larsen retrieved 'Samarra horizon' wares from 15 rural sites in his survey of Bahrain (1983 p. 271ff) and a similar pattern is evident from small sites elsewhere in Ras al-Khaimah, Oman, and the Eastern Province of Saudi Arabia (e.g. Costa & Wilkinson 1987 p. 185f; Kennet 2002A; Whitcomb 1975, pls. 3b, 4a; Whitcomb 1978, pl. 78; Whitcomb 1987, figs. H, I). It is therefore misleading to consider the Abbasid component of the well-assemblage as anything out of the ordinary.

Fig. 790. 2:5.

Fig. 791. 2:5.

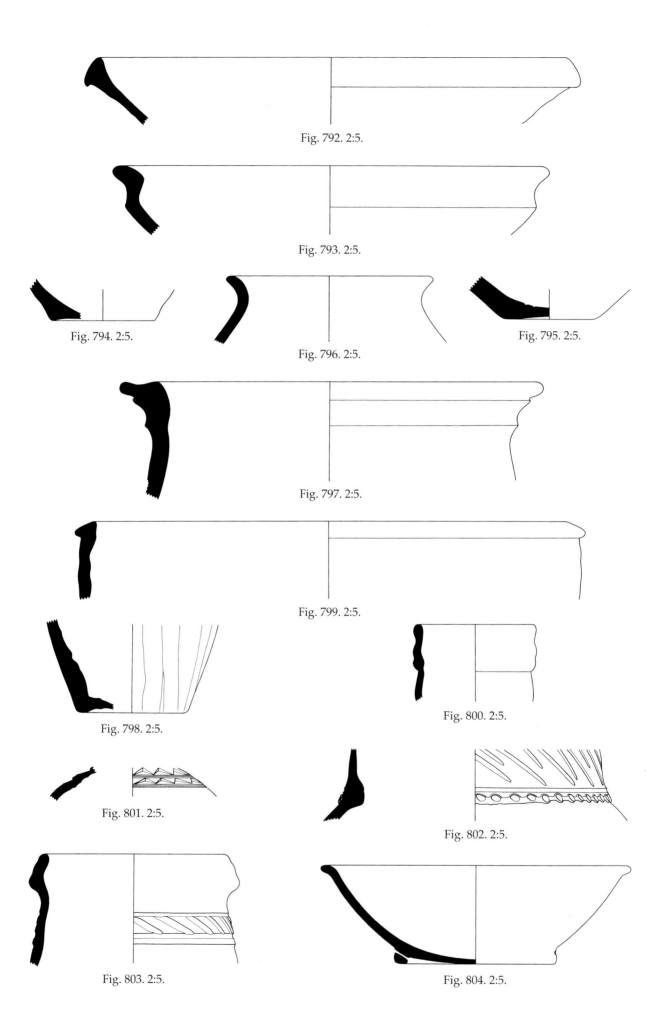

Fig. 792. 2:5.

Fig. 793. 2:5.

Fig. 794. 2:5.

Fig. 796. 2:5.

Fig. 795. 2:5.

Fig. 797. 2:5.

Fig. 799. 2:5.

Fig. 798. 2:5.

Fig. 800. 2:5.

Fig. 801. 2:5.

Fig. 802. 2:5.

Fig. 803. 2:5.

Fig. 804. 2:5.

16. Parthian-Sasanian Sculpture

Nine fragments of late pre-Islamic sculpture in the round and one fragment of an inscription were found during the excavations at the Barbar Temple. All fragments are made of oolitic limestone that occurs on the nearby island of Jiddah (fig. 2). According to the analysis of Vesta S. Curtis one fragment seems to be part of a human arm, while two are parts of shoes. The rest of the sculpture fragments cannot be further identified.

All ten fragments were found east of the central temple platforms in area III excavated in 1955 (fig. 7). A drawing of the northern soil wall of the area, section 12, was made in 1956, and the area was partly re-examined in 1959. The objects are numbered 517.FM, AKH and AKP.

517.FM: one fragment of an arm, was found in area III 1955, at approximately coordinate –24 or –25, and approximately below layer 20 in layer 6 in section 12.

517.AKH: one fragment of a shoe, one unidentified fragment of sculpture, and one fragment of an inscription, were found in 1959 in the northern soil wall of area III excavated in 1955, "in a late pit dug through the temple layers", probably corresponding to the general disturbance of the area around layer 20 in section 12.

517.AKP, one fragment of a shoe and five unidentified fragments of sculpture, were found in 1959 in the northern soil wall of area III excavated in 1955, "in a late pit dug through the temple layers", probably corresponding to the general disturbance of the area around layer 20 in section 12.

The following description and conclusion by Vesta S. Curtis has been excerpted from a manuscript by Curtis & Andersen (in prep.):

Fragment of human arm bent at the elbow (fig. 805) (517.FM). Length 31 cm, width 11 cm. The hand is broken off and parts are missing inside the elbow. A pattern of dots arranged in one vertical and three horizontal lines indicates the decoration on the sleeve of the garment. Traces of diagonal folds are visible on the upper arm. The break inside the arm as well as the angle of the elbow and the rows of

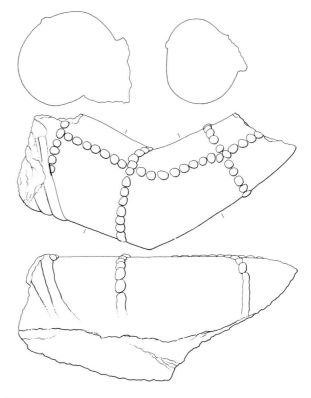

Fig. 805.

dotted pearl (?) decoration indicate that the fragment belonged to a right arm, which was held close
to the body.

The statue may have originally been clad in a
type of garment, which consisted of a long-sleeved
tunic or jacket. It is possible that this was combined
with a cloak, as folds on the upper arm indicate an
outer garment. This type of costume was often combined with trousers in the Parthian and also Sasanian periods. Also common in late Parthian and
Sasanian art was elaborate decoration on the
sleeves of tunics and jackets. Statues and reliefs
from the late Parthian period at Masjid-i Solaiman,
Bard-i Nichandeh, Susa, Assur and Hatra, and also
Palmyra and Dura Europos of the late second and
early third century AD show this type of appliqué
work or embroidery on tunics and trousers (Curtis
1998 pl. IVa, b; 2000 pls. 5, 9 and III; 2001 pls. VIIIX-
XI). Similar decoration is also popular on Indo-
Scythian and Kushan-period sculpture to the east of
the Parthian empire (Rosenfield 1967 pls. 16, 20).

Fragment of a shoe (fig. 806) (517.AKH). Length 16.5
cm, width 11cm. It is broken just above the ankle
and at the toes. The sole and the right side of the
shoe are plain, while the top and inner side are decorated with a design of dots and lines. The lines are
arranged in squares and one line runs diagonally
across the ankle. At the meeting point of the diagonal and horizontal lines at the side of the foot some
other carved lines are visible. These may have been
part of a decorative clasp, perhaps made of metal.

Fragment of the front part of a shoe broken on three
sides (fig. 807) (517.AKP). Length 8 cm, width 8 cm.
The decoration consists of a line of dotted pearls at
the top of the foot. The surface treatment on either
side of the decorative strip is different: to the right
the surface is well carved, while the other side is
less well treated. This piece is not part of the above
described fragment (fig. 806), as the breaks do not
match, but both fragments could belong to one and
the same statue.

The first described fragment (fig. 806) is decorated on the left side. This indicates that the shoe
was meant to be viewed from that side, but the second fragment (fig. 807) has its decoration above the
toes; the surface treatment to the right side of the
dotted pattern indicates that the right side was visible to the viewer. As the two shoe fragments were
to be seen from the side rather than the front, and as
one piece seems to belong to the right foot (fig. 806)
and the other to the left foot (fig. 807), we can assume that the feet were pointing out and therefore
the inside of each shoe, which was visible, was decorated. The actual statue was probably placed
against a wall, as was the custom with dedicatory
statues from Hatra, for example, where the back of

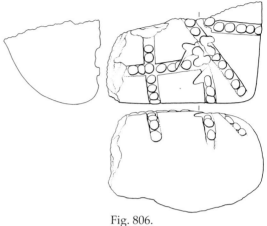

Fig. 806.

the statues were often left unpolished (Matthiesen
1992 p. 213-215).

In late Parthian art the decoration on tunics and
trousers is often repeated on shoes. This is notice-
able at Palmyra, Dura Europos and Hatra, and also
at Masjd-i Solaiman and Bard-i Nichandeh (Math-
iesen 1992 figs. 28, 82; Curtis 2000 p. 33, fig. 9, pl. III;
2001 pls. VIII a-b, Xa, e, XIb). Also popular at this
time and in the Sasanian period are shoes and boots
decorated with round clasps on the ankles (Curtis
2001 pl. Xe; Trever and Lukonin 1987 no. 17). This
was also fashionable in Indo-Scythian and Kushan
art of the first and second centuries AD (Rosenfield
1967 pl. 120).

The frontal pose and gesture of adoration with
one raised hand are characteristic of the art of the
late Parthian-period (Safar and Mustafa 1974 pls. 1,
9, 25-33, 251, 326-7; Curtis 1994 pls. I-III; 2001 pl. X).
At Bard-i Nichandeh and Masjid-i Solaiman standing male figures sometimes hold a cone, a palm leaf
or a cornucopia in their left hand (Ghirshman 1977
II: pls. XXIV, 4; XXV; XXXVII). The cornucopia is
also depicted at Tang-i Sarvak (Vanden Berghe and
Schippmann 1985 pl. 28).

Worshipping figures with the raised right hand
are also popular on funerary stele from graveyards
in Bahrain (Lombard 1999 cat. nos. 358-359, 361).
There is a striking resemblance between these and
Elymaian reliefs of the late second and early third
centuries from Bard-i Nichandeh and Masjid-i Solaiman in southwestern Iran (cf. Curtis 1994 pl. I).
Human figures at these two sites are represented
frontally. Sometimes only one foot appears in pro-

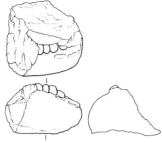

Fig. 807.

Fig. 808.

file (Ghirshman 1977, II: pls. 32, 33), but mostly both feet are in profile and face outwards (Ghirshman 1977, II: pls. XXV, XXXVI:1, LXXXIII:1-2). Elymaian rock reliefs, especially at Shimbar and Tang-i Sarvak, depict figures with both feet turned out (Vanden Berghe and Schippmann 1985 figs. 4, 6, 8, 11). This pose remains popular also throughout the Sasanian period. For example, the Narseh relief at Naqsh-i Rustam of the late third century shows male and female figures with both feet facing opposite directions (Herrmann 1977 pls. 11-13). The same pose is adopted on the fifth century relief of Ardashir II at Taq-i Bustan (Ghirshman 1962 pl. 233). Figures with feet pointing in opposite directions appear also on Sasanian silver plates (Trever and Lukonin 1987 nos. 17, 19).

One of the most popular themes in late Parthian art is worshipping figures who are shown either in a pose of adoration , e.g. Hatra, Masjid-i Solaiman and Bard-i Nichandeh (Ghirshmann 1977, II: pls. XXIV: 4; XXV, XXVIII:1; LXXXII: 1-4; LXXXV; Safar and Mustafa 1974 pl.197) or are shown sacrificing over an altar, e.g at Bisitun, Bard-i Nichandeh, Shimbar, Tang-i Sarvak and Ashur (Andrae and Lenzen 1933 p. 109, fig. 46; Curtis 2001 pl. VIII; Ghirshmann 1977, II: pl. XIII, 3; Vanden Berghe and Schippmann 1985 pls. 22, 39, 45). It is possible that the fragments of sculpture from the Barbar Temple may have belonged to a worshipping figure, as this tradition was popular in the Mesopotamian and Iranian world in the second and early third centuries AD.

From the very limited evidence presented by the small pieces of sculpture from the Barbar Temple site, it is almost impossible to determine their exact date, but it would not be far-fetched to suggest a late Parthian/early Sasanian date of perhaps the third or fourth century AD, particularly in view of the close parallels with Elymaian material of the early third century AD from southwestern Iran.

Inscription (fig. 808) (517.AKH). Length 12.6 cm, width 16 cm. Probably in Aramaic (Professor Mark Geller, personal communication). It is difficult to establish whether this fragmentary inscription was part of a statue base, as known from the sculpture of Hatra (Safar and Mustafa 1974 pls. 4, 197) or not, but in any case it is likely that it belonged to the same figure as the above fragments.

Conclusion

The Sasanian pottery found on the site (see chapter 15) indicates activities throughout the Sasanian period at the Barbar site, but the pottery alone does not give any idea of the nature of these activities. However, the recovery of the sculpture fragments suggest that it was not only a settlement of local peasants working in the surrounding gardens, but could have been a place of some religious or secular importance, possibly in the third or fourth century AD.

17. Other Finds

Gold

Temple I 1955

Band of smooth sheet gold, slightly wrinkled, narrowing towards the ends, which are partly or totally bent over (517.FF) (fig. 809). Found together with copper vessel (517.CB) (fig. 657) in clay level of Temple I, at level 2.72 (plan 1 and section 5:17, black triangle).

Temple II
Area XII 1959

Two fragments of smooth sheet gold, 0.15 mm thick (517.ALK) (fig. 810). From layer of clay immediately below plinth stones north of the staircase, plans 1 and 6:47-52. It is uncertain whether the gold fragments are related to the plinth stones or derive from the clay core of Temple I.

Gold nail, with rectangular head and rhomboid section, flattening towards the end, which is damaged (517.AMA) (fig. 811). Found together with many copper nails in clay level between plinth stones north of the staircase, plans 1 and 6:47-52.

Area III 1959

Gold nail (fig. 812) and fragment of crumpled sheet gold (fig. 813), embedded in corroded lump of copper nails (517.AKO) (fig. 814). The nail weighs 0.6 g. The sheet is 0.5 mm thick, weighs 0.15 g and has part of a square hole punched through it, which is c. 4 mm wide. The edges of the square hole have been scratched by the instrument that produced the hole.[1] The gold nail has probably been used to fasten gold sheet to an object of another material, like wood. The head of this particular nail is only c. 2.5 × 3 mm and cannot have produced this particular hole, which may have been pre-punched by another instrument before a nail was hammered in, i.e. the procedure followed when attaching copper sheeting to a wooden base, cf. above, p. 282.

The fragment has one original edge preserved, which is cut straight, while the other edges are ragged, as if the sheet had been ripped off.[2] In line with the evidence from the copper sheet and nails, the half-punched hole can be explained by this piece of sheet having been partly covered by another sheet. Found in disturbed area just east of the staircase, plan 6:45.

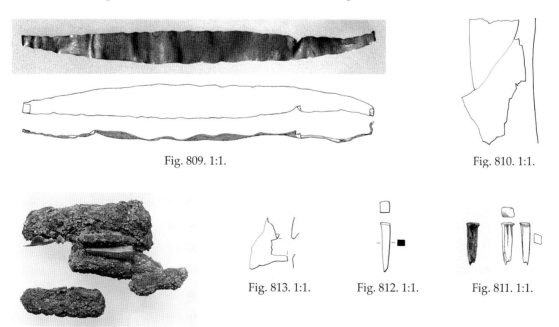

Fig. 809. 1:1.

Fig. 810. 1:1.

Fig. 813. 1:1.　　Fig. 812. 1:1.　　Fig. 811. 1:1.

Fig. 814. 1:1.

[1] Observed at 10× magnification by conservator Helle Strehle.
[2] Observed at 10× magnification by conservator Helle Strehle.

Lapis-lazuli, carnelian and other stones

1954

Two fragments of cylindrical bead of lapis-lazuli (517.BZ) (fig. 815). From sand layer in "Pit of offering" of Temple II (fig. 695:4 and 7).

A lingam-shaped amulet or games piece of lapis-lazuli. From sand layer in "Pit of offering" of Temple II (fig. 695:5). The object has disappeared, but it is sketched in the diary (fig. 816), and in the preliminary publication (Glob 1954a p. 152) there is a reference to similar shapes in the Indus civilization, namely Marshall 1931 pl. CLV:16-17 and Mackay 1938, pl. 139:21 and 140:12.

Area IV 1959

Piece of lapis-lazuli, 0.7 × 0.7 × 0.9 cm, with just one polished side (517.AMH). From one of the pits in the southwestern part of the floor of Temple I, plan 2:1.

Area IX 1959

Flat, biconical turqoise bead (517.ALF) (fig. 817). Found just below the floor of Temple I, at a place where the floor was demolished.

Worked piece of lapis-lazuli (517.ALN) (fig. 818). Found near the bottom of the clay level of Temple I, plan 1.

Area XII 1959

Two circular pieces of lapis-lazuli, probably inlay of eye, representing the iris. One with a rounded back, the other with a peg behind to serve for attachment in a soft substance (517.ALI) (fig. 819). From clay level immediately below plinth stones, north of the staircase, plans 1 and 6:47-52. It is uncertain whether the lapis-lazuli pieces are related to the plinth stones or derive from the clay core of Temple I.

Area IV 1960

Double-conic bead of limestone (517.APM) (fig. 820). From Temple IIb context.

1961, clay level of Temple Ia

Slender barrel-shaped bead of carnelian (517.ARK) (fig. 821). Found 1 m deep in the clay level at the base of Temple Ia, in the southwestern corner, near stone vessel (517.ARJ) (figs. 69-71, plan 1).

Area V 1961

Double-conic bead of limestone (517.AQZ) (fig. 822). From undatable context.

Northeast Temple

Cylindrical lapis-lazuli bead (681.AZ) (fig. 823). Found in the spoils from the southeast quadrant of the temple.

Slender barrel-shaped carnelian bead (681.BV) (fig. 824). From level above demolished outer wall in southeast quadrant.

Flat, biconical carnelian bead (681.CB) (fig. 825). From level above demolished northern wall in northwest quadrant.

Flat, biconical carnelian bead (681.EX) (fig. 826). From southwest quadrant.

Biconical carnelian bead (517.AQN) (fig. 827). Surface find from the southeast corner quadrant of the NE-temple.

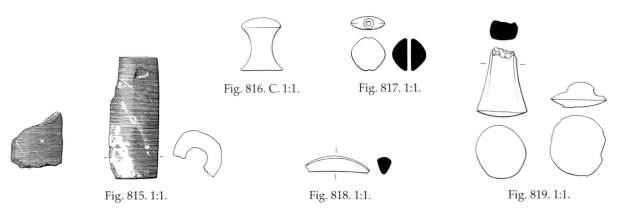

Fig. 815. 1:1.

Fig. 816. C. 1:1.

Fig. 817. 1:1.

Fig. 818. 1:1.

Fig. 819. 1:1.

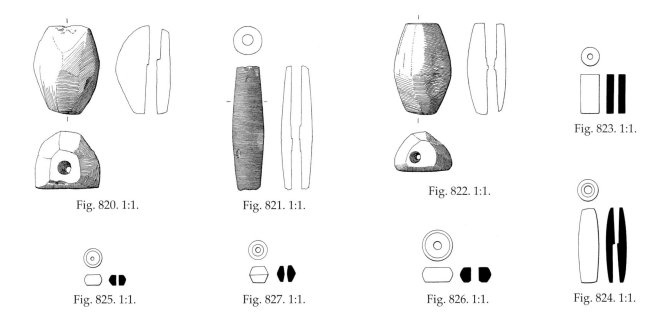

Fig. 820. 1:1.

Fig. 821. 1:1.

Fig. 822. 1:1.

Fig. 823. 1:1.

Fig. 825. 1:1.

Fig. 827. 1:1.

Fig. 826. 1:1.

Fig. 824. 1:1.

Ivory and shell

Area III 1961

Three fragments of worked ivory, one with decoration of dot-and-circles (517.ARO) (fig. 828). From undatable context.

1954

Worked piece of large conch of ellipsoid shape with central perforation, probably inlay of eye, the piece representing the white of the eyeball (517.I) (fig. 829). The edge of the perforation is slanting as if to receive an inlay of the iris, similar to the two lapis-lazuli pieces mentioned above (fig. 819). Found above the "Pit of offering" of Temple II, plan 3:16.

1955

Two mother-of-pearl shells (517.BM and DY) from uncertain contexts.

Area VII 1957

Worked piece of small conch with natural hole (517.ABO) (fig. 830). From Temple IIb context.

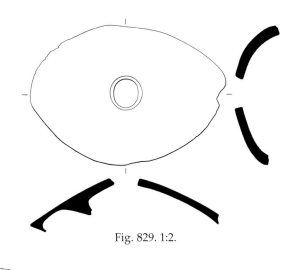

Fig. 829. 1:2.

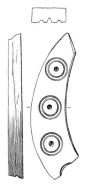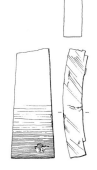

Fig. 828. 1:1.

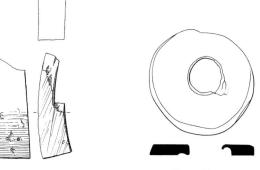

Fig. 830. 1:1.

Steatite vessels

1955

Rim-sherd with spout and row of dotted double circles between horizontal lines; the breaks have been sawn (517.FC) (fig. 831). Found between the upper platform floors of Temple I and II.

1956

Side-sherd, 0.8 cm thick, with two perforations and cutting marks on the outside (cf. Frifelt 2001 fig. 298) (517.SJ). Uncertain context.

Area VI 1957

Side-sherd, 1.4 cm thick (517.AAZ). Temple I context.

Area VIII 1957

Side-sherd, 0.5 cm thick (517.ABD). Temple IIb context.

Area IX 1957

Side-sherd, 0.8-1.4 cm thick (517.ABT). Temple I context.

Two side-sherds, 0.7 cm and 1.6 cm thick (517.ADS). Uncertain context.

Area XVII 1957

Side-sherd, 1.8 cm thick (517.AEL). Temple I context.

Area XVIII 1957

Rim-sherd, polished inside and out (517.AEN) (fig. 832). Uncertain dating.

Side-sherd, 1.6 cm thick, the breaks have been sawn (517.AER). Uncertain context.

Area III 1958

Side-sherd, 0.8 cm thick (517.AHN). Temple I context.

Side-sherd, 1.7- 2.4 cm thick and 32 cm in diameter (517.AJA). Found below Temple I floor, until 1 m below floor.

Two rim-sherds (517.AJI) (fig. 833). From clay level of Temple I.

Area VII 1958

Side-sherd, 1 cm thick (517.AHD). Found between the upper platform floors of Temple I and II.

Area II 1959

Rim-sherd with row of dotted double circles between horizontal lines (517.AKE) (fig. 834). From Temple IIb context.

Area III 1959

Side-sherd, 0.7-1.2 cm thick, with two perforations (517.ALR). Temple I context.

Area VIII 1959

Side-sherd, 0.6-0.8 cm thick (517.ALV). Uncertain dating.

Area VIII 1959

Three side-sherds, 0.8 cm, 1.2 cm, and 1.5-2 cm (517.AMD). Uncertain dating.

Area XV 1960

Side-sherd, 1.8 cm thick (517.AOT). Temple I context.

Area I 1960

Side-sherd, 1.7-2.1 cm thick (517.AOZ). Uncertain dating.

Two side-sherds, 0.6 and 1 cm thick (517.APH). Uncertain dating.

Rim-sherd with two rows of incised triangles forming a band, worn (517.AQC) (fig. 835) (cf. David 2002 fig. 11:6). Uncertain dating.

Area II 1960

Side-sherd, polished inside and outside (517.APC). Uncertain dating.

Side-sherd, 0.4 cm thick (517.APQ). Uncertain context.

Area III 1960

Side-sherd, 0.9 cm thick (517.APA). Uncertain dating.

Rim-sherd (517.APX) (fig. 836). Uncertain dating.

Area IV 1960

Base-sherd, sooted (517.AQH) (fig. 837). Uncertain dating.

Area I 1961

Side-sherd, 0.5-0.9 cm (517.ARS). From Temple IIb context.

Area V 1961

Base-sherd, 0.8-1.3 cm (517.ARH) (fig. 838). Uncertain dating.

1961

Side-sherd, 0.6 cm thick (517.AQM). Found in Temple I context below the floor, plan 3:54.

Summary. No complete or almost complete steatite vessel was found at the Barbar Temple, but 7 rim-sherds of which 3 were decorated, 2 base-sherds and 25 undecorated side-sherds, of which 2 had re-pair holes. Of these, 9 sherds were sampled and analysed by Kohl et al. (1979 Appendix A, nos. 236-244). The context and dating information on these scattered pieces is scarce.

The large diameter and thin wall of several of these vessels, which are not seen in for instance the repertoire from Qala'at al-Bahrain (*Qala'at 1* figs. 1898-1921), are probably due to the special temple context.

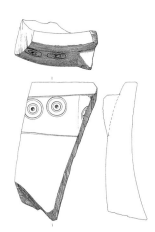

Fig. 831. 1:2.

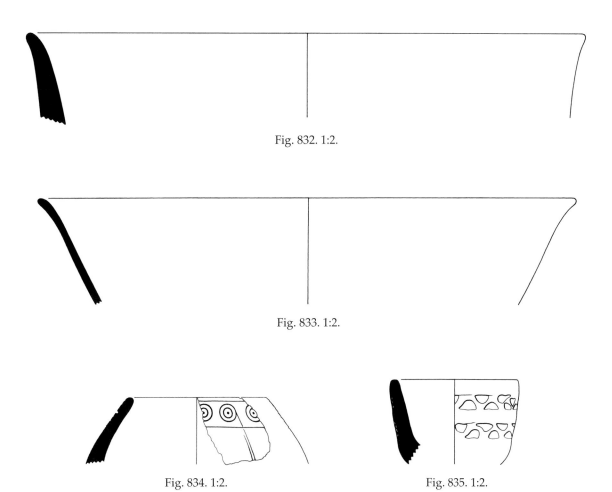

Fig. 832. 1:2.

Fig. 833. 1:2.

Fig. 834. 1:2.

Fig. 835. 1:2.

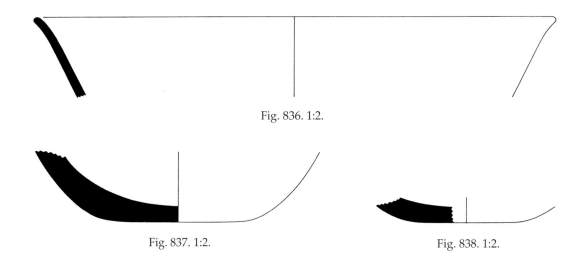

Fig. 836. 1:2.

Fig. 837. 1:2.   Fig. 838. 1:2.

Flint, stone and plaster

Very little *flint* was found at the site, and only 1 denticulated microblade, found on the surface, and 8 coarse flakes and chips were registered.

Fragment of whetstone? with three polished surfaces, $3.4 \times 7.9 \times 1.3$ cm (517.AKV).

24 *hammer-stones* (cf. *Qala'at 1* p. 403) were registered and 1 anvil-stone with a polished side (cf. *Qala'at 1* p. 404); random scatter.

15 fragments of hammer-stones, pestles, etc. with crushed or polished surfaces.

Door-stone of *oolitic limestone*, $16.5 \times 22 \times 8$ cm, diameter of hole 6.5 cm, depth 2.5 cm. No context information (517.S).

Phallos-shaped object of oolitic limestone, very uneven surface, without clear traces of working. Found in 1955, probably in a Temple II context (517.EL) (fig. 839). The shape is known in small size, in lapis-lazuli (fig. 816), and in large size, cf. Appendix 6.

Fragment of cut oolitic limestone, $10.5 \times 14 \times 5.5$ cm, with cut rectangular hole (517.AHG). From rubble layer below flagged floor of Temple II, area III 1958.

Fragment of ashlar in oolitic limestone, re-used as mortar, $15.5 \times 14 \times 11.5$ cm, depression 5.5 cm deep (517.AME). Area VI 1959.

Fragment of grindstone of farush, $24 \times 26 \times 9.5$ cm (517.AHX). Found in rubble layer below Temple II floor.

Fragment of large asymmetrical vessel of *plaster*, 3 cm thick (517.T). Found 1954 in flagged floor of Temple II platform.

Lumps of yellowish-white, very fine-grained material (517.BO). Analysis reveals that it consists of almost pure lime, $CaCO_3$ (no gipsum, $CaSO_4$) and very little sand.[3] Possibly found below the Temple II floor.

Fragment of conical block of plaster with impressions in the centre of a bundle of what may be palm-leaf ribs (517.ADQ) (fig. 840). Area VIII 1957, level c. 5.00, a Temple IIb context.

Fragment of wall plaster, $14 \times 23 \times 4.5$ cm, with small, c. 2 cm, corroded copper pieces, embedded (517.AHY). Found in 1958 area III, inner wall of chamber on Temple I floor, plan 2:13.

Fragment of plaster, 15×22 cm and 7 cm thick, with impression of woven mat (517.FL) (fig. 841). Found in 1955 without context information.

A conical jar stopper of plaster with a diameter of 6.5 cm and a curved lid of plaster, 3×12.5 cm (517.AEN).

Several fragments of plaster with impressions of palmwood and palm-leaf ribs (517.AHZ). Found in rubble layer below flagged floor of Temple II platform, area III 1958.

---

[3] Examined by conservators Anne Cappeln and Helle Strehle

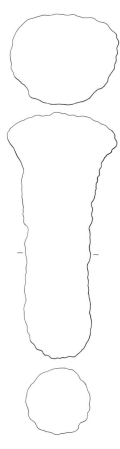

Fig. 839. 1:2.

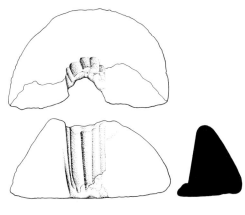

Fig. 840. 1:5.

Fig. 841. 1:3.

Miscellanea

1961

Fragment of club in alabaster (517.ARX) (fig. 842). Found in the northern part of the temple in undatable context.

1958 area III

Lump of bitumen, 5.5 × 6.5 cm, and 3 cm thick with one flat side and one side impressed with reeds (517.AHC). Found in disturbed layer below level of flagged floor of Temple II.

1959 area I/II

Worked piece of steatite with incision (of animal?) (517.AKC) (fig. 843). Uncertain context.

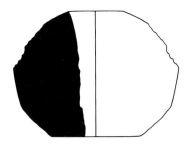

Fig. 842. 1:2.

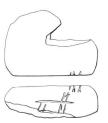

Fig. 843. 1:2.

18. Conclusion

The first Danish archaeological mission to Bahrain took place from December 1953 to May 1954, and the systematic survey of the island that was carried out during these five months was rewarded with conspicuous results: On the north coast of Bahrain, the tell of *Qala'at al-Bahrain* was identified, and trial excavations gave evidence of settlement going back to the 3rd mill. BC (Glob 1954c); a number of the famous burial mounds were excavated (Bibby 1954b); the first stamp seal was reported from Bahrain (Glob 1954b fig. 5); a small temple well was uncovered at Umm as-Sujur (Bibby 1954a); and a large temple complex at the village of Barbar was located (Glob 1954a). For the first time, the outlines of *an archaeological Dilmun culture* were uncovered, a counterpart to the Dilmun of the Mesopotamian cuneiform sources (cf. Oppenheim 1954). The following six years of excavation revealed the Barbar temple to be the jewel in the crown of the Dilmun culture.

The Barbar Temple complex, its architecture, stratigraphy and find material, has been dealt with extensively in the preceding chapters, and it remains here to add some interpretative considerations.

The temple architecture consists of three main structural parts, most clearly seen in the second phase of the temple, Temple II: a central elevated platform with a double altar, connected by a processional staircase to a pool towards the west – a deep-lying chamber built around a freshwater spring – and by a ramp to a court towards the east with abundant evidence of fire (fig. 4) (see chapter 1). This main structure can also be traced in Temple I (fig. 3) but only partly in Temple III, which was almost completely demolished (fig. 5).

There is a remarkable continuity between Temples I and IIa-b (and as far as the evidence has been preserved also Temple III), not just in these main structures, but also in the placement of minor features – evidence of a marked continuity in the cult of the place. In the following, an attempt will be made to elucidate the functions and meanings that were attached to the different structural parts of the temple, followed by some thoughts about communal consumption in the temple, the role of the temple in Dilmun society and the relationship to Mesopotamia.

The central platform

The double altar. The focal point of the central platform of Temple II is a double structure constructed of well-dressed ashlars. It is only partly preserved, and the upper surfaces of the stones are clearly, through different shallow dressings, prepared to receive one or more upper courses, which have completely disappeared (plan 3:18, figs. 105-107).

Different interpretations of this structure have been suggested, e.g. offering tables (Glob 1968 p. 62; Mortensen 1971a p. 394), places where sacred palm trees were planted (During Caspers 1973b p. 78), plinths for twin statues (Bibby 1996 p. 51) and finally, the interpretation suggested above (p. 96): a double altar (cf. Andersen 1986 p. 170).

The clue to the original shape of the structure may be derived from three features: the round shape in plan, the concave side in section and the smoothness of the vertical external surfaces. The round shape can be seen on plan 3:18, two round structures partly embedded into a "base", cf. above, p. 94-96. The outside vertical face of the structures is not completely vertical, but slightly concave in the preserved course. In the western circle, where the stones are c. 50 cm high, the curvature is 0.5–1 cm deep (fig. 55) and very smooth, i.e. much more smooth than otherwise found for the façade ashlars of the temple, where the individual cutting-marks are either clearly visible or the surface roughly eroded (see below). On the outside face of the double structure, all traces of shaping have been obliterated, and the surface "feels" smooth.

The two round structures have these three features in common with a round monolith found buried under the adjacent floor (figs. 61-64) (plan 3:AD), the difference being primarily one of size. The monolith is 1.22 m in diameter and 43 cm high, whereas the double structures are each c. 2.5 m in diameter, and this greater size may be the reason why their basal parts have been constructed of several stones, rather than one.

Two fragments of a similar smooth-surfaced monolith with a diameter of 87 cm were found below the floor of Temple II (figs. 108-109, cf. above, p. 96). Besides, a complete smooth monolith with a diameter of 35 cm and a height of 17 cm is known from the contemporary settlement at Saar (Lombard 1999 Cat. 68). Using these monoliths as analogy, the round structures can be reconstructed as having had a total height of around 1 m, possibly capped with two huge slabs with concave surfaces.

It is remarkable that the two round structures have different heights, the western c. 50 cm and the eastern c. 25 cm above floor level. Perhaps this means that also their original upper surfaces were at different levels and that the gods that were presumably worshipped here had a different relative standing in the local pantheon.

A detail of construction should be noted: the two altars are not constructed directly upon the flagged floor. They are founded below the floor, and the floor flags are fitted to the side of the altar blocks. A certain primacy of the altars may be stressed here, perhaps also a continuity with an earlier altar on the same spot. Part of a similar construction in roughly shaped blocks was in fact uncovered on the floor of Temple I, immediately below the double structure (plan 2:23, figs. 55-60).

A further two round structures, built of smaller stones mortared with plaster, were excavated on the Temple I floor (plan 2:24-25, figs. 59-60) in the same, northeastern, area of the platform. The upper part of these cylinders is not preserved, but they may have been shaped like or even carried such monoliths.

The two round structures on the Temple I floor and the double structure of Temple II have in common the existence of nearby *drains*, which may give an indication of their function. It is, indeed, striking that the floors around these round structures were equipped with drains (plans 2:6-7 and 3:15) that took their beginning in immediate proximity (figs. 59-60, 104). They led to the edge of the platform, at exactly the same spot in both Temples I and II (plans 2:6 and 3:2-3, fig. 38). In the case of Temple II the drain runs down a vertical cutting in the outer face of the platform wall (plan 3:2, figs. 90 and 103). From here the drains continue further east in subterranean channels leading many metres away from the temple (cf. plan 7:24, sections 12:H-I and 13:C). On the west side of the temple similar drains can be related to both Temple I and II and in the case of Temple II followed for more than 20 m (plans 1:35-36 and 3:67-68).

If these drains were simply meant to carry rainwater away from the upper platform, they would hardly have had their entry so close to these obviously important structures. And if the drains were intended to be used only for libations of wine, beer or the like they would hardly have been so extensive. It is more likely that they had some other specific purpose related to the round structures, a purpose that will be elucidated below.

First, the hypothesis that the round structures were altars used for bloody sacrifices shall be suggested. The throat of the sacrificial animal was cut over the altar, the welling blood itself being a libation to the god. Such a procedure would subsequently, especially in a hot climate like Bahrain's, necessitate a thorough cleaning of the altar and the surrounding floor with water, and the dirty effluent would have to be removed.

This may then be the reason why the drains take their beginning close to the altars. They should facilitate the removal of the contaminated water. Incidentally, this may also explain why the western drain (plan 3:67) turns off towards the north-west, straight away from the pool: to prevent the polluted water from seeping into the well-chamber.

In this context, the so-called *edge-ground potsherds* must be discussed. They are found in their hundreds at the Barbar Temple, but never at the Northeast Temple or at Qala'at al-Bahrain. The edge of the sherd, either one part or all the way around, has been ground smooth on a hard surface allowing a well-defined transition between the ground edge and the side of the sherd. It is suggested that these sherds were used to scrape off the coagulated blood from the altars and the flagged or plastered floors around the altars.

A special feature of the altars should be noted: their circular shape may be broken by a protruding part, cf. figs. 58 and 61. Also the two cylindrical stone blocks in the altar construction on the oval platform (plan 3:50) (figs. 162-166) both have a narrow offset band on the side. On the top one of them had a raised edge running around the block, but open at the offset band. Furthermore, the altarstone found up against the northern oval platform wall of Temple IIb should be noted in this context (plan 5:3, fig. 181). Its upper side was not just finely cut, but polished to erase all tool-marks, and along the edges a groove was pricked out which had a central outlet (cf. *Qala'at 1* fig. 2039).[1]

These details seem compatible with the idea of a bloody sacrifice. The altar's concave upper surface, the rim and the groove contained the blood on the altar and at the protruding or offset band the overflow was led down the frontal side of the altar.

The "bench". Just east of the double altar an upright stone slab was found during excavation, standing in a shallow cutting in the stone floor, and at a distance of 1.1 m a similar slab was found lying beside a similar cutting. Possibly these slabs supported a short bench (plan 3:19-21, fig. 251). Was this in-

---

[1] Note the resemblance of these two pieces to much later South Arabian offering or libation tables (IMA 1997 p. 80, 93, 128 and 143).

tended for a statue of the god or a priest impersonating the god, so that the god could partake in the sacrificial ceremonies?

Close to the "bench" stood a cubical stone with a round hollow on the upper surface (plan 3:22, fig. 251). A similar object is known from the temple court at Tell F3 in Failaka, where it has been interpreted as a censer (Kjærum 1986b p. 81, figs. 11-12).

In this connection reference may be made to finds of several vessels of alabaster or calcite (figs. 761-765) and finely carved steatite (figs. 832-833 and 836) which may have contained offerings to the gods, such as food, drink and oil for annointing.

Pierced stones. A few metres south-west of the altars was a row of 3 stones with a rounded top, pierced with a circular hole, embedded in the Temple II floor (plan 3:27-29, figs. 112-117) (see above, p. 97-98). Another similar stone was lying loose by the altar (plan 3:25, figs. 105-107), and a fifth pierced stone, a little different in shape and with a ring-cutting, was found in the western part of the central platform (plan 3:30, fig. 118). One of the upright standing stones had a projection in the form of an animal's head (plan 3: 28, fig. 114).

Mortensen has noted that similar stones, originally functioning as anchors, have been found erected in temples at Ras Shamra and Byblos in the Levant, and at Saqqara, in Egypt, in front of the tomb of Mereruka (1986 p. 184), but the formal similarities are very general (cf. McCaslin 1980 fig. 35). The irregular lower part of the Barbar stones (fig. 116) suggests that they were designed to be partly buried in the floor and not to function as anchors in any practical sense. Also, they do not have the traces of wear around the edges of the holes that wet ropes would soon leave on a rather soft limestone. So, if they were anchors, it can only have been in a symbolic sense. For a more likely contemporary anchor found at Qala'at al-Bahrain, see *Qala'at 1* fig. 2034.

The intensity of wear on the pierced stones is by far most prominent on the stone with the ring-cutting. The traces of wear are, however, found on the *outside* of the stone, especially the corners and small sides (see fig. 118), whereas the edges of the circular piercing are sharp and unworn. On the other stones, the wear is less marked, but again concentrated on the outer edges, and only on one stone is it found also on the edges of a hole; otherwise the edges of the holes are without traces of wear (*contra* Mortensen 1986 p. 184). These wear traces could simply have been produced by tying ropes around the stones, ropes that could have been for tethering sacrificial animals as suggested by Glob (1955 p. 192).

The Eastern Court

The route of the sacrificial animals to the altars probably passed via the cobbled road, coming in from the north (plan 7:21) and up the ramp (plan 7:18-19) to the central platform, and it may be noted that a ramp is more suitable as an accessway for livestock than a stair. After the sacrifice the animals were probably brought down into the Eastern Court for further processing, as will be argued below.

The dark, charcoal-coloured, powdery layers which are very conspicuous for the Eastern Court, not just inside the court but also outside, have been interpreted as the ashy remains from the cooking over a fire of the animals sacrificed at the temple. The table-like constructions (plan 7:4 and 16, fig. 228), related both to the oval and the earlier round phase of the court (see above, p. 181), probably served for cutting up the animals, as earlier suggested (Mortensen 1956 p. 197). In this context it may be relevant to note that inside and south of the court one knife and three daggers were found (figs. 721-725), which is a remarkably high number of cutting-instruments compared to other metal objects from this area (cf. above, p. 275).

The Eastern Court was completely and very carefully excavated. The number of bones found here is thus high, and Bangsgaard's analysis (see Appendix 1) has interestingly showed that, apart from three fragments from the diaphysis of a radius (one from sheep or goat and two from cattle), all bones are either from the distal part of the leg (metapodium or carpal/tarsal bones) or from the mandible or the cranium, i.e. parts of the body which carry very little meat and are often discarded after butchering. This supports the interpretation of the Eastern Court as a place for butchering (and cooking) the sacrificed animals.

The find of many half-globular beakers (figs. 504-513) in and around the court indicates that some consumption probably also took place in this area.

The well and the pool

In all phases of the temple, I-III, there was a well, positioned towards the south-west (figs. 2-5); indeed, in Temple IIa-b and III the same well-shaft was utilized (see above, p. 68-70, plans 3:38 and 8:8-11, figs. 74, 79, 248, 250).

In at least Temples I, IIa and IIb the well was accompanied by a pool, i.e. a chamber built around a freshwater spring (see above, p. 71, plan 6, figs. 185-201), positioned near the well, but further north-west (figs. 2-3).

No pool was ascertained for Temple III, but it may have been demolished together with almost all of this temple. It would, at any rate, have been necessary to re-position the pool with the construction of Temple III. The west wall of the central platform of the new temple advanced 5 m towards the west, and the height of the platform was increased, making it impossible to reach the water in the pool of Temple II without the staircase becoming too steep. With a gradient as the Temple II stair and an estimated height of the Temple III platform of 4 m, the staircase would have reached the groundwater level of c. 5.50 c. 20 m from the platform wall, i.e. at least 5 m west of the Temple II pool.

The presence of two plinth-stones north of the Temple III platform (plan 8:3-4, figs. 242-245) points, however, to a likely position of a staircase leading down to a pool related to Temple III, in analogy with the plinth-stones along the pool staircase of Temple II (plan 6:47-54, fig. 203).

The existence of two separate accesses to water in Temples I-II and probably also III, is striking and demands an explanation. The two structures must have had very different functions, and it is suggested here that the well furnished the temples with water for drinking and cleaning, i.e. relatively mundane functions, whereas the pool was associated with quite different ideas.

This interpretation is based on the following considerations: the modest architecture of the wells and of the staircases leading down to the different phases of the well *versus* the outstanding architecture of the pool and the staircase leading down to the pool (figs. 185-213); the similarity of the well to contemporaneous wells found at Qala'at al-Bahrain (*Qala'at 1* plan 3:1 and 19); and the copious quantities of storage vessel sherds found in the area around the well against the meagre pottery found in the pool area.

The whole structure of the temple points to the upper platform as being an especially holy area, but Andersen is undoubtedly right in pointing out that the eminent staircase, leading from the platform down to the pool, accords to the pool an equal importance, which is underlined by the quality of the stonework in the pool itself (see above, p. 8).

This staircase is a dominant feature of the temple, outstanding in its size, the quality of the building material and the execution (see above, p. 159). It is c. 1.75 m wide, constructed of large slabs and must have been c. 15 m long, with c. 30 steps (cf. section 33). The upper part, above the level of the oval platform, has been free-standing, whereas the lower part has been below the ground, embedded in the oval platform, and indeed the whole pool was probably roofed over. At the beginning of the subterranean part foundations for a portal were uncovered (plan 6:55-56, figs. 218-219).

The two lowest steps of the staircase leading down to the pool (plan 6:34-35, fig. 205) must have been either constantly or often submerged in water or at least splashed with water, and were severely worn (cf. levels on plan 6 and section 33), whereas

the other steps of the staircase which have been at a distance to the water were not visibly worn. The limestone is more soft and susceptible to wear when wet than when dry.

The staircase can probably be termed a processional stair. Something important should occur between the pool and the uppermost platform. One suggestion could be that the divinity actually lived in the spring and had to be brought – perhaps in the shape of a statue or personified by a priest – up to the altar to receive its/his sacrifices. The special structure of the temple seems to be designed to bring these two elements together: the convention saying that the god should be worshipped at a high place and the natural fact that the fresh water, where the god had his abode, issued below ground.

Apart from the ceremonial staircase, there was a second, more seclusive, access to the pool: through the east room (plan 6:2) to a worn threshold (plan 6:11) in front of a round basin (plan 6:13, figs. 194-195). Andersen describes this basin as well-like (see above, p. 151) and, indeed, the drum construction is found similarly in the wells at Barbar (fig. 250), Umm as-Sujur (see Appendix 5) and Qala'at al-Bahrain (*Qala'at 1* figs. 232-233). But, in this case the drums are truncated as if to facilitate access from the threshold. The upper drum has openings to the left and right. To the right a very special stone vessel with three holes in the lower side was placed on two stone blocks (plan 6:15, figs. 196-198). The east room, the separate access to the pool, the round basin and the stone vessel could be related to rituals preparing the statue of the god or the priest personifying the god for the grand procession from the pool up the ceremonial staircase.

When ascending the pool staircase, leaving the subterranean part and entering into the open, one was met on both sides of the staircase with copper-plated wooden objects slotted into stone plinths (plan 6:47-54, figs. 210-217, see above, p. 270-274). Poles carrying holy emblems have been suggested, but the cuttings in the plinth-stones are too shallow (15-20 cm) to hold poles, and the remains of the copper-plated objects do not even fit closely into the slots. The way the stones are arranged in pairs, with each stone having two holes, and the interval between the four holes of each row, suggests that the idea is for a four-legged animal to stand there so that the body of the animal would have added stability to the construction. One of the stones has an extra hole (plan 6:48), and its position suggests that it was intended to stabilize a particularly long tail,[2] perhaps of a bull.[3] This indicates that the animals had their backs towards the platform wall and were facing those ascending the staircase. Similar plinth-stones, one with a third "tail-hole", lie, as mentioned above, in front of the northern terrace wall of Temple III (plan 8:4).

A shell eye inlay, found in the "Pit of offering" (plan 3:16) may originally have belonged to one of the animals (fig. 829). The edge of the perforation is slanting, as if to receive an iris inlay, similar to two lapis-lazuli pieces found in the area (figs. 819).

If this reconstruction of a number of animal statues on both sides of the staircase and their orientation is trusted, then it indicates that the most important movement was up the staircase: To bring the statue or the representation of the god from his deep hidden abode up to the altar on the upper platform to accept his offerings was the most important ceremonial event, and during this procedure the god was received by the animal statues.

The oval terrace

Whereas the central platform, the ceremonial staircase and the pool stand out in exclusive importance, the oval platform is characterized by a number of smaller and therefore perhaps less important installations.

West of the temple a series of stone pillars was found. On a small platform attached to the oval terrace wall of Temple IIb were three standing stones (plan 3:60-62, fig. 169). Two of them consisted of plinth-stones with inset pillars. Apparently these pillar-stones had broken and were therefore encapsulated with a casing of smaller stones set in plaster (figs. 171-175). Interestingly enough, this shape seems to be imitated in the third, central, pillar (figs. 176-177). Further to the north-west lay two similar, but damaged, sets of plinth and pillar (plan 3:64 and 66, figs. 179-180), as well as a parallel to the central pillar on the platform (section 21:E, fig. 158).

Close by the stair leading up to the oval platform is an altar (plan 3:50, figs. 162-165), and to the north an altar stone which seems to have been walled into the oval terrace wall (plan 5:3, fig. 181).

A special context was uncovered on the oval platform to the north-east. Between two parallel walls (section 31, figs. 182-183) was a burnt layer with many bones burnt at high temperatures and a stamp-seal impressed token (Kjærum, see above, p. 300, fig. 787). The same layer lay in heaps outside the two walls, and here five more tokens were found (figs. 783-786, 788). A further token was found in an adjacent area (fig. 789). Perhaps this was a place where special kinds of temple refuse were destroyed (cf. Bangsgaard in Appendix 1).

The question of the main entrance to the temple may be raised in this context. There are some indications that the southern front of the temples was "the fine side" and that the primary entrance would have been here. The walls enclosing the oval platforms of both Temples IIa and IIb (plan 3:31, 41) have a marked height towards the south – and in the case of Temple IIb well-dressed ashlars

have been lavishly used (fig. 132) – whereas they are quite low towards the north. There is, in fact, already a stair up against the southern wall of the Temple IIa oval wall (plan 3:33), suggesting that the main entrance to the temple was from the south. This may perhaps be corroborated by several tenuous indications that the northern side was the "back side" of the temple: the just described area on the northern part of the oval platform where refuse may have been burnt; the fact that the drains issuing from the central platform turn off towards the north; and the interpretation of the cobbled road leading from the north on to the ramp by the Eastern Court as access for sacrificial animals.

Stone masonry

The building material for Temple II consists of ashlars cut in *oolitic limestone*,[4] a type of limestone found on Jiddah Island, lying off the northwest coast of Bahrain, less than 10 km from Barbar. The geology of Jiddah comprises "a sequence of siltstone, limestone and sandstone overlain by a limestone cap rock, where only the sandstone and limestone cap rock outcrop on the island…. The cap rock … consists of a massive light grey to brownish white, fine to medium grained, moderately strong to strong sandy oolitic limestone … The limestone ranges in thickness from 0.5 m in the south, to about 11 m beneath the old prison block in the centre of the island."[5] Numerous quarrying traces have been found on Jiddah (fig. 87), and it is likely that the ashlars were transported by sea from there to the coast 500 m north of Barbar (Glob 1954a p. 150).

The *ashlars* would have received their rough shape at the quarry, whereas layers of fine limestone chippings found at several places on the Barbar site indicate that the final shaping of the blocks took place during the construction of the walls (cf. sections 2A:18 and 4:9). A clear difference can be noted between the dressing of façade walls that were intended to be in full view, and the dressing of foundation walls that were out of sight, submerged in the ground.

[2] Cf. the copper-plated bulls from the al-Ubaid temple which have their tails reaching all the way down to the ground (Hall & Wolley 1927 p. 76, pl. XXVII: nr. T.O. 321).

[3] On the local stamp seals long-tailed animals are almost always bulls, e.g. Kjærum 1983 no. 174, pers. comm. Poul Kjærum, June 2003.

[4] Determined by Magdy Nassif, Institute of Geology, Aarhus University.

[5] Cited from a geological report by McClelland-Suhaimi Ltd for the Bahrain Ministry of Housing 1991.

To the façade walls belong the walls of the pool (figs. 185-201), the face of the Temple IIb oval terrace wall (figs. 132, 149-156), the outer walls of the central platform of Temple II (fig. 96) and the walls, both inside and outside, on top of this platform (plan 3:8-10). All these walls exhibit clear cutting-traces, which on close inspection can be seen to have been left by an adze with a cutting edge 7-8 cm wide (cf. figs. 659 and 664), directed by a right-handed workman (see for instance figs. 190-191). The lines that can be seen on the façade of the ashlars, going from upper left to lower right, indicate where the chip was broken off, and they are not, as supposed by Doe (1986 p. 189, fig. 52), evidence of a left-handed stonecutter.

On the façade walls the orientation of the cutting-traces is the same on all ashlars of a wall, indicating that the wall received the final trimming after the stones had been placed, whereas the cutting-traces on the ashlars of the foundations are purely random and less careful, indicating that their final dressing took place before they were put in place and that they were not intended to be in full view.

Communal consumption

1. The evidence from the pottery. There are remarkable differences between the pottery found at the Barbar temple and that found at the contemporary city of Qala'at al-Bahrain, in spite of the many general and specific similarities that have been used for dating purposes in chapter 11. In particular, the Barbar temple lacks luxury pottery of all kinds – wheel-made, painted, or imported wares – and these differences may probably be related to the social context of the temple rituals.

Firstly, the pottery found at Barbar belongs almost exclusively to the local, so-called Barbar tradition, with only a few sherds referable to other traditions. At the contemporary city of Qala'at al-Bahrain, only 4 km from Barbar, 6% of all rim sherds in period IIa belong in the Mesopotamian tradition (*Qala'at 1* fig. 390), and although no exact calculations have been made, the percentage for Barbar in the contemporary Temple I phase is clearly much lower, since almost all Mesopotamian sherds found there are illustrated in this volume (figs. 394-407). The percentage for Umm an-Nar rim sherds in period IIa at Qala'at al-Bahrain is low (0.4%) (*Qala'at 1* fig. 390), but it is distinctly lower at Barbar (figs. 391, 408-416). All through period IIa-c at Qala'at al-Bahrain the percentage of Eastern pottery is stable (1.1-1.6 %) (*Qala'at 1* fig. 390), but there is hardly a single sherd from the Eastern traditions present at Barbar. Fig. 616 may be an exception, but could just as well be a local imitation.

Secondly, focusing on the pottery belonging to the Barbar tradition found at the temple, it is conspicuous how a number of types that appear commonly at contemporaneous Qala'at al-Bahrain (*Qala'at 1*) are either very rare or completely absent at Barbar. This applies to the sieve-necked jar (type B7-8), which is present only in a few examples; small jars with red wavy lines (types B22-23) have not been found; rims of type B30 are not found combined with flat plates as at Qala'at al-Bahrain, but with large bowls instead; painted wheel-made goblets, cups and jars (types B62-72) are not found, and painted pottery in general is extremely rare.

It is also striking to contrast the coarse drinking-beakers and goblets from the temple found either in the foundations for Temple I (figs. 269-275) or in the Eastern Court of Temple IIb (figs. 504-513) with the fine, painted, wheel-made goblets of Qala'at al-Bahrain (*Qala'at 1* figs. 194-200).

The types absent from the Barbar temple are precisely those types that in the analysis of the pottery from Qala'at al-Bahrain were described as a set of pottery related to serving, eating and drinking (*Qala'at 1* p. 177). In the light of the Barbar material we may now add that this particular set of pottery at Qala'at al-Bahrain may have been related to high-prestige activities within the household, such as entertainment of guests, i.e. consumption which had an aspect of showing off towards social competitors and which therefore necessitated investment in luxury products.

Conversely, the lack of these items at Barbar may indicate that consumption here was not a household or family-based activity that involved social competition, but that the separate households were in this context subsumed under a larger community. This means that we should not think in terms of each household bringing its own food and drink to the temple, but rather that cooking and eating was a communal affair organized within the context of the temple. As a first example of such a communal consumption, may be referred to the many beakers lying in the clay level of Temple Ia with additional offerings.

The lack of flat plates and the occurrence of large bowls perhaps indicate special dishes not served in a private household or perhaps other ways of serving and eating.

2. The evidence from the animal bones. Analyses show that cattle bones make up a much larger proportion in relation to sheep or goat at Barbar than at Qala'at al-Bahrain, the percentage of cattle being even further reduced at the Saar village (see Bangsgaard in Appendix 1, fig. 10).

That more cattle than sheep/goat was consumed at Qala'at al-Bahrain than at Saar may be explained by a higher status and greater wealth of the inhabitants of the capital than of the village, with reference to a higher quality being generally accorded to beef than mutton and goat's meat. In line with this argumentation, the predominance of cattle at the Barbar temple can be explained by assuming that temple consumption required the finest quality possible.

Alternatively, one might suggest that cattle had a special significance in the cult of the temple, perhaps being closely related to one of the gods worshipped there.

The large frequency of cattle bones found at the Barbar temple is at any rate an indication that eating was done in large groups, since a dead ox will feed about 8 times more people than a slaughtered sheep, and, in a hot climate, it requires many more consumers if the meat is not to rot (Uerpmann & Uerpmann 1997 p. 261-262).

It may be added that bulls are often depicted at or by altars on stamp seals (e.g. Kjærum 1983 no. 83 and 87).

The stamp-seals

9 stamp-seals, 1 seal-impressed potsherd and 7 seal-impressed tokens were found at the Barbar temple. Considering that this is a one-period site excavated during 8 seasons, this is a very low number compared to the 21 stamp-seals and 3 seal-impressions found in a rather small area of contemporaneous private houses by the northern city wall of Qala'at al-Bahrain (Kjærum 1994), the 95 stamp-seals, 220 sealings, and 14 tokens found at the contemporaneous settlement of Saar (Crawford 2001), and the 367 stamp-seals uncovered at the contemporaneous Tell F3 and Tell F6 on Failaka (Kjærum 1983).

Apparently, the economic functions that were related to the use of stamp-seals did not apply to the Barbar temple to any large extent, if at all. In this connection it may also be noted that storerooms seem to be lacking at the temple (Qala'at 2 p. 41. Cf. also Crawford, Killick & Moon 1997 p. 54).

The five stamp-seals (figs. 773-777) found scattered in the sand layer at the bottom of the pool, could, if accidentally lost, indicate that sealing took place around this area. There are indications that access to the pool was regulated at two points, at a portal by the entrance to the subterranean part of the staircase (plan 6:55-56, see above, p. 168-171) and further down the stairs, where the evidence suggests that the pool was closed by a wall (plan 6:12) and a door at the second step from the bottom (cf. section 33:F and K, see above, p. 165). If such doors were secured by sealings, a number of seals were bound to be lost over the years. The alternative interpretation that the seals are votive finds is not particularly likely, since other votive finds are lacking from the area.

The temple and the State

The investment of man-hours and material resources in the construction of the Barbar temples sets them aside as something requiring a large organization like the city wall around Qala'at al-Bahrain (Qala'at 1 p. 32ff), the monumental buildings in the centre of Qala'at al-Bahrain (Qala'at 2 p. 13) and the so-called Royal mounds at Ali (Reade & Burleigh 1978). It is hardly a coincidence that all these large monuments appear at the beginning of Qala'at al-Bahrain period II, and this has been interpreted as evidence for the formation of a state in Bahrain (Højlund 1989).

From the first to the last phase of the Barbar temple there is evidence of increasing investment of resources. The size of the temples increases substantially from Temples Ia to Ib, IIa, IIb and III, and to this should be added that the Northeast Temple may be contemporaneous with Temple III. The changes between Barbar Temple I and II seem to be particularly noteworthy. Temples Ia-b make use of the same materials as private houses, normal-sized burial mounds, and the early phases of the city wall at Qala'at al-Bahrain, i.e. uncut stone, clay and plaster, with the use of plaster as mortar appearing in Temple Ib. The introduction of large quantities of well-dressed ashlars in Temple II undoubtedly marks a gigantic increase of resource investment that is continued in Temple III and in the Northeast Temple. This epoch-making event may be roughly dated to the transition between Qala'at al-Bahrain period IIa and IIb and underlines what has already been perceived as a transition between two very different stages in the Dilmun society, Qala'at al-Bahrain period IIa and periods IIb-c (Højlund 1989 p. 53; 1993 p. 3-4; Qala'at 1 p. 469-475; Qala'at 2 p. 40-41).

The few existing indications for at date of the last building phase of the temple, Temple III, point towards early period IIc at Qala'at al-Bahrain. The evidence for dating the last building phase of monumental structures in the centre of Qala'at al-Bahrain is likewise slender, but points at Qala'at al-Bahrain period IIb/c (Qala'at 2 p. 40-41). A firmer dating of these monuments and their disuse would be of great interest for evaluating the apparent collapse of the Dilmun state.

The Mesopotamian connection

No inscriptions or other written evidence were found at the Barbar Temple, and the preceding interpretation of the temple has therefore relied primarily on the material evidence. Considering the close relations between Dilmun and Mesopotamia and the many examples of Mesopotamian influence in Bahrain, there is, however, reason to consider whether Mesopotamian sources may throw some light on the monument.

Mortensen referred to similarities between the oval Eastern Court and the oval platform of Temple II and the three Mesopotamian oval temples of Khafajah, al-Ubaid and al-Hiba, dating to the Early Dynastic period (1956 p. 197; 1971a p. 396). This relation seemed the more likely, since the best parallels to the pottery beakers found in the clay level of Temple Ia seemed to be found in Mesopotamian cities and temple deposits of the Early Dynastic period I (Mortensen 1971a p. 395). As it has now been shown that the Barbar Temple is separated from the Early Dynastic period by several hundred years (Mortensen 1986 and *Qala'at 1* p. 172), these parallels seem of a more superficial nature and less relevant. But the possibility may still be considered whether the Barbar temples "reflect archaic [Mesopotamian] traditions expressed in the architecture as well as in the pottery and in the tradition of scattering votive beakers … " (Mortensen 1986 p. 185), traditions that could perhaps have been kept alive in the Eastern province of Saudi Arabia at places like Tarut Island.

It has been suggested that the Mesopotamian goddess Ninhursag might be connected to the Barbar temple, because of the alleged similarities to the temples of Khafajah and al-Ubaid, both dedicated to this goddess (Mortensen 1971a p. 395, note 4), but the revision of the chronology of the Barbar temple, making it several hundred years later, has made this hypothesis less plausible. A further suggestion may also be mentioned, namely that the village of Barbar lying close to the temple received its name because the temple was an é - b a b b a r, i.e. a temple of the god Šamaš (Potts 1983b p. 128).

Of primary importance is, however, that Andersen in his interpretation of the pool chamber of the Barbar Temple refers to Mesopotamian written sources on the god Enki and his abode, the *abzu*. "The clue to our problem may be given by some striking features of the Barbar Temple. The temple was situated at a freshwater spring, indicating the numinous power which gave the impulse for the cult at Barbar. Over this spring was built a basin

and we know that a water-cult took place here. If we in this case want to draw a conclusion, the most obvious interpretation would be that this unique structure represents an 'abzu'. The temple-abzu is well known from the texts but it has been extremely difficult to identify in excavations. As the special dwelling of Enki, the god of the subterranean freshwater ocean, also called 'abzu', this deity then is reflected in an outstanding way. As a deep, quiet, hidden place the abzu is the abode of Enki as the god of wisdom. He there administers the 'mes' and as the Lord of the Abzu he is also the god of the springs which dispense freshwater and fertility." (Andersen 1986 p. 175-176).

The Mesopotamian textual sources on Enki and his *abzu* (Sjöberg 1995) supply us with a frame of interpretation for the pool chamber of the Barbar temple that is hard to overlook, and in this connection it is irrelevant if the actual name of the god worshipped at Barbar was Enki or perhaps Inzak. As Nashef has pointed out, there is no textual evidence that Enki was worshipped in Dilmun, whereas the texts suggest that Inzak and Meskilak were worshipped as the main deity pair there (Nashef 1986 p. 348 and note 36). There may, however, easily have been similarities between the cults of Enki and Inzak, something that may be mirrored in the close relationship between the two gods (Nashef 1986 p. 345-346).

Andersen also mentions the reference in the myth *Enki and Ninmach* to the 'clay above the abzu', from which, according to this myth, man was created by Enki, Ninmach and Nammu, and he suggests that the clayish foundation of the Barbar Temple may be an expression of this idea (Andersen 1986 p. 176-177).

According to the Mesopotamian creation myth known as *Enki and Ninhursag* or the *Myth of Dilmun*, the god Enki gave abundant fresh water to Dilmun (cited below after André-Salvini 1999 p. 46-47). Whether this belief was also prevalent in Dilmun – perhaps related to a god by another name – we do not know, but the temple at Barbar indicates that this may have been the case (cf. Bibby 1986b p. 194):

Ninsikilla spoke to her father Enki:…
My city has no water in its channels […]
[Her father Enki replied to Ninsikila:]
[Let the Sun make water rise up from the gates of the Earth […]
Let Dilmun have abundant water to drink!
Let the saltwater wells become freshwater wells
And let your city become the "house on the edge of the quay" (a warehouse)…
And he gave Dilmun water in abundance…
The fields and the ground produced barley…
Dilmun truly became the "house on the edge of the quay" of the land,
And, in the sunlight of that day, it was so!